Temples
of the Most High

Temples
of the Most High

COMPILED BY N. B. LUNDWALL

□

Being A Compilation of:

The Dedicatory Prayers of Temples Erected in the Present Dispensation.

Their Historical and Physical Description.

Faith-Promoting Incidents and Manifestations of Divine Acceptance.

Sermons and Historical Data Pertaining to Temples which are yet to be Erected.

Information Pertaining to Records and Historical Places that are held Sacred by Latter-day Saints; the Efficacy and Sacredness of Temple Ordinances.

Discourses by the Prophet Joseph, Brigham Young, Orson Pratt, Parley P. Pratt, John Taylor, Wilford Woodruff and others, on the Eternity of Intelligence and the Immortality of the Soul.

Concordance and References pertaining to Temples, Temple Work and Kindred Historical Subjects.

□

BOOKCRAFT
Salt Lake City, Utah
1968

23rd Printing, 1977

LITHOGRAPHED IN U.S.A.
BY

PUBLISHERS PRESS

SALT LAKE CITY, UTAH

ILLUSTRATIONS

ACKNOWLEDGEMENT

Sincere gratitude is expressed to those who have contributed in the compilation and publishing of this book, viz:

To Dr. John A. Widtsoe for his kindly interest and suggestions in reading the manuscript; also to Elder Joseph Fielding Smith for suggestions imparted.

To Alvin F. Smith for his whole-hearted generosity in the use of books in the Historian's Office, this being true not only of this work, but of all publications printed in the past by the Compiler; also to A. William Lund for like consideration.

To those who have contributed articles, namely, Herman R. Bangerter, Nephi L. Morris, LeRoi C. Snow, E. C. McGavin, Bion Tolman, Ariel L. Crowley, J. Hatten Carpenter, Herber Jarvis, Mathias F. Cowley, Pres. Edward J. Wood, Patriarch John F. Nash, John Fetzer and Nellie T. Taylor.

To Wilford C. Wood for furnishing pictures of the Far West and Independence Temple sites, and Adam-ondi-Ahman.

To The Little Brown Company of Boston for permission to use paragraph quoted from "Figures of the Past," by Josiah Quincy, in Chapter XV.

To the very fine generosity and courtesy of The Architectural Forum engineering magazine of New York City, for furnishing the cuts, etchings and write-up on the Kirtland Temple.

To the National Geographic Magazine for information tendered.

To the Librarian of Congress, Fine Arts Department, for pictures of the Kirtland Temple.

To Frank C. Pomeroy, of Mesa, Arizona, for data published by him in the Genealogical and Historical Magazine.

To the following named Presidents of Temples who have contributed information concerning the Temples over which they preside: To President Edward J. Wood, Alberta Temple; to President Harold S. Snow, of the St. George Temple; to President Charles R. Jones, of the Arizona Temple, and to President Joseph Quinney, Jr., of the Logan Temple.

To S. O. Bennion, C. W. Birkinshaw and James Hill of the Deseret News Press; to T. Albert Hooper, Manager of the Deseret Book Company; to Howard J. Gerber and Glen F. Gale, of the Typesetting Service Company, and to J. P. Ridges Engraving Company, for their cooperation and assistance.

To the hundreds who have expressed their interest and given their patronage to all publications issued by the Compiler of this book.

INTRODUCTION

This book is presented to the public as the companion volume to THE VISION, a work published in 1939, the Table of Contents for which is listed herein. Both books are compilations of rare, inspirational, and very inaccessible writings of such great men as Joseph Smith, the Prophet, Brigham Young, Orson Pratt, Parley P. Pratt, Wilford Woodruff, Orson Hyde, John Taylor, Lorenzo Snow, Pres. Joseph F. Smith, Heber C. Kimball and others. The quality of this compilation will speak for itself and needs no comment. Like THE VISION, the TEMPLES OF THE MOST HIGH is dedicated to the cause of truth and righteousness. It is hoped that its distribution will be far and wide; that its pages will inspire many souls; that the downcast may be cheered by its message; that the careless and indifferent, yea, also those who have stepped aside from the path that the Gospel directs, may return to the fold and again partake of the joy and happiness that once was theirs; that those who know not the truth concerning the Latter-day Saints may search its pages and be brought into the channel through which divine revelation may come to them. Those who are timid about using their own minds may derive strength by reading the following paragraph which was also incorporated in the Introduction given in THE VISION.

"I wish to notice this. We read in the Bible, that there is one glory of the sun, another glory of the moon, and another glory of the stars. In the Book of Doctrine and Covenants, the glories are called, telestial, terrestrial, and celestial, which is the highest. These are worlds, different departments, or mansions, in our Father's house. Now those men, or those women, who know no more about the power of God, and the influence of the Holy Spirit, than to be led entirely by another person, suspending their own understanding, and pinning their fate upon another's sleeve, will never be capable of entering into the celestial glory, to be crowned as they anticipate; they will never be capable of becoming Gods. They cannot rule themselves to say nothing of ruling others, but they must be dictated to in every trifle, like a child. They cannot control themselves in the least, but James, Peter, or somebody else must control them. They never can become Gods, nor be crowned as rulers with glory, immortality, and eternal lives. They never can hold scepters of glory, majesty, and power in the celestial kingdom. Who will? Those who are valiant and inspired with the true independence of heaven, who will go forth boldly in the service of their God, leaving others to do as they please, determined to do right, though all mankind besides should take the opposite course. Will this apply to any of you? Your own hearts can answer."

Pres. Brigham Young, *Journal of Discourses*, Vol. 1, p. 312.

TABLE OF CONTENTS

(Figures in parentheses designate pages on which the
sub-headings are given.)

Chapter I

THE KIRTLAND TEMPLE

DEDICATORY PRAYER

('Given by revelation to Joseph, the Seer, and repeated in the Kirtland Temple at the time of its dedication, March 27th, 1836.)

Thanks be to Thy name, O Lord God of Israel, who keepest covenant and showest mercy unto Thy servants who walk uprightly before Thee, with all their hearts;

Thou who hast commanded Thy servants to build a house to Thy name in this place. (Kirtland.)

JOSEPH SMITH, THE PROPHET

And now Thou beholdest, O Lord, that Thy servants have done according to Thy commandment.

And now we ask Thee, Holy Father, in the name of Jesus Christ, the Son of Thy bosom, in whose name alone, salvation can be administered to the children of men, we ask Thee, O Lord, to accept of this house, the workmanship of the hands of us, Thy servants, which Thou didst command us to build;

For Thou knowest that we have done this work through great tribulation; and out of our poverty we have given of our substance, to build a house to Thy name, that the Son of man might have a place to manifest Himself to His people.

And as Thou hast said in a revelation, given to us, calling us Thy friends, saying, "Call your solemn assembly, as I have commanded you;

And as all have not faith, seek ye diligently, and teach one another words of wisdom; yea, seek ye out of the best books, words of wisdom, seek learning even by study, and also by faith.

Organize yourselves; prepare every needful thing, and establish a house, even a house of prayer, a house of fasting, a house of faith, a house of learning, a house of glory, a house of order, a house of God.

That your incomings may be in the name of the Lord, that your outgoings may be in the name of the Lord, that all your salutations may be in the name of the Lord, with uplifted hands unto the Most High.

And now, Holy Father, we ask Thee to assist us, Thy people, with Thy grace, in calling our solemn assembly, that it may be done to Thy honor, and to Thy divine acceptance.

And in a manner that we may be found worthy, in Thy sight, to secure a fulfillment of the promises which Thou hast made unto us, Thy people, in the revelations given unto us;

That Thy glory may rest down upon Thy people, and upon this Thy house, which we now dedicate to Thee, that it may be sanctified and consecrated to be holy, and that Thy holy presence may be continually in this house.

And that all the people who shall enter upon the threshold of the Lord's house, may feel Thy power, and feel constrained to acknowledge that thou hast sanctified it, and that it is Thy house, a place of Thy holiness.

And do Thou grant, Holy Father, that all those who shall worship in this house, may be taught words of wisdom out of the best books, and that they may seek learning even by study, and also by faith, as Thou hast said;

And that they may grow up in Thee, and receive a fulness of the Holy Ghost and be organized according to Thy laws, and be prepared to obtain every needful thing;

And that this house may be a house of prayer, a house of fasting, a house of faith, a house of glory and of God, even thy house;

That all the incomings of Thy people, into this house, may be in the name of the Lord;

That all the outgoings from this house may be in the name of the Lord;

And that all their salutations may be in the name of the Lord, with holy hands, uplifted to the Most High;

And that no unclean thing shall be permitted to come into Thy house to pollute it;

And when Thy people transgress, any of them, they may speedily repent, and return unto Thee, and find favor in Thy sight, and be restored to the blessings which Thou hast ordained to be poured out upon those who shall reverence Thee in Thy house.

And we ask Thee, Holy Father, that Thy servants may go forth from this house, armed with Thy power, and that Thy name may be upon them, and Thy glory be round about them, and Thine angels have charge over them;

And from this place they may bear exceedingly great and glorious tidings, in truth, unto the end of the earth, that they may know that this is Thy work, and that Thou hast put forth Thy hand, to fulfill that which Thou hast spoken by the mouths of the prophets, concerning the last days.

We ask Thee, Holy Father, to establish the people that shall worship, and honorably hold a name and standing in this thy house, to all generations and for eternity;

That no weapon formed against them shall prosper; that he who diggeth a pit for them shall fall into the same himself;

That no combination of wickedness shall have power to rise up and prevail over Thy people upon whom Thy name shall be put in this house;

And if any people shall rise against this people, that Thine anger be kindled against them,

And if they shall smite this people, Thou wilt smite them, Thou will fight for Thy people as Thou didst in the day of battle, that they may be delivered from the hands of all their enemies.

We ask Thee, Holy Father, to confound, and astonish, and bring to shame and confusion, all those who have spread lying reports abroad, over the world against Thy servant or servants, if they will not repent, when the everlasting gospel shall be proclaimed in their ears,

And that all their works may be brought to naught, and be swept away by the hail, and by the judgments which Thou wilt send upon them in Thine anger, and there may be an end to lyings and slanders against Thy people;

For Thou knowest, O Lord, that Thy servants have been innocent before Thee in bearing record of Thy name, for which they have suffered these things;

Therefore we plead before Thee a full and complete deliverance from under this yoke;

Break it off, O Lord, break if off from the necks of Thy servants, by Thy power, that we may rise up in the midst of this generation and do Thy work.

O Jehovah, have mercy upon this people, and as all men sin, forgive the transgressions of Thy people, and let them be blotted out forever.

Let the anointing of Thy ministers be sealed upon them with power from on high;

Let it be fulfilled upon them, as upon those on the day of Pentecost, let the gift of tongues be poured out upon Thy people, even cloven tongues as of fire, and the interpretation thereof,

And let Thy house be filled, as with a rushing mighty wind, with Thy glory.

Put upon Thy servants the testimony of the covenant, that when they go out and proclaim Thy word, they may seal up the law, and prepare the hearts of Thy saints for all those judgments Thou art about to send, in Thy wrath, upon the inhabitants of the earth, because of their transgressions, that Thy people may not faint in the day of trouble.

And whatsoever city Thy servants shall enter, and the people of that city receive their testimony, let Thy peace and Thy salvation be upon that city, that they may gather out of that city the righteous, that they may come forth to Zion, or to her Stakes, the places of Thine appointment, with songs of everlasting joy;

And until this be accomplished, let not Thy judgments fall upon that city.

And whatsoever city Thy servants shall enter, and the people of that city receive not the testimony of Thy servants, and Thy servants warn them to save themselves from this untoward generation, let it be upon that city according to that which thou hast spoken by the mouths of Thy Prophets;

But deliver Thou, O Jehovah, we beseech Thee, Thy servants from their hands, and cleanse them from their blood.

O Lord, we delight not in the destruction of our fellow men. Their souls are precious before Thee;

But Thy word must be fulfilled; help Thy servants to say, with Thy grace assisting them, Thy will be done, O Lord, and not ours.

We know that Thou hast spoken by the mouth of Thy prophets terrible things concerning the wicked, in the last days—that thou wilt pour out Thy judgments without measure;

Therefore, O Lord, deliver Thy people from the calamity of the wicked; enable Thy servants to seal up the law, and bind up the testimony, that they may be prepared against the day of burning.

We ask Thee, Holy Father, to remember those who have been driven (by the inhabitants of Jackson County, Missouri) from the lands of their inheritance, and break off, O Lord, this yoke of affliction that has been put upon them.

Thou knowest, O Lord, that they have been greatly oppressed and afflicted by wicked men, and our hearts flow out with sorrow, because of their grievous burdens.

O Lord, how long wilt thou suffer this people to bear this affliction, and the cries of their innocent ones to ascend up in Thine ears, and their blood come up in testimony before Thee, and not make a display of Thy testimony in their behalf?

Have mercy, O Lord, upon that wicked mob, who have driven Thy people, that they may cease to spoil; that they may repent of their sins, if repentance is to be found;

But if they will not, make bare Thine arm, O Lord, and redeem that which Thou didst appoint a Zion unto Thy people!

And if it cannot be otherwise, that the cause of Thy people may not fail before Thee, may Thine anger be kindled, and Thine indignation fall upon them, that they may be wasted away, both root and branch, from under heaven;

But inasmuch as they will repent, Thou art gracious and merciful, and wilt turn away Thy wrath, when Thou lookest upon the face of Thine anointed.

Have mercy, O Lord, upon all the nations of the earth, have mercy upon the rulers of our land, may those principles which were so honorably and nobly defended, viz., the Constitution of our land, by our fathers, be established for ever;

Remember the kings, the princes, the nobles, and the great ones of the earth, and all people, and the churches, all the poor, the needy, and afflicted ones of the earth.

That their hearts may be softened, when Thy servants shall go out from Thy house, O Jehovah, to bear testimony of Thy name, that their prejudices may give way before the truth, and Thy people may obtain favor in the sight of all.

That all the ends of the earth may know that we Thy servants have heard Thy voice, and that Thou hast sent us,

That from among all these, Thy servants the sons of Jacob may gather out the righteous to build a holy city to Thy name, as Thou hast commanded them.

We ask Thee to appoint unto Zion other Stakes, besides this one which Thou hast appointed, that the gathering of Thy people may roll on in great power and majesty, that Thy work may be cut short in righteousness.

Now these words, O Lord, we have spoken before Thee, concerning the revelations and commandments which Thou hast given unto us, who are identified with the Gentiles;

But Thou knowest that Thou hast a great love for the children of Jacob, who have been scattered upon the mountains, for a long time, in a cloudy and dark day;

We therefore ask Thee to have mercy upon the children of Jacob, that Jerusalem, from this hour, may begin to be redeemed,

And the yoke of bondage may begin to be broken off from the house of David.

And the children of Judah may begin to return to the lands which Thou didst give to Abraham, their father;

And cause that the remnants of Jacob, who have been cursed and smitten, because of their transgression, be converted from their wild and savage condition, to the fulness of the everlasting gospel,

That they may lay down their weapons of bloodshed, and cease their rebellions;

And may all the scattered remnants of Israel, who have been driven to the ends of the earth come to a knowledge of the truth, believe in the Messiah, and be redeemed from oppression, and rejoice before Thee.

O Lord, remember Thy servant, Joseph Smith, Junior, and all his afflictions and persecutions, how he has covenanted with Jehovah, and vowed to Thee, O mighty God of Jacob, and the commandments which Thou hast given unto him, and that he hath sincerely striven to do Thy will.

Have mercy, O Lord, upon his wife and children, that they may be exalted in Thy presence, and preserved by Thy fostering hand:

Have mercy upon all their immediate connections, that their prejudices may be broken up, and swept away as with a flood, that they may be converted and redeemed with Israel, and know that Thou art God.

Remember, O Lord, the presidents, even all the presidents of Thy Church, that Thy right hand may exalt them, with all their families, and their immediate connections, that their names may be perpetuated, and had in everlasting remembrance, from generation to generation.

Remember all Thy Church, O Lord, with all their families, and all their immediate connections, with all their sick and afflicted ones, with all the poor and meek of the earth, that the kingdom which Thou hast set up without hands, may become a great mountain, and fill the whole earth;

That Thy Church may come forth out of the wilderness of darkness, and shine forth fair as the moon, clear as the sun, and terrible as an army with banners,

And be adorned as a bride for that day when Thou shalt unveil the heavens, and cause the mountains to flow down at Thy presence, and the valleys to be exalted, the rough places made smooth; that Thy glory may fill the earth,

That when the trumpet shall sound for the dead we shall be caught up in the cloud to meet Thee, that we may ever be with the Lord,

That our garments may be pure, that we may be clothed upon with robes of righteousness, with palms in our hands, and crowns of glory upon our heads, and reap eternal joy for all our sufferings.

O Lord God Almighty, hear us in these our petitions, and answer us from heaven, Thy holy habitation, where thou sittest enthroned, with glory, honor, power, majesty, might, dominion, truth, justice, judgment, mercy, and an infinity of fullness, from everlasting to everlasting.

O hear, O hear, O hear us, O Lord, and answer these petitions, and accept the dedication of this house unto Thee, the work of our hands, which we have built unto Thy name!

And also this Church, to put upon it Thy name; and help us by the power of Thy Spirit, that we may mingle our voices with those bright, shining seraphs around Thy throne, with acclamations of praise, singing, Hosanna to God and the Lamb;

And let these Thine anointed ones be clothed with salvation, and Thy saints shout aloud for joy. Amen, and Amen.

Doc. and Cov. Section 109.

Physical and Historical Description

The cornerstones of the Kirtland Temple were laid on July 23, 1833. "It was commenced in June, 1833, under the immediate direction of the Almighty, through His servant, Joseph Smith, whom He called in his boyhood, like Samuel of old, to introduce the fulness of the everlasting gospel.

At that time the Saints were few in number, and most of them very poor; and had it not been for the assurance that God had spoken, and had commanded that a house should be built to His name, of which He not only revealed the form but also designated the dimensions, an attempt towards building that Temple under the then existing circumstances, would have been by all concerned, pronounced preposterous. ***

Its dimensions are eighty by fifty-nine feet; the walls fifty feet high, and the tower one hundred and ten feet. The two main halls are fifty-five by sixty-five feet in the inner court. The building has four vestries in front, and five rooms in the attic, which were devoted to literature and for meetings of the various quorums of the Priesthood.

There was a peculiarity in the arrangement of the inner court which made it more than ordinarily impressive—so much so that a sense of sacred awe seemed to rest upon all who entered. Not only the Saints, but strangers also, manifested a high degree of reverential feeling. Four pulpits stood, one above another, in the center of the building, from north to south, both on the east

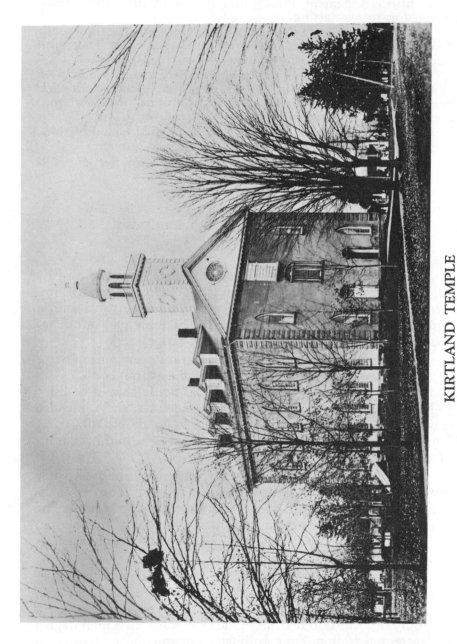

KIRTLAND TEMPLE

Site dedicated in June, 1833. Temple dedicated on March 27, 1836, by Joseph Smith the Prophet.

KIRTLAND TEMPLE
General view looking west, second floor.

and west ends. *** In front of each of these two rows of pulpits was a sacrament table, for the administration of that sacred ordinance. In each corner of the court was an elevated pew for the singers—the choir being distributed into four compartments. In addition to the pulpit curtains were others, intersecting at right

KIRTLAND TEMPLE
General view looking east, first floor.

angles, which divided the main ground-floor hall into four equal sections, giving to each one half of one set of pulpits.

From the day the ground was broken for laying the foundation of the Temple, until its dedication on the 27th of March, 1836, the work was vigorously prosecuted.

With very little capital except brain, bone, and sinew, combined with unwavering trust in God, men, women, and even children, worked with their might. While the brethren labored in their departments, the sisters were actively engaged in boarding and clothing workmen not otherwise provided for—all living as abstemiously as possible, so that every cent might be appropriated to the grand object, while their energies were stimulated by the prospect of participating in the blessings of a house built by the direction of the Most High, and accepted by Him.

Life of Joseph, the Prophet, by Edward W. Tullidge, pp. 187-189

The Kirtland Temple—An Historic American Building
(By Permission)

The Temple is 59 x 79 feet in size, contains a partly excavated basement, two full stories and an attic. The long axis of the building lies east and west with the front facing east. The exterior walls up to the cornice line are of stone, covered, except for the exposed stone foundation, stone quoins at the corners and the stone frieze of the cornice, with stuccoed plaster which contains bits of broken glass, china, etc., collected, according to tradition, by the women of the Church and used to produce a sparkle on the wall surfaces. The gables, dormers and tower are of frame construction. The original roof was covered with handmade wood shingles. The exterior trim around the door and window openings is of stone in long lengths, neatly and accurately tooled. The interior framing construction is of hewn and sawed material, following the usual heavy construction of that period. The interior trim, stairs, pews, pulpits, doors, etc., are of native wood hand-molded, carved and painted.

The first story is the apostolic floor, the second the church floor, and the attic the school and quorum floor. The first and second stories each contain two groups of nine pulpits, that at the east end being for the Aaronic order and the opposite one for the Melchizedek order. The pulpits are raised in tiers above

KIRTLAND TEMPLE
General View Looking West, Second Floor

KIRTLAND TEMPLE
General View Looking North, First Floor

the main floors. The seating arrangements in these two stories consist of stalls with doors, and movable pews in each stall, making possible the use of the entire auditorium from either pulpit. The second story auditorium and the schoolroom story were originally used for instruction purposes in connection with preparation for the ministry, priesthood and missionary work.

The workmanship, moldings, carvings, etc., show unusual skill in execution. Many motives are used in the various parts, varying in outline, contour and design, but blended harmoniously. This phase of the work indicates facility in adapting the design to meet varying conditions, as for instance the change in outline of moldings and in design and size of carving on the spiral stairs. It is not probable that all of the workmen engaged on the building were skilled artisans and yet the result is so harmonious as to raise the question if they may not have been inspired as were the builders of the cathedrals of old.

The Architectural Forum Master Detail Series, March, 1936, New York City

---

Faithfulness of Women and Men
By Heber C. Kimball

At this time the brethren were laboring night and day building the house of the Lord. Our women were engaged in spinning and knitting in order to clothe those who were laboring at the building, and the Lord only knows the scenes of poverty, tribulation, and distress which we passed through in order to accomplish this thing. My wife toiled all summer in lending her aid towards this accomplishment. She had a hundred pounds of wool, which, with the assistance of a girl, she spun in order to furnish clothing for those engaged in the building of the Temple, and although she had the privilege of keeping half the quantity of wool for herself, as a recompense for her labor, she did not reserve even so much as would make her a pair of stockings, but gave it for those who were laboring at the house of the Lord. She spun and wove and got the cloth dressed, and cut and made up into garments, and gave them to those men who labored on the Temple; almost all the sisters in Kirtland labored in knitting, sewing, spinning, etc., for the purpose of forwarding the work of the Lord, while we went up to Missouri to endeavor to reinstate our brethren on their lands, from which they had been driven. Elder Rigdon when addressing the brethren upon the importance of building this house, spake to this effect, that we should use every effort to accomplish this building by the time appointed, and if we did, the Lord would accept it at our hands, and on it depends the salvation of the church and also of the world. Looking at the sufferings and poverty of the church, he frequently used to go upon the walls of the building both by night and day and frequently wetting the walls with his tears, crying aloud to the Almighty to send means whereby we might accomplish the building. After we returned from our journey to the west, the whole church united in this undertaking and every man lent a helping hand. Those who had no teams went to work in the stone quarry and prepared the stones for drawing to the house, President Joseph Smith, Jr., being our foreman in the quarry, and the Presidency, High Priests, and Elders all alike assisting. Those who had teams assisted in drawing the stone to the house. These all laboring one day in the week, brought as many stones to the house as supplied the masons through the whole week. We continued in this manner until the walls of the house were reared. The committee who were appointed by revelation to superintend the building of the house, were Hyrum Smith, Reynolds Cahoon, and Jared Carter. These men used every exertion in their power to forward the work.

Times and Seasons, Vol. 6, pp. 367-8.

Manifestations of Divine Acceptance

Visions manifested to Joseph Smith, the Prophet, and Oliver Cowdery, in the Temple at Kirtland, Ohio, April 3, 1836. The occasion was that of a Sabbath day meeting. The Prophet prefaces his record of the manifestations with these words: In the afternoon, I assisted the other presidents in distributing the Lord's Supper to the Church, receiving it from the Twelve, whose privilege it was to officiate at the sacred desk this day. After having performed this service to my brethren, I retired to the pulpit, the veils being dropped, and bowed myself with Oliver Cowdery, in solemn and silent prayer. After rising from prayer, the following vision was opened to both of us.—Personal manifestations of the Lord Jesus Christ—His acceptance of the Temple. Visitation of Moses and his commitment of the keys of the gathering.—Visitation by Elias and his conferment of authority.—Visitation of Elijah in direct fulfillment of Malachi's prediction.

The veil was taken from our minds, and the eyes of our understanding were opened.

We saw the Lord standing upon the breastwork of the pulpit, before us; and under His feet was a paved work of pure gold, in color like amber.

His eyes were as a flame of fire; the hair of His head was white like the pure snow; His countenance shone above the brightness of the sun; and His voice was as the sound of the rushing of great waters, even the voice of Jehovah, saying:

"I am the first and the last; I am he who liveth, I am he who was slain; I am your advocate with the Father.

"Behold, your sins are forgiven you; you are clean before me; therefore, lift up your heads and rejoice.

"Let the hearts of your brethren rejoice, and let the hearts of all my people rejoice, who have, with their might, built this house to my name.

"For behold, I have accepted this house, and my name shall be here; and I will manifest myself to my people in mercy in this house.

"Yea, I will appear unto my servants, and speak unto them with mine own voice; if my people will keep my commandments and do not pollute this holy house.

"Yea, the hearts of thousands and tens of thousands shall greatly rejoice in consequence of the blessings which shall be poured out, and the endowment with which my servants have been endowed in this house.

"And the fame of this house shall spread to foreign lands; and this is the beginning of the blessings which shall be poured out upon the heads of my people. Even so, Amen."

After this vision closed, the heavens were again opened unto us; and Moses appeared before us, and committed unto us the keys of the gathering of Israel from the four parts of the earth, and leading of the ten tribes from the land of the north.

After this, Elias appeared, and committed the dispensation of the Gospel of Abraham, saying that in us and our seed all generations after us should be blessed.

After this vision had closed, another great and glorious vision burst upon us; for Elijah the prophet, who was taken to heaven without tasting death, stood before us, and said:

"Behold, the time has fully come, which was spoken of by Malachi—testifying that he (Elijah) should be sent before the great and dreadful day of the Lord comes—To turn the hearts of the fathers to the children, and the children to the fathers, lest the whole earth be smitten with a curse — Therefore, the keys of this dispensation are committed into your hands; and by this ye may know that the great and dreadful day of the Lord is near, even at the doors."

Doc. & Cov., Sec. 110, 14-16.

January 21, 1836: The Presidency then took the seat in their turn, according to their age, beginning at the oldest, and received their anointing and blessing under the hands of Father Smith. And in my turn, my father anointed my head, and sealed upon me the blessings of Moses, to lead Israel in the latter days, even as Moses led him in days of old; also the blessings of Abraham, Isaac and Jacob. All of the Presidency laid their hands upon me, and pronounced upon my head many prophecies and blessings, many of which I shall not notice at this time.

The heavens were opened before us, and I beheld the celestial kingdom of God, and the glory thereof, whether in the body or out I cannot tell. I saw the transcendent beauty of the gate through which the heirs of that kingdom will enter, which was like unto circling flames of fire; also the blazing throne of God, whereon were seated the Father and the Son. I saw the beautiful streets of that kingdom, which had the appearance of being paved with gold. I saw Fathers Adam and Abraham, and my father and mother, my brother, Alvin, that has long since slept, and marveled how it was that he had obtained an inheritance in that kingdom, seeing that he had departed this life before the Lord had set His hand to gather Israel the second time, and had not been baptized for the remission of sins. Thus came the voice of the Lord unto me, saying:

"All who have died without a knowledge of this Gospel, who would have received it if they had been permitted to tarry, shall be heirs of the celestial kingdom of God; also all that shall die henceforth without a knowledge of it, who would have received it with all their hearts, shall be heirs of that kingdom, for I, the Lord, will judge all men according to their works, according to the desires of their hearts."

And I also beheld that all children who die before they arrive at the years of accountability, are saved in the celestial kingdom of heaven. I saw the Twelve Apostles of the Lamb, who are now upon the earth, who hold the keys of this last ministry, in foreign lands, standing together in a circle, much fatigued, with their clothes tattered and feet swollen, with their eyes cast downward, and Jesus standing in their midst, and they did not behold Him. The Savior looked upon them and wept.***

Also, I saw Elder Brigham Young standing in a strange land, in the far south and west, in a desert place, upon a rock in the midst of about a dozen men of color, who appeared hostile. He was preaching to them in their own tongue, and the angel of God standing above his head, with a drawn sword in his hand, protecting him, but he did not see it. And I finally saw the Twelve in the celestial kingdom of God. I also beheld the redemption of Zion, and many things which the tongue of man cannot describe in full.

Many of my brethren who received the ordinance with me saw glorious visions also. Angels ministered unto them as well as to myself, and the power of the Highest rested upon us, the house was filled with the glory of God, and we shouted Hosanna to God and the Lamb. My scribe also received his anointing with us, and saw, in a vision, the armies of heaven protecting the Saints in their return to Zion, and many things which I saw.

The Bishop of Kirtland with his Counselors, and the Bishop of Zion with his Counselors, were present with us, and received their anointings under the hands of Father Smith, and this was confirmed by the Presidency, and the glories of heaven were unfolded to them.

We then invited the High Councilors of Kirtland and Zion into our room, and President Hyrum Smith anointed the head of the President of the Councilors in Kirtland, and President David Whitmer, the head of the President of the Councilors of Zion. The President of each quorum then anointed the heads of his colleagues each in his turn, beginning at the oldest, The visions of heaven were opened to them also. Some of them saw the face of the Savior, and others were ministered unto by holy angels, and the spirit of prophecy and revelation was poured out in mighty power; and loud Hosannas, and glory to God in the highest, saluted the heavens, for we all communed with the heavenly hosts. And I saw in my vision all of the Presidency in the celestial kingdom of God and many others that were present. Our meeting was opened by singing, and prayer was offered by the head of each quorum; and closed by singing, and invoking the benediction of heaven, with uplifted hands. Retired between one and two o'clock in the morning.

History of Church, Vol. 2, pp. 380-2.

President Rigdon arose to conclude the services of the evening by invoking the blessing of heaven upon the Lord's anointed, which he did in an eloquent manner; the congregation shouted a long Hosanna; the gift of tongues fell upon us in mighty power, angels mingled their voices with ours while their presence was in our midst, and unceasing praises swelled our bosoms for the space of half-an-hour.

I then observed to the brethren, that it was time to retire. We accordingly closed our interview and returned home at about two o'clock in the morning, and the Spirit and visions of God attended me through the night.

History of Church, Vol. 2, p. 383.

March 27, 1836: Brother George A. Smith arose and began to prophesy, when a noise was heard like the sound of a rushing mighty wind, which filled the Temple, and all the congregation simultaneously arose, being moved upon by an invisible power; many began to speak in tongues and prophesy; others saw glorious visions; and I beheld the Temple was filled with angels, which fact I declared to the congregation. The people of the neighborhood came running together (hearing an unusual sound within and seeing a bright light like a pillar of fire resting upon the Temple), and were astonished at what was taking place. This continued until the meeting closed at eleven P. M.

History of Church, Vol. 2, p. 428.

An Elect Lady Testifies

My brother (President Lorenzo Snow) spent most of the winter of 1837-8 in Kirtland, where he witnessed many marvelous manifestations of the power of God; also exhibitions of the power and opposition of the adversary. During the time he became intimately acquainted with Joseph Smith, the Prophet, and with his father, the Patriarch—with the Twelve Apostles and other leading men in the Church. In his journal he speaks of the fast meetings, prayer and testimony meetings in the Temple, as follows:

There we had the gift of prophecy—the gift of tongues—the interpretation of tongues—visions and marvelous dreams were related—the singing of heavenly choirs was heard, and wonderful manifestations of the healing power, through the administration of the Elders, were witnessed. The sick were healed—the deaf made to hear, the blind to see, and the lame to walk, in very many instances. It was plainly manifest that a sacred and divine influence—a spiritual atmosphere pervaded that holy edifice. Yes, indeed, for the Son of God, in His glory, had honored it with His royal presence. His voice, like the sound of many waters, was heard saying:

"I am the first and the last, I am he who liveth, I am he that was slain, I am your advocate with the Father."* * *

No language can describe my feelings when, for the first time, I stood up in one of those pulpits to address an audience—a pulpit on the breastwork of which, only a short time before, this holy Personage stood—His hair as white as pure snow, His eyes as a flame of fire—where also Moses, Elias and Elijah came and committed the keys of their dispensations to Joseph Smith.

Public meetings were regularly held in the Temple, after its dedication, on Sundays; and on the first Thursday in each month a fast meeting, commencing at or before 10 a.m. and closing at 4 p.m.*** On the aforementioned days, Father Smith (the Prophet's father) was in the habit of entering the Temple very early in the morning, and there offering up his prayers to God, in that holy place, before the rising of the sun, after having told the Saints, publicly, that they were welcome to come as early as they pleased. The result was that many assembled before the hour of 10 a.m. and did not leave till after 4 p.m.

At one of these meetings, an insane woman came into the quarter of the house where I had convened; she came before the opening services, and her tongue ran incessantly, making so much confusion as to render it improper, if not impossible, for the pre-

siding Elder to commence religious services. The more she was
coaxed and supplicated to be silent the more impetuous she became. At length, Elder John P. Greene, who was appointed to
preside in that department, requested the congregation to kneel
down and all simultaneously pray to God, vocally, that the evil
spirit which was actuating that woman might be bound. The
request was immediately complied with, and when we arose from
our kneeling position Brother Greene, addressing the unfortunate woman (who was then silent), said: "Sister, you may now
speak, for thou wilt not speak unless thou shalt speak by the
Spirit of God." She instantly arose to her feet, and, in a sputter-
ing, stammering manner, tried to speak, but could not, and flew
out of the Temple like a dart, and we saw no more of her that
day.

     I will relate one more remarkable circumstance which trans-
pired in that interesting season—a circumstance which was not
confined to either section of the Temple, but was witnessed by
the many who were congregated on that day; and certainly all
now living who were present on that occasion will remember. It
is a testimony of answer to prayer that never can be forgotten.
Father Smith presided over the meeting in the northwest section
of the Temple, and after the meeting was opened by singing, he
was mouth in prayer, and in course of supplication he very earnestly prayed that the Spirit of God might be poured out as on
the day of Pentecost—that it might come "as a rushing mighty
wind." Some time after in the midst of the exercises of the forenoon, it did come; and whether Father Smith had forgotten what
he had prayer for or whether, in the fervency of his heart, when
praying he did not realize what he prayed for, I never ascer-
tained, but when the sound came and filled the house, with an
expression of great astonishment he raised his eyes, exclaiming,
"What! Is the house on fire?" But presently he comprehended
the cause of his alarm, and was filled with unspeakable joy.

Biography and Family Record of Lorenzo Snow, by Eliza R. Snow Smith, pp. 11-14.

Dedicatory Services as Described by Heber C. Kimball

     This building the Saints commenced in 1833, in poverty,
and without means to do it. In 1834 they completed the walls,
and in 1835-36 they nearly finished it. The cost was between six-

ty and seventy thousand dollars. A committee was appointed to gather donations; they traveled among the churches and collected a considerable amount, but not sufficient, so that in the end they found themselves between thirteen and fourteen thousand dollars in debt. This house was 80x60 feet, and 57 feet high to the eaves. It was divided into two stories, each 22 feet high, and arched overhead. Ten feet were cut off from the front by a partition, and used as an entry or outer court, which also contained the stairs. This left the main room 55x65 feet in the clear, both below and above. In each of these rooms were built two pulpits, one in each end. Each pulpit consisted of four different apartments; the fourth standing on a platform raised a suitable height above the floor; the third stood directly behind and elevated a little above the fourth; the second in rear of and elevated above the third; and in like manner the first above the second. Each of these apartments was just large enough and rightly calculated to seat three persons, and the breastwork in front of each of these three last mentioned was constituted of three semicircles, joining each other, and finished in good style. The fourth or lower one, was straight in front, and had an elegant table leaf attached to it, that could be raised at pleasure for the convenience of administering the sacrament, etc. These pulpits were alike in each end of the house. One was for the use of the Melchizedek or High Priesthood and the other for the Aaronic or Lesser Priesthood. The first or highest apartment was occupied by the First President over the whole Church; the second apartment by the Melchizedek High Priesthood; the third by the President of the High Priests' quorum; and the fourth by the President of the Elders and his two counselors. The highest apartment of the other pulpit was occupied by the Bishop of the Church and his two counselors; the next by the President of the Priests and his two counselors; the third by the President of the Teachers and his two counselors; and the fourth by the President of the Deacons and his two counselors.

Each of these apartments had curtains hanging from the ceilings overhead down to the top of the pulpit, which could be rolled up or dropped down at pleasure, and when dropped down would completely exclude those within the department from the sight of all others. The room itself was finished with slips and seats so calculated that by slipping the seats a little the congregation could change their faces toward either pulpit they chose;

for in some cases the High Priesthood would administer, and in other cases, the Lesser Priesthood would administer. The room was also divided into four compartments by means of curtains or veils hanging from the ceiling overhead down to the floor, which could be rolled up at pleasure, so that the house could be used all in one or divided into four rooms and used for different purposes. Thus the house was constructed to suit and accommodate the different quorums of the Priesthood and worship peculiar to the Church. The first story or lower room was dedicated for divine worship alone. The second story was finished similar in form to the first, but was designed wholly for instructing the Priesthood, and was supplied with tables and seats instead of slips. In the attic five rooms were finished for the convenience of schools and for different quorums of the Church to meet in. There was no baptismal font in this temple, the ordinance of baptism for the dead not having been revealed. At the time of dedication the first story was finished, also the attic, but the second story was in an unfinished condition.

At the dedication an address was delivered by Elder Rigdon from Matthew 8th chapter, 18 to 20 verses, more particularly the 20th. He spoke two hours and a half. The tenor of his discourse went to show the toils, sufferings, privations, and hardships the brethren and sisters had to endure while building this house, and compared it with the sufferings of the Saints in the days of the Savior. After the address the voice of the assembly was taken in reference to receiving and upholding the several presidents of the different quorums in their standing. The vote was unanimous in the affirmative in every instance. A hymn was sung, and then we had an interesting address from President Joseph Smith, and closed with a dedication prayer written by the Prophet.

During the ceremonies of the dedication, an angel appeared and sat near President Joseph Smith, Sr., and Frederick G. Williams so that they had a fair view of his person. He was a very tall personage, black eyes, white hair, and stoop-shouldered; his garment was whole, extending to near his ankles; on his feet he had sandals. He was sent as a messenger to accept of the dedication. During the whole of the dedication each quorum was placed in its respective station. Everything was conducted in the best of order, and profound silence maintained.

We had been commanded to prepare ourselves for a solemn

assembly. At length the time arrived for this assembly to meet; previous to which the Prophet Joseph exhorted the Elders to solemnize their minds, by casting away every evil from them, in thought, word and deed, and to let their hearts become sanctified, because they need not expect a blessing from God without being duly prepared for it, for the Holy Ghost would not dwell in unholy temples. This meeting took place soon after the house of the Lord had been dedicated.***

When the Prophet Joseph had finished the endowments of the First Presidency, the Twelve and the Presiding Bishops, the First Presidency proceeded to lay hands upon each one of them to seal and confirm the anointing; and at the close of each blessing the whole of the quorums responded to it with a loud shout of Hosanna! Hosanna! etc.

While these things were being attended to, the beloved disciple, John, was seen in our midst by the Prophet Joseph, Oliver Cowdery and others. After this all the quorums arose in order, together with the three Presidencies; and the Twelve then presented themselves separately and individually before the First Presidency, with hands uplifted towards heaven, and asked God whatever they felt to desire; and after each individual petition the whole of the quorums answered aloud, Amen! Hosanna! Hosanna! Hosanna! To God and the Lamb forever and ever, amen, and amen!

The 6th day of April being the day appointed for fasting and prayer, all the Elders, Priests, Teachers and Deacons, numbering about four hundred, met together in the House of the Lord to attend to further ordinances; none being permitted to enter but official members who had previously received their washings and anointings. Water being provided, the First Presidency, after girding themselves with towels, proceeded to wash the feet of the Twelve. After they got through, the Twelve girded themselves and washed the feet of the Seventies. They then took their seats, each quorum seating themselves in their respective places and continued in fasting and prayer, prophesying and exhortation until evening. A sufficient quantity of bread having been provided to feed this whole assembly, it was broken by the First Presidency of the Church and the Twelve, after which the congregation knelt while a benediction was pronounced upon it by the First Presidency; and afterwards the Twelve took it and administered to the congregation. Then wine, also being provided, was blessed by the First Presidency and in like manner served to the congregation by the Twelve. This order of things is similar to that which was attended to by the Savior amongst His disciples, previous to His ascension. The meeting continued on through the night; the spirit of prophecy was poured out upon the assembly, and cloven tongues of fire sat upon them, for they were seen by many of the congregation. Also angels administered to many, for they were also seen by many.

This continued for several days and was attended by a marvelous spirit of prophecy. Every man's mouth was full of prophesying, and for a number of days or weeks our time was spent in visiting from house to house, administering bread and wine and pronouncing blessings upon each other to that degree that from the external appearances one would have supposed that the last days had truly come, in which the Spirit of the Lord was poured out upon all flesh, as far as the Church was concerned, for the sons and daughters of Zion were full of prophesying. In this prophesying great blessings were pronounced upon the faithful, and also great cursings upon the ungodly, or upon those who had smitten us. During this time many great and marvelous visions were seen, one of which I will mention which Joseph the Prophet had concerning the Twelve. His anxiety was and had been very great for their welfare, when the following vision was manifested to him, as near as I can recollect:

He saw the Twelve going forth and they appeared to be in a far distant land. After some time they unexpectedly met together, apparently in great tribulation, their clothes all ragged, and their knees and feet sore. They formed into a circle and all stood with their eyes fixed upon the ground. The Savior appeared and stood in their midst and wept over them, and wanted to show himself to them, but they did not discover him. He (Joseph) saw until they had accomplished their work and arrived at the gate of the celestial city; there Father Adam stood and opened the gate to them, and as they entered he embraced them one by one and kissed them. He then led them to the throne of God, and then the Savior embraced each one of them and kissed them, and crowned each one of them in the presence of God. He saw that they all had beautiful heads of hair and all looked alike. The impression this vision left on Brother Joseph's mind was of so acute a nature that he never could refrain from weeping while rehearsing it.

Life of Heber C. Kimball, by Orson F. Whitney, pp. 100-6.

The Poverty of the Saints in Kirtland

By Daniel Tyler

At that time (1835-6) perhaps two thousand people, or even less, constituted the entire Church of Jesus Christ of Latter-day Saints, and they were mostly of the poorer class. A few well-to-do farmers composed the so-called wealthy portion of the Church. Those who had a little property, as a rule, clung to it, leaving those who were dependent upon their labor for their daily food to build the house of the Lord.

How often have I seen those humble, faithful, servants of the Lord, after toiling all day in the quarry, or on the building, when the walls were in course of erection, weary and faint, yet with cheerful countenances, retiring to their homes with a few pounds of corn meal that had been donated. And in the case of those who lacked a cow to give a little milk, the corn meal was sometimes, for days together, all that they and their families had to subsist on. When a little flour, butter or meat came in, they were luxuries. Sometimes a little New Orleans Molasses, not as good as our sorghum, would be donated, but oftener the hands had to seek a job elsewhere to get a gallon or so, and then return to the labor on the temple.

To show how little interest the few who had means took in building the temple, and supplying the wants of the hands, one instance only need be mentioned. I think it was father Fisher, who, by some accident, fell from the scaffold, and was disabled for performing manual labor. He could manage, by the labor of his boys, to get a little corn, but corn bread was dry food. He went to the prophet and asked him what he should do, and was told to get up a subscription paper and present to those who were best able to donate, and raise money enough to buy a cow, which would cost from ten to twelve dollars. He did as directed, and received the full sum of seventy-five cents. One person gave fifty and another twenty-five cents. This so disgusted the prophet that he preferred a charge against them before the High Council "for a lack of charity to the Church, and benevolence to the poor." One of them made a humble acknowledgment, and the other was disfellowshipped.

Juvenile Instructor, vol. 15.

Revelations Received by Joseph the Seer at Kirtland

Twenty-seven years ago on the fifth of this month (May), in the year 1834, a company started for Kirtland to redeem Zion. Brother Heber C. Kimball and my brother, Joseph, were in that camp. There had not been ordained any Twelve Apostles nor any Seventies, although there was a revelation pertaining to the Apostles and Seventies. There were High Priests but no high priests quorum. I am relating this as a little matter of history that will no doubt be interesting to those who were not there.

After we returned from Missouri, my brother, Joseph Young, and myself had been singing after preaching in a meeting and when the meeting was dismissed, Brother Joseph said: "Come go down to my house with me." We went and sang to him a long time and talked with him. He then opened the subject of the Twelve and Seventies for the first time I ever thought of it. He said: "Brethren, I am going to call out Twelve Apostles. I think we will get together by and by, and select Twelve Apostes and select a quorum of Seventies from those who have been up to Zion out of the camp boys." In 1835, the last of January, or in February, or about that time, we held our meetings from day to day, and Brother Joseph called out Twelve Apostles at that time. He had a revelation when we were singing to him. Those who were acquainted with him knew when the Spirit of revelation was upon him, for his countenance wore an expression peculiar *to* himself while under that influence. He preached by the Spirit of revelation and taught in his council by it and those who were acquainted with him could discover it at once, for at such times there was a peculiar clearness and transparency in his face. He followed up that revelation until he organized the Church and so along until the baptism of the dead was revealed.

Brigham Young, J. D. 9:89.

Saints Witnessing Great Manifestations, Soon Apostatized

Among the first principles that were revealed to the children of men in the last days was the gathering; the first revelations that were given to the Church were to command them to gather, and send Elders to seek out a place for the gathering of the Saints. What is the gathering for? Why was it that the Savior wished the children of Israel to gather together? It was that they might become united and provide a place wherein He could reveal unto them keys which have been hid from before the foundation of the world; that He could unfold unto them the laws of exaltation, and make them a kingdom of Priests—even the whole people, and exalt them to thrones and dominions in the celestial world.

For this purpose, in 1833, the Saints commenced to build a Temple in Kirtland, the cost of which was not less than one hundred thousand dollars. A mere handful of Saints commenced that work, but they were full of faith and energy, and willing, as they supposed, to sacrifice everything for the building up of Zion. In a few weeks some of them apostatized; the trials were too great, the troubles were too severe. I know persons who apostatized because they supposed they had reasons; for instance, a certain family, after having traveled a long journey, arrived in Kirtland, and the Prophet asked them to stop with him until they could find a place. Sister Emma, in the meantime, asked the old lady if she would have a cup of tea to refresh her after the fatigues of the journey, or a cup of coffee. This whole family apostatized because they were invited to take a cup of tea or coffee, after the Word of Wisdom was given.

Another family, about the same time, apostatized because Joseph Smith came

down out of the translating room, where he had been translating by the gift and
power of God, and commenced playing with his little children. Some such trials as
these, you know, had to be encountered. I recollect a gentleman who came from
Canada, and who always had been a Methodist, and had always been in the habit of
praying to a God who had no ears and as a matter of course had to shout and halloo
pretty hard to make Him hear. Father Johnson asked him to pray in their family
worship in the evening, and he got on such a high key, and hallooed so loud that he
alarmed the whole village. Among others, Joseph came running out, saying, "What
is the matter? I thought by the noise that the heavens and the earth were coming
together," and said to the man, "that he ought not to give way to such an enthusiastic
spirit, and bray so much like a jackass." Because Joseph said that, the poor man put
back to Canada, and apostatized; he thought he would not pray to a God who did
not want to be screamed at with all one's might.

We progressed in this way while we were building the Kirtland Temple. The
Saints had a great many traditions which they had borrowed from their fathers, and
laid the foundations, and built that Temple with great toil and suffering, compared
with what we have now to endure. They got that building so far finished as to be
dedicated; this was what the Lord wanted. He wished them to provide a place wherein
He could reveal to the children of men those principles that will exalt them to eternal
glory, and make them Saviors on Mount Zion. Four hundred and sixteen Elders,
Priests, Teachers, and Deacons met in the Kirtland Temple on the evening of its
dedication. I can see faces here that were in that assembly. The Lord poured His
Spirit upon us and gave us some little idea of the law of anointing, and conferred
upon us some blessings. He taught us how to shout Hosanna, gave Joseph the keys
of the gathering together of Israel, and revealed to us, what, why the fact of it was,
He dare not trust us with the first key of the Priesthood. He told us to wash ourselves,
and that almost made the women mad, and they said, as they were not admitted
into the Temple while this washing was being performed, that some mischief was
going on, and some of them were right huffy about it.

We were instructed to wash each other's feet, as an evidence that we had borne
testimony of the truth of the Gospel to the world. We were taught to anoint each
other's head with oil in the name of the Lord, as an ordinance of anointing. All
these things were to be done in their time, place, and season. All this was plain and
simple, yet some apostatized because there was not more of it, and others because
there was too much.

On the evening after the dedication of the Temple, hundreds of the brethren
received the ministering of angels, saw the light and personages of angels, and bore
testimony of it. They spake in new tongues, and had a greater manifestation of the
power of God than that described by Luke on the day of Pentecost. Yet a great
portion of the persons who saw these manifestations, in a few years, and some of
them in a few weeks, apostatized. If the Lord had on that occasion revealed one
single sentiment more, or gone one step further to reveal more fully the law of
redemption, I believe He would have upset the whole of us. The fact was, He dare
not, on that very account, reveal to us a single principle further than He had done,
for He had tried, over and over again, to do it. He tried at Jerusalem; He tried away
back before the flood; He tried in the days of Moses; and He had tried, from time to
time, to find a people to whom He could reveal the law of salvation, and He never
could fully accomplish it; and He was determined this time to be so careful, and

advance the idea so slowly, to communicate them to the children of men with such great caution that, at all hazards, a few of them might be able to understand and obey. For, says the Lord, My ways are not as your ways, nor My thoughts as your thoughts; for as the heavens are higher than the earth, so are My ways than your ways, and My thoughts than your thoughts. * * *

Now if the Lord had considered it wisdom, on the day of the Kirtland endowment and great solemn assembly, to come forward and reveal to the children of men the facts that are laid down plainly in the Bible, and had told them that, without the law of sealing, no man could be exalted to a throne in the celestial kingdom, that is, without he had a woman by his side; and that no woman could be exalted to the celestial world without she was exalted with a man at her head; that the man is not without the woman, nor the woman without the man in the Lord; had He revealed this simple sentiment, up would have jumped some man, saying, "What! Got to have a woman sealed to me in order to be saved, in order to be exalted to thrones, dominions, and eternal increase?" "Yes." "I do not believe a word of it, I cannot stand that, for I never intended to get married, I do not believe in any of this nonsense." At the same time, perhaps somebody else might have had faith to receive it. Again up jumps somebody else, "Brother Joseph, I have had two wives in my lifetime, cannot I have them both in eternity?" "No." If he had said yes, perhaps we should all have apostatized at once.

Now I will illustrate this still further. The Lord did actually reveal one principle to us there, and that one principle was apparently so simple, and so foolish in their eyes, that a great many apostatized over it, because it was so contrary to their notions and views. It was this, after the people had fasted all day, they sent out and got wine and bread, and blessed them, and distributed them to the multitude, that is, to the whole assembly of the brethren, and they ate and drank, and prophesied, and bore testimony, and continued so to do until some of the High Council of Missouri stepped into the stand, and, as righteous Noah did when he awoke from his wine, commenced to curse their enemies. You never felt such a shock go through any house or company in the world as went through that. There was almost rebellion because men would get up and curse their enemies; although they could remember well that it is written that Noah cursed his own grandson, and that God recognized that curse to such an extent that, at this day, millions of his posterity are consigned to perpetual servitude.

Many men are foolish enough to think that they can thwart the power of God, and can liberate the sons of Ham from that curse before its time has expired. Some of the brethren thought that it was best to apostatize, because the spirit of cursing was with men who had been driven from Missouri by mob violence. Yet every word that they prophesied has been fulfilled. They prophesied that the bones of many of those murderers should bleach on the prairie, and that birds should pick out their eyes, and beasts devour their flesh. Men who have traversed the plains of Mexico, California, Nebraska, and Kansas, have often seen the fulfillment of that prophecy in the most marvelous manner. We have seen their names upon trees, on the heads of old trunks, and bits of boards; the names of men that I knew, and I knew just as well, in the Kirtland Temple, what would be their fate, as I know now. But that tried us, some of us were awfully tried about it. The Lord dared not then reveal anything more; He had given us all we could swallow; and persecution raged around us to such an extent that we were obliged to forsake our beautiful Temple, and flee into the state of Missouri.

By George A. Smith, J. D., Vol. 2:214-16.

The Great Apostasy

During the time my brother (Lorenzo Snow) was on this, his first mission, a great change had been going on in Kirtland, in the midst of the Saints. A spirit of speculation had crept into the hearts of some of the Twelve, and nearly, if not every quorum, was more or less infected. Most of the Saints were poor, and now prosperity was dawning upon them—the Temple was completed, and in it they had been recipients of marvelous blessings and many who had been humble and faithful to the performance of every duty—ready to go and come at every call of the Priesthood were getting haughty in their spirits, and lifted up in the pride of their hearts. As the Saints drank in the love and spirit of the world, the Spirit of the Lord withdrew from their hearts, and they were filled with pride and hatred toward those who maintained their integrity. They linked themselves together in an opposing party—pretended that they constituted the Church and claimed that the Temple belonged to them and even attempted to hold it.

Warren Parrish,[1] who had been a humble, successful preacher of the Gospel, was the ringleader of this apostate party. One Sabbath morning, he, with several of his party, came into the Temple armed with pistols and bowie-knives, and seated themselves together in the Aaronic pulpits, on the east end of the

---

[1] "Then came the financial crash of 1837, by which so many of the banking and business houses of the country were prostrated. Nearly all the banks, one after another, suspended specie payment, 'and the gold and silver rose in value in direct ratio with the depreciation of paper currency.' The Kirtland Bank shared a similar fate to many others and went down in the whirlpool of financial ruin. One of the causes alleged for the failure was malfeasance of some of those who were entrusted with the funds of the Bank. Heber says that Warren Parrish, one of the clerks, afterwards acknowledged that he took $20,000, and there was strong evidence that he took more. Those of integrity in the Church replaced the stolen money at the expense of all they had. A counterfeit, falsely reputed to have been issued by the Bank, was also used by its enemies, as a means to effect its overthrow." Life of Heber C. Kimball, By Orson F. Whitney, pkp. 112-3.

Cause of Failure of Kirtland Bank, By George A. Smith:

[1a]Some time after the finishing of the Temple, the brethren under the direction of the Prophet had established a bank in Kirtland, the paper to be redeemed by specie, and secured by real estate. The directors of that bank were members of the Church, and they were determined to sustain the credit of that money. The question has sometimes been asked, how much has that bank failed for; it did not fail for a single dollar, and yet when it failed there was perhaps a hundred thousand dollars of the bankpaper out in circulation. Warren Parrish was the teller of the bank, and a number of other men who apostatized were officers. They took out of its vault, unknown to the President or Cashier, a hundred thousand dollars, and sent their agents around among the brethren to purchase their farms, wagons, cattle, horses and everything they could get hold of. The brethren

KIRTLAND TEMPLE

First Floor. Looking West. On the middle pulpit of the center
row, stood the Redeemer as given in the 110th Section of
the Doctrine and Covenants, April 3, 1836.

would gather up this money and put it into the bank, and those traitors would steal it and send
it out to buy again, and they continued to do so until the plot was discovered and payments stopped.
It was the cursed apostates—their stealing and robberies, and their infernal villainies that prevented
that bank being conducted as the Prophet designed. If they had followed the counsel of Joseph,
there is not a doubt that it would have been the leading bank in Ohio, probably of the nation.
It was founded upon safe principles, and would have been a safe and lasting institution.

Temple, while Father Smith and others, as usual occupied those of the Melchizedek Priesthood on the west. Soon after the usual opening services one of the brethren on the west stand arose, and just after he commenced to speak, one on the east interrupted him. Father Smith, presiding, called to order—he told the apostate brother that he should have all the time he wanted, but he must wait his turn—as the brother on the west took the floor and commenced first to speak, he must not be interrupted. A fearful scene ensued—the apostate speaker becoming too clamorous that Father Smith called for the police to take that man out of the house, when Parrish, John Boynton, and others, drew their pistols and bowie-knives and rushed down from the stand into the congregation, J. Boynton saying he would blow out the brains of the first man who dared to lay hands on him. Many in the congregation, especially women and children, were terribly frightened—some tried to escape from the confusion by jumping out of the windows. Amid screams and shrieks, the policemen, in ejecting the belligerents, knocked down a stovepipe, which fell helter-skelter among the people; but, although bowie-knives and pistols were wrested from their owners, and thrown hither and thither to prevent disastrous results, no one was hurt, and after a short, but terrible scene to be enacted in a Temple of God, order was restored, and the services of the day proceeded as usual.

Biography and Family Record of Lorenzo Snow, by Eliza R. Snow Smith, pp. 20-21.

Five of the quorum of the Twelve [2, 3, 4, 5] were in this apostasy, and some in every organized quorum became disaffected.

[2]Character of Those Who Apostatized   By G. A. Smith.—After the organization of the Twelve Apostles and so far finishing of the Kirtland Temple as to hold a solemn assembly and confer the Kirtland endowment therein, the spirit of apostasy became more general and the shock that was given to the Church became more severe than on any previous occasion. The Church had increased in numbers and the elders had extended their labors accordingly; but the apostasy commenced in high places. One of the First Presidency, several of the Twelve Apostles, High Council, Presidents of Seventy, the Witnesses of the Book of Mormon, Presidents of Far West, and a number of others standing high in the Church were all carried away in this apostasy; and they thought there was enough of them to establish a pure religion that would become universal.

This attempted organization was under the direction of Warren Parrish, who had been a traveling elder in the Church and who sustained a high reputation in the Southern States as an eloquent preacher and had for some time been employed by Joseph as a clerk. He undertook to organize those elements into a church and he was told by them that all the talented men among the Elders were ready to join them. They named, for instance, Lyman Johnson, John F. Boynton, William E. McLellan, Hazen Aldrich, Sylvester Smith, Joseph Coe, Orson Johnson, W. A. Cowdery, M. F. Cowdery and others, amounting to something like thirty who had been prominent Elders in the Church.

They were going to renounce the Book of Mormon and Joseph Smith and take the "Mormon" doctrines to overthrow all the religions in the world and unite all the Christian churches in one general band and they to be its great leaders. What success did this great apostasy meet with. Brother Kimball, when on a mission in 1844 (this apostasy took place in 1837-8), while crossing Fox River on the ferry, encountered Warren Parrish. He was a grave-looking man—straight-jacketed fellow, dressed in black, with a white handkerchief around his neck. Says he: "Elder Kimball, will you have the goodness not to say to the people here that I ever was a Mormon? I am a Baptist minister. I am preaching in that meetinghouse for a salary of $500 a year. If they find out I have been a Mormon it would hurt my influence very much indeed." Where was the big church he had tried to build up? He had tried pleading law, that failed; peddling bogus money, and that failed, like his big church speculation. And where was the origin of this? I recollect waking up late one evening when I was quite a young man and hearing my father and one of the brethren talk. Being a little disposed to listen, I learned that there had been considerable difficulty between Parrish and one of the brethren. That was when he was in good standing in the Church. He had been too kind with the brother's wife. Then I learned the commencement of his apostasy.

You may go to every one of these men—I care not which one; you cannot put your finger on any one of these thirty men but what you will find that the spirit of adultery or covetousness had got possession of their hearts, and when it did the Spirit of the Lord left them. They had not sense enough to repent and put away their iniquity, but suffered themselves to be overthrown with the spirit of darkness; and they have gone to hell and there they may lift up their eyes asking for some relief or benefit from those they once tried to destroy, but if they get the privilege of waiting on a servant to those who have kept the laws of heaven they will be exceedingly thankful and fortunate.

J. D., Vol. 7:115.

[3]I have seen the day when it was as much as our lives were worth to sustain Joseph Smith—the apostates were so thick around us and persecution was so great. The day was when Brother Brigham was the only Apostle on the earth with the exception of Joseph and Sidney and Hyrum that could say to Brother Heber: Go and you shall be blessed. I am reckoning Brother Hyde with us for he went with me on that mission to England. In connection with Brother Joseph, Brother Hyrum and Brother Sidney, Brother Brigham said: "Go, Brother Heber, and in the name of Israel's God you shall be blessed and it shall prove the salvation of thousands."

John Boynton, one of the Twelve, came to me and said: "If you are such a damn fool as to listen to Joseph Smith, the fallen Prophet, and go to England under these perilous circumstances, if I knew you were shipwrecked on Van Dieman's Land, I would not assist you to get you from that land." I will speak to Lyman Johnson's credit: I will give every man credit for the good he does. Lyman Johnson steps up and says: "Brother Heber, I do not feel so, I am sorry you are going and consider you are foolish; but if you are determined to go I will help you all that is in my power." And he took from his shoulders a good nice camlet cloak and put it on to mine; and that was the first cloak I ever had. This was in the month of June, 1837. I was then destitute of the comforts of life and that cloak I wore three times across the sea and Parley P. Pratt wore it four times; and in all it crossed the sea seven times. It seemed as though it would never wear out. Those circumstances were the most trying circumstances that ever I was brought into. Joseph had to flee from that land to save his body from being slain, and so had Brother Brigham and every other man who would sustain the Prophet, the apostasy was so great, and they were most hellish in their wickedness.

I went and filled the mission according to the words of the Prophet of the Living God and was gone eleven months and two days from Kirtland, being on that land eight months and two days, in which time there were about two thousand souls added to the Church and Kingdom of God, with the help of Elders Willard Richards, Orson Hyde and Joseph Fielding. When I came back from England there were but a few living in Kirtland. There was one little society of men that pretended to take the lead and oversight of the people and they were guided by a peep stone.—Heber C. Kimball. Journal of Discourses, Vol. 6:65.

[4]When I got to Kirtland the brethren were engaged in building the house of the Lord. The commandment to build the house, and also the pattern of it was given in a revelation to Joseph Smith, Jr., Sidney Rigdon, and Frederick G. Williams, and was to be erected by a stated time. The church was in a state of poverty and distress, in consequence of which it appeared almost impossible that the commandment could be fulfilled, at the same time our enemies were raging and threatening destruction upon us, and we had to guard ourselves night after night, and for weeks

Whenever the spirit of speculation—a grasping for the things of the world—obtained, the light of the Spirit of God departed, and impenetrable darkness ensued. Some even became so blind as to seek to depose the Prophet of God. At length the hostility of the belligerent party assumed such threatening attitude that, late in the autumn of 1837, Joseph Smith and Sidney Rigdon had to flee for their lives; and at a moment's warning, started for Missouri. But their absence did not check the persecution waged by those apostate brethren—others became the target of their malice. Through their influence, the aged Father Smith was served with a State's warrant, but fortunately for him he was placed in the custody of Luke Johnson, who, although one of the apostates, was adverse to the bitter spirit of persecution which characterized others. Naturally of a jovial turn, he was more inclined to ridicule than hostility. Having been somewhat conversant with law usages, he volunteered his services as legal adviser for Father Smith, although his custodian. He privately told Father Smith's friends that the suit was instigated through malice—that he knew Father Smith was innocent, and he was determined to do all he could for him; and he was true to his word.* * *

Before closing the subject, I think a further notice is due the unantagonistic apostate, Luke Johnson. I happened to meet him the day after the scene in the court room—he enquired after his released prisoner, and after hearing that he reached his destination all right, he, in a jocose manner, related the foregoing circumstances, and closed with, "Father Smith will bless me for it, all the days of his life." To which, when I repeated it to Father Smith on my return home, he replied in the affirmative, and Luke Johnson is the only one of those five Apostles that re-

were not permitted to take off our clothes, and were obliged to lay with our fire locks in our arms. —Diary of Heber C. Kimball. Times and Seasons, 6:771.

5 The Real Spirit of an Apostate: William E. McLellin wanted to know where Heber C. Kimball was. Someone pointed me out to him as I was sitting on the ground. He came up to me and said: "Brother Heber, what do you think of the fallen Prophet now? Has he not led you blindfolded long enough? Look and see for yourself; poor, your family stripped and robbed, and your brethren in the same fix; are you satisfied with Joseph," I replied: "Yes, I am more satisfied with him a hundred-fold than ever I was before, for I see you in the very position that he foretold you would be in; a Judas to betray your brethren, if you did not forsake your adultery, fornication, lying and abominations. Where are YOU? What are you about? You and Hinckle, and scores of others; have you not betrayed Joseph and his brethren into the hands of the mob, as Judas did Jesus? Yes, verily, you have; I tell you Mormonism is true and Joseph is a true prophet of the living God; and you with all others that turn therefrom will be damned and go to hell, and Judas will rule over you."—Life of Heber C. Kimball by Orson F. Whitney, p. 230.

turned to the Church. He was re-baptized, and lived a faithful member—was much respected, and died an honorable death in the midst of his friends, in Salt Lake City.

Biography and Family Record of Lorenzo Snow, by Eliza R. Snow, pp. 22-24.

Apostasy and Pollution of the House of the Lord

Shortly after the completion of the house, Joseph and Martin Harris took a short tour through the eastern country. When they arrived at Palmyra, on their return, Joseph had a vision, which lasted until he besought the Lord to take it from him; for it manifested to him things which were painful to contemplate. It was taken from before his eyes for a short time, but soon returned again, and remained until the whole scene was portrayed before him.

On his arrival at home, the brethren seemed greatly pleased to see him. The next day he preached a sermon, and the following is a part of his remarks:

"Brethren, I am rejoiced to see you, and I have no doubt but that you are glad to see me. We are now nearly as happy as we can be on earth. We have accomplished more than we had any reason to expect when we began. Our beautiful house is finished, and the Lord has acknowledged it, by pouring out His Spirit upon us here, and revealing to us much of His will in regard to the work which He is about to perform. Furthermore, we have everything that is necessary for our comfort and convenience, and, judging from appearances, one would not suppose that anything could occur which would break up our friendship for each other, or disturb our tranquility. But, brethren, beware; for I tell you in the name of the Lord, that there is an evil in this very congregation, which, if not repented of, will result in setting many of you (who are here this day) so much at enmity against me, that you will have a desire to take my life, and you even would do it, if God should permit the deed. But, brethren, I now call upon you to repent, and cease all your hardness of heart, and turn from those principles of death and dishonesty which you are harboring in your bosoms, before it is eternally late, for there is yet room for repentance."

He continued to labor with them in this way, appealing to them in the most solemn manner until almost everyone in the house was in tears, and he was exhausted with speaking.

In the fall of 1836, a bank was established in Kirtland. Soon after the sermon, above mentioned, Joseph discovered that a large amount of money had been taken away by fraud, from this bank. He immediately demanded a search warrant of Esquire F. G. Williams, which was flatly refused. "I insist upon a warrant," said Joseph, "for if you will give me one, I can get the money, and if you do not, I will break you of your office." "Well, break it is, then," said Williams, "and we will strike hands upon it." "Very well," said Joseph, "from henceforth I drop you from my quorum, in the name of the Lord."

Joseph then went to Cleveland, in order to transact some business pertaining to the bank; and as he was absent the ensuing Sunday, my husband preached to the people. In speaking of the bank affair, he reflected somewhat sharply upon Warren Parrish. Although the reflection was just, Parrish was highly incensed, and made an attempt to drag him out of the stand. My husband appealed to Oliver Cowdery, who was justice of the peace, to have him brought to order; but Oliver never moved from his seat. William seeing the abuse which his father was receiving, sprang forward and caught Parrish, and carried him in his arms nearly out of the house. At this John Boynton stepped forward, and drawing a sword from his cane, presented it to William's breast, and said, "if you advance one step further, I will run you through." Before William had time to turn himself, several gathered around who threatened to handle him severely, if he should lay the weight of his finger upon Parrish again. At this juncture of affairs, I left the house, not only terrified at the scene, but likewise sick at heart, to see that the apostasy of which Joseph had prophesied, was so near at hand."

History of the Prophet Joseph, by his Mother, Lucy Smith, pp. 211-213.

The Kirtland Temple Defiled

By E. Cecil McGavin

[By *Permission*]
(From Improvement Era, October, 1940.)

It was agreed by all persons interviewed that a door was made in the basement wall between two buttresses of the foundation and a gentle incline was spaded through the ornamental shrubs and flowers to provide a portal through which cattle, sheep, and swine could be driven into the basement to share its warmth, while the palatial rooms above were used to suit the fickle fancy of the villagers.

It was related by many of the oldest residents of the dwarfed village that when the inclement winter set in, when the assembly room on the ground floor was not needed for any meeting of the citizens, it, too, was transformed into a stable to shelter the livestock of the neighborhood. The low benches were removed from their wooden enclosures and used for firewood, while sheep were herded into the small pews in the sacred room where the voices of angels had been heard but a short season before.

Upon the pulpit where the Lord had stood, and where Moses, Elijah, and Elias had appeared when they restored additional keys of the kingdom of God, stores of hay and straw were piled by the crude farmers, who whistled or cursed as they did their chores in the house which had been built for God.

For a few seasons the villagers were loath to use the Temple during the winter months except as a barn for their cattle. The builders of the Temple had made no provision for heating its large high-ceilinged rooms. During the long meetings in winter in the historic building, each person had been expected to provide his own method of heating. The metal bed warmers from the various homes had been filled with hot stones and placed on the floor as a footstool. Blankets or quilts had been wrapped about the worshipers as they sat through the long services. Small canvas bags had been filled with warm sand and brought to the temple to temper the cold.

But in the summer months, after the Temple was defiled, it

became the scene of the gay festivities of the hamlet. The cattle were taken from the building when spring came, and the citizens took possession of the house. The second story had been equipped originally, exactly like the ground floor — with its ornamented pulpits at each end of the room, and choir benches in the four corners, and the boxed-in benches covering the floor.

The citizens removed all the furnishings of the second floor, converting the large room into a playhouse, though the pews were reserved on the lower floor to protect their sheep at lambing time. The second story became a rendezvous for mischief-makers and pleasure-seekers. Dances, games, shows, and other types of entertainment were resorted to. When traveling troups of entertainers came to the dwindling town, the second story in the former Temple awaited their acts while wide-eyed citizens shouted their hearty approval. Partly-clad entertainers danced upon the low platform where once had stood the majestic pulpits adorned in white and gold. The Temple was opened to the animated preachers from the camp meetings and revivals. Politicians visited the historic house prior to elections and solicited the votes of the people who lived among the hills of Kirtland.

A few years later, the third story, where the School of the Prophets had formerly convened, was converted into a school. For many years these five rooms were used by the public schools of Ohio. One boy who attended school in the attic of the Temple later became president of the United States—James A. Garfield learned his three R's in that historic house.

Even the outside walls of the Temple did not escape the covetous gaze of vandals. The stone walls were covered with a strange plaster which all builders wished to duplicate, but the man who had perfected the formula had passed away. The man who had prepared the plaster for the outside walls had asked the Saints to contribute their broken glass and chinaware to be pulverized and mixed with the plaster. China closets and cupboards were almost denuded in an effort to get enough material containing the tiny particles of china and glass that glistened in the sunshine as if the walls were set with countless precious stones.

Engineers, architects, designers, all sought to learn the secret of the durable plaster which gave the building such sparkling beauty. When such admirers visited the building, they scraped from its wall large samples of the plaster that they might take it to their laboratories and learn the secret of its composition. Other souvenir collectors took long poles and broke off fragments that they might keep as a memento of their visit to the House of the Lord. Today there are only a few small patches of the original plaster upon the walls. The fragments of glass and chinaware still sparkle.

Hundreds of yards of heavy white cloth had been used for curtain material inside the Temple, lowered from rollers attached to the ceiling. These curtains had been used to divide the two large rooms into smaller ones when the various quorums of the Priesthood met in quorum capacity for deliberation. Soon after the Temple fell into profane hands, the white curtains disappeared from the hallowed house and were divided among the people as the spoils of victory. They were used to repair quilts and bed ticks, clothing, broken windows, and even to cover holes in houses and sheds.

Soon after the Saints had fled from Kirtland, the Church leaders tried to prevent such vandalism by selling or leasing the Temple to responsible parties, but all such efforts were fruitless. At the time of the exodus from Nauvoo a determined effort was made to dispose of the Temples at Nauvoo and Kirtland. While the Saints were camped at Garden Grove, we read from the Journal History of the Church:

> The council decided that the trustees might sell the Temples at Nauvoo and Kirtland and all other property of the Church to help the poor Saints to move westward. The council considered that the Temple would be of no benefit to the Saints if they could not possess their private dwellings, and when the time should come that they should return and redeem their inheritances, they would secure it from unjust claims, mobs, fire, etc., more effectually than for the Church to retain it in their hands.

In 1845, President Brigham Young received a letter from one of the Saints in Kirtland from which we quote:

> The apostates were doing everything they could to injure the Saints. They have broken into the House of the Lord, and taken possession of it, and were trying to take possession of the Church farm.
>
> Journal History, October 22, 1845.

The St. Louis *Luminary* (February 17, 1855) published an article containing this information:

> We called at Kirtland—found some tolerably good Saints considering circumstances, and many apostates. They have all become "rappers" and deny the Christ.

They have taken possession of the Temple, and they are no better off than thieves and robbers.

In December, 1882, the *Contributor* told of Richard W. Young's then recent visit to Kirtland. Since the key to the temple could not be found, Elder Young and his companions were obliged to take turns standing on each other's shoulders and looking through the broken windows of the despoiled building. We read:

> We found the interior preserved in much the same order as described by veteran Saints, and saw above on the ceiling of the main room the wires along which the curtains used to slide. The lower one of the three pulpits was strangely decorated with a few of the paraphernalia of a Protestant church, and held an open Bible. The building is in poor repair; much of the interior woodwork has been taken away for firewood, and the sashes contain more broken than undamaged panes of glass. Paint it has not seen for a generation at least.

And thus the Kirtland Temple suffered abuse for nearly half a century. In 1880, the Reorganized Church became interested in restoring it as nearly as possible to its original simplicity and beauty. They have spent a great sum of money for this purpose.

Though its present owners have no vision of Temple work and do not possess the keys which were restored in the holy house, they keep it in good preservation. They even refused a tempting offer from John D. Rockefeller, who wanted to purchase the elaborate panels and windows directly behind the pulpits in front of the building. However, he was permitted to reproduce the desired portion and place it in a magnificent cathedral he was having erected in New York City.

The Temple at Kirtland has served its purpose and has ceased to be a House of the Lord. It was but a stepping stone to greater and more complete temples wherein the sacred ordinances of the Priesthood could be administered. The courage and faith of the Saints enabled them to turn their backs upon despoiled Temples and private dwellings and face the distant West where they would build and enjoy the most sacred fruits of their labor—the Temples of God.

It must have been a source of sorrow to the Saints in the West to know how the former Temples at Kirtland and Nauvoo were being defiled. The spirit of the Pioneers is revealed in the

words of President Young when he learned that the Temple at
Nauvoo had been burned. Lifting his hand toward heaven and
as if looking beyond the sky he exclaimed, "Good, Father, if
You want it to be burned up." Later he said of the burning of
the Temple:

I would rather see it burnt than to see it in the hands of devils. I was thankful
to see the Temple of Nauvoo on fire. Previous to crossing the Mississippi River, we
had met in the Temple and handed it over to the Lord God of Israel. I hoped to see
it burned before I left but I did not. I was glad when I heard of its being destroyed
by fire, and its walls having fallen in, and said, "Hell, you cannot now occupy it."
When the temple is built here, I want to maintain it for those of the Priesthood; if
this cannot be, I would rather not see it built, but go into the mountains and administer there in the ordinances of the Holy Priesthood, which is our privilege. I would
rather do this than to build a Temple for the wicked to trample under their feet.

Journal of Discourses, VIII:203.

Chapter II

THE NAUVOO TEMPLE

Physical and Historical Description

After the exterminating order of Governor Lilburn W. Boggs of Missouri which was dated October 27, 1838 (see *History of the Church*, Vol. 3, p. 175), the Saints were compelled to flee from that State, and made Illinois their refuge from the blood-thirsty Christian mobocats who had burned, pillaged and destroyed thousands of homes and murdered many hundreds of men, women and children. Coming to Commerce, Illinois, later named Nauvoo, in 1839, the swampy and uninhabitable regions were soon reclaimed and Nauvoo became a thriving, prosperous and beautiful commonwealth.

On January 19, 1841, the Prophet Joseph received a revelation, commanding the Saints to erect a Temple for the purpose of revealing keys and powers of the Priesthood and for the salvation of the living and the dead. This revelation was as follows:

And again, verily I say unto you, Let all my saints come from afar;

And send ye swift messengers, yea, chosen messengers and say unto them; come ye, with all your gold, and silver, and your precious stones, and with all your antiquities; and with all who have knowledge of antiquities, that will come, may come and bring the box tree, and the fir tree, and the pine tree, together with all the precious trees of the earth;

And with iron, with copper, and with brass, and with zinc, and with all your precious things of the earth, and build a house to my name, for the Most High to dwell therein;

For there is not a place found on earth that he may come and restore again that which was lost unto you, or which he hath taken away, even the fullness of the Priesthood;

For a baptismal font there is not upon the earth, that they, my saints, may be baptized for those who are dead:

For this ordinance belongeth to my house, and cannot be acceptable to me, only in the days of your poverty, wherein ye are not able to build a house unto me.

But I command you, all ye my saints, to build a house unto me; and I grant unto you a sufficient time to build a house unto me, and during this time your baptisms shall be acceptable unto me.

But behold, at the end of this appointment, your baptisms for your dead shall not be acceptable unto me; and if you do not these things at the end of the appointment, ye shall be rejected as a church, with your dead, saith the Lord your God.

For verily I say unto you, that after you have had sufficient time to build a house to me, wherein the ordinance of baptizing for the dead belongeth, and for which the same was instituted from before the foundation of the world, your baptisms for your dead cannot be acceptable unto me.

For therein are the keys of the Holy Priesthood, ordained that you may receive honor and glory.

And after this time, your baptisms for the dead, by those who are scattered abroad, are not acceptable unto me, saith the Lord;

For it is ordained that in Zion, and in her Stakes, and in Jerusalem, those places which I have appointed for refuge, shall be the places for your baptisms for your dead.

And again, verily I say unto you; How shall your washings be acceptable unto me, except ye perform them in a house which you have built to my name?

For this cause I commanded Moses that he should build a tabernacle, that they should bear it with them in the wilderness, and to build a house in the land of promise, that those ordinances might be revealed which had been hid from before the world was;

Therefore, verily I say unto you, that your anointings, and your washings, and your baptisms for the dead, and your solemn assemblies, and your memorials for your sacrifices, by the sons of Levi, and for your oracles, in your most holy places, wherein you receive conversations, and your statutes and judgments, for the beginning of the revelations and foundation of Zion, and for the glory, honor, and endowment of all her municipals, are ordained by the ordinance of my holy house which my people are always commanded to build unto my holy name.

And verily I say unto you, Let this house be built unto my name, that I may reveal mine ordinances therein, unto my people;

For I design to reveal unto my church, things which have been kept hid from before the foundation of the world, things that pertain to the Dispensation of the Fulness of Times;

And I will show unto my servant Joseph all things pertaining to this house, and the Priesthood thereof; and the place whereon it shall be built;

And ye shall build it on the place where you have contemplated building it, for that is the spot which I have chosen for you to build it;

If ye labor with all your might, I will consecrate that spot that it shall be made holy;

And if my people will hearken unto my voice, and unto the voice of my servants whom I have appointed to lead my people, behold, verily I say unto you, they shall not be moved out of their place.

But if they will not hearken to my voice, nor unto the voice of these men whom I have appointed, they shall not be blest, because they pollute mine holy grounds, and mine holy ordinances, and charters, and my holy words which I give unto them.

And it shall come to pass, That if you build a house unto my name, and do not do the things that I say, I will not perform the oath which I make unto you, neither fulfill the promises which ye expect at my hands, saith the Lord;

For instead of blessings, ye, by your own works, bring cursings, wrath, indignation, and judgments upon your own heads, by your follies, and by all abominations, which you practice before me, saith the Lord.

Verily, verily I say unto you, That when I give a commandment to any of the sons of men, to do a work unto my name, and those sons of men go with all their might, and with all they have, to perform that work, and cease not their diligence, and their enemies come upon them, and hinder them from performing that work; behold, it behooveth me to require that work no more at the hands of those sons of men, but to accept of their offerings;

And iniquity and transgression of my holy laws and commandments, I will visit upon the heads of those who hindered my work, unto the third and fourth generation, so long as they repent not, and hate me, saith the Lord God.

Therefore for this cause have I accepted the offerings of those whom I commanded to build up a city and a house unto my name, in Jackson County, Missouri, and were hindered by their enemies, saith the Lord your God:

And I will answer judgment, wrath, and indignation, wailing, and anguish, and gnashings of teeth upon their heads, unto the third and fourth generation, so long as they repent not and hate me, saith the Lord your God.

And this I make an example unto you, for your consolation concerning all those who have been commanded to do a work, and have been hindered by the hands of their enemies, and by oppression, saith the Lord your God;

For I am the Lord your God, and will save all those of your brethren who have been pure in heart, and have been slain in the land of Missouri, saith the Lord.

And again, verily I say unto you, I command you again to build a house to my name, even in this place, that you may prove yourselves unto me that ye are faithful in all things whatsoever I command you, that I may bless you, and crown you with honor, immortality, and eternal life.

Doc. & Cov. Sec. 124:25-55.

On the eleventh anniversary of the organization of the Church, April 6, 1841, approximately 10,000 people from Nauvoo and surrounding sections were present to witness the laying of the four cornerstones of this Temple. It was an occasion marked by military display, sixteen companies of the Nauvoo Legion being assembled about the Temple foundation in a hollow square, within which were the visitors, the choir and band. The First Presidency of the Church laid the southeast cornerstone, the Prophet Joseph laying the stone in its proper place, and saying:

"This principal cornerstone in representation of the First Presidency, is now duly laid in honor of the Great God; and may the same be accompanied speedily; that the Saints may have a place to worship God, and the Son of Man have where to lay His head."

The southwest cornerstone was placed by officers of the High Priests; the northwest cornerstone was laid by the High Council, and the northeast stone by the Bishops.

The Lord had revealed that baptisms for the dead in the Mississippi River were acceptable only in the days of their poverty when no baptismal font was available for that purpose, but as soon as the font was available in the Temple, baptisms in the river should be discontinued. At the conference of the Church held in Nauvoo, on October 2, 1841, the Prophet made this announcement: "There shall be no more baptisms for the dead, until the ordinance can be attended to in the Lord's House, and the Church will not hold another General Conference until they can meet on said house, for thus saith the Lord."

On November 8, 1841, the baptismal font was ready for dedication in the Temple, baptisms in the river having been discontinued.

On Sunday, November 21, 1841, "The council met in council at Brigham Young's house, and at four o'clock they repaired to the baptismal font in the Temple, where President Brigham Young, Elders Heber C. Kimball and John Taylor baptized about forty persons for their dead, Elders Willard Richards, Wilford Woodruff and George A. Smith confirmed them. These were the first baptisms for the dead in the font in the Lord's House. From this time forth, as long as the Saints remained in Nauvoo, baptisms for the dead were performed in the Temple."

(Essentials in Church History by Joseph Fielding Smith, pp. 310-1.)

On October 30, 1842, the construction of the walls of the Temple had so far progressed that the first meeting was held in it. On May 24, 1845, the capstone was laid under the direction of President Brigham Young and the other members of the Twelve, the Prophet Joseph and Hyrum having been murdered in cold blood on June 27, 1844. By October 5, 1845, the construction had progressed to the extent that the autumnal conference was held within its walls. During the month of December, 1845, and the early months of 1846, many of the Saints received their blessings and endowments, and on April 30th of that year, the Temple was privately dedicated by Joseph Young, senior president of the First Seven Presidents of Seventy, now known as the First Council of the Seventy. On the following day, May 1st, the building was officially dedicated by Apostles Orson Hyde and Wilford Woodruff according to the order of the Holy Priesthood as revealed through Joseph the Prophet. The approximate cost of this magnificent structure was $1,000,000, paid for by tithing of money, labor, and from free will offerings.

After the Saints had left Nauvoo, in the severity of winter, in February and March, 1846, enroute to the Rocky Mountains, the mob took possession of Nauvoo and the Temple. The Temple was most sacred to the Saints and the mobocrats feared that if it continued to stand it would be a bond between its exiled builders and the city from which they had been so cruelly driven. On November 18, 1848, one Joseph Agnew set fire to this sacred structure, at which time all was destroyed except the walls. An attempt was made by the Icarians, a French communistic society, to rebuild the walls, but on May 27, 1850, a tornado leveled them completely, and the stones were removed to other places for building and souvenir purposes, until not one stone was left upon another. After the removal of the Saints from Nauvoo the fields and gardens reverted well nigh to the primitive wilderness and swampy conditions which the Saints had first met with in the settling of this beautiful location.

The Temple was 128 feet long by 88 feet wide and 65 feet high in the clear. The top of the spire was 165 feet above the ground and bore the figure of a flying herald sounding a trumpet. The plan of construction was that of a solid and stable four-walled building, two and a half stories high, with a hexagonal tower at the front rising in four terraces and a dome. It was constructed of a light-gray limestone, of a hardness that permitted it to be easily tooled and adapted to ornamental finish.

On the outside were thirty pilasters, nine on each side and six at each end. At its base each pilaster presented in hewn relief the crescent moon, and ended above in a capital of cut-stone depicting the face of the sun allegorically featured, with a pair of hands holding horns. Above the capitals was a frieze or cornice in which appeared thirty star stones. Further details of construction are incorporated in the other articles in this Chapter.

The architecture of the Temple was revealed of God to Joseph as will be noted in the revelation that is herein printed. On pages 196-7 of the *Documentary History of the Church*, Vol. 6, is the following interesting item:

"In the afternoon, Elder William Weeks (whom I had employed as architect of the Temple), came in for instruction. I instructed him in relation to the circular windows designed to light the offices in the dead work of the arch between stories. He said that round windows in the broad side of a building were a violation of all the known rules of architecture, and contended that they should be semi-circular — the building was too low for round windows. I told him I would have the circles, if he had to make the Temple ten feet higher than it was originally calculated; that one light at the center of each circular window would be sufficient to light the whole room; that when the whole building was thus illuminated, the effect would be remarkably grand. I wish you to carry out my designs. I have seen in vision the splendid appearance of that building illuminated, and will have it built according to the pattern shown me."

The Temple Similar to Ancient Construction

(Letter written by W. W. Phelps to William Smith, dated Nauvoo, Ill.
December 25, 1844.)

"The Temple is up as high as the caps of the pilasters, and it looks majestically, and especially to me, when I know that the tithing, 'the mites of the poor,' thus speaks of the glory of God. All the description that is necessary to give you now, is that this splendid model of Mormon grandeur, exhibits thirty hewn stone pilasters which cost about $3,000 apiece. The base is a crescent new moon; the capitols, near fifty feet high, the sun, with a human face in bold relief, about two and a half feet broad, ornamented with rays of light and waves, surmounted by two hands holding two trumpets. It is always too much trouble to describe an unfinished building. The inside work is now going forward as fast as possible. When the whole structure is completed it will cost some five or six hundred thousand dollars; and as Captain Brown of Tobasco, near the ruins of Palenque, said: 'It will look the nearest like the splendid remains of antiquity in Central America of anything I have seen, though not half as large.'

"The Temple is erected from white limestone, wrought in a superior style: is 128 by 83 feet square; near 60 feet high; two stories in the clear, and two half stories in the recesses over the arches; four tiers of windows; two gothic and two round. The two great stories will each have two pulpits, one at each end; to accommodate the Melchizedek and Aaronic priesthoods; graded into four rising seats; the first for the presidents of the elders, and his two counselors; the second for the president of the high priesthood and his two counselors; the third for the Melchizedek president and his two counselors, and the fourth for the president over the whole church (the first president) and his two counselors. The highest seat is where the scribes and Pharisees used to crowd in 'to Moses' seat.' The Aaronic pulpit at the other end the same.

"The font in the basement story is for the baptism of the living, for health, for remission of sin, and for the salvation of the dead, as was the case in Solomon's temple, and all temples that God commands to be built.* * *

"The steeple of our temple will be high enough to answer for a tower—between 100 and 200 feet high."

Times and Seasons, Vol. 5, p. 759.

NAUVOO TEMPLE

Cornerstones laid on April 6, 1841. Temple dedicated on May 1, 1846, by Elders Orson Hyde and Wilford Woodruff.

The Nauvoo Temple

By Orson F. Whitney

On the 19th of January, 1841, came a revelation urging upon the Saints the imperative necessity for the erection of a Temple at Nauvoo. In that revelation the Lord says: "For a baptismal there is not upon the earth, that they, my saints, may be baptized for those who are dead." (Doc. and Cov. 124:29.) The Temple at Kirtland, Ohio, which was built several years before the date of this revelation, had no baptismal font, the time not having then arrived for this kind of work to begin. It was in the Kirtland Temple, however, that the keys of Elijah were restored, by virtue of which the work for the dead was afterwards inaugurated.

River Baptisms: When the revelation of January 19th was given, baptisms for the dead were being performed in the Mississippi River, the Lord permitting it for a season, with the understanding that after the Saints had had sufficient time to build a Temple and place a baptismal font therein, the river baptisms should be discontinued.

The cornerstones of the Nauvoo Temple were laid on the 6th of April, 1841, and in the ensuing October the building was so far advanced that it could be used for baptismal purposes; a font having been put in the basement, and the incomplete structure boarded over.[1] This signalized the discontinuance of the river baptisms.

First Baptisms in the Temple: A month later, or on the 8th of November, Brigham Young, who was then president of the Twelve Apostles, dedicated the baptismal font, and on the 21st of that month, the first baptisms for the dead were performed in the Nauvoo Temple. This labor went on there as long as the Saints remained in Illinois, and it has been continued in all the Temples since erected by them.   Improvement Era, Vol. 28:191-2.

---

[1]*The Construction of the Baptismal Font.* The font was constructed of pine timber, and put together of staves tongued and grooved, oval shaped, sixteen feet long east and west, and twelve feet wide, seven feet high from the foundation, the basin four feet deep; the moulding of the cap or base was formed of beautiful carved wood in antique style, and the sides were finished with panel work. There were steps leading up and down into the basin in the north and south sides, guarded by side railings. The font stood upon twelve oxen, four on each side and two at each end, their heads, shoulders and forelegs projecting out from under the font. They were carved out of pine plank,

View showing the well which supplied the baptismal font. This well
was in the basement of the Nauvoo Temple. To the left, Pres. David
O. McKay; to the right, Elder George D. Pyper.

glued together, and copied after the most beautiful five-year-old steer that could be found in the
country. *** The oxen and ornamental mouldings of the font were carved by Elder Elijah Fordham,
from New York. *** The font was inclosed by a temporary frame building, sided up with split
oak clap-boards, with a roof of the same material, but was so low that the timbers of the first story
of the temple were laid above it. The water was supplied from a well thirty feet deep in the east
end of the basement. This font was built for the baptism for the dead until the temple could be
completed, when a more durable one was to take its place. Millennial Star, Vol. XVIII:744;
D.H.C., Vol. 4:446.

First Meeting in the Temple

On Sunday, the 5th day of October (1845), through the
indefatigable exertions, unceasing industry, and heaven blessed
labors, in the midst of trials, tribulations, poverty, and worldly
obstacles, solemnized, in some instances, by death, about five

thousand Saints had the inexpressible joy and great gratification to meet for the first time in the House of the Lord in the city of Joseph. From mites and tithing, millions had risen up to the glory of God, as a Temple where the children of the last kingdom could come together and praise the Lord.

It certainly afforded a holy satisfaction to think that since the 6th day of April, 1841, when the first stone was laid, amidst the most straitened circumstances, the Church of Jesus Christ of Latter-day Saints had witnessed their bread cast upon waters, or more properly, their obedience to the commandments of the Lord, appear in the tangible form of a Temple, entirely enclosed, windows in, with temporary floors, pulpits, and seats to accommodate so many persons, preparatory to a General Conference; no General Conference having been held for three years past, according to the declaration of our martyred Prophet:

"There shall be no more baptisms for the dead, until the ordinance can be attended to in the font of the Lord's House; and the church shall not hold another general conference, until they can meet in said house. For thus saith the Lord."

Brigham Young opened the services of the day in a dedicatory prayer, presenting the Temple, thus far completed, as a

Certificate belonging to Elder George B. Gardner, of Woodruff, Arizona.

monument to the Saints' liberality, fidelity, and faith—concluding: "Lord, we dedicate this house, and ourselves unto Thee."
The day was occupied most agreeably in hearing instructions
and teachings, and offering up the gratitude of honest hearts, for
so great a privilege as worshipping God, within instead of without an edifice, whose beauty and workmanship will compare
with any house of worship in America, and whose motto is
"HOLINESS TO THE LORD."   Times and Seasons, Vol. 6, pp. 1017-8.

The Capstone of the Temple Laid

After a little more than four years of hard labor, in truly
troublesome times, and not, too, without the loss of the best
blood in the Church, on the morning of the 24th ult., at a little
past 6, a goodly number of Saints had the honor and glory to
witness the capstone of the Temple laid in its place. The morning was cool, clear, and beautiful; the Saints felt glorious, the
band upon the top of the walls played charmingly, and when
the stone was placed there and a united *Hosanna to God and
the Lamb, amen and amen"* shouted three times, which not only
gave joy on earth, but filled the heavens with gladness!

The Twelve and other authorities of the Church were
present to witness and conduct this interesting scene. Like the
event when God finished His work and rested (so said President Young), as it was the seventh day of the week the Saints
might do the same.

A new hymn was sung, and as the prophets have written
for our instruction, so the "headstone" was brought forward
with shouting—grace, grace unto it; and may the God of Israel,
with His Almighty power, grant that the Saints may have peace
to obtain their endowment therein. Amen.
                                        Times and Seasons, Vol. 6, p. 926.

Manifestations of Divine Acceptance

The Lord gave a commandment that a Temple should be
built to His name. It seemed almost impossible for so poor a
people to build such a temple in their poverty, but the Lord

never requires more of men than they can perform if they will go to with their might and trust in Him.*** At the conference on the 6th of April, I witnessed the laying of the cornerstones of the Temple which was done according to the order of the Priesthood. An immense crowd of people were present on that occasion—all filled with joy and rejoicing.*** The Temple progressed with the Saints that could work at it steady. The Prophet Joseph worked with his own hands, quarrying the stone for its walls when his enemies were not pursuing him. No man knows what he suffered through persecution.

Joseph Smith did more for the salvation of the human family in the short time that he lived than any other man that ever lived in the world, Jesus Christ excepted. He lived to be 39 years old and endured a continued scene of persecution and oppression from the time that the Angel of the Lord appeared to him, until the time of his death. He bore testimony to the work of the Lord through life and sealed his testimony with his own blood. I have been with the Prophet Joseph and heard his instruction weekly and sometimes daily. The last time I heard him speak in public he spoke to the Legion (Nauvoo Legion). After telling what he had passed through and what he had suffered from men because he preached the Gospel of Jesus Christ, he said: "From my boyhood up to the present time I have been hunted like a roe upon the mountains. I have never been allowed to live like other men. I have been driven, chased, stoned, whipped, robbed, mobbed, imprisoned, persecuted, accused falsely of everything bad. I have suffered till the Lord knows I have suffered enough."* * *

The teaching of the Twelve was to build the Temple and finish the work that Joseph had begun. The people were obedient to counsel and exerted themselves to do all they could do to accomplish the work. * * * Our enemies were not satisfied with what they had done, so they continued their depredations. In the small settlements in the country the mobs collected, drove our brethren from their homes, burned their houses and grain and killed some who could not get out of the way. In the fall, the mob collected in the south part of the country and in about two weeks they burned 200 houses to ashes. The inhabitants had to flee to Nauvoo to save their lives. A great amount of grain and property was destroyed, cattle and hogs were stolen and killed almost without number. Old Father Durfee was shot and killed by the mob while he was trying to save his property from the flames. Many others died from exposure after being robbed and driven into the wood. Their sufferings were so great that they could not endure it.

The Saints gathered into Nauvoo, labored and toiled to finish the Temple. Our enemies at the same time were planning to drive us from our city and from the United States. In the fall the Temple was dedicated to the Lord, thus far completed. Prayer pronounced by President B. Young. The building was finished with the exception of a little inside work which was done during the winter.

Most of the Saints, men and women, had the privilege of receiving their endowments, learning the order of the Priesthood, the fall and redemption of man, in the Temple, in the city of Joseph. Nauvoo was called by that name after the death of Joseph. I think it was in the month of January that I and my brother, Charles, received our endowments. The building was filled up in the nicest style. It was built according to the pattern that the Lord gave to Joseph. *It was accepted of the Lord, and His holy angels have ministered unto many therein and now because of persecution we must leave it and in leaving it we leave a monument of our industry which was reared in our poverty. It was the finest building in all the western country.*

At the west end about one hundred feet from the ground was the following inscription in large gold letters:

THE HOUSE OF THE LORD, BUILT BY THE CHURCH OF
JESUS CHRIST OF LATTER-DAY SAINTS
COMMENCED APRIL 6TH, 1841.
HOLINESS TO THE LORD

At the east end of the House, inside, was arched the following sentence:

"THE LORD HAS BEHELD OUR SACRIFICE, COME AFTER US"

From the Diary of John Pulsipher.

Lucifer As An Employer of Mechanics

So many of the mechanics quit work from sheer necessity and went elsewhere to seek employment that the question of how and when the Temple was ever to be completed became more of a problem every day.

Charles Lambert and one of his fellow mechanics (W. W. Player), who also was an Englishman, and a man of faith, discussed this problem between themselves, and voluntarily pledged themselves to continue at work until the Temple was built whether they were paid for their services or not. It is one thing, however, for a man to deny himself and quite another to deny a dependent wife and children the comforts or necessities of life.

Charles Lambert had married during the first year of his residence in Nauvoo and undertaken the support of two brothers and a sister of his wife, who had recently been orphaned and were helpless. He felt keenly his responsibility, and wished for money as he never had done before. While feeling thus he was passing along the street in Nauvoo one day when he met a well-dressed, genteel stranger who inquired if his name was Charles Lambert. On being told that it was, he said his name was Higgins, and that his home was in Missouri. With an ingratiating smile, he said, 'I have heard of your skill as a workman, and want you to go to Missouri and work for me. You are not appreciated or properly paid here. If you will quit the Temple and go and work for me you can name your own price and you will be sure of your pay. You see I have plenty of money with which to pay you.' Suiting the action to the word he thrust his hand into his pocket, and drew it out full of $10.00 and $20.00 gold pieces, which he displayed in a tempting manner, and urged him to accept his offer and not to submit any longer to the unfair treatment accorded him at the Temple. With a gesture of impatience called forth by the intimation of unfairness, Father Lambert thanked the stranger for his offer, but said he couldn't think of accepting it. He said he had no complaint to make of his treatment at the Temple, and the price others would pay for work they wished done would not influence him in the matter, as he intended to continue on at the Temple from principle. Bidding the stranger 'good-day' he turned to continue his walk along the street, but almost immediately the query arose in his mind as to how the stranger knew his name, and where he got his information from about his skill as a mechanic, and turned to take a final look at the stranger, when lo! he was nowhere to be seen. He had disappeared as completely as if the ground had opened and swallowed him, and yet he had not had time by any ordinary means of locomotion to get out of sight. His opinion was, and remained so up to the day of his death, that he had been talking with no other than Satan, the prince of tempters, and though he had not yielded to his tempting offer he was vexed with himself for listening to him at all, and especially to his insinuations about the Temple management. *Gems of Reminiscence, Seventeenth Book of Faith Promoting Series, pp. 173-5.*

Nauvoo Tribulations

By President Brigham Young

But what of the Temple in Nauvoo? By the aid of sword in one hand, and trowel and hammer in the other, with firearms at hand, and a strong band of police, and the blessing of heaven, the Saints, through hunger, and thirst, and weariness, and watchings, and prayings, so far completed the Temple, despite the devices of the mob, that many received a small portion of their endowment, but we know of no one who received it in its fulness. And then, to save the lives of all the Saints from cruel murder, we moved westward, and being led by the all-searching eye of the Great Jehovah, we arrived at this place.

"Of our journey hither, we need say nothing, only God led us. Of the sufferings of those who were compelled to, and did, leave Nauvoo in the winter of 1846, we need say nothing. Those who experienced it know it, and those who did not, to tell them of it would be like exhibiting a beautiful painting to a blind man. *Journal of Discourses, Vol. 2, p. 32.*

Have You Such Faith, Latter-day Saints?

By President Brigham Young

Every time we put forth our ability to do good and build up the Kingdom of God according to the means the Lord bestows upon us, our means and ability will be doubled and trebled; yes, we shall receive ten-fold, and, as Joseph said, an hundred-fold. Have we witness of this? Yes, plenty of witnesses. I will mention one little circumstance. When we were finishing the Temple in Nauvoo, the last year of our stay there, I rented a portion of ground in what was called the church farm, which we afterwards deeded to Sister Emma. Brother George D. Grant worked for me then, and planted the corn, sowed the oats, and said this, that and the other must be attended to. They called for teams to haul for the Temple, and could not get them. Says I, put my teams on the Temple, if there is not a kernel of grain raised. I said I would trust in God for the increase, and I had as good corn as there was on the farm, though it was not touched from the time we put it in to the time of gathering. I proved the fact; I had faith.

The poor miserable apostates[2] there prophesied, and the gentiles prophesied, and all creation of wickedness seem to agree that the Temple should not be finished; and I said that it should, and the house of Israel said that it should,[3] and the angels of God said—"we will help you." Many of you remember[4] my setting my foot on the capstone and addressing the people. We completed the Temple, used it a short time, and were done with it. On the 5th and 6th of February, 1846, we committed the building into the hands of the Lord, and left it; and when we heard that it was burned, we were glad of it.

The Deseret News, Vol. 2, March 13, 1861.

---

[2]*Traitors Will Return Like Prodigal Sons.* While we were building the Temple, in Kirtland, we were poor, and in worse circumstances than we are now, or ever will be; for at that time we were persecuted and were under the necessity of lying upon the floor with our firelocks by our sides to sustain ourselves, as there were mobs gathering all around us to destroy us, and prevent us from building the Temple. And when they were driven, every man that was in the church, arose, and we took our firelocks, to reinstate our brethren, and in the night we laid upon the floor; we laid upon Brother Joseph's floor, and upon Sidney Rigdon's floor, so as to be ready to keep our enemies at bay; and we laid on Sidney Rigdon's floor many a night to save his life, and to save the lives of his family; and he is now exerting every effort to take away our lives; but he will see the day when he will be glad to come into the cellar kitchen and become a cook, and to black the boots and shoes of the servants of God; and it will be the case with thousands of others. They will be glad to black our boots and to lick the dust that is under our feet, and this is nothing to what will come to pass. I might stand here all day, and tell you things of the future, and you would not believe the half of it.

Remarks of Heber C. Kimball, City of Joseph, April 8, 1845.
Times and Seasons, 6:972.

---

[3]*Supplications Till Early Morning.* God is favoring us day by day; and leading our enemies as a horse is led by the reins. For what purpose? In order that He may carry on His work, and erect that building. I presume that the servants of God, for the sake of having that accomplished, would go into the wilderness in this case and wear sheepskins and goatskins for their apparel; and live upon bread and water, for the sake of having that building built (the Temple) and the Nauvoo House. These are my feelings by night and by day. It is uppermost in my mind, and I know it is

with my brethren. You are not aware of the feelings that they have in their bosoms on this account. They meet together and have all the time labored, in the night and in the day; in the night to offer up their prayers before God. Many times we do not go to bed until three o'clock in the morning, calling on the Father in the name of Jesus, to protect us, until that house shall be built; and to lead our enemies away, and turn everything in our favor.

Remarks by Heber C. Kimball, delivered at Nauvoo, June 1, 1845.
Times and Seasons, Vol. 6:987.

The Sisters Always Faithful. By the counsel of the Twelve, Mrs. Hyrum Smith and Mrs. Thompson request all those sisters who have received paper to collect the penny subscription, to forward them as soon as possible that they may be able to ascertain whether all those employed as collectors have been faithful; as it appears that there is suspicion resting upon a certain individual of having kept the money which she had collected. They would say for the satisfaction of the sisters that about one thousand dollars have been received, and most of the sisters with whom they have conversed, seemed inclined to continue paying their cent a week until the temple is finished; and money being wanted to purchase other things besides glass and nails, they invite all those who are able and feel so disposed to pay up for the present year; and as there are some poor sisters who are extremely anxious to throw in their mite who cannot possibly raise money, they would say that any kind of useful articles will be received from such.

Mary Smith and Mercy R. Thompson.

Times and Seasons, 6:847.

Who But Saints Could Endure This?

That foundation stone was laid (at Far West) and the Saints, as I said, fled into Illinois,[5] and there laid the foundation of a Temple at Nauvoo, Illinois, the finest building then in the western country, and the admiration of everybody. The Saints erected it in the midst of poverty, destitution, sickness, death, and, I may say, with the sword or rifle in one hand and the trowel in the other, their enemies surrounding them on every hand. They had slain Joseph and Hyrum, and attempted to destroy others of the servants of God, and they were continually burning and destroying the houses and property of the Saints, and were determined to expel them from the State. But in the midst of these tribulations the Saints continued their labors until that Temple was roofed in, and until within its walls they could attend to the ordinances for the living and the dead.

By George Q. Cannon. Journal of Discourses, Vol. 14:320.

[5]I have often thought of the shortness of the period after the death of Joseph, which was continued in building that house. He died, as you well know, or was murdered, on the 27th of June, 1844. Before 1845 had passed away the Saints were receiving their endowments in that house. The walls were completed, it was roofed, the spire finished, and the upper story so far completed that the Elders could go in and administer in the ordinances of God's house—the sealings, washings

and anointings, and in the performance of those ceremonies and ordinances which were necessary for our growth, increase and perfection as a people; and when it is recollected that all this was done in a very short period over one year, it bears testimony to the zeal of the Saints and the mighty exertions they made to fulfill the word of God and the requirements He made of us as a people, that we and our dead might not be rejected. But we were not permitted to enjoy that house, we were not permitted to continue receiving blessings there; the enemies of God's kingdom were upon us, and we were compelled to abandon it and our houses, and it fell a sacrifice to the wickedness of the wicked and it was burned with fire—probably a better fate than to have it stand and be defiled by the wicked.   By George Q. Cannon, J. D. 14:124.

Great Spiritual Heights Obtainable

By Brigham Young

The Lord has led this people all the while in this way, by giving them here a little and there a little; thus He increases their wisdom, and he that receives a little and is thankful for that shall receive more and more, and more, even to the fullness of the eternal Godhead; there is no stopping place, but the weak capacity of man cannot understand it unless the Spirit of the Eternal God is in their hearts, and then they can comprehend but a little of it. In this is the glory, power, and excellency of the gospel of the Son of God to poor, weak, finite man. Look, O ye Latter-day Saints, at the nations of the earth, Christendom, look at them; but look at ourselves (although we have received a great deal, yet who are there here that have seen Jesus Christ, that have beheld angels, that have conversed with the spirits of just men made perfect, and the assembly of the church of Enoch and with God, the judge of all? Who is there here that has been caught up to the third heavens and gazed upon the order and glory of the celestial world? Don't you see, brethren, we have yet a great deal to learn, but it is not our privilege to be filled with all the fullness of Godliness? When you receive all that is for you, you will say, O, the blindness of Christendom! O, the ignorance of the world; even the Latter-day Saints that have assembled themselves together at the April conference in the year eighteen hundred and forty-five, will say, what am I? * * *

And I would say, as no man can be perfect without the woman, so no woman can be perfect without a man to lead her.

I tell you the truth as it is in the bosom of eternity; and I say so
to every man upon the face of the earth; if he wishes to be saved
he cannot be saved without a woman by his side.

Remarks delivered in Temple, April 6, 1845.　Times and Seasons, Vol. 6:954-5.

The Mormons

(A lecture delivered before the Historical Society of Pennsylvania, March 26, 1850.)

By Thomas L. Kane

A few years ago, ascending the Upper Mississippi in the
autumn, when its waters were low, I was compelled to travel by
land past the region of the Rapids. My road lay through the
half-breed tract, a fine section of Iowa, which the unsettled state
of its land-titles had appropriated as a sanctuary for coiners,
horse thieves, and other outlaws. I had left my steamer at Keo-
kuk, at the foot of the Lower Falls, to hire a carriage, and to
contend for some fragments of a dirty meal with the swarming
flies, the only scavengers of the locality. From this place to
where the deep water of the river returns, my eye wearied to
see everywhere sordid, vagabond and idle settlers, and a country
marred without being improved, by their careless hands.

I was descending the last hillside upon my journey, when a
landscape in delightful contrast broke upon my view. Half en-
circled by a bend of the river, a beautiful city lay glittering in the
fresh morning sun, its bright new dwellings, set in cool green
gardens ranging up around a stately dome-shaped hill, which
was crowned by a noble marble edifice, whose high tapering
spire was radiant with white and gold. The city appeared to
cover several miles, and beyond it in the background, there
rolled off a fair country, chequered by the careful lines of fruitful husbandry. The unmistakable marks of industry, enterprise,
and educated wealth, everywhere, made the scene one of singular and most striking beauty.

It was a natural impulse to visit this inviting region. I pro-
cured a skiff, and rowing across the river, landed at the chief
wharf of the city. No one met me there. I looked and saw no

one. I could hear no one move; though the quiet everywhere was such that I heard the flies buzz, and the water ripples break against the shallow of the beach. I walked through the solitary streets. The town lay as in a dream, under some deadening spell of loneliness, from which I almost feared to wake it. For plainly it had not slept long. There was no grass growing up in the paved ways. Rains had not entirely washed away the prints of dusty footsteps.

Yet I went about unchecked. I went into empty workshops, ropewalks, and smithies. The spinner's wheel was idle; the carpenter had gone from his workbench and shavings, his unfinished sash and casing. Fresh bark was in the tanner's vat, and the fresh-chopped lightwood stood piled aginst the baker's oven. The blacksmith's shop was cold; but his coal heap, and ladling pool, and crooked water horn were all there, as if he had just gone off for a holiday. No work people anywhere looked to know my errand. If I went into the gardens, clinking the wicketlatch loudly after me, to pull the marigolds, heart's-ease, and lady-slippers, and draw a drink with the water-sodden well-bucket and its noisy chain; or, knocking off with my stick the tall heavy-headed dahlias and sunflowers, hunted over the beds for cucumbers and love-apples no one called out to me from any opened windows, or dog sprang forward to bark and alarm. I could have supposed the people hidden in the houses, but the doors were unfastened, and when at last I timidly entered them, I found dead ashes white upon the hearths, and had to tread a tiptoe, as if walking down the aisle of a country church to avoid rousing irreverent echoes from the naked floors.

On the outskirts of the town was the city graveyard. But there was no record of plague there, nor did it in anywise differ much from other Protestant American cemeteries. Some of the mounds were not long sodded; some of the stones were newly set, their dates recent, and their black inscriptions glossy in the mason's hardly-dried lettering ink. Beyond the graveyard, out in the fields, I saw, in one spot hard by where the fruited boughs of a young orchard had been roughly torn down, the still smouldering embers of a barbecue fire, that had been constructed of rails from the fencing round it. It was the latest sign of life there. Fields upon fields of heavy-headed yellow grain lay rotting ungathered upon the ground. No one was at hand to take in their rich harvest. As far as the eye could reach, they stretched away—they, sleeping too, in the hazy air of autumn.

Only two portions of the city seemed to suggest the import of this mysterious solitude. On the southern suburb, the houses looking out upon the country showed, by their splintered wood-work and walls battered to the foundation, that they had lately been the mark of a destructive cannonade. And in and around the splendid Temple, which had been the chief object of my admiration, armed men were barracked, surrounded by their stacks of musketry, and pieces of heavy ordnance. These chal-lenged me to render an account of myself, and why I had had the temerity to cross the water without a written permit from a leader of their band.

Though these men were generally more or less under the influence of ardent spirits; after I had explained myself as pass-ing stranger, they seemed anxious to gain my good opinion. They told me the story of the Dead City; that it had been a notable manufacturing and commercial mart, sheltering over 20,000 persons; that they had waged war with its inhabitants for several years, and had been finally successful only a few days before my visit, in an action fought in front of the ruined suburb; after which, they had driven them forth at the point of the sword. The defense, they said, had been obstinate, but gave way on the third day's bombardment. They boasted greatly of their prowess, especially in this battle, as they called it; but I dis-covered they were not of one mind as to certain of the exploits that had distinguished it; one of which as I remember, was, that they had slain a father and his son, a boy of fifteen, not long resident of the fated city, whom they admitted to have borne a character without reproach.

They also conducted me inside the massive sculptured walls of the curious Temple, in which they said the banished inhabit-ants were accustomed to celebrate the mystic rites of an unhal-lowed worship. They particularly pointed out to me certain features of the building, which, having been the peculiar objects of a former superstitious regard, they had as a matter of duty, sedulously defiled and defaced. The reputed sites of certain shrines they had thus particularly noticed, and various sheltered chambers, in one of which was a deep well, constructed they believed with a dreadful design. Beside these they led me to see a large and deep-chiseled marble vase or basin, supported upon twelve oxen, also of marble, and of the size of life, of which they told some romantic stories. They said, the deluded persons, most of whom were immigrants from a great distance, believed their Deity countenanced their reception here of a baptism of regeneration, as proxies for whomsoever they held in warm affection in the countries from which they had come. That here parents "went into the water" for their lost children, children for their parents, widows for their spouses, and young persons for their lovers. That thus the Great Vase came to be for them associated with all dear and distant memories, and was therefore the object, of all others in the building, to which they attached the greatest degree of idolatrous affection. On this account the victors had so diligently desecrated it, as to render the apartment in which it was contained too noisome to abide in.

They permitted me also to ascend into the steeple, to see where it had been lightning-struck on the Sabbath before; and to look out, East and South, on wasted farms like those I had seen near the city, extending till they were lost in the distance. Here, in the face of pure day, close to the scar of the Divine wrath left by the thunderbolt were fragments of food, cruises of liquor, and broken drinking vessels, with a bass drum and a steamboat signal bell of which I afterwards learned the use with pain.

It was after nightfall when I was ready to cross the river on my return. The wind had freshened since the sunset; and the water beating roughly into my little boat, I headed higher up the stream than the point I had left in the morning, and landed where a faint glimmering light invited me to steer.

Here among the dock and rushes, sheltered only by the darkness, without a roof between them and the sky, I came upon a crowd of several hundred human creatures whom my movements roused from uneasy slumber upon the ground. * * *

Dreadful indeed was the suffering of these forsaken beings. Cowed and cramped by cold and sunburn alternating as each weary day and night dragged on, they were almost all of them, the crippled victims of disease. They were there because they had no homes nor hospital, nor poorhouse, nor friends to offer them any. They could not satisfy the feeble cravings of their sick; they had not bread to quiet the fractious hunger-cries of their children. Mothers and babes, daughters and grandparents, all of them alike, were bivouacked in tatters, wanting even covering to comfort those whom the sick-shiver of fever was searching to the marrow.

These were Mormons famishing in Lee County, Iowa, in the fourth week of the month of September, in the year of our Lord, 1846. The city—it was Nauvoo, Illinois. The Mormons were the owners of that city and the smiling country around. And those who had stopped their ploughs, who had silenced their hammers, their axes, their shuttles and their workshop wheels; those who had put out their fires, who had eaten their food, spoiled their orchards, and trampled underfoot their thousands of acres of unharvested bread; these—were the keepers of their dwellings, the carousers in their temple—whose drunken riot insulted the ears of their dying.

I think it was as I turned from the wretched night-watch of which I have spoken, that I first listened to the sounds of revel of a party of the guard within the city. Above the distant hum of voices of many, occasionally rose distinct the loud oath-tainted exclamation, and the falsely intonated scrap of vulgar song; but lest this requiem should go unheeded, every now and then, when their boisterous orgies strove to attain a sort of ecstatic climax, a cruel spirit of insulating frolic carried some of them into the high belfry of the Temple steeple, and there with the wicked childishness of inebriety, they whooped and shrieked, and beat the drum that I had seen, and rang in charivaric unison their loud-tongued, steamboat bell.

They were, all told, not more than six hundred and forty persons who were thus lying on the river flats. But the Mormons in Nauvoo and its dependencies had been numbered the year before at over 20,000. Where were they? They had last been seen carrying in mournful trains their sick and wounded, halt and blind, to disappear behind the western horizon, pursuing the phantom of another home. Hardly anything else was known of them; and people asked with curiosity, what had been their fate—what their fortunes. Millennial Star, Vol. 13, pp. 113-116.

Fruits of Mobocracy

It was a sorry sight that met our youthful gaze the evening following the visit to the abandoned and dismantled Mormon Temple in September, 1846. Between two hundred and three hundred Mormons, men, women and children, driven out of Nauvoo the day before, were encamped in an open space a little above Montrose. Unquestioned we wandered among the tents and witnessed the sorrow that brooded over the households there assembled. Scattered about were numerous adjuncts of refined and comfortable living, elegant furniture, paintings,here and ther e a piano or a harp, finely upholstered sofas and chairs and many tasteful and convenient things which well-to-do persons would surround themselves with in well-ordered homes. There was a mingling of all ages, from the gray haired sire and matron to the babe in arms. And there were some sick; and an air of desolation and bereavement over-shadowed all, that left its impression upon our minds as one of the most pitiful sights, short of the carnage of a battlefield, that one ever beheld. When we left the scene near midnight repose was gathering over the weird scene, broken only by prayers that were being offered in the tents—prayers for safety and deliverance—prayers for their persecutors.

By J. D. Miller, who was one of those marshalled into the militia by Governor Ford of Illinois to "protect" the Saints against the mob at Nauvoo. Contributor, Vol. 11:78.

The Twelve Impart Counsel Filled with Benevolence

Let it not be supposed that the sick and destitute are to be denied the blessings of the Lord's House; God forbid; His eye is ever over them for good. He that hath not, and cannot obtain, but saith in his heart, if I had, I would give freely, is accepted as freely as he that gives of his abundance. The Temple is to be built by tithing and consecration, and everyone is at liberty to consecrate all they find in their hearts so to do; but the tithing required, is one-tenth of all anyone possessed at the commencement of the building, and one-tenth part of all his increase from that time until the completion of the same, whether it be money, or whatever he may be blessed with. Many in this place are laboring every tenth day for the house, and this is their tithing of their income, for they have nothing else; others would labor the same, but they are sick, therefore, excusable; when they get well, let them begin; while there are others who appear to think their own business of more importance than the Lord's. Of such we would ask, who gave you your time, health, strength, and put you into business? And will you not begin quickly to return with usury that which you have received? Our God will not wait always.   D. H. C., Vol. 4:473-4.

The Poverty of the Saints in Nauvoo

By Daniel Tyler

The Saints then were more numerous (in Nauvoo) than when commanded to build the Kirtland temple, but even then it was difficult for many of the people to subsist. They had been robbed of all their property, in Missouri, only two years previous, and after settling at Nauvoo (then called Commerce), with its swamps and sloughs, they had endured much sickness, such as ague, chills and fever. The swamps, however, were finally drained and the place became more healthful.

Provisions were cheap, corn being only twenty-five cents per bushel; but the trouble was to get the twenty-five cents. Wheat was about thirty to fifty cents, but where was the money? It seemed almost impossible to get either provisions or clothing. There was no grain market, even at the low prices. Thousands of bushels of corn were taken to New Orleans in flat boats, a distance of nearly two thousand miles, and sold at such a low figure, as to scarcely pay for the trouble of shipping it.

The few who had money (if there were any such), could live on "hog and hominy" without much expense; but, as a whole, the Church was very poor. Indeed, such was the condition of the people, that many aged and infirm sisters who needed a little tea, sugar or coffee, might be seen at the counter of the store, calling for one cent's worth of either or all of said articles.

A neighbor of mine speaks of seeing a farmer with a large pontoon wagon, containing forty bushels of unshelled corn, which he wanted to trade for a pair of boots, worth four dollars, but none of the merchants were buying corn, nor had any of the poor Saints four dollars to buy the load, so he had to haul it home again, a distance of twenty or thirty miles.

The poor who were in health, when they could find labor, worked for something to eat. There was, however, but little call for labor, compared with the influx of immigration. Those having a little means, of course, had to build, and some employment was thereby created for a few mechanics and laborers. The prophet counseled the brethren to do all they could in those severe times, for the poor; and the Bishops called on the merchants and others having means, to lend a helping hand. But these necessary calls came so often, that some of the merchants refused aid.

Juvenile Instructor, Vol. 15.

New Altar Dedicated in Nauvoo Temple

This afternoon the new altar was used for the first time, and four individuals and their wives were sealed. The altar is about two and one-half feet high, two and one-half feet long and about one foot wide, rising from a platform about eight or nine inches high and extending out on all sides about a foot, forming a convenient place to kneel upon. The top of the altar and the platform for kneeling upon are covered with cushions of scarlet damask cloth; the sides of the upright part or body of the altar are covered with white linen. The Twelve and the Presiding Bishops with their wives were present at the dedication of the altar this afternoon.   Journal History, January 7, 1845.

The Sealing Power in the Priesthood

By Joseph the Prophet

(Sunday, January 21, 1844, Nauvoo: Preached at the southeast corner of the Temple to several thousand people, although the weather was somewhat unpleasant. My subject was the sealing of the hearts of the fathers to the children, and the hearts of the children to the fathers.)

What shall I talk about today, I know what Brother Cahoon wants me to speak about. He wants me to speak about the coming of Elijah in the last days. I can see it in his eye. I will speak upon that subject then.

The Bible says, "I will send you Elijah the Prophet before the coming of the great and dreadful day of the Lord; and he shall turn the hearts of the fathers to the children, and the hearts of the children to the fathers, lest I come and smite the earth with a curse."

Now, the word turn here should be translated bind, or seal. But what is the object of this important mission, or how is it to be fulfilled? The keys are to be delivered, the spirit of

Elijah is to come, the Gospel to be established, the Saints of God gathered, Zion built up, and the Saints to come up as saviors on Mount Zion.

But how are they to become saviors on Mount Zion? By building their Temples, erecting their baptismal fonts, and going forth and receiving all the ordinances, baptisms, confirmations, washings, anointings, ordinations and sealing powers upon their heads, in behalf of all their progenitors who are dead, and redeem them that they may come forth in the first resurrection and be exalted to thrones of glory with them, and herein is the chain that binds the hearts of the fathers to the children, and the children to the fathers, which fulfills the mission of Elijah. And I would to God that this Temple was done now, that we might go into it, and go to work and improve our time, and make use of the seals while they are on earth.

The Saints have not too much time to save and redeem their dead, and gather together their living relatives, that they may be saved also, before the earth will be smitten, and the consumption decreed falls upon the world.

I would advise all the Saints to go with their might and gather together all their living relatives to this place, that they may be sealed and saved, that they may be prepared against the day that the destroying angel goes forth; and if the whole Church should go to with all their might to save their dead, seal their posterity, and gather their living friends, and spend none of their time in behalf of the world, they would hardly get through before night would come, when no man can work; and my only trouble at the present time is concerning ourselves, that the Saints will be divided, broken up, and scattered, before we get our salvation secure; for there are so many fools in the world for the devil to operate upon, it gives him the advantage oftentimes.

The question is frequently asked, "Can we not be saved without going through with all those ordinances, etc?" I would answer, No, not the fullness of salvation. Jesus said, "There are many mansions in my Father's house, and I will go and prepare a place for you." House here named should have been translated kingdom; and any person who is exalted to the highest mansion has to abide a celestial law, and the whole law too. (Excerpts.)   D. H. C., Vol. 6:183-4.

The True Order of Dedicating Temples

If the strict order of the Priesthood were carried out in the building of Temples, the first stone will be laid at the southeast corner, by the First Presidency of the Church. The southwest corner should be laid next. The third, or northwest corner next; and the fourth or northeast corner the last.

The First Presidency should lay the southeast cornerstone, and dictate who are the proper persons to lay the other corner-stones.

If a Temple is built at a distance, and the First Presidency are not present, then the Quorum of the Twelve Apostles are the proper persons to dictate the order for that Temple; and in the absence of the Twelve Apostles, then the presidency of the stake will lay the southeast cornerstone. The Melchizedek Priest-hood laying the cornerstones on the east side of the temple, and the Lesser Priesthood those on the west side.

Rise and Fall of Nauvoo, by B. H. Roberts, pp 95-6.

(See Addenda "C" for confession of Joseph Agnew, "Burning of Nauvoo Temple.")

Baptism for the Dead Performed in the Mississippi River

(Excerpt from Sermon delivered at the General Conference, April 6, 1891.)
By Pres. Wilford Woodruff

Joseph Smith himself (many of you may recollect the time) went into the Mississippi River one Sunday night after meeting, and baptized a hundred. I baptized another hundred. The next man, a few rods from me, baptized another hundred. We were strung up and down the Mississippi, baptizing for our dead. But there was no recorder, we attended to this ordinance without waiting to have a proper record made. But the Lord told Joseph that he must have recorders present at these baptisms —men who could see with their eyes and hear with their ears, and record these things. Of course, we had to do the work over again. Nevertheless, that does not say the work was not of God.

The Deseret Weekly, Vol. 42:554, April 25, 1891.

Robert Horne Witnessed Baptisms Performed in the Mississippi River

At one time I brought with me some boxes of glass that had been given me by a brother in the Philadelphia branch for Brother Joseph. At Alton I got a man named Dan Janes to take them up to Nauvoo on his boat, which he promised to do after much questioning. Some time afterwards I saw the Elders baptizing for the dead in the Mississippi River. This was something new to me, and the beauty of this great principle dawned upon me. I had never heard of such a doctrine then. Orson Pratt was baptizing. Brother Joseph stood on the banks holding a child in his arms. He was tall and stately and looked so grand, and he seemed clothed with such majesty that I had not the impudence to speak to him and ask if he had received those boxes of glass.

Millennial Star, 55:584.

The above picture is that of two Mormon Elders (Herbert Halls and Albert J. Jex) near one of the twenty-four sun stones constructed for the Nauvoo Temple, each of which cost $300.

In a reply letter to N. B. Lundwall (dated April 11, 1960, from Quincy, Ill.), from Mr. George Irwin, President of the Historical Society of Quincy and Adams County, Mr. Irwin states:

"We cannot tell you how much the stone weighs as we have no record of this. The stone is 54" high and the top measures 72" wide and 19" deep. It slopes inward to a bottom measurement of 54" wide and 8" deep. You might be interested to know that the stone face itself is 27" high and 32" wide.

"There is another of these stones in the State Park at Nauvoo, Illinois, and we understand that there is one in the Smithsonian Institution. These are the only ones known still in existence. Our sun stone has been in our possession for some years, having come to us through a prominent resident of Nauvoo. We also have a few other pieces of stone from the Temple and a complete set of copper keys to the various Temple rooms, which came to us from men to whom they were entrusted by the Mormons."

Chapter III

THE ST. GEORGE TEMPLE

DEDICATORY PRAYER
By Daniel H. Wells
(April 6, 1877)

Almighty and Everlasting God, our Heavenly Father, Thou who are the God of Abraham, Isaac and Jacob, the God of Moses, of David, of Solomon; the God and Father of our Lord and Savior, Jesus Christ, the God of Joseph and of Brigham, even the God of Israel; Thou who art the Father of our spirits; it is to Thee we approach this morning to worship and to offer up our dedicatory prayer, in thanksgiving and praise for this offering, even a Temple which Thou hast enabled Thy people to rear unto Thy most Holy Name. We realize, Our Father, that we are dependent upon Thee, and that, although we are shut out from Thy presence, inheriting many weaknesses and made subject to many temptations and sins, we are Thy children and as such, we come before Thee in the depths of humility, with broken hearts and contrite spirits, praying that Thine indulgence, Thy tender mercy and compassion may be extended toward us, and that Thou wilt forgive everything which thine all-seeing and searching eye hath held amiss in us.

ELDER DANIEL H. WELLS

We thank Thee, O Lord, that Thy people whom Thou hast led to this distant land, and whom Thou hast preserved by Thine own right arm, have been permitted to establish themselves in the homes, which Thou hast given them, and that, through thy continued efforts and that through Thy continued blessings they have been enabled to gather together the materials of which this build-

ST. GEORGE TEMPLE

Site dedicated on November 9, 1871. Temple dedicated on April 6, 1877,
by Elder Daniel H. Wells.

ing is composed; to put together and erect the same, even a Temple, which we dedicate and now consecrate to Thee that it may be holy unto Thee the Lord our God, for sacred and holy purposes and that the blessing, even life for evermore, may be commanded here from heaven, even from Thy presence, and may flow through the ordinances which appertain unto Thy holy place, unto us Thy children. We pray that the blessings pertaining to our eternal salvation and to the establishing of Thy kingdom upon this, Thine earth, may be poured out upon Thy Holy Priesthood and Thy people, who shall worship and officiate in this Thy Holy House.

We dedicate and consecrate the foundation of this building upon which it stands. Cause, O Lord, that it may not give way nor yield in consequence of any destructive elements which may be in the soil, but may the nature of those elements be changed so as to become strengthening instead of weakening, that the same may always remain firm and sound.

We dedicate and consecrate the lower and upper walls of the building and the buttresses which support the same and all the materials: the stone, the lime, and the sand which compose the mortar, and all that pertains thereunto, together with the flagging, the timbers, the joints, the floors, and the foundations upon which they rest, that the same may be protected and preserved, that none of the elements, either through storms, fire or earthquakes, may have power to destroy, disturb or injure this, Thy Holy House. We also dedicate and consecrate unto Thee, all the openings, entrances, doors and windows, and their fastenings of the basement story.

We also present to Thee the Baptismal font in which is performed the ordinance of baptism for the living and for the dead, with the steps, the railings around and the oxen upon which it rests, the foundations, together with the connections and apparatus for furnishing, conveying, holding and heating, the water with all that pertains to it, dedicating and consecrating all unto Thee, the Lord, our Father and God, that they may be Holy unto Thy name.

We pray that Thy blessing may attend those of Thy servants who administer and who may officiate in the ordinances that may be performed therein in behalf of Thy people, and in behalf of those our progenitors, our relatives and friends, who have gone before us to the spirit world, so far as we may be enabled and permitted to officiate for them. We dedicate also to Thee the rooms of this building in the first, second and third stories, with the pillars and supports thereof, including the side rooms, with the partition wall for the purposes for which they may be used, by the Priesthood, for prayer, for worship for councils or meetings, or for administering the Holy Ordinances of Thy house, that they may be holy unto Thee, the Lord our God. We also dedicate the roof and the tower with its dome, its covering and walls and the battlements around and above the roofs with the timbers and frames and supports upon which the roof and tower rest, and are made permanent, and the fastenings and all that appertain thereto and the materials of which they are composed.

We dedicate also the entrances, the steps and the circular stairs, with the railings and banisters thereunto attached. Grant, O Lord, that the roof which covers all, may shield and protect the building from the storms which may come upon it. We dedicate the pipes which convey the water from the room with their fastenings and the materials of which they are composed. We also dedicate the chimneys, flues, conduits, and sewers and openings for ventilation; also all the doors, windows and glass, the hinges and nails and screws, the door locks and handles, the windows, weights and cords and fastenings of every kind; and all the paint, putty, plaster, whitewash and all the ornamental work within and without, everything used in the construction and completion of the entire building, from the foundations unto the top thereof that all may be holy unto the Lord our God.

Holy Father, we dedicate unto Thee the furniture and utensils used in the holy washing, anointings and ceremonies of this Thy Holy House; also the curtains and frames for partitions; together with the altars and their cushions and the tables and chairs, stools and desks that all may be sanctified for the use and purposes intended. We dedicate also the tower on the outside, containing the fountain, also the aqueduct and pipes conveying water thereunto.

We dedicate the block of land upon which this Temple is situated and the fence which encloses it, with its opening and gates, the hinges, hangings and fastenings and the materials of which they are composed, also the roads and walks leading thereto and through the same.

We dedicate and consecrate the pulpits with the cushions thereon, and the ornamental fringe around, together with the steps, railings and banisters and the seats, with the cushions on them; and the floors, and the foundations upon which they stand. May nothing unholy, impure ever enter here but may the same be Holy unto the Lord our God.

Especially do we pray that Thy power may rest upon Thy servants who may occupy these pulpits when they shall minister by virtue of their holy calling, either in preaching, in counseling or in transacting business pertaining to the welfare of Thy Church and kingdom here upon earth. We implore Thy blessings upon the various congregations of Thy people who may assemble in this House from time to time, both in their incomings and outgoings and may Thy blessing and Thy spirit dwell herein and rest upon them for their comfort and edification, and abide richly in their hearts, that they may learn further of Thy ways and walk in Thy paths. We desire also to commend these Thy servants and people to Thy kind care and keeping, that they may be preserved unto Thee from the powers of the wicked and ungoldly, and from the powers of all evil and opposing influences, from whose grasp Thou hast heretofore delivered us in bringing us here to these valleys and the fastnesses of these mountains. We acknowledge Thee and the great deliverance Thou hast wrought out for us, and we pray Thee, O God, in the name of Jesus, to accept of these Thy servants and the people and preserve and keep us in Thy most holy keeping. Let the ministering angels from Thy presence attend us, and let Thy grace and power be upon us that we may walk in the paths of purity and holiness, and be enabled to bring forth Thy purposes and establish Thy kingdom in all its fullness, administering in all the ordinances pertaining to Thy House; and also send forth salvation to all the children of men, scattered abroad upon the face of the whole earth, for their redemption from sin and bondage, even from gross darkness.

We now ask, our Father, that we Thy servants and people may be acceptable unto Thee, praying Thee to grant that Thy Holy Spirit may pervade each heart before Thee, that our worship may be such as Thou delightest to behold and that the revelations of Thy mind and will may continue to be made manifest through Thy servant Brigham, and all of Thy servants upon whom Thou hast conferred the authority of the Holy Priesthood.

We feel not to multiply words before Thee, for language is inadequate to express the fullness of the feelings and emotions of our souls in being thus privileged to meet before Thee in this sacred, this holy place.

Accept, O God, of this tribute of our hearts, and let Thy peace and blessing dwell and abide here in this Holy Temple, which we now, with uplifted hearts and hands, present and consecrate and dedicate entire as a sacred offering unto Thee for Thine acceptance. May it stand as a monument of purity and holiness as long as the earth shall remain, commemorative of Thy great goodness toward us, Thy people, and Thy name shall have the honor, the praise and glory, for we ask all in Jesus' name, and unto Thee and our blessed Lord and Savior, and to the Holy Spirit be all power, might and dominion worlds without end. Amen.

Journal History, April 6, 1877.

Physical and Historical Description

The question of erecting a Temple in the rock-ribbed valley of St. George was with the people from the beginning of its settlement, and after presenting the construction of a Temple to his counselors, Heber C. Kimball and George A. Smith, and to the

NAME OF THE DEAD.	WHEN AND WHERE BORN.						WHEN DIED.			WHEN BAPTIZED.			WHERE BAPTIZED.	NAME OF HEIR OR PROXY.	RELATIONSHIP OF HEIR OR PROXY TO THE DEAD.
	DAY.	MO.	YR.	TOWN.	COUNTY.	COUNTRY.	DAY.	MO.	YR.	DAY.	MO.	YR.			
304 Charlotte McAllister						Eng							In the Church		
305 Martha Wood McAllister						"							"		
306 Edward Wm Huff McAllister	28	Oct	1822	Philadelphia	Phil⁰	Penn							"	"	
307 Mary Jane Albert Attinger McAllister				"	"	"							"	"	
308 Francis Michal Jones	31	Mar	1824	Mansfield	Notts	Eng	24	Sep	1861	21	Jan	1862			
309 Mary Ann Leili Mules															
310 Martha Baker Eldredge				London	Mid.	Eng							In the Church		
311 George Washington	22	Feby	1732			Virg.	11	Dec	1799	21	Aug	1877	St George	Jr Tr McAllister	Friend
312 John Washington							"	"	"	"	"	"	"	"	"
313 Sir Henry Washington							"	"	"	"	"	"	"	"	"
314 Lawrence Washington							"	"	"	"	"	"	"	"	"
315 Augustine Washington							"	"	"	"	"	"	"	"	"
316 Mr Washington Father of Augustine							"	"	"	"	"	"	"	"	"
317 Lawrence Washington							"	"	"	"	"	"	"	"	"
318 Van. Park Custis							"	"	"	"	"	"	"	"	"
319 John Park Custis							"	"	"	"	"	"	"	"	"
320 James Madison	16	Mar	1751			Virg.							"	"	"
321 James Monroe	2	Apl	1759			"							"	"	"
322 John Quincy Adams	11	July	1767			Mass							"	"	"

NAME OF THE DEAD.	WHEN AND WHERE BORN.						WHEN DIED.			WHEN BAPTIZED.			WHERE BAPTIZED.	NAME OF HEIR OR PROXY.	RELATIONSHIP OF HEIR OR PROXY TO THE DEAD.
	DAY.	MO.	YR.	TOWN.	COUNTY.	COUNTRY.	DAY.	MO.	YR.	DAY.	MO.	YR.			
323 Andrew Jackson	15	Mar	1767			S. C.	8	Jun	1845	21	Aug	1877	St George	Jr T. McAllister	Friend
324 Wm Henry Harrison	9	Feby	1773			Virg	4	Apl	1841	"	"	"	"	"	"
325 John Tyler	20	Mar	1790			"	17	Jan	1862	"	"	"	"	"	"
326 James Knox Polk	2	Nov	1795			N. C.	15	Jun	1849	"	"	"	"	"	"
327 Zachary Taylor	24	Nov	1770			Virg	9	July	1850	"	"	"	"	"	"
328 Millard Fillmore	7	May	1800			N. Y.	8	Mar	1874	"	"	"	"	"	"
329 Franklin Pierce	23	Nov	1804			N. H.	8	Oct	1869	"	"	"	"	"	"
330 Abraham Lincoln	12	Feby	1809			Ky	15	Apl	1865	"	"	"	"	"	"
331 Andrew Johnson	27	Apl	1808			N. C.	31	July	1875	"	"	"	"	"	"
332 Nathan Thompson s				Kingston		N. H.				22	Apl	1879	"	Wm H Thompson	"
333 Levi Thompson s	18	Nov	1767	"		"				"	"	"	"	"	"
334 Nathan Thompson s	6	Sep	1770	"		"				"	"	"	"	"	"
335 Samuel Thompson s	2	May	1773	"		"				"	"	"	"	"	"
336 Richard Thompson s	18	Sep	1775	"		"				"	"	"	"	"	"
337 William Thompson s				Stratham		"				"	"	"	"	"	"
338 William Thompson Jr s				"		"				"	"	"	"	"	"
339 Levi Thompson s	29	Nov	1779	"		"	21	May	1866	"	"	"	"	"	"

Photostatic copies of private records of J. D. T. McAllister which were

BAPTIZED.	CONFIRMED.	WITNESSES.	RECORDER.	ENDOWMENTS.					ORDAINED.		SEALED.	
BY WHOM				DAY.	MO.	YR.	WHERE.	BY WHOM.	WHAT OFFICE.	BY WHOM.	DAY. MO. YR.	WHERE.
				5	Sep	1877	St George	Jno. Wells				
				6	"	"	"	Anne Thos Wells				
				7	"	"	"	Ann Hawley McAllister				
				12	"	"	"	Ellen Hawley McAllister				
				9	Nov	"	"	Mary Scrimshire				
				20	Feby	1878	"	Ellen S. Vance				
				"	"	"	"	Susanna Patrick Angus				
				"	"	"	"	Eliza Patrick				
W. Woodruff	Wm Fawcett	A.P. Winsor	A.K. Whitehead	22	Aug	1877	"	Jos. McAllister	Pst.	W. Woodruff		
"	"	Jos. Harman	"	"	"	"	"	John Lyth	Eld.	Wm Fawcett		
"	"	"	"	"	"	"	"	Peter Perkins	"	Jos. Harman		
"	"	"	"	"	"	"	"	Thos. Day	"	Wm Fawcett		
"	"	"	"	"	"	"	"	Hugh S. Gowans	"	Jos. McAllister		
"	"	"	"	"	"	"	"	Chas. A. Terry	"	"		
"	"	"	"	"	"	"	"	Wm Richey	"	W. Woodruff		
"	"	"	"	"	"	"	"	H. M. Bigler	"	"		
"	"	"	"	"	"	"	"	David Moss	"	Wm Fawcett		
"	"	"	"	22	Aug	1877	"	John F. Smith	"	Wm Fawcett		
"	"	"	"	"	"	"	"	Henry Eyring	"	W. Woodruff		
				"	"	"	"	Wm Vance		"		

BAPTIZED.	CONFIRMED.	WITNESSES.	RECORDER.	ENDOWMENTS.					ORDAINED.		SEALED.	
BY WHOM				DAY.	MO.	YR.	WHERE.	BY WHOM.	WHAT OFFICE.	BY WHOM.	DAY. MO. YR.	WHERE.
W. Woodruff	Wm Fawcett	A.P. Winsor	A.K. Whitehead	22	Aug	1877	St George	Jos. Harman	Elder	Wm Fawcett		
"	"	Jos. Harman	"	23	"	"	"	M. F. Farnsworth	"	Wm Fawcett		
"	"	"	"	"	"	"	"	Mathew Clayton	"	"		
"	"	"	"	"	"	"	"	Geo Coombs	"	"		
"	"	"	"	"	"	"	"	H. C. D. Riding	"	J. L. Smith		
"	"	"	"	"	"	"	"	J. D. McAllister	"	W. Woodruff		
"	"	"	"	"	"	"	"	David Mustard	"	Jno. Pimm		
"	"	"	"	"	"	"	"	Wm F. Smith	"	J. L. Smith		
"	"	"	"	"	"	"	"	A. K. Whitehead	"	W. Woodruff		
Jos. Hammond	J. D. McAllister	Geo Woodward	"	25	Apl	1879	"	Chr. Peterson	"	Jno. Pimm		Thompson
"	"	Jos. Harman	"	25	June	"	"	Josiah G. Hardy	"	C. A. Terry		
"	"	"	"	25	Apl	"	"	Jos. S. Allen	"	H. Bigler		
"	"	"	"	25	June	"	"	Saml B. Hardy	"	H. Granger		
"	"	"	"	"	"	"	"	Wm Roberts	"	C. A. Terry		
"	"	"	"	"	"	"	"	Thos. Webb	"	G. Woodward		
"	"	"	"	"	"	"	"	Jas. McLellan	"	J. L. Smith		
"	"	"	"	"	"	"	"	T. M. Thomas	"	H. Granger		

furnished by his son Martin L. McAllister of St. George, Utah.

council of the Twelve, President Brigham Young wrote, under date of April 15, 1871, that the time had at last arrived when a Temple should be built.

After preliminary surveys to determine where rock, lime, sand and lumber could be obtained, it was finally decided to break ground for the building on November 6, 1871, but inclement weather and the unfinished state of the surveying made it necessary to postpone this until November 9, on which day the site was dedicated by George A. Smith, upon which occasion appropriate ceremonies were conducted among which was the "Hosanna Shout." Work on the excavations began immediately, but the task was rendered difficult as several springs of alkali water were discovered and the seepage threatened to ruin the foundations. To obviate this difficulty a pile driver was improvised out of a cannon of the Mexican War which was filled with lead and surrounded with cottonwood bark which was firmly fastened on by means of steel bands to prevent splitting. A frame and device for hoisting this thousand-pound weight was constructed and after the water and mud were excavated from the place where the foundation was to be, hundreds of tons of volcanic rock were pounded into the earth with this great hammer, and so great was the momentum that the hammer would bounce three times before coming to rest. In this way a secure foundation was made possible. As the pile driver made firm the earth, the masons laid up the foundation of great slabs of malipi rocks. Over $100,000 was spent on the foundation alone.

On April 1, 1874, before leaving St. George for his return to Salt Lake City, President Young and others laid the cornerstones of the Temple, at which time he offered the dedicatory prayer. The principal works of the Church, a silver plate bearing the names of the Authorities of the Church, and other items, were placed in a box which was deposited in the wall at the southeast corner, twelve feet from the bottom of the foundation. The superstructure above this foundation was of red sandstone, the construction of which was under the direction of Edward Lloyd Parry, and was completed on March 5, 1875. On this day appropriate ceremonies were held, with brass band, singing, speaking and a picnic.

On January 1, 1877, the lower story of the Temple was completed sufficiently for use. Appropriate ceremonies were held and Wilford Woodruff dedicated the finished portion for appro-priate Temple work. On January 9, 1877, baptisms for the dead were administered and endowments for the dead were given two days later. During the months of January, February and March, Brigham Young spent much time explaining the rites and cere-monies of the Temple service, which had been revealed to the Prophet Joseph Smith and which were taught to Brigham Young and six others in the Brick Store at Nauvoo, Brigham Young being the last to survive of the seven thus taught by the Prophet. All of these sacred ordinances were fully expounded to all of the brethren and sisters ministering in the St. George Temple and his instructions were carefully recorded. On April 6, 1877, the forty-seventh annual conference of the Church was held in St. George, at which time the Temple was dedicated by Daniel H. Wells, the dedicatory services lasting three days, at each of which Apostle Lorenzo Snow, who had been trained under the Prophet Joseph Smith, led in the "Hosanna Shout" with solemn and beautiful dignity.

The Temple building has a magnificent appearance. The red bluffs on the north, the volcanic ridges on the east and west, the Rio Virgin, running through the valley on the south, and the beautiful city on the north and northwest, form a lovely picture with striking and vivid contrasts. The cost of the Temple has been about $500,000. The baptismal font, weighing 18,000 pounds, was presented to the Church by Brigham Young, its cost being $5,000.

The Temple is 141 feet 8 inches long, 93 feet 4 inches wide, 84 feet high to the square or parapet, and 175 feet high to the top of the vane on the tower.

During much of the year 1875, one hundred men were engaged at the Temple in construction work, one hundred were at the rock quarries, and forty were engaged in furnishing lum-ber, totaling 240 men. Over a million feet of lumber were used in constructing the building. Some of the beams were exceedingly large, being 12" by 24" by 26' to 46' long. Much of it was hauled by ox team from Mt. Trumbull, 80 miles distant. The remainder came from Pine Valley Mountain, a distance of 30 miles north of St. George, and from the Buckskin Mountains on the Kaibab Forest. Seventeen thousand tons of black vol-canic rock and red sandstone went into the building. The quarry for the black rock was on top of the first landing on the west side of the second rise on the black ridge west of St. George, the red sandstone being secured just around the west point of the red hill north of St. George.

Truman O. Angell, Church architect, drew the plans for the building; Miles P. Romney was general superintendent of construction; Edward Lloyd Parry had charge of the stone cutting and laying; William Carter of the device for pounding to solidity the foundation bottoms; George Jarvis had charge of all scaffold making and hoisting devices at the quarries and at the temple; William Burt had charge of the plastering; David Milne supervised the painting and decorating; Albert Foremaster and Et Wiltbank supervised the production and delivery of lime; Robert Gardner superintended the getting out of the lumber at Mt. Trumbull and Pine Valley; and Arch McNeil was overseer at the quarries. The mule teams of James Andrus, Edward M. Brown, Thomas Judd and Daniel D. McArthur hauled much of the stone, the larger pieces being slung under the wagons. Benjamin and Frederick Blake were the noted drivers of large ox teams that brought in the lumber from Mt. Trumbull.

Presidents of the St. George Temple:

> Wilford Woodruff, 1877-1884.
> John D. T. McAllister, 1884-1893.
> David H. Cannon, 1893-1924.
> Thomas P. Cottam, 1925-1926.
> Edward H. Snow, 1926-1932.
> George F. Whitehead, 1932-1937.
> Harold S. Snow, 1937-1963.
> Rudger C. Atkin, 1963—Present Incumbent.

No Lives Will Be Lost

The statement of facts that I here relate came under my own observation and are my own experiences, and have the same force and effect as though they were notarized under seal. I was born on the 14th day of October, 1860, in Salt Lake City, Utah. My parents' names were: my father, George Jarvis, and my mother, Ann Prior Jarvis. I was in St. George, Utah, at the time of the dedication of the site for the Temple, and saw President Brigham Young take the first shovelful of dirt from the foundation, and he stated at the time "that there would not be any persons who would lose their lives on any of the works on this Temple." I lived to see this prediction fulfilled as I saw many persons hurt but none of them died. I was within three or four feet of him when he made this statement.

One man by the name of John Burt, fell from the top of the Temple. He was plastering with my brother, George Jarvis, who had stepped off a plank. John Burt jumped from the fire wall onto the scaffold about three or four feet below and the plank broke and he went right on through, falling to the ground, some 84 feet, and fell on the scattered rock, dirt, etc., which was on the ground. The workmen rushed to him. I was on a horse not far away and came up to him also. He was conscious and was calling for his mother. In ten days he was walking around the streets of St. George and resumed his work later on, so that the fall did not disable him nor prevent him from continuing the work on the Temple. I knew of another man who fell from the top of the Temple also, Thomas Crane. Will Thayne fell 35 feet off the wall alighting across a large malipi rock on his side, but he was not killed; Pete Granger had the large frame from which the huge hammer worked and which weighed many hundreds of pounds, and which was 35 feet high, fall on him; George Lang had a huge rock on his wagon which weighed 8,000 pounds, and was driving a team of mules. His mules ran away with this rock on the wagon; he fell from the wagon and his ear was torn from his head. Yet none of these men were killed, but continued their labors on the Temple.

Upon one occasion President Brigham Young was in the Tabernacle at St. George and was speaking on the spirit world. He stated that it was not far from us and if the veil could be taken from our eyes there wouldn't be either a man, woman or child who would dare go out of "this tabernacle as the spirits of the Gadianton robbers were so thick out there. This is where they lived in these mountains," said he.

At the dedication of the Temple, as they had just left from dedicating the sealing rooms upstairs and were about to close the services, Brigham Young, having rheumatism, was brought to the stand, and in speaking near the Priesthood stand of the

Elders, he struck the stand with his knotted cane and said: "There are men present that have no more right here than the devils from hell." My brother, George Jarvis, was close to the two men he pointed to, and he said they fluttered like wounded ducks. I was not more than fifteen feet from President Young and saw and heard everything and know whereof I speak. This statement is written and signed at Mesa, Arizona, this 1st day of April, 1940.   Signed: Heber Jarvis.

Appearance of the Signers of the Declaration of Independence and Presidents of the United States to President Wilford Woodruff In the St. George Temple

---

I am going to bear my testimony to this assembly, if I never do it again in my life, that those men who laid the foundation of this American Government and signed the Declaration of Independence were the best spirits the God of Heaven could find on the face of the earth. They were choice spirits, not wicked men. General Washington and all the men that labored for the purpose were inspired of the Lord. Another thing I am going to say here, because I have a right to say it. Every one of those men that signed the Declaration of Independence with General Washington called upon me, as an Apostle of the Lord Jesus Christ, in the Temple at St. George two consecutive nights, and demanded at my hands that I should go forth and attend to the ordinances of the house of God for them. Men are here, I believe, that know of this—Brothers J. D. T. McAllister, David H. Cannon and James C. Bleak. Brother McAllister baptized me for all these men, and I then told these brethren that it was their duty to go into the Temple and labor until they got endowments for all of them. They did it. Would those spirits have called upon me, as an Elder in Israel, to perform that work if they had not been noble spirits before God? They would not. I bear this testimony because it is true. The spirit of God bore record to myself and the brethren while we were laboring in that way. * * *

(Report of President Wilford Woodruff, General Conference, April 10, 1898, pp. 89-90.)

We have labored in the St. George Temple since January, and we have done all we could there; and the Lord has stirred up our minds, and many things have been revealed to us concerning the dead. President Young has said to us, and it is verily so, if the dead could they would speak in language loud as ten thousand thunders, calling upon the servants of God to rise up and build Temples, magnify their calling and redeem their dead. This doubtless sounds strange to those present who believe not the faith and doctrine of the Latter-day Saints; but when we get to the spirit world we will find out that all God has revealed is true. We will find, to, that everything there is reality, and that God has a body, parts and passions, and the erroneous ideas that exist now with regard to Him will have passed away. I feel to say little else to the Latter-day Saints wherever and whenever I have the opportunity of speaking to them, than to call upon them to build these Temples now under way, to hurry them up to completion. The dead will be after you, they will seek after you as they have after us in St. George. They called upon us, knowing that we held the keys and power to redeem them.

I will say here, before closing, that two weeks before I left St. George, the spirits of the dead gathered around me, wanting to know why we did not redeem them. Said they: "You have had the use of the Endowment House for a number of years and yet nothing has ever been done for us. We laid the foundation of the government you now enjoy, and we never apostatized from it, but we remained true to it and were faithful to God." These were the signers of the Declaration of Independence, and they waited on me for two days and two nights. I thought it very singular that notwithstanding so much work had been done, and yet nothing had been done for them. The thought never entered my heart from the fact, I suppose, that heretofore our minds were reaching after our more immediate friends and relatives. I straightway went into the baptismal font and called upon Brother McAllister to baptize me for the signers of the Declaration of Independence, and fifty other eminent men, making one hundred in all, including John Wesley, Columbus, and others; I then baptized him for every President of the United States except three; and when their cause is just, somebody will do the work for them.

(Remarks made at General Conference, September 16, 1877.)
Journal of Discourses, Vol. 19, p. 229.

Many Saints are Glued to the Earth
By President Brigham Young

(Remarks made at the dedication of portions of the St. George Temple.
January 1, 1877.)

I cannot consent in my feelings to retire from this house without speaking to this people. Perhaps it would not be prudent to say all I have in my heart to say to those assembled. I shall say a few encouraging things to the Latter-day Saints. We are enjoying today a privilege which but few have enjoyed since the days of Adam. Solomon built a Temple for the performance of certain ordinances but through apostasy little was accomplished therein. I will not say that Enoch had no Temples in which he officiated. His people became so perfect that the Lord took them to another place that removed them from the presence of the wicked. The Latter-day Saints have been laboring for over forty years in accordance with the revelations of the Lord to Joseph Smith who was commanded to establish the kingdom by gathering the Saints by building Temples, by organizing the people as a heavenly family upon the earth. We built a Temple at Kirtland and one at Nauvoo. Joseph located the site for one in Jackson County, and for another in Far West, Missouri. From these we were driven by ruthless mobs; now we have a Temple which will be completely finished in a few days. There is enough now completed to commence work. Those who can see the spiritual atmosphere can see that many are still glued to the earth. They are lusting and longing for the things of this world, in which there is no profit. While we ought to look after temporal things, we should devote them all to the kingdom of God. Where are the hearts of the people; where are their forefathers? What are they doing for their own salvation and for that of their forefathers?

If we were awake to this great truth this house would be crowded from Monday morning until Saturday night. This Temple has been built in a warm climate where the people, including the Lamanites, can come in the winter and labor for their salvation and that of their progenitors. What do you suppose the fathers would say if they could speak from the dead? Would they not say: "We have lain here thousands of years in this prison house, bound and fettered in the association of the filthy and corrupt." If they had the power the very thunders of heaven would resound in our ears. All the angels in heaven are looking to this little handful of people. When I think upon this subject I want the tongue of seven thunders to awaken the people to action. When we closed the Endowment House many of the people of the north came to us crying. They begged the privilege to be baptized for their dead. They can now come here, do the work and bid the prisoners go free. I shall never be satisfied until Satan is conquered and driven from the face of the earth.

Life of Wilford Woodruff, by Mathias F. Cowley, pp. 494-5.

Revelations Given in the St. George Temple

(Excerpt from discourse delivered at the General Conference, April 6, 1891.)
By Pres. Wilford Woodruff

The spirit of inspiration was with Brigham Young from the day that he entered into this work till he laid down his life upon his bed. I bear testimony to these things. There never has been a time, either in these Temples or anywhere else, but the Lord has made manifest His will on any point on which light was desired. To my certain knowledge the Lord gave revelations in St. George Temple to His servants there, upon points of doctrine we did not understand. President Young was there. I was there. Brother McAllister and others labored there, and we knew these things. So I say there is no man that goes into these Temples to labor, or goes into the vineyard of the Lord to labor who, if he will live his religion and do his duty, will fail in receiving the mind and will of God. Yes, the Lord has raised up Saviors upon Mount Zion, and the Kingdom is the Lord's. It is His work. And we have the great power as Latter-day Saints to go into these temples and redeem our dead, and attend to the ordinances for them that they never heard of in their day and generation. What will be the condition of these saviors upon Mount Zion? These Saints of the Lord will hold the keys of salvation to their Father's house to the endless ages of eternity. There never will be a time when that power will be taken from them. We ought to realize these things, and we ought to prize the blessings which God has put in our hands.

The Deseret Weekly, April 25, 1891, p. 554.

Brigham Young

When the scroll shall be unfolded listing the life's labors of Brigham Young, he will be recognized as one of the world's greatest benefactors. As a leader, the world will search in vain for one who surpasses him in righteous achievement and valor, in history's great trek across an uncharted desert. He was indeed a Prophet who prophesied, a Seer who saw and a Revelator who revealed. He was, like all great men, one whom the righteous loved and whom the wicked hated.

He labored on the Kirtland Temple as superintendent in the glazing, painting, and finishing of it; he dedicated the Far West Temple site on July 4, 1938; he dedicated the completed portion of the Nauvoo Temple on October 5, 1845 and laid its capstone; he offered the dedicatory prayer on April 1, 1874, when the corner-stones of the St. George Temple were laid; he took an active and overseeing part in the choosing of the sites, or drawnig up of architectural plans, or encouraging construction of temples at St. George, Logan, Manti, and Salt Lake, in addition to his great physical labors on the Kirtland and Nauvoo Temples. His contributions in this volume attest his greatness. He was truly a worthy successor and a devoted friend to the Prophet Joseph, to the Latter-day Saints and to God.

Chapter IV

THE LOGAN TEMPLE

DEDICATORY PRAYER
By
President John Taylor
(May 17, 1884)

O God, the Eternal Father, the Creator of all things, visible and invisible, the Author of our existence, the Lord and Giver of life; we approach Thee, as Thou hast directed, in the name of Thy well beloved Son, Jesus Christ, our Savior and Redeemer, and say: "Our Father who art in heaven; hallowed be Thy name, Thy kingdom come, Thy will be done in earth as it is in heaven." We acknowledge Thy power, we bow to Thy authority and reverence Thy holy name.

We, O God, a few of Thy creatures, according to Thine instructions, and in obedience to Thy law and Thy word, have built this house unto Thee, which was contemplated and designed by Thy servant Brigham; that it may be "a house of order, a house of prayer," a place acceptable to Thee, and wherein we can worship Thee in accordance with Thy will, Thy law and the principles which Thou hast revealed; and for the manifestation of Thy will, and the teachings and administration of ordinances, and the instruction of Thy people in all principles of science and intelligence pertaining to this life, and the lives that are to come.

PRESIDENT JOHN TAYLOR

It hath pleased Thee, O Lord God, our Heavenly Father, to reveal Thyself in our days, and to make known unto us through Thy servant Joseph—by the manifestation of Thyself and Thy well beloved Son, Jesus Christ, our Savior and Redeemer, by Thine

LOGAN TEMPLE

Site dedicated on May 17, 1877. Temple dedicated on May 17, 1884, by President John Taylor.

appearing unto him, that Thou still livest by the opening of the heavens, by the brightness of Thine appearance, and by Thine own voice Thou hast manifested Thyself unto him, and pointing also to our glorious Redeemer who was present with Thee, declared Him to be Thy well beloved Son in whom Thou wast well pleased, and commanded Thy servant Joseph to hear Him.

Thou hast also been pleased through Him and through the Holy Priesthood, which have lived on the earth and still exist in the Heavens, to restore the everlasting Gospel in its fulness, richness, power and glory; with the Holy Priesthood, and the keys thereof and pertaining thereunto, together with the dispensation of the fullness of times, spoken of by all the holy Prophets since the world was; which our forefathers have waited to be revealed, that we, as well as Thy servant Joseph, might be put in possession of the knowledge of Thyself and of Thy law, through the power of the Holy Priesthood, and the everlasting Gospel which brings life and immortality to light, and opens a communication between the heavens and the earth; and through which, as Thou hast stated, "God shall give unto you (the Saints) a knowledge by His Holy Spirit, yea, by the unspeakable gift of the Holy Ghost, that has not been revealed since the world was until now."

Thou didst command Thy servant Joseph in the land of Ohio to build a house unto Thee, saying: "Organize yourselves, prepare every needful thing and establish a house, even a house of prayer, a house of fasting, a house of faith, a house of learning, a house of glory, a house of order, a house of God." And when this house was completed Thou didst manifest Thyself to Thy servant Joseph, to Oliver Cowdery, and to others of the Holy Priesthood and in the brightness of Thy glory didst reveal unto him exceedingly great and precious principles, and Thou didst send also Thine ancient servant Moses, who formerly gathered Thy people Israel from the land of Egypt, to commit the keys of gathering of latter-day Israel; and also Elias, who committed the dispensation of the Gospel of Abraham; and also Elijah the Prophet, to whom was committed the keys of the dispensation spoken of by Malachi, which was to "turn the heart of the fathers to the children, and the heart of the children to their fathers." And Thou didst then introduce a preparatory work associated with the washings and anointings of Thy people. Thou didst also command Thy servant Joseph to build a house at Nauvoo wherein further development of the Holy Priesthood might be introduced, saying: "For there is not a place found on earth that He may come and restore that which was lost unto you, or which He hath taken away, even the fullness of the Priesthood, for a baptismal font there is not upon the earth, that they, my Saints, may be baptized for those who are dead." And it is written: "Therefore, verily I say unto you, that your anointings, and your washings, and your baptisms for the dead, and your solemn assemblies, and your memorials for your sacrifices, by the sons of Levi, and for your oracles in your most holy places, wherein you receive conversations, and your statutes and judgments, for the beginning of the revelations and foundation of Zion, and for the glory, honor and endowment of all her municipals, are ordained by the ordinance of my holy house which my people are always commanded to build unto my holy name." This house was commenced by Thy servant Joseph, and completed by Thy servant Brigham and the Twelve; and in it were revealed many great and precious principles and ordinances which had previously been communicated to a chosen few before Thy servant Joseph's death. And as Thou didst give a standing commandment that Thy people were always to build houses unto Thy holy name, when Thy people came here unto this land, even the land of Zion, Thy servant Brigham, according to this commandment and Thy manifestations unto him, did build a house in St. George, in this Territory, wherein many precious principles have been developed, and much labor performed according to Thy holy ordinances, in the interests of the living and the dead; so we have now completed this, another house, which we this day dedicate and consecrate unto Thee, that we may be further prepared to carry out Thy will, to administer in Thine ordinances, to purify and instruct Thy Church, and to build up and establish Thy Zion on the earth, which Thou hast decreed should be accomplished in the dispensation of the fullness of times. We feel, O Lord God, our weakness and unworthiness before Thee, and our inability to do anything without Thy guidance and assistance; but as Thou hast given us a commandment, in common with others, we have built this house, and present it to Thee, and pray that Thou wilt accept it in the name of Thy Son Jesus Christ, our Lord and Redeemer. We dedicate the ground on which it is built, as also by which it is surrounded, known as the Temple Block; we dedicate the foundation upon which it rests, the stones, the mortar, the doors, the stairs, the windows, the floors, the fastenings, the ceilings and roof, the painting and ornamentation, the stands for the Holy Priesthood, the baptismal font and the various rooms associated therewith, and also all the rooms for the performance of ordinances and the various purposes for which they are designed, the heating apparatus, and the furniture and everything therein from the foundation to the towers thereof, unto Thee, the Lord our God, that it may be a place most holy, wherein Thine ordinances may be performed, and Thy Priesthood administered according to Thy holy law, and in accordance with Thy will and purposes pertaining to the human family. For Thou, O God, hast ordained the principles which have been developed for the blessing, salvation and exaltation of the human race, and hast appointed Thy holy ordinances for the endowment of Thy Holy Priesthood and in the interests of the living and the dead; that Thy servants may go forth to the nations of the earth endowed with power from on high, and bear a message of salvation, even as

Thy messengers to all the family of Adam, according to Thy word. And that Thy people may be prepared through the ordinances of Thine House to inherit thrones, principalities, powers, dominions and exaltations in the eternal worlds. And, also, that Thy purposes pertaining to the redemption of the dead may be carried out strictly in accordance with Thy law, that in this Thy holy house Thine ordinances may be performed in the interest of those who have died without a knowledge of the gospel; and that Thy servants and handmaidens who may officiate in Thy holy ordinances therein may thus become saviors upon Mount Zion, even according to the words of Thine ancient servant Malachi, wherein he stated that it was necessary that the hearts of the fathers should be turned to the children, and the hearts of the children to the fathers, and that according to later revelations, a welding, connecting link might bind together the living and the dead in fraternal and patriarchal relations, according to the holy order which exists with the Gods; and a bond of union and fellowship be brought about between the heavens and the earth, for Thou hast said that they without us cannot be made perfect, and that we without them cannot be made perfect; we pray Thee, therefore, O God, that those who officiate here may act prudently, wisely and intelligently, with purity, virtue and honor before Thee, and perform their duties acceptably in this Thy Temple on earth.

And we also pray Thee, O Father, that Thy Priesthod may be assisted by Thy Holy Priesthood in the heavens, that Priesthood which is after the order of the Son of God, after the order of Melchizedek, and after the power of an endless life, which administers in time and eternity, to impart unto us by Thy direction and according to Thy will, a correct knowledge of all laws, rites and ordinances, and direction how to administer and to whom to administer; that there may be a perfect union and harmony, if we are counted worthy, between the Priesthood on the earth and the Priesthood in the heavens. And that Thou wouldst teach us Thy will and Thy law, and Thine ordinances more fully and completely, and reveal unto us the abundance of truth and intelligence associated with the interests of the living and the dead; that knowing Thy will we may do Thy will on earth as it is done in heaven.

And as Thou hast said, among other things, pertaining to Thine house, that in it we were to seek diligently and teach one another words of wisdom, "Yea, seek ye out of the best books words of wisdom, seek learning by study and also by faith," and Thou hast further instructed us to "become acquainted with all good books, and with languages, tongues and people," and obtain a knowledge of nations, kingdoms, governments and laws, and Thou hast declared that there is "a time to come in which nothing shall be withheld, whether there be one God or many Gods, they shall be manifest."

"All thrones and dominions, principalities and powers, shall be revealed and set forth upon all who have endured valiantly for the Gospel of Jesus Christ and also if there be bounds set to the heavens, or to the seas, or to the dry land, or to the sun, moon or stars; all the times of their revolutions; all the appointed days, months, and years, and all the days of their days, months and years, and all their glories, laws and set times, shall be revealed in the days of the dispensation of the fullness of times. According to that which was ordained in the midst of the Council of the Eternal God of all other Gods, before this world was, that should be reserved unto the finishing and the end thereof, when every man shall enter into His eternal presence, and into His immortal rest." And, as all wisdom dwells with thee, and, as all light, truth and intelligence flow from Thee, we humbly seek unto Thee for Thy blessing to rest upon this house, that it may be indeed a house of learning under Thy guidance, direction and inspiration, as Thou didst ordain the laws of the universe, and art the Creator and Sustainer of worlds, and the Regulator of their times and seasons, we ask that in this house a more full knowledge of Thee and Thy laws may be developed, and that those things spoken of by Thy servant Joseph may begin to be made manifest. We therefore pray Thee to grant that when Thy people draw nigh unto Thee in the holy order that Thou hast appointed and revealed, that Thou will hear their prayers, and look with favor upon their supplications, which are made in accordance with Thy word, and Thy will and Thy law. And if we are accounted worthy, and it is in accordance with Thy will and purposes, and not incompatible with the holy order which exists among the Gods, and that Thou hast ordained, we pray Thee that Thy presence may be with us. We pray also that the presence of Thy Son, Jesus Christ, our Savior, may be here, and that the Holy Ghost, the Comforter, may be our guide and instructor, and that Thine angels may be permitted to visit this holy habitation and communicate with Thy Priesthood in the interests of the living and the dead.

We also pray Thee, as Thou hast revealed unto us many things, to give us a more clear knowledge of the telestial, terrestrial, and celestial glories, and the laws, regulations and bounds by which they are governed; and the duties and responsibilities connected with each, that we may be enabled more fully to comprehend our duties, responsibilities and obligations, pertaining to all men in the various conditions and associations of life, and connected also with this nation and other nations of the world, that we may be enabled to act justly, prudently, righteously and intelligently in all the various relations of life, pertaining to social, religious, political and other duties devolving upon us, and that we may comprehend always fully the relationship that we sustain to this nation, to other nations, and to the world generally in which we live, and understand more perfectly our responsibilities to the living and the dead, to the wicked and corrupt, to the honorable and upright among men; to Thee, our heavenly Father, to Jesus, the Mediator of the New Covenant, to the Ancient of Days, and to the different orders, quorums and organizations of the holy Priesthood, and to our brethren generally, in this the land of Zion.

We ask thee to bless the nation in which we live and the rulers thereof, for we are persuaded, O Lord, that while great wickedness and corruption abound in all grades of society, that there are hundreds of thousands of honorable men who are desirous to do right and maintain the principles of freedom and the liberty of men, and who do not and cannot acquiesce in the measures taken by the thoughtless and uninformed, who seem to be desirous to injure Thy people, many of whom, however, through the circulation of misrepresentation and falsehood, do not comprehend the position which Thy people occupy, nor the principles by which they are governed. Enlighten their minds, we pray Thee, and lead them in the paths of life. Bless, we pray Thee, all the upright, the pure and virtuous who are seeking to maintain and sustain the glorious principles of freedom enunciated in the Constitution of the United States, and who are opposed to tyranny, misrule and oppression; and save this nation, O God, from the infamy, under guise of law, of being the spoliators and robbers of a virtuous, inoffensive and God-fearing people, in violation of their constitutional rights, and because they fear and reverence Thee and Thy laws but may this house be preserved unto us as a holy place wherein to worship Thee, and to administer Thine ordinances, to learn Thy laws, the laws of the universe—embracing the world and other worlds; for the instruction of Thy people in the higher branches of education in all true intelligence, scientific, linguistic, natural and theological.

Bless the honest and upright throughout the world, and lead the erring in the paths of righteousness; and as Thou hast decreed that terrible judgments shall overtake the ungoldly, we leave these things, O Lord, in Thy hands, and wish to conform ourselves to Thy will.

Preserve us, O God, in these valleys of the mountains, and let not our enemies and Thine enemies triumph over Thy people, and suffer them not to bring us into bondage, for Thou, O Lord, knowest that we are seeking to do Thy will and carry out Thy laws; preserve us, therefore, in our immunities, liberties and rights, and save us from the menacing power of tyranny and oppression, for our trust, O God, is in Thee.

Bless, we pray Thee, the councils and authorities of the Church; the First Presidency, the Twelve with their council, the Patriarchs, the Presidents of Stakes, the High Councils and Bishops thereof, together with the Seventies, High Priests, Elders, Priests, Teachers, Deacons, and all the quorums and authorities of Thy Church, as also all the helps, aids and governments pertaining thereto, the Relief Societies, the Sunday School, the Primary and the Mutual Improvement Associations, and all men and women who are seeking for the welfare of Zion. Bless all our friends who are not of us, who are desirous to maintain the principles of virtue, integrity, honor and freedom. We pray Thee also to bless those who have assisted to build this house, the committee of construction, the architects, the superintendents, the workmen in all their various branches that have contributed by their industry and talent to construct this building as a habitation for Thee, our God; bless the Stakes of this Temple district, as well as all persons who have contributed of their means thereunto, or in any wise assisted in the construction thereof. Let the fear of God rest upon all Thy people. Preserve them in the principles of honor, of virtue, of truth, of integrity, and in the love of God, that they may be worthy of Thy blessings. Let the people praise Thee, O God; let all the people praise Thee. O Lord, our God, hear us in the heavens, and answer us upon the earth, that Zion may arise and shine, that the glory of God may rest upon her. That thy people may be preserved from the errors of vanity, the follies and corruptions of the world; that they may progress and excel in every principle of integrity, intelligence, virtue and purity, until Zion shall become the praise and glory of the whole earth, and Thy will be begun to be done on earth as it is in heaven. We ask this at Thy hands, and dedicate this house unto Thee, together with ourselves, our wives, our children, our houses, our lands, our flocks and herds, and our possessions, for time and all eternity, in the name of Thy Son, Jesus Christ. Amen.

Millennial Star, Vol. 46, pp. 386-391.

Physical and Historical Description

The Logan Temple, like other Temples constructed in this dispensation, is in fulfillment of prophecy, uttered, in this case, by President Wilford Woodruff.

The site for this Temple was designated by President Brigham Young and was dedicated by Orson Pratt on May 17, 1877, at which time impressive services were conducted by President Young. Elder Charles O. Card served as Superintendent of construction of the Temple from the beginning until its completion, and Truman O. Angell was the architect. On the 28th day of May excavation was begun and the cornerstones were laid on September 17, 1877, under the direction of President John Taylor of the Council of the Twelve, President Brigham Young having died on August 29th previous. The Temple was dedicated on May 17, 1884, by President John Taylor as President of the Church.

The territory covered in the district of the Logan Temple at the time of its building and dedication comprised but three stakes; viz: Cache, Box Elder and Bear Lake, with a total Church population of about 25,000. As a result of the dividing and subdividing of these stakes, there were in 1933 thirty-six stakes in the Logan Temple district, with a Church population of over 151,000, with a proportionate increase since that census.

The grounds upon which the Temple stands comprise a full city block of eight acres, to which has been added nearly two acres on the east end, which, with an elliptical frontage, gives a very attractive entrance to the Temple. The whole block is planted with beautiful trees, shrubs, lawns and flower beds, and is the admiration of all who view it.

The main building of the Temple is 171 feet long, 95 feet wide, and 86 feet high at the square, with an octagonal tower at each corner 100 feet high, and a large square tower at each end. The tower at the west end is 165 feet high, and the one at the east end is 170 feet high. Massive buttresses strengthen the walls, and the masonry is of the very best; and today there is scarcely a crack or defect to be seen in the whole building. The rock used in the construction of the building was brought from mountain quarries near by, and is a very dark silicious limestone. The lumber for the building was obtained from Logan Canyon, and was prepared at the Temple sawmill specially installed for that purpose. The building has five stories. In the basement is a beautiful font room finished in white enamel, the font being of cast iron, cast in a logan foundry, and stands upon the backs of twelve oxen, also cast in iron and bronzed, which present a very impressive appearance. The rooms of the Temple throughout correspond in a general way with the rooms of all other Church Temples; are all beautifully finished in white enamel, with chaste decorations of gold leaf and soft colors, and are representative of the best art of the day in which they were erected and compare equally well with present day decoration and finish. The Temple was seven years in building—1877 to 1884. It is difficult to estimate the exact cost of the building because of the manner in which it was built, a large portion being given in labor, farm products, and other means; but it is safe to say that it cost approximately $750,000 exclusive of the land and improvements.

Of the 20,939,792 ordinances performed in all of the Temples, since the organization of the Church, including the Nauvoo Temple and the old Endowment House in Salt Lake City, it is interesting to learn that 5,454,043 of this number were performed in the Logan Temple, being a little over 26% of all. These figures are up to December 31, 1933, and represent work performed for fifty years (1844 to 1933).

Presidents of the Logan Temple:

> Marriner W. Merrill, 1884-1906.
> William Budge, 1906-1918.
> Joseph R. Shepherd, 1918-1935.
> William A. Noble, 1935-1936.
> Joseph Quinney, Jr., 1936-1943.
> El Ray Christiansen, 1943-1952.
> A. George Raymond, 1952—Present Incumbent.

A few interesting Facts Connected with the History of the Logan Temple:

"On May 21, 1884, the first baptismal day in the Temple, there were 51 baptisms for the dead performed, Apostle Franklin D. Richards being the first person to act as proxy in this work. Those who officiated at the font for the first baptisms in the Temple were David H. Cannon, baptizer; John Taylor, Thomas Moore, George Q. Cannon and Charles O. Dunn, confirmers; Charles O. Card, Orson Smith and Frederick Smith, witnesses; Samuel Roskelley and L. John Nuttall, recorders. On July 11, 1925, there were 4,120 baptisms performed for the dead, this being the greatest number performed in one day. On May 21, 1884, there were 43 endowments given for the living and 14 for the dead, a total of 57. This was the first day upon which endowments were given. On February 22, 1930, there were 1,505 endowments given, this being the greatest number given in one day. At the beginning of work in the Temple, but one endowment session was held each day. The number of sessions held daily has increased from time to time, until today (1934) six sessions are held daily, four during the day time and two each night. On a very few occasions it has become necessary to hold seven sessions during the day and night."

Construction of Logan Temple Foretold
By Wilford Woodruff

"On the 21st of August, 1863, in company with the President of the Church, the Twelve Apostles, and a large number of Elders, and a large train of carriages, we entered the town of Logan, and we met a large number of boys and girls, young men and maidens parading the streets, the females dressed in white on one side of the road, and males in their best attire on the other side, all to celebrate the coming of President Young and his company.

"August 22nd—Sunday morning we met in a large bowery, E. T. Benson, President, and Peter Maughan, Bishop.

"There were present of the authorities of the Church, Brigham Young, H. C. Kimball, D. H. Wells, J. Taylor, W. Woodruff, G. A. Smith, Lorenzo Snow, F. D. Richards, C. C. Rich and President Joseph Young, and a large congregation of Elders and Saints. After prayer, President Young called upon W. Woodruff to speak.

"As I arose I was clothed upon with the Spirit of God, and my mind was turned toward the young people who had met us the evening before; and the following is a synopsis of some of the remarks which I made:

" 'As I am called upon this morning to address this assembly my mind leads me to speak to the young people who are before me. I wish to say to my young friends, last evening as we came into this town, we met you parading in the street, to pay proper respect to President Young and his party. You met to greet Prophets, Apostles and inspired men. This is a privilege which no other generation of young people have enjoyed for eighteen hundred years until Joseph Smith the Prophet was raised up to lay the foundation of the Church and Kingdom of God on the earth; a privilege for which I would have felt amply repaid if I had had to travel a thousand miles in the days of my boyhood on foot to have witnessed.

" 'Now, my young friends, I wish you to remember these scenes you are witnessing during the visit of President Young and his brethren. Yea, my young friends, treasure up the teachings and sayings of these prophets and apostles as precious treasure while they are living men, and do not wait until they are dead. A few days and President Young and his brethren, the prophets and apostles and Brothers Benson and Maughan, will be in the spirit world. You should never forget this visitation. You are to become men and women, fathers and mothers; yea, the day will come, after your fathers, and these prophets and apostles are dead, you will have the privilege of going into the towers of a glorious Temple built unto the name of the Most High (pointing in the direction of the bench), east of us upon the Logan bench; and while you stand in the towers of the Temple and your eyes survey this glorious valley filled with cities and villages, occupied by tens of thousands of Latter-day Saints, you will then call to mind this visitation of President Young and his company. You will say: That was in the days when Presidents Benson and Maughan presided over us; that was before New York was destroyed by an earthquake; it was before Boston was swept into the sea, by the sea heaving itself beyond its bounds; it was before Albany was destroyed by fire; yea, at that time you will remember the scenes of this day. Treasure them up and forget them not. President Young followed and said: 'What Brother Woodruff has said is revelation and will be fulfilled'."[2]

Deseret News, Vol. 33, page 678.

---

[2]Remarks delivered at Logan, Utah, on August 1, 1880, by President Wilford Woodruff—"I was thinking today of a time many years ago, when President Young and several brethren of the Twelve, were in Logan; it was a time when a railroad up to this region was not even dreamed of, the time when Brothers Ezra T. Benson and Peter Maughan presided here; when at a meeting President Young called upon me to talk to the people assembled. The night before, however, we had been met by a long line of children and young people, from three up to twenty years of age; they had come out to meet the prophet, and presented a fine sight. While talking to the people, I felt led to speak to the children and young people; and I told them that I wanted them to remember the visit which the president was making them because the day would come when they were grown up, when they would talk to one another and say that on such a day President Young and party visited us, and we were told then that we should see the day when a temple should be built in this place, from the top of which we would be able to survey the country around which would be occupied by ten thousand of our people; and you will say this was told us when Brother Benson and Brother Maughan presided here. We never thought of building a temple here at that time, it had never entered into the heart of man to do so. Brothers Benson and Maughan have been for some years now in the spirit world. Today you are engaged in building a temple which will be completed and dedicated; and when this shall be done these young people will have the opportunity of going to the top of the building and will then see what I promised to you in those early days.

"I mention this to show you how things are presented to our minds and given utterance to in our public teachings about which, at the time, we have little or no idea."

Journal of Discourses, Vol. 21:299.

Lucifer Tries to Hinder Temple Work
By President Rudger Clawson

On one occasion I heard the late Apostle Marriner W. Merrill, President of the Logan Temple, relate this extraordinary incident:

He was sitting in his office one morning, he said, when he noticed from the window a company of people coming up the hill to the Temple. As they entered the Temple grounds they presented rather a strange appearance, not only in dress but in their mode of travel. Some were riding on horses, others were in conveyances, and still others were afoot. He wondered who they could be as he was not looking for a company of such size that particular morning. They dismounted from their horses, stepped down from their conveyances, put their animals under the shade and walked about complacently as if they had a perfect right to be there.

A little later a person unknown to Brother Merrill entered the room. Brother Merrill said to him: "Who are you and who are these people who have come up and taken possession of the Temple grounds unannounced?" He answered and said: "I am Satan and these are my people." Brother Merrill then said: "What do you want? Why have you come here?" Satan replied: "I don't like the work that is going on in this Temple and feel that it should be discontinued. Will you stop it?" Brother Merrill answered and said emphatically, "No, we will not stop it. The work must go on." "Since you refuse to stop it, I will tell you what I propose to do," the adversary said. "I will take these people, my followers, and distribute them throughout this Temple district, and will instruct them to whisper in the ears of people, persuading them not to go to the Temple, and thus bring about a cessation of your Temple work." Satan then withdrew.

President Merrill, commenting on this strange interview with the Evil One, said that for quite a period of time the spirit of indifference to Temple work seemed to take possession of the people and very few came to the House of the Lord. The presumption was that Satan had carried out his threat which caused a temporary lull in Temple work.

It is not to be wondered at that Satan, who is the enemy of all righteousness, is displeased with Temple work.

Church Section, The Deseret News, Dec. 12, 1936, Vol. 344, No. 61.

The Spirit of Discernment Manifested
By Mathias F. Cowley

On one of the three days during which the Dedicatory Services of the Logan Temple were held, President John Taylor and President Charles O. Card stood at the top of the stairs leading to the assembly room and as the people were surging up the steps to get to the assembly room, President Taylor sighted a woman in the crowd whom he did not know but indicated her to President Card and said: "Don't let that woman come into the assembly; she is not worthy." Brother Card was greatly surprised and said: "Why not?" President Taylor said: "I know not but the Spirit of God said, 'She is not worthy'." And so Brother Card went down the steps and met the woman and told her she would have to go back. Brother Card said to President Taylor: "She couldn't pass the door keeper without a recommend." President Taylor replied, "That matters not; she is not worthy." She did not raise much opposition when confronted by Brother Card when she showed her ticket of admission.

Brother Card turned her back and later on he went to see her at her home and he asked her how she had gotten her recommend to go to the Temple, and she said there was a man in the ward who was not worthy of a recommend, but the Bishop gave him one, thinking it would make him feel glad to attend the dedicatory services, and also help him renew his religious duties. This woman happened to meet the man on the street and he asked her how she would like to go to the dedication of the Temple. She said she would like to but could not get a recommend. He said: "I have a recommend and will give it to you for one dollar." And so she got her recommend by paying this amount.

The thing in this matter was that the spirit of revelation was manifested in President Taylor who did not know personally the woman and had never seen her before nor ever afterwards. It was an instance in which was manifested the promise of Joseph Smith the Prophet[3] to Elder Taylor in Nauvoo when the Prophet said to him: "Elder Taylor, you have received the Holy Spirit and if you are faithful in heeding its promptings the day will come when it will be within you a fountain of continuous revelation from God."

I was at the dedication of the Logan Temple but did not hear this but it was told to me afterwards. The following statement was uttered later by President Taylor to Brother Card and others: "Brethren, you may deceive the Bishop and you may deceive the Presidents of the Stake, and you may deceive the General authorities of the Church, but you cannot deceive the Lord Jesus Christ nor the Holy Ghost. You know yourselves better than anybody else and if there is anything wrong in you, now is the time to repent and make yourselves square with the Lord; and if you do not repent, the time will come when you will be humbled, and the higher up you get the greater will be your fall."

(The foregoing statement was dictated to the Compiler of this book in Los Angeles during the forepart of March, 1940, while Elder Cowley was visiting in California, and residing at 1536 North Hoover Street.)

---

[a]*Statement by President John Taylor:* I well remember a remark that Joseph Smith made to me upwards of forty years ago. Said he: "Elder Taylor, you have been baptized, have had hands laid upon your head for the reception of the Holy Ghost, and you have been ordained to the Holy Priesthood. Now, if you will continue to follow the leadings of that Spirit it will always lead you right. At times it might be contrary to your judgment; never mind that, follow its dictates; and if you be true to its whisperings it will in time become in you a principle of revelation, so that you will know all things."   Journal of Discourses, Vol. 19:153-4.

MANTI TEMPLE

Site Dedicated on April 25, 1877. Temple Dedicated on May 21, 1888, by Elder Lorenzo Snow.

Chapter V

THE MANTI TEMPLE

DEDICATORY PRAYER
By Apostle Lorenzo Snow
(May 21, 1888)

Almighty and Eternal Father, Creator of heaven and earth, and all that they contain, Thou who art the God and Father of our Lord and Savior Jesus Christ, and of the spirits of all living; to Thee, Thy believing children here present bring our offering and beseech Thee to grant Thy listening ear while we dedicate this Temple unto Thy most holy name.

We realize our weakness, our utter feebleness and inability to advance the interests and honor of Thy name upon the earth, except Thou dost guide us by Thy Holy Spirit; therefore, we humble ourselves in Thy presence, and earnestly entreat Thee to forgive us our sins and all vanity and unworthiness which Thy purity and perfection have discovered in any one of us, inasmuch as we are truly penitent therefor, and ready to forgive those who trespass against us.

We praise and adore Thee for having restored to earth again the fulness of the Everlasting Gospel, wherein Thou didst break the silence of ages by speaking to Thy servant Joseph Smith, while yet in the days of his youth, and by Thy presence and Thine own voice didst declare unto Him Thy well Beloved Son, our Savior, in whose name alone immortality and eternal life can be obtained; and Thou didst teach, discipline and empower Him to bring forth thy glorious latter-day work—the dispensation of the fullness of times.

PRESIDENT LORENZO SNOW

With the record of the Prophet Mormon, Thou didst entrust him with the Urim and Thummim, by which the unlettered youth was enabled to translate the language in which it was engraven though long since lost to the human family, and thereby revealed the origin, prosperity and downfall of the mighty nations that inhabited this hemisphere for more than twenty-five centuries of time, and also informing us that the pure gospel of a crucified and risen Redeemer had been delivered to, and His Church established among them.

We praise Thy name for revealing this knowledge which the wisdom of the world was unable to discover. Also that Thou didst authorize Thy servant Joseph to baptize for the remission of sins, by sending John the Baptist to ordain Joseph to that power; giving him also a promise that this ministry should abide in the earth until the sons of Levi shall again offer unto Thee, O Lord, an offering in righteousness.

In the plentitude of Thine everlasting love Thou didst also send Thine Apostles Peter, James and John, who conferred the Melchizedek Priesthood and apostleship, which enabled the Prophet Joseph to organize Thy Church and set in order all its appointments, offices and ordinances with its gifts and blessings, as in the former dispensations.

Everlasting praise to Thy Holy name for sending line upon line and precept upon precept, and continuing to reveal the abundance of peace and truth by sending Moses to confer the spirit with power to gather the House of Israel, and Elijah, to turn the hearts of the fathers to their children and the hearts of the children to their fathers, that the whole earth might not be smitten with a curse.

When these manifestations of Thine unfathomable love to Thy Saints stirred up the envious hate of the ungoldly to bloody persecution, imprisonment of Thy servants, and finally to extermination from the State of their chosen homes, Thine own right hand brought deliverance to Thy Saints, and gave them a happy respite while they built the beautiful Nauvoo. But there the wrath of the ungodly waxed furious again while Thou didst fill Thy servant Joseph with revelations of Thy will for the upbuilding of Zion and the exaltation of the righteous until nothing could subdue their insatiable fury but the life-blood of Joseph and Hyrum and the expulsion of Thy people from the nation; yet Thy loving kindness failed not, and the heart of the savage Indians was moved to give us a kindly welcome.

We glorify Thy great and Holy name, Almighty Father, for these communications of intelligence and power to man in the flesh again, and that the Spirit, forseeing the hatred of the wicked that would be aroused by the developments thereof, moved Thy servant Joseph to seal all these keys of power and intelligence which he had received upon the heads of his brethren the Apostles, with commandment that they should build up Thy kingdom and establish its righteousness in the earth till Thy Son, our Savior, shall come.

Thy people being under a sense of these weighty obligations, and being driven out from among men, it seemed proper to Thee to make Thy servant Brigham mighty in wisdom and strength to lead Thy people in safety, and after a year and a half's journey in the desert among savage tribes, Thou didst give us rest in these valleys of the Rocky Mountains. In all these tribulations Thine ear heard and Thine own arm brought answers of deliverance to the supplications of Thine afflicted children. Nor wast thou weary of their necessities and entreaties, but didst soften the rigor of unfriendly elements, and didst cause the clouds to scatter refreshing showers, the hills to yield their treasures of snow, and springs of living water to come forth from the dry and parched ground. The labor of the husbandman has been crowned with plenty for man and beast, and much wherewith to bless the stranger. The everlasting hills have yielded their rich treasures of iron, lead, silver, and gold, while lightning and steam have contributed to gather Thy sons from afar and Thy daughters from the ends of the earth in swiftest ships, and without disaster.

How can we declare the multitude of all Thy mercies which Thou hast shown to Thy dependent, covenant children who have put their trust in Thee, for time would fail to mention the threatening famine by reason of the cricket, the locust and the grasshopper, when Thou didst send the gulls that swallowed them up, and the lives of Thy people were saved; or the earthquakes which have engulfed islands, provinces and cities, with the multitudes of their inhabitants, while Thy people have dwelt safely in this volcanic region, unharmed and undisturbed thereby; neither is the din of war heard in all our borders.

We praise Thy Holy name for all the mighty work Thou didst enable Thy chief apostle, Brigham, to perform; that he was moved to build and to appoint Temples according to Thy holy commandment in various cities of the land, and to designate that one should occupy this delightful spot. Since it has pleased Thee to take him to Thyself, Thine other chief apostle, John Taylor, was inspired and with his brethren did lay the foundations of this House, and with the free-will offerings of Thy Saints had reared it nearly to completion when his precious life was cut short by cruel persecution. We who are spared and are permitted to come together now dedicate this Temple unto Thee. We most earnestly pray that Thou wilt accept of this our offering in the all-prevailing name of Thy Son Jesus Christ, our Lord and Savior.

We dedicate the ground and the hill on which it stands, that the same may be holy unto the Lord our God; that its steps, its terraces, its trees and shrubbery, with all its adornments and its approaches may be the pathways of the just to the House of the Lord, the Temple of our God. Let the foundation of this House be made permanent and never be moved from its place. May the stones and the cement of which the building is composed become compact and strong as if it were one solid rock.

We consecrate the basement of the lower story, which is in
likeness of the home of the dead, with its baptismal font, for the
service of the living and the dead, with its steps, the oxen on which
the font rests, its seats, its rooms for changes, with all its doors and
windows, their hangings and fastenings, the furniture and all that
appertains to it. May the fountain which supplies it continue a living spring that shall never fail, and the stream become as a river of
life to Thy believing penitent children; that they who shall be
buried therein may effectually die unto sin, and in coming forth
may as certainly arise to lives of righteousness and faith, the spirit
bearing witness of the blood of Christ which cleanseth from all
sin; and when the ordinance is performed for the dead, that they
may realize its efficacy as if they had received it themselves while
in the flesh, and be judged in like manner.

We dedicate and consecrate unto Thee and the service of Thy
Saints, the lower and upper main courts, with all other apartments
in this building which are sheltered by its roof, according to the
various uses for which they have been designed, with their stands,
their altars, their desks, the stairs by which they are reached, their
doors and windows, their hangings and fastenings, together with
floors, partitions, ceilings, finishings, furnishings and ornamenta-
tions, also all apparatus and fixtures for ventilating, warming,
lighting and seating the same, whether they are for public worship, administering in the holy sacraments and ordinances of this
Holy Temple or for private prayer and secret devotion; also all
rooms that are used for study and learning words of wisdom from
the best books, or by lectures and the experience of righteous and
learned men able to teach the will and ways of the Lord, all these
we dedicate unto Thee that all may be most holy and acceptable
unto the Lord our God.

Wilt Thou accept and bless these sacred altars which have
been erected by the offerings of Thy devoted Saints? And when
Thy people shall approach Thee in Thine own appointed way,
then do Thou hearken and hear their supplications; grant them
deliverance from their adversaries; succor them in their temptations; give them knowledge of the ancestry of their generations
that they may go forth in the holiness and power of Thine ordinances and as saviors on Mt. Zion redeem the generations of their
dead and bring many sons and daughters unto Thee in Thy kingdom.

When Thy sons and daughters shall desire to plight their
faith with each other unto Thee in a covenant of everlasting life
and shall obtain admittance here in Thy holy courts, then O Lord,
be pleased to accept their offerings; sanctify them, that they may
be clean from all unrighteousness; clothe Thy servants with the
habiliments of the Priesthood, and here at the shrine of Thy love
seal them Thine by Thy Holy Spirit of promise until the day of
their redemption, the resurrection of their bodies, as purchased by

the blood of Christ Thy Son. May this holy Temple be to them as one of the gates of heaven, opening into the straight and narrow path that leads to endless lives and eternal dominion.

We dedicate the stands in the eastern portion of the building for the occupancy and ministration of the holy Melchizedek Priesthood, which has the keys of all spiritual blessings, is of the order of Thy Son Jesus Christ, and holds the power of endless lives.

We also consecrate the stands in the west of the building for the occupancy and ministration of the Aaronic Priesthood, which is an appendage to the Melchizedek Priesthood and holds the keys of temporal blessings.

We beseech Thee, our Heavenly Father, to inspire Thy ministering servants who shall instruct Thy people from these stands, that they may rightly divide the words of truth and give to each member of Thine household his portion of meat in due season, that from the treasures of Thy store house the riches of eternal life may exalt Thy children to a knowledge of Thyself.

May he who shall preside over the ministrations in this holy Temple, and all who labor with him, be greatly blessed with the understanding of Thy perfect law and all the applications thereof to the conditions of Thy people. When any difficult matter shall require his consideration, may the voice of Thy Holy Spirit give to him the revelations of Thy will, that all the ministrations of this Thy House and all the ordinances performed may be sanctioned in heaven, Thy holy habitation.

We dedicate to Thee the records which are and shall be kept of all the ordinances administered here in this Temple. May the recorders who shall have the care and labor of making and keeping them be abundantly blessed with wisdom and knowledge, that the same may be truthfully and faithfully kept and be found worthy of all acceptation, that Thy people may be righteously judged according to all that shall be written therein. We earnestly pray that they may be preserved most holy unto Thee from all violence and desecration, until they shall have accomplished the full object and purpose of their creation.

O Lord God of our fathers, of the prophets, and of Thy people, we beseech Thee accept the dedication of this Temple, with all that appertains to it, including the foundation and the towers thereof, unto Thyself.

May this delightful location be known as a holy hill of Zion, among Thy people. Graciously be pleased to place Thy name upon this House. Let the power of Thy Spirit be felt by all who shall enter within its portals. Give Thine angels charge concerning it, that it shall never be possessed by Thine enemies, neither be defiled by the wicked and ungodly, nor even be injured by any destructive elements, but grant that it may stand and endure as a monument of the obedience and love of Thy people, and to the honor of Thy holy name for ages yet to come in holiness to the Lord.

We praise Thee for Thy goodness in enabling Thy servants to translate and send abroad the fulness of Thy Gospel as contained in the Book of Mormon into so many languages of the various nations of the earth; do Thou bless the humble efforts of Thy faithful servants in all the various peoples and tongues among whom it has penetrated that they may bear a faithful testimony of the truth that has sprung out of the ground, and of the righteousness that has looked down from heaven.

Have Thou mercy upon Judah and Jerusalem; hasten the going forth of this sacred record to the Hebrews of all nations; raise up men and means to carry the glad tidings of Thy returning favor to that afflicted people. Wilt Thou hear and answer the prayers of Thy servants and turn away the barrenness of their land? Make it very fertile as in days of old; turn the hearts of the exiles to Thy promises made to their fathers, and let the land of Jerusalem become inhabited as towns without walls for the multitude of men and cattle therein, that they may rebuild their city and temple, that the glory of the later house may be greater than that of the former house.

We render thanks and praise to Thy holy name for the measure of Thy Spirit sent forth among the scattered remnants of the seed of Joseph; that they are pleased and comforted at hearing of the record of their fathers; that, where they have opportunity, they incline to the arts of peace and self support. O, may the power of the Gospel, through obedience, enable them to be relieved from the terrible curse which is upon them, break forth into the light of Zion, and obtain a fulfillment of the promises made unto their fathers.

We beseech Thee, let Thy peculiar blessings rest upon Thy servants, the Twelve Apostles, according to the arduous and important labor and presidency which have developed upon them by the death of Thy servant, President John Taylor. Wilt Thou strengthen Thy servant who is called to preside over them and the Church with continual inspiration of the Holy Spirit; preserve him in health, accept the labors of his life and fill him with the spirit and power of his holy apostleship. May the apostles be united in the bond of perfectness with each other and prevail with Thee for abundance and richness of Thy word, to dispense to Thy people. Preserve them from the hands of their enemies until they shall accomplish their work. Give them power to send Thy Gospel to all nations, kindreds, tongues and peoples, to gather Thine elect from all lands, to build up Thy Zion and establish Thy righteousness in the earth, and to attain to the power of their calling and apostleship in the flesh.

O Lord, bless the Patriarchs whom Thou hast appointed in the land of Zion. May they have power to seal blessings upon Thy people by inspiration, as did the ancient fathers, that their blessings may be fulfilled upon the heads of their descendants and of Thy people.

Bless the Seventies with their Presidency, to magnify their calling in all lands where their lots may be cast, or where they may be appointed to labor, that Thine Elders may praise Thee and all the ends of the earth hear of the salvation of our God.

Bless those who preside over the various missions in all the earth, that they may dispense the Gospel by all proper means within their reach, by writing, by publishing, by sending Thine Elders to all places where the word of God may have free course and be glorified by the obedience of the honest in heart.

Endow Thou Thy servants, the High Priests, with all the gifts and qualifications of their holy calling.

We pray Thee to bless the Stakes of Zion which Thou hast established. May their Presidents, Counselors, High Councils, with the High Priests, the Seventies, the Elders and all that constitute the authorities of Thy Church, abide in the revelation of Thy Will, that Zion may lengthen her cords and strengthen her stakes in all righteousness.

Enable the Bishops and High Councils to decree justice and judgment in equity and truth, that the Wards and Stakes of Zion may be built up in holiness, that we may be Thy people and Thou be our God. Bless with them the Priests, Teachers and Deacons, the standing ministry to Thy Church, that they may be vigilant to put away iniquity from Thy Church, that Thou mayest bestow upon Thy people the fulness of Thy favor, Thine everlasting love.

We pray for Thy blessing upon the Relief Societies, the Young Ladies' and Young Men's Associations, the Sabbath Schools, and the Primaries, with all those who are appointed to superintend and preside over them; that they may be abundantly blessed in relieving the sufferings of the destitute and sorrowful, arresting the wayward, and inspiring them with love for pure intelligence, and educating them in the way of life and faith, that our youth may find Thee early, and the aged be established in Thy righteousness forever.

We dedicate ourselves, with our wives, our children, our houses and lands, our flocks and herds, our gardens and vineyards, with all that we are and have, unto Thee, the Lord our God, for time and for all eternity, and for the accomplishment of the work which Thou hast given us to do.

Heavenly Father, Thou hast seen the labors of Thy Saints in the building of this House. Their motives and their exertions are all known to Thee. The hearts of the children of men and every thought thereof are open to Thy sight. Thy people have sought to do Thy will in rearing and adorning this great structure. They have contributed freely of the means which Thou hast given them for its erection, and the hands of the committee and of the superintendent and assistant superintendent have been strengthened and their hearts been gladdened thereby. Even the children of Thy people have shown delight in helping to purchase the curtains, the carpets and the furniture of this House. We this day present it to Thee, O Lord our God, as the fruit of the tithings and free will offerings of Thy people. Accept this, we beseech Thee, and let Thy choice blessings rest down upon every man, woman and child who has contributed to the building and adorning of this Temple. Bless them with increased faith and with all the blessings of heaven and earth in due season; that in heavenly gifts, in their basket and in their store, in their children, in their flocks and in their herds, in their fruits of the earth, and in the conveniences and comforts of life, they may abound and ever increase. If there are any of Thy people, O Father, who have not had the means to assist in this work, but have felt in their hearts to sustain it and to say that they gave not because they had not, but would gladly give if they had, let these same blessings rest down upon them also, and condescend to accept the desires of their hearts as free-will offerings unto Thee. Show favor unto all who have helped to forward this work by good wishes, good words or good deeds. Remember Thou and bless, we entreat Thee, the committee, and the architect and superintendent, and his assistant superintendent, and all the workmen and their foremen in every department who have labored in preparing the ground upon which the House stands, or the materials of which it is composed, or in constructing and bringing it to completion. Reward them, we ask Thee, for their faithfulness and diligence, and grant that the recollection of their labors may be a source of pleasure to them and their children after them.

O Lord God, who dwellest in the heaven of heavens, look down from Thy holy habitation, we beseech Thee, in great mercy and tender compassion upon Thy Zion which Thou hast founded. We turn to Thee with all our hearts for that help and succor which Thou alone canst give. We are beset with peril. We are surrounded with danger. The powers of evil are aroused against us. The foes of Thy Zion are numerous and mighty, while Thy people are but few and feeble. Floods of falsehood, slander and unjust accusations sweep over the land, concerning Thy Saints. By these means many of our fellow-citizens have been poisoned against us. They have urged the enactment of laws to ensnare us, to confiscate the property which we have constructed unto Thee, and to overflow the plan of salvation which Thou hast revealed to us. Through the delusion of lies and the binding effect of prejudice, our fellow-citizens would deny us our rights, would consign us to prison, would wrest from us our property, would threaten us with utter destruction.

Holy Father, Thou knowest how false are the accusations against us. We appeal to Thee for deliverance. Turn aside the wrath of man. Break the bands which encircle us. Destroy the traps which are spread for our feet. Let the light of eternal truth shine upon us and illumine our pathway. Vindicate us by Thy power, and let not the wicked aspersions of our enemies prevail. Show to the world, especially to our nation, the true character of Thy people. Enlighten the minds of the officers of our government, soften their hearts, and give them power to check all spirit of persecution and disposition to justify oppression and approve of unjust judgments. Help them to comprehend the true principles of liberty and to enforce the same for the benefit of all people throughout the land. Open their eyes to see the wrongs that are being committed against Thy people. Awaken them to a sense of justice. Give to the Chief Executive, to his cabinet and to the Congress and the courts of our nation, the firmness, courage and comprehension of justice necessary to maintain just and righteous government in the land, that all the people may rejoice.

Restrain and control the words and acts of preachers, lecturers and writers who endeavor to create anger and hostility against Thy people. Take from all such the power to blind the eyes of the nation by misrepresentation and falsehood, or to inflame the people to sanction acts of anger against the innocent.

As Thou hast in the past overruled the violence of mobs and the cruelty of the wicked for the glory of Thy name and the salvation of Thy people, we ask Thee, Righteous Father, to so control this present persecution that Thy purposes may be accomplished in the redemption of Thy Zion. Be with and sustain Thy people in their afflictions. In their imprisonments, in their exile, in the unjust confiscation of their property and in the endurance of all the wrongs to which they are subjected, give them grace and patience and fortitude. May no murmuring at Thy providences ever escape their lips. Reveal to Thy people the salvation which awaits us.

O God, before Thee in this Thy Holy House, do we this day confess our sins. We acknowledge our shortcomings and imperfections. We are full of faults and errors. We accept the afflictions which we are now enduring as being permitted by Thee to make us more worthy of our high calling. We humbly pray Thee to forgive us. Blot out our transgressions, that they shall not appear against us any more. Condescend to let Thy favor and the light of Thy countenance rest upon us. Make known Thy will more and more plainly unto all Thy Saints. Uphold us in all righteousness as the people whom Thou hast chosen. Suffer us not to be put to shame; but show the inhabitants of the earth the truth of our testimony concerning Thee and Thy work.

Now, Holy Father, we ask Thee in the name of Jesus Christ, Thy beloved Son, to hear and answer this our prayer. We entreat Thee to accept this dedication of this House. Sanctify it and make it holy. The ordinances performed therein by Thy servants and handmaids, may they be in Thy sight as though performed by Thyself.

And to Thy name be the honor and glory and praise for ever and ever, through Jesus Christ, our Reedeemer, Amen.
—Millennial Star, Vol. 50, No. 25, pp. 385-392.

Physical and Historical Description

Like all Temples erected in this Dispensation, the Manti Temple stands stately and majestic, and its location is most beautiful. The terraces, which at first surrounded it, have given place to beautiful lawns and shrubs. The cement stairway has been removed, to be replaced with a smaller approach, and the remaining space covered with lawns.

The Temple is built upon a solid hill or mountain of rock, from which also the Temple is built. Along the base of the range which hems Sanpete Valley on the east, there is an underlying oolitic stratum, manifest in knolls or hills which are covered with a few feet of earth. On one of these the Manti Temple is built, commanding a superb view of the country north and south of that part of the valley lying to the west of it. Like all Temples erected by the Latter-day Saints, it faces the east, though the view is right into the mountain range.

The site of the Temple was selected by President Brigham Young. During its construction, Brigham Young, John Taylor and Wilford Woodruff have occupied the Presidency of the Church. Ground was broken on April 25, 1877, and the site dedicated on that day by President Brigham Young. The cornerstones were laid on April 14, 1879. The structure is 171 feet 6 inches long and 92 feet wide. It is 79 feet high to the square. The walls are 3 feet 6 inches thick at the base, with 4-foot buttresses. The walls taper to 3 feet at the square and the buttresses to about 2 feet 6 inches. There are two towers, the one on the east being 179 feet in height, the one on the west being 169 feet. These towers are thirty feet square at the base. The interior of the Temple is practically the same as that in the others that have been erected. Adjoining the structure proper on the north is a building 100 feet long by 40 feet wide, in which is placed the apparatus for heating.* An additional Annex to the west has been added to the annex as at first constructed which provides adequate office room for the recording department and for linen room. During the past five years (1935-40) a large amount of remodeling has been done which has increased the space used for ordinance work, and also provided steel lockers for both men and women.

The buildings are heated by steam. Water is supplied through pipes from a spring some distance from the Temple. The public highway runs past the Temple, from which the ascent to the ground floor is over thirty feet. A drive, beginning at the north, passing under part of the east edge of the building and finding an outlet on the south, makes this ascent easy. The Temple is of oolitic stone, and is of a warm cream color. The towers have ample window facilities. It is impossible to imagine a more commanding eminence for a Temple and one affording greater opportunity for artistic and delightful surroundings. W. H. Folsom of Salt Lake City, was the architect and superintendent, who carried the construction through to completion, with Edward L. Parry as master mason and William Asper as designer of stairways* and interior decorator. The Temple is 125 miles from Salt Lake City. The main room has a seating capacity of about 1,500 persons.

The approximate cost was $1,000,000. The dedicatory prayer was offered by Apostle Lorenzo Snow on May 21, 1888.

Presidents of the Manti Temple:
  Daniel H. Wells, 1888-1891.
  Anthon H. Lund, 1891-1893.
  John D. T. McAllister, 1893-1906.
  Lewis Anderson, 1906-1933.
  Robert D. Young, 1933-1943.
  Lewis R. Anderson, 1943-1959.
  A. Bent Peterson, 1959—Present Incumbent.

*Note: A letter from Pres. Lewis R. Anderson (June, 1945) states: The heating plant has been moved from the Annex basement to a building immdiately to the east of the Annex. A distinctive feature of the Manti Temple is the two spiral stairways, which have no center support, located in the west tower of the Temple. No other Temple has this. There are only five such stairways in the United States, which includes the two in this Temple. There are 150 steps in each stairway, the height from floor to ceiling being 95 feet for each.

Manifestations of Divine Acceptance

The Manti Temple has been a source of inspiration to me from the day I first set eyes upon it, which was in July, 1887. At that time I was in a sheep camp on the mountains west of Ephraim about sunset, and looking over the Sanpete valley I saw the Temple in the distance; and although I uttered a silent prayer that sometime I might enter its portals, I little realized then that I should be called to labor there as a Recorder, which I have for the past twenty-nine years. I had left London in March, 1886, for Australia and after much traveling finally landed in San Francisco in February, 1887, and thence to Salt Lake City.

Events connected with the site of the Temple have increased my faith greatly. After some discussion by certain of the Church leaders, ground was broken for its erection on April 25, 1877, by President Brigham Young. He stated that the angel Moroni had dedicated this spot for the erection of a Temple and on this site it should be built.[1] The wisdom of this selection has been fully vindicated in the years that have followed. A natural spring to the east was in readiness to provide water for the grounds and for use inside the Temple. Years ago parties endeavored to appropriate the waters of this spring but failed. Providence intervened as its waters were needed for this sacred edifice. As years have elapsed the volume of flow has increased as extensions required more water.

The towers of this Temple are seen many miles distant as one enters the valley from either the north or south. The beauties of the surroundings of the Temple appeal to visitors and they are greatly impressed with the beauty of what they have seen. This beauty is dependent on the water from the spring mentioned.

On August 8, 1888, I had the privilege of entering the Temple and received my blessings. During the past fifty years I have met and conversed with many people who have related to me many faith-promoting incidents pertaining to their labors for their kindred who have passed beyond.

Up to June, 1905, outside of a few near relatives which I had known as a boy in England, and for whom I had performed the Temple work, my vicarious work was very meager. I could obtain but little information concerning my ancestors, but from 1905, in fulfillment of a blessing given under the Spirit in tongues, I have gathered over 20,000 Carpenter and Hatton names of my kindred and have completed the work for them.

On the 15th of April, 1908, I went to the Temple with my wife, and on that day we were sealed for some ten couples of my Carpenter kindred. Among them was a certain Warncombe Carpenter and his wife, Eleanor Taylor. During the ceremony a most peculiar feeling came over me, one I had never experienced before—a sensation of warmth in my chest which extended upwards which brought tears to my eyes and I melted through the intensity of its effects. This feeling I did not experience when being sealed for the other nine couples. I realized that Warncombe and his wife were permitted to show their gratitude to us for the work performed for them and gave us a taste of the joys of heaven, for I had never tasted such exquisite joy before, but have since on seven or eight occasions. As we went home my wife and I talked over this experience and she had experienced the same feeling as I. We likened this to the feelings expressed by the two disciples who were going to Emmæus, and who, after meeting the Savior, remarked: Did not our bosoms burn within us?

This Warncombe Carpenter was born about 1623 at Dilwyn, Hereford, England, and died November 2, 1669. He belonged to the main branch of the Carpenter family who had lived there before 1300, and were a cadet branch of the *Carpentier* family from Cambrai, in French Flanders, and from which the Carpenter families of England originated. Warncombe was an officer in the Cavalier army and fought at the battle of Naseby in 1645, for King Charles 1, and carried the wounds received to his death. One of his sons was the famous general known as Lord George Carpenter, the ancestor of the Earl of Tyrconnel.

I give this incident as a testimony of the fact that when we say our dear ones are dead, they still live as the same individuals though in another sphere, and are cognizant of the work being done for them and which is necessary for their progression; and they are sometimes permitted, as in this case, to show their gratitude for services performed for them, and which they could not do for themselves in the sphere to which they have departed.   J. Hatten Carpenter, Manti, Utah, May 10, 1940.

---

[1]*Temple Site Dedicated by Moroni:* "At the conference held in Ephraim, Sanpete County, June 25, 1875, nearly all the speakers expressed their feelings to have a temple built in Sanpete County, and gave their views as to what point and where to build it, and to show the union that existed, Elder Daniel H. Wells said: 'Manti,' George Q. Cannon, Brigham Young, Jr., John Taylor, Orson Hyde, Erastus Snow, Franklin D. Richards, Lorenzo Young and A. M. Musser said, 'Manti stone quarry.' I have given the names in the order in which they spoke. At 4 p.m. that day President Brigham Young said: 'The Temple should be built on Manti stone quarry.' Early on the morning of April 25, 1877, President Brigham Young asked Brother Warren S. Snow to go with him to the Temple hill. Brother Snow says: 'We two were alone; President Young took me to the spot where the Temple was to stand; we went to the southeast corner, and President Young said: 'Here is the spot where the prophet Moroni stood and dedicated this piece of land for a Temple site and that is the reason why the location is made here, and we can't move it from this spot; and if you and I are the only persons that come here at high noon today, we will dedicate this ground.' "

Life of Heber C. Kimball, by Elder Orson F. Whitney, page 447.

Heavenly Voices Are Heard: "On the first day, just as Professor Smyth was concluding the voluntary—a selection from Mendelssohn—a number of the Saints in the body of the hall and some of the brethren in the west stand heard most heavenly voices singing. It sounded to them as angelic, and appeared to be behind and above them, and many turned their heads in that direction wondering if there were not another choir in some other part of the building. There was no other choir, however, * * * Some of the Saints saw the spirits of Presidents Young and Taylor, J. M. Grant, and others in the Temple, and the heads of some of the speakers were surrounded by a halo of heavenly light during the services. The Saints enjoyed a heavenly feast extending through the three days, and many shed tears of joy while listening to the testimonies and admonitions of the servants of God. There can be no question but that God has accepted the Manti Temple at the hands of His Saints and will bless all who have in any degree assisted to build it or who, not having the means to assist, have said in their hearts, 'I would have helped if I could.' "

Millennial Star, Vol. 50, No. 26, p. 405.

The Prophet Joseph Was Present

"When we dedicated the Temple at Manti, many of the brethren and sisters saw the presence of spiritual beings, discernible only by the inward eye. *The Prophets Joseph, Hyrum, Brigham and various other Apostles that have gone were seen and not only this, but the ears of many of the faithful were touched, and they heard the music of the heavenly choir.*" By Franklin D. Richards, Genealogical Magazine, Vol. 15:148.

Deceased Relatives Hold Conversation

"I remember one day in the temple at Manti, a brother from Mount Pleasant rode down to the temple to take part in the work, and as he passed the cemetery in Ephraim, he looked ahead (it was early in the morning), and there was a large multitude all dressed in white, and he wondered how that could be. Why should there be so many up here; it was too early for a funeral, he thought; but he drove up and several of them stepped out in front of him and they talked to him. They said, 'Are you going to the temple?' 'Yes.' 'Well, these that you see here are your relatives and they want you to do work for them.' 'Yes,' he said, 'but I am going down today to finish my work. I have no more names and I do not know the names of those who you say are related to me.' 'But when you go down to the temple today you will find there are records that give our names.' He was surprised. He looked until they all disappeared, and drove on. As he came into the temple, Recorder Farnsworth came up to him and said, 'I have just received records from England and they all belong to you.' And there were hundreds of names that had just arrived, and what was told him by these persons that he saw was fulfilled. You can imagine what joy came to his heart, and what a testimony it was to him that the Lord wants this work done." By President Anthon H. Lund.

Chapter VI

THE SALT LAKE TEMPLE

DEDICATORY PRAYER
By
President Wilford Woodruff
(April 6, 1893)

Our Father in heaven, Thou has created the heavens and the earth, and all things that are therein; Thou most glorious One, perfect in mercy, love, and truth, we, Thy children, come this day before Thee, and in this house which we have built to Thy most holy name, humbly plead the atoning blood of Thine Only Begotten Son, that our sins may be remembered no more against us forever, but that our prayers may ascend unto Thee and have free access to Thy throne, that we may be heard in Thy holy habitation. And may it graciously please Thee to hearken unto our petitions, answer them according to Thine infinite wisdom and love, and grant that the blessings which we seek may be bestowed upon us, even a hundred fold, inasmuch as we seek with purity of heart and fullness of purpose to do Thy will and glorify Thy name.

PRES. WILFORD WOODRUFF

We thank Thee, O Thou Great Eloheim, that Thou didst raise up Thy servant, Joseph Smith through the loins of Abraham, Isaac and Jacob, and made him a Prophet, Seer, and Revelator, and through the assistance and administrations of angels from heaven, Thou didst enable him to bring forth the Book of Mormon, the stick of Joseph, in the hand of Ephraim, in fulfillment of the prophecies of Isaiah and other prophets, which record has been translated and published in many languages. We also thank Thee, our Father in heaven, that Thou didst inspire Thy servant and give him power on the earth to organize Thy Church in this

SALT LAKE TEMPLE

Ground consecrated on February 14, 1853. Temple dedicated on April 6, 1893,
by President Wilford Woodruff.

goodly land, in all its fullness, power and glory, with Apostles, Prophets, Pastors and Teachers, with all the gifts and graces belonging thereto, and all this by the power of the Aaronic and Melchizedek Priesthood, which Thou didst bestow upon him by the administration of holy angels, who held that Priesthood in the days of the Savior. We thank Thee, our God, that Thou didst enable Thy servant Joseph to build two temples, in which ordinances were administered for the living and the dead; that he also lived to send the gospel to the nations of the earth and to the islands of the sea, and labored exceedingly until he was martyred for the word of God and the testimony of Jesus Christ.

We also thank Thee, O our Father in heaven, that Thou didst raise up Thy servant Brigham Young, who held the keys of the Priesthood on the earth for many years, and who led Thy people to these valleys of the mountains, and laid the corner-stone of this great Temple and dedicated it unto Thee; and who did direct the building of three other temples in these Rocky Mountains which have been dedicated unto Thy holy name, in which temples many thousands of the living have been blessed and the dead redeemed.

Our Father in heaven, we are also thankful to Thee for Thy servant John Taylor, who followed in the footsteps of Thy servant Brigham, until he laid down his life in exile.

Thou hast called Thy servants Wilford Woodruff, George Q. Cannon, and Joseph F. Smith to hold the keys of the Presidency and priesthood this day, and for these shepherds of Thy flock we feel to give Thee thanksgiving and praise. Thy servant Wilford is bound to acknowledge Thy hand, O Father, in the preservation of his life from the hour of his birth to the present day. Nothing but Thy power could have preserved him through that which he has passed during the eighty-six years that Thou hast granted him life on the earth.

For the raising up of the Twelve Apostles, we also thank Thee, our God, and for the perfect union which exists among us.

We thank Thee, O Lord, for the perfect organizations of Thy Church as they exist at the present time.

O Lord, we regard with intense and indescribable feelings the completion of this sacred house. Deign to accept this the fourth temple which Thy covenant children have been assisted by Thee in erecting in these mountains. In past ages Thou didst inspire with Thy Holy Spirit Thy servants, the prophets, to speak of the time in the latter days when the mountain of the Lord's house should be established in the tops of the mountains, and should be exalted above the hills. We thank Thee that we have had the glorious opportunity of contributing to the fulfillment of these visions of Thine ancient seers, and that Thou hast condescended to permit us to take part in the great work. And as this portion of

Thy servants' words has thus so marvelously been brought to pass, we pray Thee, with increased faith and renewed hope, that all their words with regard to Thy great work in gathering Thine Israel and building up Thy kingdom on earth in the last days may be as amply fulfilled, and that, O Lord, speedily.

We come before Thee with joy and thanksgiving, with spirits jubilant and hearts filled with praise, that Thou hast permitted us to see this day for which, during these forty years, we have hoped, and toiled, and prayed, when we can dedicate unto Thee this house which we have built to Thy most glorious name. One year ago we set the capstone with shouts of Hosanna to God and the Lamb. And today we dedicate the whole unto Thee, with all that pertains unto it that it may be holy in Thy sight; that it may be a house of prayer, a house of praise and of worship; that Thy glory may rest upon it; that Thy holy presence may be continually in it; that it may be the abode of Thy Well-Beloved Son, our Savior; that the angels who stand before Thy face may be the hallowed messengers who shall visit it, bearing to us Thy wishes and Thy will, that it may be sanctified and consecrated in all its parts holy unto Thee, the God of Israel, the Almighty Ruler of Mankind. And we pray Thee that all people who may enter upon the threshold of this, Thine house, may feel Thy power and be constrained to acknowledge that Thou hast sanctified it, that it is Thy house, a place of Thy holiness.

We pray Thee, Heavenly Father, to accept this building in all its parts from foundation to capstone, with the statue that is on the latter placed, and all the finals and other ornaments that adorn its exterior. We pray Thee to bless, that they decay not, all the walls, partitions, floors, ceilings, roofs and bridging, the elevators, stairways, railings and steps, the frames, doors, windows, and other openings, all things connected with the lighting, heating, and sanitary apparatus, the boilers, engines, and dynamos, the connecting pipes and wires, the lamps and burners, and all utensils, furniture and articles used in or connected with the holy ordinances administered in this house, the veils and the altars, the baptismal font and the oxen on which it rests, and all that pertains thereto, the baths, washstands and basins. Also the safes and vaults in which the records are preserved, with the records themselves, and all books, documents, and papers appertaining to the office of the recorder, likewise the library with all the books, maps, instruments, etc., that may belong thereto. We also present before Thee, for Thine acceptance, all the additions and buildings not forming a part of the main edifice, but being appendages thereto; and we pray Thee to bless all the furniture, seats, cushions, curtains, hangings, locks, and fastenings, and multitudinous other appliances and appurtenances found in and belonging to this Temple and its annexes with all the work or ornamentation thereon, the painting and plastering, the gilding and bronzing, the fine work in wood and metal of every kind, the embroidery and needlework, the pictures and statuary, the carved work and canopies. Also the materials of which the buildings and their contents are made or composed—the rock, lime, mortar and plaster, the timbers and lath, the wood of various trees, the gold and silver, the brass and iron, and all other metals, the silk, wool, and cotton, the skins and furs, the glass, china, and precious stones, all these and all else herein we humbly present for Thine acceptance and sanctifying blessing.

Our Father in heaven, we present before Thee the altars which we have prepared for Thy servants and handmaidens to receive their sealing blessings. We dedicate them in the name of the Lord Jesus Christ, unto Thy most holy name, and we ask Thee to sanctify these altars, that those who come unto them may feel the power of the Holy Ghost resting upon them, and realize the sacredness of the covenants they enter into. And we pray that our covenants and contracts which we make with Thee and with each other may be directed by Thy holy Spirit, be sacredly kept by us, and accepted by Thee, and that all the blessings pronounced may be realized by all Thy Saints who come to these altars, in the morning of the resurrection of the just.

O Lord, we pray Thee to bless and sanctify the whole of this block or piece of ground on which these buildings stand, with the surrounding walls and fences, the walks, paths and ornamental beds, also the trees, plants, flowers and shrubbery that grow in its soil; may they bloom and blossom and become exceedingly beautiful and fragrant; and may Thy Spirit dwell in the midst thereof, that this plot of ground may be a place of rest and peace, for holy meditation and inspired thought.

Preserve these buildings, we beseech Thee, from injury or destruction by flood or fire; from the rage of the elements, the shafts of the vivid lightning, the overwhelming blasts of the hurricane, the flames of consuming fire, and the upheavals of the earthquake, O Lord, protect them.

Bless, we pray Thee, Heavenly Father, all who may be workers in this house. Remember continually Thy servant who shall be appointed to preside within its walls; endow him richly with wisdom of the Holy Ones, with the spirit of his calling, with the power of his Priesthood, and with the gift of discernment. Bless, according to their calling, his assistants and all who are associated with him in the performance of the ordinances—baptisms, confirmations, washings, anointings, sealings, endowments, and ordinations which are performed herein, that all that is done may be holy and acceptable unto Thee, Thou God of our salvation. Bless the recorders and copyists, that the records of the Temple may be kept perfect, and without omission and errors, and that they may also be accepted of Thee. Bless, in their several positions, the engineers, watchmen, guards, and all others who have duties to perform in connection with the house, that they may perform them unto Thee with an eye single to Thy glory.

Remember also in Thy mercy all those who have labored in the erection of this house, or who have, in any way, by their means or influence aided in its completion; may they in no wise lose their reward.

O Thou God of our fathers, Abraham, Isaac, and Jacob, whose God Thou delightest to be called, we thank Thee with all the fervor of overflowing gratitude that Thou hast revealed the powers by which the hearts of the children are being turned to their fathers and the hearts of the fathers to the children, that the sons of men, in all their generations can be made partakers of the glories and joys of the kingdom of heaven. Confirm upon us the spirit of Elijah, we pray Thee, that we may thus redeem our dead and also connect ourselves with our fathers who have passed behind the veil, and furthermore seal up our dead to come forth in the first resurrection, that we who dwell on the earth may be bound to those who dwell in heaven. We thank Thee for their sake who have finished their work in mortality, as well as for our own, that the prison doors have been opened, that deliverance has been proclaimed to the captive, and the bonds have been loosened from those who were bound. We praise Thee that our fathers, from last to first, from now, back to the beginning, can be united with us in indissoluble links, welded by the Holy Priesthood, and that as one great family united in Thee and cemented by Thy power we shall together stand before Thee, and by the power of the atoning blood of Thy Son be delivered from all evil, be saved and sanctified, exalted and glorified. Wilt Thou also permit holy messengers to visit us within these sacred walls and make known unto us with regard to the work we should perform in behalf of our dead. And, as Thou has inclined the hearts of many who have not yet entered into covenant with Thee to search out their progenitors, and in so doing they have traced the ancestry of many of Thy Saints, we pray Thee that Thou wilt increase this desire in their bosoms, that they may in this way aid in the accomplishment of Thy work. Bless them, we pray Thee, in their labors, that they may not fall into errors in preparing their genealogies; and furthermore, we ask Thee to open before them new avenues of information, and place in their hands the records of the past, that their work may not only be correct but complete also.

O Thou Great Father of the spirits of all flesh, graciously bless and fully qualify those upon whom Thou hast placed a portion of Thine authority, and who bear the responsibilities and powers of the priesthood which is after the order of Thy Son. Bless them all from first to last from Thy servant who represents Thee in all the world to the latest who has been ordained to the Deacon's office. Upon each and all confer the spirit of their calling, with a comprehension of its duties and a loving zeal to fulfill them. Endow them with faith, patience and understanding. May their lives be strong in virtue and adorned with humility; may their ministrations be effectual, their prayers be availing and their teachings the path of salvation. May they be united by the Spirit and power of God in all their labors, and in every thought, word and act, may they glorify Thy name and vindicate the wisdom that has made them kings and priests unto Thee.

For Thy servants of the First Presidency of the Church we first of all pray. Reveal, in great clearness, Thy mind and will unto them in all things essential for the welfare of Thy people; give them heavenly wisdom, abounding faith, and the power and gifts necessary to enable them to preside acceptably unto Thee over the officers and members of Thy Church. Remember in love Thy servant whom Thou hast called to be a Prophet, Seer, and Revelator to all mankind, whose days have been many upon the earth; yet lengthen out his span of mortal life, we pray Thee, and grant unto him all the powers and gifts, in their completeness, of the office Thou hast conferred upon him; and in like manner bless his associates in the Presidency of Thy Church.

Confer upon Thy servants, the Twelve Apostles, a rich endowment of Thy Spirit. Under their guidance may the gospel of the kingdom go forth into all the world, to be preached to all nations, kindreds, tongues, and people, that the honest in heart in every land may hear the glad tidings of joy and salvation. Overrule, we pray Thee, in the midst of the governments of the earth, that the barriers that now stand in the way of the spread of Thy truths may be removed, and liberty of conscience be accorded to all peoples.

Remember in loving kindness Thy servants, the Patriarchs. May they be full of blessings for Thy people Israel. May they bear with them the seeds of comfort and consolation, of encouragement and blessing. Fill them with the Holy Spirit of promise, and be graciously pleased to fulfill their words of prophecy, that Thy name may be extolled by the people of Thy Church and their faith in Thee and in the promises of Thy ministering servants be increasingly strengthened.

With Thy servants of the Twelve, bless their associates, the Seventies; may they be powerful in the preaching of Thy word and in bearing it to the four quarters of the earth. May an ever-widening way be opened before them until they shall have raised the gospel standard in every land and proclaimed its saving truths in every tongue, that all the islands and the continents may rejoice in the testimony of the great work Thou art in these later days performing on the earth.

Bless abundantly, O Lord, the High Priests in all the varied duties and positions to which Thou hast called them. As standing ministers of Thy word in the multiplying Stakes of Zion wilt Thou endow them richly with the spirit of their exalted callings. As Presidents, Counselors, Bishops, members of High Councils, and in every other office which their Priesthood gives them the right to fill may they be righteous ministers of Thy holy law, loving fathers of the people, and as judges in the midst of the Saints may they deal out just and impartial judgment tempered with mercy and love.

So also, in their various callings, confer precious gifts of wisdom, faith and knowledge upon Thy servants, the Elders, Priests, Teachers, and Deacons, that all may diligently perform their parts in the glorious labors Thou hast called Thy Priesthood to bear.

Forget not, we beseech Thee, Thy servants the missionaries, who are proclaiming the saving truths that Thou hast revealed for man's redemption to the millions who are now overshadowed by deep spiritual darkness. Preserve them from all evil, deliver them from mob violence, may they want no good thing, but be greatly blessed with the gifts and powers of their ministry. Rember also their families, that they may be sustained and comforted by Thee and be cherished and cared for by Thy Saints.

We pray Thee for the members of Thy Holy Church throughout all the world, that Thy people may be so guided and governed of Thee, that all who profess to be and call themselves Saints may be preserved in the unity of the faith, in the way of truth, in the bonds of peace, and in holiness of life. Strengthen the weak, we pray Thee, and impart Thy Spirit unto all.

Our Father, may peace abide in all the homes of Thy Saints; may holy angels guard them; may they be encompassed by Thine arms of love; may prosperity shine upon them, and may the tempter and the destroyer be removed far from them. May the days of Thy covenant people be lengthened out in righteousness, and sickness and disease be rebuked from their midst. May the land they inhabit be made fruitful by Thy grace, may its waters be increased and the climate be tempered to the comfort and need of Thy people; may drought, devastating storms, cyclones, and hurricanes be kept afar off, and earthquakes never disturb the land which Thou hast given us. May locusts, caterpillars and other insects not destroy our garden and desolate our fields; but may we be a people blessed of Thee in our bodies and spirits, in our homes and habitations, in our flocks and herds, in ourselves and our posterity, and in all that Thou hast made us stewards over.

Now we pray for the youth of Zion—the children of Thy people; endow them richly with the spirit of faith and righteousness and with increasing love for Thee and for Thy law. Prosper all the institutions that Thou hast established in our midst for their wellbeing. Give to our Church Schools an ever-increasing power for good. May the Holy Spirit dominate the teachings given therein and also control the hearts and illumine the minds of the students. Bless marvelously Thy servants, the General Superintendent, and all the principals, teachers and other officers, and also those from the General Board of Education of Thy Church. Remember, like-wise in Thy loving kindness the Sunday Schools, with all who, either as teachers or scholars, belong thereto; may the influence of the instruction given therein broaden and deepen, to Thy glory and the salvation of Thy children, until the perfect day. Bless the members of the General Board of the Deseret Sunday School Union with the wisdom necessary for the proper fulfillment of their duties, and for the accomplishment of the purposes for which this board was created.

We also uphold before Thee the Young Men's and Young Ladies' Mutual Improvement Associations, with all their officers, general and local, and the members. May they be prospered of Thee, their membership be enlarged, and the good that they ac-complish increase with every succeeding year. For the Primaries and Religion Classes we also seek Thy constant blessing and guid-ing care; may the spirit of instruction be poured out upon the presidents and associate officers and the teachers. May they keep peace with the rest of the educational establishments in Thy Church; so that from their earliest years our children may be dili-gently brought up in the ways of the Lord, and Thy name be magnified in their growth in virtue and intelligence.

Nor would we forget, O Lord, the normal training classes among Thy people, whether these classes be connected with the Church Schools, the Improvement Associations, or the Sunday Schools. Grant that these classes may be the means of spreading true education throughout all the borders of the Saints by the crea-tion of a body of teachers who will not only be possessed of rare intelligence but be filled also with the spirit of the gospel and be powerful in the testimony of Thy truth and in implanting a love for Thee and Thy works in the hearts of all whom they instruct.

We would hold up before Thee, O Lord, the Relief Societies, with all their members; and all those who preside in their midst according to their callings and appointments, general or local. Bless the Teachers in their labors of mercy and charity, who, as ministering angels, visit the homes of the sick and the needy, bear-ing succor, consolation and comfort to the unfortunate and sor-rowful. And bless, we beseech Thee, most merciful Father, the poor of Thy people, that the cry of want and suffering may not ascend unto Thee from the midst of Thy Saints whom Thou hast blessed so abundantly with the comforts of this world. Open up new avenues by which the needy can obtain a livelihood by honest industry, and also incline the hearts of those blessed more abun-dantly, to give generously of their substance in this respect, less favored brethren and sisters, that Thou mayest not have reason to chide us for the neglect of even the least among Thy covenant children.

O God of Israel, turn Thy face, we pray Thee, in loving kindness toward Thy stricken people of the House of Judah. Oh, deliver them from those that oppress them. Heal up their wounds, comfort their hearts, strengthen their feet, and give them ministers after Thine own heart who shall lead them as of old, in Thy way. May the days of their tribulation soon cease, and they be planted by Thee in the valleys and plains of their ancient home; and may Jerusalem rejoice and Judea be glad for the multitude of her sons and daughters, for the sweet voices of children in her streets, and the rich outpouring of Thy saving mercies upon them. May Israel no more bow the head, or bend the neck to the oppressor, but may his feet be made strong on the everlasting hills, never more, by violence, to be banished therefrom, and the praise and the glory shall be Thine.

Remember in like pity the dwindling remnants of the House of Israel, descendants of Thy servant Lehi. Restore them we pray Thee, to Thine ancient favor, fulfill in their completeness the promises given to their fathers, and make of them a white and delightsome race, a loved and holy people as in former days. May the time also be nigh at hand when Thou wilt gather the dispersed of Israel from the islands of the sea and from every land in which Thou hast scattered them, and the ten tribes of Jacob from their hiding place in the north, and restore them to communion and fellowship with their kinsmen of the seed of Abraham.

We thank Thee, O God of Israel, that Thou didst raise up patriotic men to lay the foundation of this great American government. Thou didst inspire them to frame a good constitution and laws which guarantee to all of the inhabitants of the land equal rights and privileges to worship Thee according to the dictates of their own consciences. Bless the officers, both judicial and executive. Confer abundant favors upon the President, his Cabinet, and Congress. Enlightened and guided by Thy Spirit may they maintain and uphold the glorious principles of human liberty. Our hearts are filled with gratitude to Thee, our Father in heaven, for Thy kindness unto us in softening the hearts of our fellow citizens, the people of this nation, toward us. That which Thou hast done has been marvelous in our eyes. We thank Thee that Thou didst move upon the heart of the President of our nation to issue a general amnesty. Thou hast removed prejudice and misunderstanding from the minds of many of the people concerning us and our purposes, and they are disposed to treat us as fellow citizens, and not as enemies. In this holy house we feel to give Thee glory therefore, and we humbly ask Thee to increase this feeling in their hearts. Enable them to see us in our true light. Show unto them that we are their friends, that we love liberty, that we will join with them in upholding the rights of the people, the Constitution and laws of our country; and give unto us and our children an increased disposition to always be loyal, and to do everything in our power to maintain Constitutional rights and the freedom of all within the confines of this great Republic.

Remember in mercy, O Lord, the kings, the princes, the nobles the rulers, and governors and the great ones of the earth, and likewise all the poor, the afflicted and the oppressed, and indeed, all people, that their hearts may be softened when Thy servants go forth to bear testimony of Thy name, that their prejudices may give way before the truth, and Thy people find favor in their eyes. So control the affairs of the nations of the earth, that the way be prepared for the ushering in of a reign of righteousness and truth. We desire to see liberty spread throughout the earth, to see oppression cease, the yoke of the tyrant broken, and every despotic form of government overthrown by which Thy children are degraded and crushed, and prevented from enjoying their share of the blessings of the earth, which Thou hast created for their habitation.

O God, the Eternal Father, Thou knowest all things. Thou seest the course Thy people have been led to take in political matters. They have, in many instances, joined the two great national parties. Campaigns have been entered upon, elections have been held, and much party feeling has been engendered. Many things have been said and done which have wounded the feelings of the humble and the meek, and which have been a cause of offense. We beseech Thee, in Thine infinite mercy and goodness, to forgive Thy people wherein they have sinned in this direction. Show them, O Father, their faults and their errors, that they may see the same in the light of Thy Holy Spirit, and repent truly and sincerely, and cultivate that spirit of affection and love which Thou art desirous that all the children of men should entertain one for another, and which Thy Saints, above all others, should cherish. Enable Thy people hereafter to avoid bitterness and strife, and to refrain from words and acts in political discussions that shall create feeling and grieve Thy Holy Spirit.

Heavenly Father, when Thy people shall not have the opportunity of entering this holy house to offer their supplications unto Thee, and they are oppressed and in trouble, surrounded by difficulties or assailed by temptation and shall turn their faces towards this Thy holy house and ask Thee for deliverance, for help, for Thy power to be extended in their behalf, we beseech Thee, to look down from Thy holy habitation in mercy and tender compassion upon them, and listen to their cries. Or when the children of Thy people, in years to come, shall be separated, through any cause, from this place, and their hearts shall turn in remembrance of Thy promises to this holy Temple, and they shall cry unto Thee from the depths of their affliction and sorrow to extend relief and deliverance to them, we humbly entreat Thee to Turn Thine ear in mercy to them; hearken to their cries, and grant unto them the blessings for which they ask.

Almighty Father, increase within us the powers of that faith delivered to and possessed by Thy Saints. Strengthen us by the memories of the glorious deliverances of the past, by the remembrance of the sacred covenants that Thou hast made with us, so that, when evil overshadows us, when trouble encompasses us, when we pass through the valley of humiliation, we may not falter, may not doubt, but in the strength of Thy Holy name may accomplish all Thy righteous purposes with regard to us, fill the measure of our creation, and triumph gloriously, by Thy grace, over every besetting sin, be redeemed from every evil, and be numbered in the kingdom of heaven amongst those who shall dwell in Thy presence forever.

And now, our Father, we bless Thee, we praise Thee, we glorify Thee, we worship Thee, day by day we magnify Thee, and give Thee thanks for Thy great goodness towards us, Thy children, and we pray Thee, in the name of Thy Son Jesus Christ, our Savior, to hear these our humble petitions, and answer us from heaven, Thy holy dwelling place, where Thou sittest enthroned in glory, might, majesty, and dominion, and with an infinitude of power which we, Thy mortal creatures, cannot imagine, much less comprehend. Amen and Amen. Contributor, Vol. 14:292.

Physical and Historical Description

No object in Salt Lake City excites greater interest in the minds of strangers than the Temple, which has been erected by the Church of Jesus Christ of Latter-day Saints. It elicits expressions of wonderment because of its beautiful yet massive proportions, unique architecture, and evident costliness. Numerous questions are asked concerning the structure, the purposes for which it has been built, and why none but members of the Church are permitted to enter its precincts. This article has been compiled, from authentic sources, to satisfy all reasonable inquiries in relation to these matters.

Four days after the arrival of the Pioneers on the barren site of this now lovely city, July 28, 1847, President Brigham Young, while walking over the ground with some of his associates, suddenly stopped, and, striking the point of his cane into the parched soil, exclaimed, "Here we will build the Temple of our God." His prophetic words were noted by his companions, and Apostle (afterwards President) Wilford Woodruff drove a wooden stake into the small hole made by the point of President Young's cane. On the evening of the same day, the ten acres selected for the Temple Block were marked out, and it was decided that the future city should surround that square.

In April, 1851, the members of the Church—assembled in general conference—voted unanimously to build the Temple. February 14, 1853, after the site for the great structure was surveyed, the block was solemnly dedicated, and ground broken for the foundation of the Temple. On April 6th of the same year the cornerstones of the Temple were laid, with impressive ceremonies, amid great rejoicing of the assembled multitude.

Unknown to those who surveyed the site for the building, the wooden stake driven into the ground by Wilford Woodruff, on the 28th of July, 1847, marked the center of the plot laid out by them.

It should ever be remembered that this magnificent structure was planned and its erection begun by a small number of despoiled and destitute people, at a time when they were struggling for existence in the midst of adverse surroundings. We shall not enumerate the many seemingly insurmountable obstacles which, from time to time, hindered the progress of the stupendous undertaking; but it may well be said that the completed Temple is a monument of faith and work unparalleled in the world's history.

The Temple is built of gray granite taken from a mountain of that enduring material at the mouth of Little Cottonwood canyon, twenty miles southeast of the city. Many blocks of granite in the walls are so large that four yoke of oxen were required to haul each of them, occupying four days in transit. This process of hauling rocks by ox-team, from the quarry to the Temple site, was so slow and expensive that President Young decided to have a canal constructed to carry the rock by boats. Accordingly, the canal was dug, at great cost, from the mouth of Little Cottonwood canyon across the bench land, to an outlet in City Creek, near the Temple block. But in 1873, before the canal was sufficiently completed to be made available for the main purpose

in view, a line of railroad was laid which supplanted this contemplated use of the canal. The latter has since been used to
great advantage in conveying a large supply of water from Jordan River to the City.

Some idea of the massiveness of the building, and of the
enormous amount of rock used in its construction, may be obtained from the following figures: Foundation, or footing wall,
sixteen feet wide and eight feet deep; basement walls, eight feet
thick; upper story walls, six feet thick. The extreme length of
the building is 186½ feet; extreme width, 118½ feet. Height of
side walls on main bulding, 107½ feet; east center tower, 210
feet high; west center tower, 204 feet. Inverted arches are constructed in the foundation, to distribute evenly the enormous
pressure of the massive walls. The entire area is 21,850 feet.

The architecture of the Temple is composite and original.
The six towers, three on the east and three on the west, are built
entirely of granite. Within each of the four corner towers there
is a spiral staircase. There are 172 granite steps, and four land-
ings, in each of these stairways. Each step is six feet long, and
weighs over 1,700 pounds.

On the capstone of the east center tower is a hammered
copper statue, twelve feet five and one-half inches in height,
heavily gilded with pure gold leaf. It represents the angel Moroni, blowing a trumpet, proclaiming the restoration of the Gospel.

The largest dressed rocks in the building are known as the
"Earth Stones." They are at the base of the buttresses, near the
level of the ground, on each side of the basement windows, fifty
of them in all. Each of these blocks of granite is five and one-
half feet high, four and one-half feet wide, and twenty inches
thick, and weighs over three tons. On each of them is carved, in
bas-relief, a globe three feet eleven inches in diameter. They
cost, when finished, about $300 each.

The "Moon Stones" are also fifty in number, inserted in
the buttresses in line with the top of the first row of oval windows. These stones are carved to represent the different phases
of the moon.

On the buttresses above the "Moon Stones," in line with

the top of the upper row of oval windows, are the "Sun Stones," fifty in number.

Nearly all the keystones of the windows and doors in the building are ornamented with a beautifully cut five-pointed star. There are also stars carved on the face of a large number of other granite stones prominent in various parts of the structure.

On the facade of the middle tower at the west end of the building, in line with the battlements, is carved the seven stars forming the constellation of Ursa Major, the Great Bear, or dipper, with the pointers directed, as nearly as possible, toward the North Star.

The keystones of the lower windows of the east and west center towers have inscribed on them the words of the Lord, "I am Alpha and Omega." Below these keystones is carved the emblem of Clasped Hands, and on the stones at the top of the upper windows in the same towers is depicted the awe-inspiring symbol of the All-Seeing Eye.

At the top of the buttresses of the east center tower are carved representations of rays of light emanating from clouds. * * * The stones representing rays of light streaming from the midst of clouds indicate Gospel Light dispelling the clouds of error which had enshrouded the world: "For, behold, the darkness shall cover the earth, and gross darkness the people, but the Lord shall arise upon thee, and His glory shall be seen upon thee."

The stones representing the sun, earth, moon and numerous stars, are allegorical emblems of the conditions to which the resurrected souls of mankind will be assigned when all are judged "according to their works."

"There are also celestial bodies, and bodies terrestrial; but the glory of the celestial is one, and the glory of the terrestrial is another. There is one glory of the sun, and another of the moon, and another of the stars; for one star differeth from another star in glory. So also is the resurrection of the dead." (I Cor. 15.)

The depicted constellation of Ursa Major, with the pointers directed to the North Star, is intended to remind those in doubt concerning the true way, that they should follow the path indicated by the Priesthood.

The Clasped Hands are emblematic of the strong union and brotherly love characteristic of Latter-day Saints, through which they have been enabled to accomplish so much both at home and abroad.

The grand truth recorded in the Scriptures, "The eyes of the Lord are in every place, beholding the evil and the good," is expressed by the symbol of the All-Seeing Eye.

The following words are inscribed on a stone tablet on the east center tower of the Temple:

HOLINESS TO THE LORD

THE HOUSE OF THE LORD BUILT BY THE

CHURCH OF JESUS CHRIST OF LATTER-DAY SAINTS.

COMMENCED APRIL 6, 1853;

COMPLETED APRIL 6, 1893.

Elders' Journal, Vol. 3:81-83.

President Brigham Young, and Counselors, with Patriarch John Smith, laid the southeast cornerstone on April 6, 1853, the former delivering the oration, and President Heber C. Kimball offering the prayer. The southwest cornerstone was laid by Presiding Bishop Edward Hunter, his counselors and the presiding authorities of the Lesser Priesthood, Bishop Hunter delivering the oration and Bishop Alfred Cordon offering the prayer. The northwest cornerstone was next put into place by the Presidency of the High Priests' Quorum and the Presidency and High Council of the Stake, John Young delivering the oration and George B. Wallace offering the prayer. The Twelve Apostles, the Presidency of the Seventies and the Elders' Quorums officiated at the fourth corner, the northeast, Parley P. Pratt delivering the oration and Orson Hyde offering the prayer.

The capstone was laid on April 6, 1892. The Temple was dedicated on April 6, 1893, by President Wilford Woodruff.

The Dedicatory Services continued twice each day from April 6th to the 18th, again on April 23rd and 24th, the 21st and 22nd being reserved for Sunday School children.

Presidents of the Salt Lake Temple:

Lorenzo Snow, 1893-1898.

Joseph F. Smith, 1898-1911.

Anthon H. Lund, 1911-1921.

George F. Richards, 1921-1938.

Stephen L. Chipman, 1938-1945.

Joseph Fielding Smith, 1945-1949.

Robert D. Young, 1949-1953

ElRay L. Christiansen, 1953-1961.

Willard E. Smith, 1961-1964.

Howard S. McDonald, 1964—Present Incumbent.

Spiritual Communication

Discourse by Elder Parley P. Pratt, Delivered on the North-East Corner Stone of the Temple at Great Salt Lake City, after the Twelve Apostles, the First Presidency of the Seventies, and the Presidency of the Elders' Quorum had laid the Stone, April 6, 1853.

"And when they shall say unto you, seek unto them that have familiar spirits, and unto wizards that peep and mutter; should not a people seek unto their God? for the living to hear from the dead?"

The foregoing text was copied by Nephi, from the Book of Isaiah, about six hundred years before Christ, and is now contained in the second Book of Nephi, chap. ix.

For the last few years the world has been disturbed very much by alleged communications from the world of spirits. "Mesmerism," "Clairvoyance," "Spiritual Knockings," "Writing Mediums," etc., are said to be channels of communication between the living and the dead. How often one meets with an invitation to seek to some *"medium"*—to someone "familiar with spirits," in order to hear from a deceased father, mother, husband, wife, or other relative or friend.

On the other hand, these alleged communications from the spirit world are zealously opposed, on the ground that there is no such philosophy in nature; that there can be no medium of communication between the living and those who have passed the vale of death; and that, therefore, all alleged communications from that source must necessarily be false.

It becomes the Saints to be able on this, as on all other subjects, to judge correctly and understandingly, by their knowledge of the principles of true philosophy, and of the laws of God and nature.

If on the one hand we admit the principle of communication between the spirit world and our own, and yield ourselves to the unreserved or indiscriminate guidance of every spiritual manifestation, we are liable to be led about by every wind of doctrine, and by every kind of spirit which constitute the varieties of being and of thought in the spirit world. Demons, foul or unclean spirits, adulterous or murderous spirits, those who love or make a lie, can communicate with beings in the flesh, as well as those who are more true and virtuous.

Again—The spirits who are ignorant, uncultivated, and who remain in error, can communicate through the same medium as those better informed.

To illustrate this subject, we will consider the telegraphic wire as a medium of communication between New York and Boston.

Through this medium a holy Prophet or Apostle could communicate the holy and sacred words of truth; while through the same, could be communicated words of truth in relation to news, business transactions, the sciences, etc.; and also every species of lie, error, imposition, fraud, etc. Hence, if the people of New York should submit to the guidance of beings in Boston, who communicate with them by telegraph or other mediums, they would be guided by a mixture of intelligence, truth, error, falsehood, etc., in every conceivable variety. So with communications from the spirit world, if we once credit the philosophy of fact of an existing medium of communication.

If, on the other hand, we deny the philosophy or the fact of spiritual communication between the living and those who have died, we deny the very fountain from which emanated the great truths or principles which were the foundation of both the ancient and modern Church.

Who communicated with Jesus and His disciples on the holy mount? Moses and Elias, from the invisible world. Who bestowed upon the Apostles the commission to preach the Gospel to every creature in all the world? He that had passed the vale of death, and had dwelt in the spirit world, yea, he that had ascended far on high above the realms of death, and far beyond all the principalities and powers of the spirit world, and had entered, and been crowned, in the mansions of immortal flesh.

Who communicated with the beloved disciple on the Isle of Patmos, and revealed these sublime truths contained in his prophetic book? He that liveth and was dead, through his angel, who declared to John—Behold, I am thy fellow-servant, and of thy brethren the Prophets, that have the testimony of Jesus.

Who communicated with our great modern Prophet, and revealed through him as a medium, the ancient history of a hemisphere, and the records of the ancient dead? Moroni, who had lived upon the earth fourteen hundred years before. Who ordained Joseph the Prophet, and his fellow-servant, to the preparatory Priesthood, to baptize for the remission of sins? John the Baptist, who had been beheaded! Who ordained our first founders to the Apostleship, to hold the keys of the kingdom of God, in these the times of restoration? Peter, James, and John, from the eternal world. Who instructed him in the mysteries of the Kingdom, and in all things pertaining to Priesthood, law, philosophy, sacred architecture, ordinances, sealings, anointings, baptisms for the dead, and in the mysteries of the first, second and third heavens many of which are unlawful to utter? Angels and spirits from the eternal worlds.

Who revealed to him the plan of redemption, and of exaltation for the dead who had died without the Gospel? and the keys and preparations necessary for holy and perpetual converse with Jesus Christ, and with the spirits of just men made perfect, and with the general assembly and Church of the first-born, in the *holy of holies?* Those from the dead!

Again—How do the Saints expect the necessary information by which to complete the ministrations for the salvation and exaltation of their friends who have died?

By one holding the keys of the oracles of God, as a medium through which the living can hear from the dead.

Shall *we*, then, deny the principle, the philosophy, the fact of communication between worlds? No! Verily no!

The spiritual philosophy of the present age was introduced to the modern world by Joseph Smith. The people of the United States abandoned him to martyrdom, and his followers to fire and sword, and plunder and imprisonment, and final banishment to these far-off mountains and deserts, simply because a medium of communication with the invisible world had been found, whereby the living could hear from the dead. No sooner had the people and nation, thus guilty of innocent blood, completed the banishment of the Saints from their midst, than they began to adopt some of the same principles of spiritual philosophy, although in a perverted sense of the word.

Editors, statesmen, philosophers, priests, and lawyers, as well as the common people, began to advocate the principle of converse with the dead, by visions, divination, clairvoyance, knocking and writing mediums, etc. This spiritual philosophy of converse with the dead, once established by the labors, toils, sufferings, and martyrdom of its modern founders, and now embraced by a large portion of the learned world, shows a triumph more rapid and complete—a victory more extensive, than has ever been achieved in the same length of time in our world.

A quarter of a century since, an obscure boy and his few associates, in the western wilds of New York, commenced to hold converse with the dead. Now, vision, new revelation, clairvoyance, mediums, oracles, etc., are talked of and advocated as far as the modern press extends its influence, or steam its power of locomotion.

An important point is gained, a victory won, and a countless host of opposing powers vanquished, on one of the leading or fundamental truths of "Mormon" philosophy, viz.—*"That the living may hear from the dead."*

But notwithstanding these great victories of truth over error, ignorance, and superstition, in certain points of spiritual philosophy, yet much remains to be done, ere pure, uncontaminated truth will reign triumphant, and darkness and error surrender their last stronghold on the earth.

The fact of spiritual communications being established, by which the living hear from the dead—being no longer a question of controversy with the well informed, we drop that point, and call attention to the means of discriminating or judging between the lawful and the unlawful mediums or channels of communication—between the holy and impure, the truths and falsehoods thus communicated.

The words of the holy Prophet in our text, while they admit the principle of the living hearing from the dead, openly rebuke, and sharply reprove, persons for seeking to those who have familiar spirits, and to wizards that peep and mutter, and remind us that a people should seek unto their God for the living to hear from the dead!

By what means, then, can a people seek unto their God, for such an important blessings as to hear from the dead?

And how shall we discriminate between those who seek to Him, and those who seek the same by unlawful means?

In the first place, no person can successfully seek to God for this privilege, unless he believes in direct revelation in modern times.

Secondly, it is impossible for us to seek Him successfully, and remain in our sins. A thorough repentance and reformation of life are absolutely necessary, if we would seek to Him.

Thirdly, Jesus Christ is the only name given under heaven, as a medium through which to approach to God. None, then, can be lawful mediums, who are unbelievers in Jesus Christ, or in modern revelation, or who remain in their sins; or who act in their own name, instead of the name appointed.

And, moreover, the Lord has appointed a Holy Priesthood on the earth, and in the heavens, and also in the world of spirits; which Priesthood is after the order or similitude of His Son; and has committed to this Priesthood the keys of holy and divine revelation, and of correspondence, or communication between angels, spirits, and men, and between all the holy departments, principalities, and powers of His government in all worlds.

And again—The Lord has ordained that all the most holy things pertaining to the salvation of the dead, and all the most holy conversations and correspondence with God, angels, and spirits, shall be had only in the sanctuary of His holy Temple on the earth, when prepared for that purpose by His Saints; and shall be received and administered by those who are ordained and sealed unto this power, to hold the keys of the sacred oracles of God.

To this same principle the prophets of Isaiah and Micah bear testimony, saying, that in the last days all nations shall go up to the house (or Temple) of the Lord, in order to be taught in His ways, and to walk in His paths; for out of Zion shall go forth the law, etc. Now it is evident that the people of all nations in the last days would be utterly unable to learn the ways of the Lord to perfection, in any other place except in a holy Temple erected among the mountains. For if the oracles, and most holy ordinances, and the keys or the mysteries, could be had elsewhere, or in any and every place, the people would never take the pains to resort to one house amid the mountains in order to learn of His ways, and to walk in His paths.

It is, then, a matter of certainty, according to the things revealed to the ancient Prophets, and renewed unto us, that all the animal magnetic phenomena, all the trances and visions of clairvoyant states, all the phenomena of spiritual knockings, writing mediums, etc., are from impure, unlawful, and unholy sources; and that those holy and chosen vessels which hold the keys of Priesthood in this world, in the spirit world, or in the world of resurrected beings, stand as far aloof from all these improper channels, or unholy mediums, of spiritual communication, as the heavens are higher than the earth, or as the mysteries of the third heaven, which are unlawful to utter, differ from the jargon of sectarian ignorance and folly, or the divinations of foul spirits, abandoned wizards, magic-mongers, jugglers, and fortune-tellers.

Ye Latter-day Saints! Ye thousands of the hosts of Israel! Ye are assembled here today, and have laid these Corner Stones, for the express purpose that the living might hear from the dead, and that we may prepare a holy sanctuary where *"the people may seek unto their God, and for the living to hear from the dead,"* and that heaven and earth, and the world of spirits may commune together—that the kings, nobles, presidents, rulers, judges, priests, counselors, and senators, which compose the general assembly of the Church of the first-born in all these different spheres of temporal and spiritual existence, may sit in grand Council, and hold a Congress or court on the earth, to concert measures for the overthrow of the "mystery of iniquity," the thrones of tyrants, the sanctuaries of priestcraft and superstition, and the reign of ignorance, sin, and death.

Saints! These victories will be achieved, and Jesus Christ and his Saints will subdue all opposing powers, and attain to universal empire in heaven and on earth, as sure as innocent blood was ever shed on Mount Calvary, or the official seal broken on the door of the tomb of the Son of God. This day's work, in laying these Corner Stones for a temple amid the mountains, is one advancing step in the progress of the necessary preparations for these mighty revolutions.

Let Zion complete this Temple, let it be dedicated to, and accepted by the Almighty, let it be preserved in holiness according to the laws of the Holy Priesthood, and Zion shall not want for a man to stand before the Lord, and to receive the oracles, and administer in His holy sanctuary, and to administer the keys of His government upon the earth.

> While sun, or moon, or stars shall shine.
> Or principalities endure.

If the Saints accomplish these things, and fail not to keep the commandments of Jesus Christ and the counsels of his servants, the kingdoms of the world shall never prevail against them from this time forth and forever.

But remember, O ye Saints of the Most High! *remember* that the enemy is on the alert. That old serpent and his angels, who have ruled this lower world, with few exceptions, for so many ages, will not tamely, and without a struggle, submit to have the kingdom, and seat of government, and sanctuary of our God, again erected on our planet, no more to be thrown down or subdued, till every square yard of the vast domain shall be reconquered by its rightful owners. No! From the moment the ground was broken for this Temple, those inspired by him (Satan) have commenced to rage; and he will continue to stir up his servants to anger against that which is good, but, if we are faithful, the victory is ours, in the name of Jesus Christ. Amen.

J. of D., Vol. 2, pp. 43-47.

The Powers of Evil Will Rage

In after years, President Kimball predicted, in relation to this Temple that when its walls reached the square the powers of evil would rage and the Saints would suffer persecution. The walls of the Salt Lake Temple "reached the square" in November, 1882, eight months after the passage by Congress of the celebrated "Edmunds Law." One year later, in November, 1883, occurred the trial of Rudger Clawson for polygamy under the provisions of that law, in the Third District Court of Utah Territory. This, the first gun of the campaign, was the signal for the inauguration of an anti-Mormon crusade which, for bitterness and cruelty, takes rank in the history of religious persecution with the deeds of the Dark-Ages. Thus was fulfilled another prediction of the Prophet Heber, fifteen years after his mortal eyes were closed in death.   Life of Heber C. Kimball, by Orson F. Whitney, p. 409.

The Salt Lake Temple Seen in Vision in July, 1847
By President Brigham Young

I scarcely ever say much about revelations, or visions, but suffice to say, five years ago last July I was here, and saw in the spirit the Temple not ten feet from where we have laid the chief cornerstone. I have not inquired what kind of a Temple we should build. Why? Because it was represented before me. I have never looked upon that ground, but the vision of it was there. I see it as plainly as if it was in reality before me. Wait until it is done. I will say, however, that it will have six towers to begin with, instead of one. Now do not any of you apostatize because it will have six towers, and Joseph only built one. It is easier for us to build sixteen than it was for him to build one. The time will come when there will be one in the center of Temples we shall build and on the top, groves and fish ponds. But we shall not see them here, at present.   J. D. Vol. 1:113.

Salt Lake Temple Seen in Vision Before Exodus
By President Wilford Woodruff

When in the western country, many years ago, before we came to the Rocky Mountains, I had a dream. I dreamed of being in these mountains, and of seeing a large fine looking temple erected in one of these valleys which was built of cut granite stone. I saw that temple dedicated, and I attended the dedicatory services, and I saw a good many men that are living today in the midst of this people. And I saw them called of God and sent forth into the United States and to Babylon, or what is called the Christian world, to bind up the law and seal up the testimony against the nations of the earth, because they had rejected the testimony of Jesus and of the establishment of the kingdom of God upon the earth. When the foundation of that temple was laid I thought of my dream, and a great many times since. And whenever President Young held a council of the brethren of the Twelve and talked of building the temple of adobe or brick, which was done, I would say to myself, "No, you will never do it"; because I had seen it in my dream built of some other material. I mention these things to show you that things are manifested to the Latter-day Saints sometimes which we do not know anything about only as they are given by the Spirit of God.   J. D. Vol. 21:299-300.

Salt Lake Temple to Endure Through the Millenium
By President Brigham Young

I want to see the Temple built in a manner that it will endure through the Millennium. This is not the only Temple we shall build; there will be hundreds of them built and dedicated to the Lord. This Temple will be known as the first Temple built in the mountains by the Latter-day Saints. And when the Millennium is over, and all the sons and daughters of Adam and Eve, down to the last of their posterity, who come within the reach of the clemency of the Gospel, have been redeemed in hundreds of Temples through the administration of their children as proxies for them, I want that Temple to stand as a proud monument of the faith, perseverance and industry of the Saints of God in the mountains, in the nineteenth century.

J. D., Vol. 10:254. See also J. D. Vol. 11:372.

The Redeemer Appears to President Lorenzo Snow
By LeRoi C. Snow

For some time President Woodruff's health had been failing. Nearly every evening President Lorenzo Snow visited him at his home on South 5th East Street. This particular evening the doctors said President Woodruff was failing rapidly and they feared he would not live much longer.

Lorenzo Snow was then President of the Council of Twelve and was greatly worried over the possibility of succeeding President Woodruff, especially because of the terrible financial condition of the Church. Referring to this condition, President Heber J. Grant has said: "The Church was in a financial slough of despond, so to speak, almost financially bankrupt—its credit was hardly good for a thousand dollars without security."

My father went to his room in the Salt Lake Temple, where he was residing at the time. He dressed in his robes of the Priesthood, went into the Holy of Holies, there in the House of the Lord and knelt at the sacred altar. He plead with the Lord to spare President Woodruff's life, that President Woodruff might outlive him and that the great responsibility of Church leadership would never fall upon his shoulders. Yet he promised the Lord that he would devotedly perform any duty required at his hands. At this time he was in his eighty-sixth year.

Soon after this President Woodruff was taken to California, where he died Friday morning at 6:40 o'clock, September 2, 1898. President George Q. Cannon at once wired the sad information to the President's office in Salt Lake City. Word was forwarded to President Snow who was in Brigham City. The telegram was delivered to him on the street in Brigham. He read it to President Rudger Clawson, then president of Box Elder Stake, who was with him, went to the telegraph office and replied that he would leave on the train about 5:30 that evening. He reached Salt Lake City about 7:15, proceeded to the President's office, gave some instructions and then went to his private room in the Salt Lake Temple.

President Snow put on his holy temple robes, repaired again to the same sacred altar, offered up the signs of the Priesthood, and poured out his heart to the Lord. He reminded the Lord how he had plead for President Woodruff's life and that his days might be lengthened beyond his own; that he might never be called upon to bear the heavy burdens and responsibilities of Church leadership. "Nevertheless," he said, "Thy will be done. I have not sought this responsibility but if it be Thy will, I now present myself before Thee for Thy guidance and instruction. I ask that Thou show me what Thou wouldst have me do."

After finishing his prayer he expected a reply, some special manifestation from the Lord. So he waited—and waited—and waited. There was no reply, no voice, no visitation, no manifestation. He left the altar and the room in great disappointment. He passed through the Celestial room and out into the large corridor leading to his own room where a most glorious manifestation was given President Snow. One of the most beautiful accounts of this experience is told by his granddaughter, Allie Young Pond.

"One evening when I was visiting Grandpa Snow in his room in the Salt Lake Temple, I remained until the doorkeepers had gone and the nightwatchman had not yet come in, so Grandpa said he would take me to the main front entrance and let me out that way. He got his bunch of keys from his dresser.

"After we left his room and while we were still in the large corridor, leading into the Celestial room, I was walking several steps ahead of Grandpa when he stopped me, saying: 'Wait a moment, Allie. I want to tell you something. It was right here that the Lord Jesus Christ appeared to me at the time of the death of President Woodruff. He instructed me to go right ahead and reorganize the First Presidency of the Church at once and not wait as he had done after the death of the previous presidents, and that I was to succeed President Woodruff.'

"Then Grandpa came a step nearer and held out his left hand and said: 'He stood right here, about three feet above the floor. It looked as though He stood on a plate of solid gold.'

"Grandpa told me what a glorious personage the Savior is and described His hands, feet, countenance and beautiful White Robes, all of which were of such a glory of whiteness and brightness that he could hardly gaze upon Him.

"Then Grandpa came another step nearer me and put his right hand on my head and said: 'Now, granddaughter, I want you to remember that this is the testimony of your grandfather, that he told you with his own lips that he actually saw the Savior here in the Temple and talked with Him face to face.'

"Then we went on and Grandpa let me out of the main front door of the Temple."

During the M. I. A. June conference in 1919 at the officers' testimony meeting in the Assembly Hall, I related Allie Young Pond's experience and testimony. President Heber J.

Grant immediately arose and said: "In confirmation of the testimony given by Brother LeRoi C. Snow quoting the granddaughter of Lorenzo Snow, I want to call attention to the fact that several years elapsed after the death of the Prophet Joseph Smith before President Young was sustained as the president of the Church. After the death of President Young, several years elapsed again before President Taylor was sustained, and again when he died several years elapsed before President Woodruff was sustained.

"After the funeral of President Wilford Woodruff the Apostles met in the office of the First Presidency and Brother Francis M. Lyman said: 'I feel impressed although one of the younger members of the quorum, to say that I believe it would be pleasing in the sight of the Lord if the First Presidency of the Church was reorganized right here and right now. If I am in error regarding this impression, President Snow and the senior members of the council can correct me.'

"President Snow said that he would be pleased to hear from all the brethren upon this question, and each and all of us expressed ourselves as believing it would be pleasing to the Lord and that it would be the proper thing to have the Presidency organized at once.

"When we had finished, then and not until then did Brother Snow tell us that he was instructed of the Lord in the Temple the night after President Woodruff died, to organize the Presidency of the Church at once. President Anthon H. Lund and myself are the only men now living who were present at that meeting." The Deseret News, Saturday, April 2, 1938.

Chapter VII

THE HAWAIIAN TEMPLE

DEDICATORY PRAYER
By President Heber J. Grant
(November 27, 1919)

O God, the Eternal Father, we, Thy servants and handmaidens, thank Thee, in the name of Jesus Christ, Thy well-beloved Son, with all the power of our being, that we are privileged this day to be present in this beautiful land, to dedicate into Thy Most Holy Name, a temple of the Living God.

We thank Thee, O God, the Eternal Father, that Thou and Thy Son, Jesus Christ, didst visit the boy, Joseph Smith, Jr., and that he was instructed by Thee, and Thy beloved Son.

We thank The that Thou didst send Thy servant, John the Baptist, and that he did lay his hands upon Joseph Smith and Oliver Cowdery and ordain them to the Aaronic, or Lesser Priesthood.

We thank Thee for sending Thy servants Peter, James, and John, apostles of the Lord Jesus Christ, who ministered with the Savior in the flesh and after His crucifixion, and that they did ordain Thy servants Joseph Smith and Oliver Cowdery apostles of the Lord Jesus Christ, and bestowed upon them the Holy Melchizedek Priesthood, by which authority and apostleship we do dedicate unto Thee, this day, this holy edifice.

PRESIDENT HEBER J. GRANT

We thank Thee for the integrity and the devotion of Thy servants, the Prophet and the Patriarch, Joseph Smith and Hyrum Smith. We thank Thee that they labored all the days of their lives, from the time of the restitution of the Gospel of Jesus Christ until the day of their martyrdom, and that they sealed their testimony with their blood.

HAWAIIAN TEMPLE

Site Dedicated on June 1, 1915. Temple Dedicated on November 27, 1919, by President Heber J. Grant.

We thank Thee for Thy servants Brigham Young, John Taylor, Wilford Woodruff, Lorenzo Snow, and Joseph F. Smith, who have severally stood at the head of Thy Church since the martyrdom of Thy servant Joseph Smith, and who have led and directed Thy people by the inspiration of Thy Holy Spirit, and who have sent forth representatives to proclaim the everlasting gospel in nearly every land and clime.

We thank Thee for all the faithful members of the First Presidency of the Church, and for the Apostles, in this last dispensation; and for each and all of the faithful men who have held office as general authorities of the Church.

O God, our Eternal Father, we pray Thee to bless the Presidency of Thy Church, Thy servants Heber J. Grant, Anthon H. Lund, and Charles W. Penrose. May these men, O Father, be guided by the unerring counsels of Thy Holy Spirit, day by day. May they be even as a three-fold cord that cannot be broken. May they see eye to eye in all matters for the upbuilding of the Church of Jesus Christ upon the earth.

Bless, O Father, each and all of the Apostles, the Presiding Patriarch, the First Council of the Seventy, and the Presiding Bishopric.

Bless, we beseech Thee, those who preside in all the stakes of Zion, and in all the wards and branches of the Church.

Bless those who preside over the missions of the Church throughout the world together with all Thy servants and handmaidens who have gone forth to proclaim to the peoples of the world the restoration again to the earth of the plan of life and salvation.

Bless those, O Father, who preside in the temples that have been erected to Thy Holy Name in the land of Zion. Bless, also, those who preside and who labor in the Church schools which have been established from Canada on the north to Mexico on the south.

O God, accept of the gratitude and thanksgiving of our hearts, for the very wonderful and splendid labors performed in the land of Hawaii by Thy servants President George Q. Cannon and Joseph F. Smith. We thank Thee for their devotion to the gospel and to the people of this land. We thank Thee for raising up Thy servant Elder J. H. Napela, that devoted Hawaiian, who assisted Thy servant President Cannon in the translation of the Book of Mormon, which is the sacred history of the Nephites, the Lamanites, and the Jaredites. We thank Thee that the plates containing the Book of Mormon were preserved so that they could be translated, and that Thy words to the Prophet Joseph Smith might be fulfilled; namely, "That the Lamanites might come to the knowledge of their fathers, and that they might know the promises of the Lord, and that they may believe the gospel and rely upon the merits of Jesus Christ, and be glorified through faith in His name, and that through their repentance they might be saved."

We thank Thee, that thousands and tens of thousands of the descendants of Lehi, in this favored land, have come to a knowledge of the gospel, many of whom have endured faithfully to the end of their lives. We thank Thee, our Father and our God, that those who are living and who have embraced the gospel are now to have the privilege of entering into this holy house, and laboring for the salvation of the souls of their ancestors.

We thank Thee that on this occasion the widow of Thy beloved servant, George Q. Cannon, even Thine handmaiden, Sister Sarah Jenne Cannon, is present with us today, and is permitted to participate in these dedicatory services.

We thank thee, O Father in Heaven, for our families, our friends, our relatives, and for all the many blessings which Thou hast bestowed upon us.

We thank Thee for all of the temples that have been erected in this last dispensation, and we pray Thy choice blessings to be and abide with all those who minister therein. We pray that that same sweet spirit which is present in all of the temples, may abide with those who shall labor in this holy house.

We thank Thee, O Father, this day, that the promise made in a dream to Thy servant William W. Cluff, by Thy Prophet Brigham Young, that the day would come when a temple should be erected in this land, is fulfilled before our eyes.

We thank Thee, O God, that Thy faithful and diligent servant, President Joseph F. Smith, was moved upon, while in this land, on the birthday of Thy servant President Brigham Young, in the year 1915, to dedicate this spot of ground for the erection of a temple to the Most High God.

We thank Thee for the long and faithful and diligent labors of Thy servant President Samuel E. Woolley, who has so faithfully presided over this mission for these many years. We thank Thee for his labors in the erection of this temple, and beseech Thee, O Father, that Thou wilt bless him and all of his associate workers.

We pray Thee, O Father, to bless the son of Thy beloved servant President Joseph F. Smith, E. Wesley Smith, who now presides over the Hawaiian mission. May the missionary spirit be and abide with him. May he have that same splendid love for the people of this land which his dear departed father possessed.

We now thank Thee, O God, our Eternal Father, for this beautiful temple and the grounds upon which it stands, and we dedicate the grounds and the building, with all its furnishings and fittings, and everything pertaining thereunto, from the foundation to the roof thereof, to Thee, our Father and our God. And we humbly pray Thee, O God, the Eternal Father, to accept of it and to sanctify it, and to consecrate it through Thy Spirit for the holy purposes for which it has been erected.

We beseech Thee that no unclean thing shall be permitted to enter here, and that Thy Spirit may ever dwell in this holy house

and rest mightily upon all who shall labor as officers and workers
in this house, as well as all who shall come here to perform ordinances for the living or for the dead.

May Thy peace ever abide in this holy building, that all who
come here may partake of the spirit of peace, and of the sweet
and heavenly influence that Thy Saints have experienced in other
temples, and that has also been experienced in visiting the monument and cottage erected at the birthplace of Thy servant Joseph
Smith, the great latter-day prophet.

May all who come upon the grounds which surround this temple, in the years to come, whether members of the Church of
Christ or not, feel the sweet and peaceful influence of this blessed
and hallowed spot.

And now that this temple is completed and ordinance work
will soon be commenced, we beseech Thee, O Father, that Thou
wilt open the way before the members of the Church in these
lands, as well as of the natives of New Zealand, and of all the
Pacific islands, to secure the genealogies of their forefathers, so
that they may come into this holy house and become saviors
unto their ancestors.

We thank Thee, O God, our Eternal Father, that the land of
Palestine, the land where our Savior and Redeemer ministered in
the flesh, where He gave to the world the plan of life and salvation, is now redeemed from the thralldom of the unbeliever, and
is in the hands of the great, enlightened and liberty-loving empire
of Great Britain. We acknowledge Thy hand, O God, in the
wonderful events which have led up to the partial redemption of
the land of Judah, and we beseech Thee, O Father, that the Jews
may, at no far distant date, be gathered home to the land of
their forefathers.

We thank Thee that Thy servants, the Prophets Joseph Smith
and Brigham Young, were moved upon to send holy apostles to
Jerusalem to dedicate that land for the return of the Jews.

We acknowledge Thy hand, O God, our Heavenly Father, that
one of the benefits of the great and terrible world war, through
which the nations of the earth have recently passed, will be the
opportunity for the Jews to return to the land of their fathers.

We thank Thee, our Father in Heaven, for the victory which
came to the armies of the Allies, and we beseech Thee that that
victory may lead to increased liberty and peace throughout all
the nations of the earth.

We pray for Thy blessings to be upon the kings, and upon the
nobles, and upon the rulers in all nations, that they may have it
in their hearts to administer justice and righteousness and to give
liberty and freedom to the peoples over whom they rule.

We thank Thee that Thou didst inspire the noble men who
wrote the Constitution of our beloved country, and we beseech
Thee that the principles of that inspired document may ever be

maintained; that the people may overcome selfishness and strife, and contention, and all bitterness, and that they may grow and increase in the love of country, in loyalty and patriotism, and in a determination to do that which is right and just.

We thank Thee for this land of liberty in which we dwell, which Thou hast said is choice above all other lands. We do thank Thee, O God our Father, for the noble men who have presided over our country from the days of George Washington until the present time.

We pray Thee to bless Woodrow Wilson, the president of these United States. Touch him with the healing power of Thy Holy Spirit and make him whole. We pray that his life may be precious in Thy sight, and may the inspiration that comes from Thee ever abide with him.

We pray for the vice-president of the United States, for the members of the president's cabinet, for the senators and congressmen, and for all the officers of this great and glorious government in every state and territory, and in every land where the United States bears rule. We also remember before Thee, all those who have been selected to administer the law in this favored land of Hawaii.

We beseech Thee, O God in heaven, that the people of the United States of America may ever seek to Thee for guidance and direction, that Thy declaration and promise that this is a land choice above all other lands, and shall be protected against all foes, provided the people serve Thee, may be realized and fulfilled, and that the people may grow in power and strength and dominion, and, above all, in love of Thy truth.

We thank Thee, O God, that Thy Son, our Redeemer, after being crucified and laying down His life for the sins of the world, did open the prison doors and proclaim the gospel of repentance unto those who had been disobedient in the days of Noah, and that He subsequently came to the land of America, where He established His Church and chose disciples to guide the same.

We thank Thee for restoring again to the earth the ordinances of the gospel of Thy Son Jesus Christ whereby men and women can be, in very deed, saviors upon Mount Zion, and where they can enter into Thy holy temples and perform the ordinances necessary for the salvation of those who have died without a knowledge of the gospel.

We thank Thee, O Father, above all things upon the face of the earth, for the gospel of Thy Son Jesus Christ, and for the Priesthood of the living God, and that we have been made partakers of the same, and have an abiding knowledge of the divinity of the work in which we are engaged.

We thank Thee for the words of Thy Son Jesus Christ to the Prophet Joseph Smith and Sidney Rigdon: "This is the gospel, the glad tidings which the voice out of the heavens bore record unto us, that He came into the world, even Jesus, to be crucified for the world, and to bear the sins of the world, and to sanctify the world, and to cleanse it from all unrighteousness, that through him all might be saved whom the Father had put into his power and made by him; who glorifies the Father and saves all the works of his hands."

We thank Thee, O Father, that Thou didst send Thy Son Jesus Christ, to visit Thy servants Joseph Smith and Oliver Cowdery in the Kirtland temple, the first temple ever erected by Thy people in this last dispensation. We thank Thee for the words of our Redeemer: "I am the first and the last. I am He who liveth. I am He who was slain. I am your advocate with the Father. Behold your sins are forgiven you, you are clean before me, therefore, lift up your heads and rejoice, and let the hearts of your brethren rejoice, and let the hearts of all my people rejoice, who have with their might, built this house to my name, for behold, I have accepted this house, and my name shall be here, and I will manifest myself to my people in mercy in this house."

We thank Thee, O God, that Thou hast accepted, by the testimony of Thy Holy Spirit, all of the temples that have been erected from the days of Kirtland until this present one.

We also thank Thee for sending Thy servants, Moses and Elias and Elijah, to the Kirtland temple, and delivering to Thy servants, Joseph and Oliver, the keys of every dispensation of the gospel of Jesus Christ from the days of Father Adam down to the present dispensation, which is the dispensation of the fulness of times.

We thank Thee, that Elijah has appeared and that the prophecy of Thy servant Malachi, that the hearts of the fathers should be turned to the children, and the hearts of the children to the fathers, lest the earth be smitten with a curse, has been fulfilled in our day, and that our hearts in very deed, go out to our fathers; and we rejoice beyond our ability to express that we can, through the ordinances of the gospel of Jesus Christ, become saviors of our ancestors.

We thank Thee, O God, with all our hearts and souls for the testimony of Thy servants Joseph Smith and Sidney Rigdon: "And now, after the many testimonies which have been given of him, this is the testimony last of all, which we give of him, that he lives; for we saw him, even on the right hand of God, and we heard the voice bearing record that he is the Only Begotten of the Father; that by him and through him, and of him the worlds are and were created, and the inhabitants thereof are begotten sons and daughters unto God."

We thank Thee, O Father, for the knowledge that we possess in our very souls, that Thou dost live, and that Thy Son Jesus is our Redeemer, and our Savior, and that Thy servant, Joseph Smith, Jr., was and is a prophet of the true and living God. And,

O Father, may we ever be true and faithful to the gospel of Thy Son Jesus Christ, revealed through Thy servant Joseph.

We beseech Thee, O Lord, that Thou wilt stay the hand of the destroyer among the natives of this land, and give unto them increasing virility and more abundant health, that they may not perish as a people, but that from this time forth they may increase in numbers and in strength and influence, that all the great and glorious promises made concerning the descendants of Lehi, may be fulfilled in them; that they may grow in vigor of body and of mind, and above all in a love for Thee and Thy Son, and increase in diligence and in faithfulness in the keeping of the commandments which have come to them through the gospel of Jesus Christ.

We pray Thee, O Father, to bless this land that it may be fruitful, that it may yield abundantly, and that all who dwell thereon may be prospered in righteousness.

Bless all Thy people who have named Thy name in all parts of the world. Especially bless Thy people in the Valleys of the Mountains, whereunto they were led by Thy divine guidance, and where the greatest of all temples in this dispensation has been erected, and where Thou hast blessed and prospered Thy people even beyond anything that could have been expected.

Bless, O Father in Heaven, all Thy servants and handmaidens who hold responsible positions in all the various auxiliary organizations of Thy Church, whether as general, stake, ward, or mission authorities; in the Relief Societies, in the Mutual Improvement associations, in the Sunday schools, in the Primary association, and in the Religion Class organizations. Bless each and every one who is laboring for the benefit of the members, as well as the members themselves, in these associations.

We especially pray Thee, O Father in Heaven, to bless the youth of Thy people in Zion and in all the world. Shield and preserve and protect them from the adversary and from wicked and designing men. Keep the youth of Thy people, O Father, in the straight and narrow path that leads to Thee; preserve them from all pitfalls and snares that are laid for their feet. O Father, may our children grow up in the nurture and testimony of the divinity of this work as Thou has given it unto us, and preserve them in purity and in the truth.

O God, our Heavenly and Eternal Father, sanctify the words which we have spoken, and accept of the dedication of this house, we beseech Thee, in the name of Thine Only Begotten Son Jesus Christ our Redeemer. We have dedicated this house unto Thee by virtue of the Priesthood of the Living God which we hold, and we most earnestly pray that this sacred building may be a place in which Thou shalt delight to pour out Thy Holy Spirit in great abundance, and in which Thy Son may see fit to manifest Himself and to instruct Thy servants. In the name of Jesus Christ our Redeemer. Amen and Amen.

Improvement Era, Vol. 23, No. 4, February, 1920.

Physical and Historical Description

The erection of a Temple in the Hawaiian Islands has been the dream of many devoted and faithful Saints of the Polynesian Race since the Gospel was first promulgated to them in 1850 by George Q. Cannon, Joseph F. Smith, and hundreds of other faithful Elders. The native Saints looked forward to the time when the prophecy made by George Q. Cannon would be realized, namely, the erection of a Temple in those far off islands. Its fulfillment began when President Joseph F. Smith and party visited the Island of Hawaii and dedicated the site for a Temple on June 1, 1915, at Laie, on the Island of Oahu, one of the northern group of the Hawaiian Islands.

The Hawaiian Temple is located on what is known as the "Plantation of Laie," a 6,500-acre tract located about thirty-two miles north of Honolulu, purchased for the Church of Jesus Christ of Latter-day Saints by Elder Francis A. Hammond in 1865, and in part has been utilized since as a sugar plantation and the gathering place for the native Latter-day Saints of the Hawaiian group of islands. The site of the Temple is on a moderately high hill of eminence commanding an unobstructed view of the Pacific Ocean.

HAWAIIAN TEMPLE
By
Howard W. Burton, Architect

This Temple was dedicated on November 27, 1919, by President Heber J. Grant. Hyrum C. Pope and Harold W. Burton were the Architects of the Temple as originally built from 1915 to 1917. Ralph E. Woolley was superintendent of construction. The dedication of the Temple was delayed until 1919 owing to the First World War.

Additions to the Temple and the Bureau of Information made in 1938 were designed by Harold W. Burton, Architect. Ralph E. Woolley was Superintendent of Construction.

Douglas W. Burton was the Architect for the 1962 Additions to the Temple and the new Bureau of Information built during 1962. Joseph E. Wilson was Superintendent of Construction for both projects.

A striking feature of the Temple's exterior are the four sculptured panels illustrative of the four Dispensations of the Gospel, namely, the "Old Testament" Dispensation, the "New Testament" Dispensation, the "Book of Mormon" and the "Latter-Day" Dispensations. The principal characters of each of these Dispensations are clearly depicted. These four sculptures form a freize occupying the upper portion of the four faces of the central truncated tower. These sculptures are the work of Leo and Avard Fairbanks.

The Hawaiian Temple is one of the earliest examples of Architectural concrete in America. All of the architectural details, including ornamental elements, and the sculptured freizes are of concrete, cast integrally and monolithicly with the exterior walls of the building. The entire structural elements of the Temple, including its foundations, exterior and interior walls, floors, roofs, beams, columns and girders, are of reinforced concrete, laced together with steel bars, built to resist the ravishes of time.

The Temple proper is built in the form of a Crecian Cross, measuring seventy-six feet over the arms of the cross in both directions. The Temple faces east. The Annex to the Temple, as originally built, extended 23 feet in front and to the east of the Temple proper and was 76 feet wide from north to south. In 1938 the Temple Annex was increased by two extensions, one on the north and one on the south side of the Annex, increasing the width to 140 feet. In 1962 the Temple Annex was further enlarged with additions extending to the north and south, making the total width of the Annex 270 feet.

The Temple is situated on a commanding site, set among the lush greenery of Hawaii, overlooking the blue Pacific ocean, on the windward side of the Island of Oahu, forty miles from Honolulu. The Temple rests on a natural semi-circular base at an elevation of twenty-three feet above the ocean. One gets an unobstructed view of the ocean from the upper semi-circular terrace, looking eastward down through the palm-lined water court, through the forecourt of the New Bureau of Information to the main approach Avenue which is on the east and west axis of the Temple. This Avenue is a two-lane street 100 feet wide, divided in the center with tall, stately Auracia pines, native to many of the South Pacific Islands. These trees make a most harmonious contrast to the tall Royal Palms lining the water court and final approach to the Temple.

After leaving the broad avenue leading from the ocean up to the Temple, one enters the forecourt of the new Bureau of Information which connects with the gradual ascending palm-lined water court. This court is 100 feet wide and 380 feet long, divided into four separate terraces, each provided with a reflecting pool twenty feet wide and eighty feet long.

The new Bureau of Information is divided into two seperate symmetrical sections divided by a forecourt 184 feet wide from north to south and 192 feet deep from east to west. The forecourt is land-scaped with exotic tropical foilage in addition to a pool 112 feet wide and 54 feet from front to back on its center axis. An electrical water fountain presents a spectacular display of ever-changing colored water, spouting a foaming spray high above the surface of the pool.

The small original Bureau built when the Temple was erected no longer functioned adequately. Tourist travel had increased many fold. The Temple had become a major point of interest in Hawaii.

I was just saying, brethren and sisters (Brother Woolley had finished speaking to the Saints in the Hawaiian language), that this land, the land of Laie, was one of the cities of refuge in olden times and I was telling them that now it is a city of refuge indeed, both to the spirit and body of man. William W. Cluff saw in vision President Young upon this land and talked with him, and President Young told him that "upon this land we will build a Temple unto our God." Later on when President George Q. Cannon visited here, fifty years after the Gospel had been established, he told us, both at Laie and Honolulu, that the time would come when we would have a house in which to perform the ordinances necessary for the salvation of the living and the dead.

(Proceedings of the Dedication of the Hawaiian Temple on November 27, 1919.)

By Samuel E. Woolley

Presidents of the Hawaiian Temple:

William M. Waddoups.
Castle H. Murphy.
William M. Waddoups.
Albert H. Belliston.
Edward L. Clissold.
Castle H. Murphy.
Ralph E. Woolley.
Benjamin Bowring.
Ray E. Dillman, 1956-1960.
H. Roland Tietjen, 1960-1963.
Edward L. Clissold, 1963—Present Incumbent.

ALBERTA TEMPLE

Site Dedicated on July 27, 1913. Temple Dedicated on August 26, 1923, by President Heber J. Grant.

Chapter VIII

THE ALBERTA TEMPLE

DEDICATORY PRAYER

By

President Heber J. Grant
(August 26, 1923)

O God, the Eternal Father, we, Thy servants and handmaidens, thank Thee, in the name of Jesus Christ, Thy well-beloved Son, with all the power of our being, that we are privileged this day to be present in this choice land to dedicate unto Thy most Holy Name, a temple of the Living God.

We thank Thee, O God, the Eternal Father, that Thou and Thy Son, Jesus Christ, did visit the boy, Joseph Smith, Jr., and that he was instructed by Thee, and by Thy Beloved Son.

We thank Thee that Thou didst send Thy servant, John the Baptist, and that he did lay his hands upon Joseph Smith and Oliver Cowdery and ordain them to the Aaronic, or Lesser Priesthood.

We thank Thee for sending Thy servants Peter, James and John, Apostles of the Lord Jesus Christ, who ministered with the Savior in the flesh and after His crucifixion, and that they did ordain Thy servants Joseph Smith and Oliver Cowdery, Apostles of the Lord Jesus Christ, and bestow upon them the Holy Melchizedek Priesthood, by which authority and apostleship we do dedicate unto Thee, this day, this holy edifice.

We thank Thee for the integrity and the devotion of Thy servants, the Prophet and Patriarch, Joseph Smith and Hyrum Smith. We thank Thee that they labored in Thy cause all the days of their lives, from the time of restoration of the gospel of Jesus Christ until the day of their martyrdom, and that they were faithful even to the sealing of their testimony with their blood.

We thank Thee for Thy servants, Brigham Young, John Taylor, Wilford Woodruff, Lorenzo Snow, and Joseph F. Smith, who have severally stood at the head of Thy Church since the martyrdom of Thy servant Joseph Smith, and who have led and directed Thy people by the inspiration of Thy Holy Spirit, and who have sent forth representatives to proclaim the everlasting gospel in nearly every land and clime.

We thank Thee for all the faithful members of the First Presidency of the Church, and for the Apostles, in this last dispensation; and for each and all of the faithful men who have ministered as general authorities of the Church.

O God, our Eeternal Father, we pray Thee to bless the Presidency of Thy Church—Thy servants, Heber J. Grant, Charles W.

Penrose, and Anthony W. Ivins. May these men, O Father, be guided by the unerring counsels of Thy Holy Spirit, day by day. May they be even as a three-fold cord that cannot be broken. May they see eye to eye in all matters for the upbuilding of the Church of Jesus Christ upon the earth.

Bless, O Father, each and all of the Apostles, the Presiding Patriarch, the First Council of the Seventy, and the Presiding Bishopric. We particularly pray for Thy choice blessings to be with President Charles W. Penrose, and Elders Reed Smoot, Orson F. Whitney, and David O. McKay, who are unable to be present on this occasion.

Bless, we beseech Thee, those who preside in all the stakes of Zion, and in all the wards and branches of the Church, and over the various quorums of the Priesthood, whether of the Melchizedek or of the Aaronic Priesthood.

Bless those who preside over the missions of the Church throughout the world, together with all Thy servants and handmaidens who have gone forth to proclaim to the peoples of the world the restoration to the earth of the plan of life and salvation.

Bless those, O Father, who have been called to preside and labor in this temple and also in other temples that have been erected to Thy Holy Name in the land of Zion and in the Hawaiian Islands. We thank Thee for all of the temples that have been erected in this last dispensation, and we pray Thy choice blessings to be and abide with all those who minister therein. We pray that the same sweet spirit which is present in all of the temples that have heretofore been erected may abide with all those who shall labor in this holy house.

Bless those who preside and who labor in the Church schools which have been established from Canada on the north to Mexico in the south, and in the far off islands of the Pacific Ocean.

Bless, O Father in Heaven, all Thy servants and handmaidens who hold responsible positions in the various auxiliary organizations of Thy Church, whether as general, stake, ward or mission officers; in the Relief Societies, in the Sunday schools, in the Mutual Improvement associations, in the Primary association, and in the Religion Class organizations. Bless each and everyone who is laboring for the benefit of the members as well as the members themselves in these associations.

We thank Thee that Thy servant, President John Taylor, and many other residents of the Dominion of Canada, came to a knowledge of the gospel and remained steadfast to the end of their lives. We thank Thee, our Father, and our God, for those now living, who embraced the gospel in this choice land and others who have emigrated from the United States and other countries to Canada, and that they are now to have the privilege of entering into this holy house and laboring for the salvation of their ancestors.

We thank Thee, O God, for the inspiration by which Thy faithful and diligent servant, President Joseph F. Smith, was moved upon to direct the construction of a temple in this favored land; and that he had the privilege of visiting this spot of ground upon which this temple now stands, and dedicating the same for the erection of a temple to the Most High God.

We thank Thee for the long and faithful and diligent labors of Thy servant, President Charles O. Card, the pioneer in this section and after whom this city was named, and for the faithful and diligent men who have labored in the presiding offices in the stakes of Zion established here in Alberta.

We thank Thee, O God, our Eternal Father, that the land of Palestine, the land where our Savior and Redeemer ministered in the flesh where He gave to the world the plan of life and salvation, is now redeemed from the thralldom of the unbeliever, and is now under the fostering care of the great, enlightened and liberty-loving empire of Great Britain. We acknowledge Thy hand, O God, in the wonderful events which have led up to the partial redemption of the land of Judah, and we beseech Thee, O Father, that the Jews may, at no far distant date, be gathered home to the land of their fathers.

We thank Thee that Thy servants, the Prophets Joseph Smith and Brigham Young, were moved upon to send Apostles to Jerusalem to dedicate that land for the return of the Jews.

We acknowledge Thy hand, O God, our Heavenly Father, in the fact that one of the benefits of the great World War, through which the nations of the earth have recently passed, is the opportunity afforded the Jews to return to the land of their fathers.

We beseech Thee, our Father in heaven, that the victory which came to the cause of the Allies may lead to increased liberty and peace throughout all the nations of the earth.

We pray that Thy blessings may be upon kings, rulers and nobles, in all nations, that they may minister in justice and righteousness and give liberty and freedom to the peoples over whom they rule.

We thank Thee that the spirit of justice and righteousness has characterized the rulers in the British Empire, and we humbly beseech Thee that the people of this great nation and the people of the world may overcome selfishness and refrain from strife, contention, and all bitterness, and that they may grow and increase in the love of country, in loyalty and patriotism and in a determination to do what is right and just.

We beseech Thee, O God in Heaven, that the people of Canada may ever seek Thee for guidance and direction, that Thy declaration that the American continent is a land choice above all other lands, and Thy promise that it shall be protected against all foes, provided the people serve Thee, may be fulfilled, and that the people may grow in power, and strength and dominion, and, above all, in a love of Thy truth.

We thank Thee, O Father in heaven, for the splendid treatment that has been accorded by the officials in the Dominion of Canada to those of Thy people who have immigrated to this country, and we humbly pray Thee to aid Thy sons and Thy daughters who have taken upon them Thy name so to order their lives in righteousness and truth that they may retain the good will of the people this country and merit the same because of their good works.

We thank Thee, O God, that Thy Son, our Redeemer, after having been crucified and having laid down his life for the sins of the world, did open the prison doors and proclaim the gospel of repentance unto those who had been disobedient in the days of Noah, and that He subsequently came to the land of America, where he established His Church and chose disciples to guide the same.

We thank Thee for restoring again to the earth the ordinances of the gospel of Thy Son Jesus Christ, whereby men and women can be, in very deed, saviors upon Mount Zion, and where they can enter into Thy holy temples and perform the ordinances necessary for the salvation of those who have died without a knowledge of the gospel.

We thank Thee, O Father, above all things, for the gospel of Thy Son Jesus Christ, and for the Priesthood of the living God, and that we have been made partakers of the same, and have an abiding knowledge of the divinity of the work in which we are engaged.

We thank Thee for the words of Thy Son Jesus Christ to the Prophet Joseph Smith and Sidney Rigdon: "This is the gospel, the glad tidings which the voice out of the heavens bore record unto us, that he came into the world, even Jesus, to be crucified for the world, and to bear the sins of the world, and to sanctify the world, and to cleanse it from all unrighteousness, that through Him all might be saved whom the Father had put into His power and made by Him, who glorifies the Father, and saves all the works of His hands."

We thank Thee, O Father, that Thou didst send Thy son Jesus Christ, to visit Thy servants Joseph Smith and Oliver Cowdery in the Kirtland temple, the first temple erected by Thy people in this last dispensation. We thank Thee for the words of our Redeemer spoken in that temple: "I am the first and the last: I am He who liveth; I am He who was slain; I am your advocate with the Father. Behold, your sins are forgiven you; you are clean before me; therefore, lift up your heads and rejoice. Let the hearts of your brethren rejoice, and let the hearts of all my people rejoice, who have, with their might, built this house to My name. For behold, I have accepted this house, and My name shall be here; and I will manifest Myself to my people in mercy in this house."

We thank Thee, O God, that by the testimony of Thy Holy Spirit Thou hast manifested Thine acceptance of the several temples that have been erected from the days of Kirtland until this present time.

We also thank Thee for sending Thy servants, Moses and Elias, and Elijah, to the Kirtland temple, to confer upon Thy servants, Joseph and Oliver, the keys of every dispensation of the gospel of Jesus Christ from the days of Father Adam down to the present dispensation, which is the dispensation of the fulness of times.

We thank Thee that, through the visitation of Elijah, the prophecy of Thy servant Malachi—that the hearts of the fathers should be turned to the children, and the hearts of the children to the fathers, lest the earth be smitten with a curse—has been fulfilled in our day, and that our hearts in very deed go out to our fathers; and we rejoice beyond our ability to express that we can, through the ordinances of the gospel of Jesus Christ, become saviors of our ancestors.

We thank Thee, O God, with all our hearts for the testimony of Thy servants Joseph Smith and Sidney Rigdon: "And now, after the many testimonies which have been given of Him, this is the testimony, last of all, which we give of Him: that He lives! For we saw Him, even on the right hand of God; and we heard the voice bearing record that He is the only Begotten of the Father—that by Him, and through Him, and of Him, the worlds are and were created, and the inhabitants thereof are begotten sons and daughters unto God."

We thank Thee, O Father, for the knowledge which we possess, that Thou dost live, and that Thy Son Jesus Christ is our Redeemer, and our Savior, and that Thy servant, Joseph Smith, Jr., was and is a prophet of the true and living God. And, O Father, may we ever be true and faithful to the gospel of Thy Son Jesus Christ, revealed through Thy servant Joseph.

We beseech Thee, O Lord, that Thou wilt stay the hand of the destroyer among the descendants of Lehi, who reside in this land, and give unto them increasing virility and more abundant health, that they may not perish as a people, but that from this time forth they may increase in numbers and in strength and in influence, that all the great and glorious promises made concerning the descendants of Lehi, may be fulfilled in them; that they may grow in vigor of body and of mind, and above all in love for Thee and Thy Son, and increase in diligence and in faithfulness in keeping the commandments which have come to them through the gospel of Jesus Christ, and that many of them may yet have the privilege of entering this holy house and receiving ordinances for themselves and their departed ancestors.

We pray Thee, O Father, to bless this land that it may be fruitful, that it may yield abundantly, and that all who dwell hereon may be prospered in righteousness.

Bless Thy people in all parts of the world. Continue to remember Thy Saints in the Valleys of the Mountains, whereunto they were led by Thy divine guidance, and where the greatest of all temples in this dispensation has been erected, and where Thou hast blessed and prospered Thy people even beyond all that could have been expected.

We especially pray Thee, O Father in Heaven, to bless the youth of Thy people in Zion and in all the world. Shield them from the adversary and from wicked and designing men. Keep the youth of Thy people, O Father, in the straight and narrow path that leads to Thee, preserve them from the pitfalls and snares that are laid for their feet. O Father, may our children grow up in the nurture and admonition of the Lord Jesus Christ. Give unto them a testimony of the divinity of this work as Thou hast given it unto us, and preserve them in purity and in the truth.

We now thank Thee, O God, our Eternal Father, for this beautiful temple and the ground upon which it stands, and we dedicate the building, with its grounds, with all its furnishings and fittings, and everything pertaining thereunto, from the foundation to the roof hereof, to Thee, our Father and our God. And we humbly pray Thee, O God, the Eternal Father, to accept of it and to sanctify it, and to consecrate it through Thy Spirit to the holy purposes for which it has been erected.

We beseech Thee to enable us so to guard this house that no unclean thing shall enter here. May Thy Spirit ever dwell in this holy house and rest upon all who shall labor as officers and workers herein, as well as upon all who shall come here to perform ordinances for the living or for the dead.

May Thy peace ever abide in this holy building, that all who come here may partake of the spirit of peace and of the sweet and heavenly influence that Thy Saints have experienced in other temples. Protect this building from the powers and elements of destruction.

May all who come upon the grounds which surround this temple, whether members of the Church of Christ or not, feel the sweet and peaceful influence of this blessed and hallowed spot.

O God, our Heavenly and Eternal Father, sanctify the words which we have spoken, and accept of the dedication of this house, and these grounds, which we have dedicated unto Thee by virtue of the Priesthood of the Living God which we hold, and we most earnestly pray that this sacred building may be a place in which Thy Son may see fit to manifest Himself and to instruct Thy servants, and in which Thou shall delight to dwell.

All this we ask and do in the authority of the Holy Priesthood and in the name of Thine Only Begotten Son, Jesus Christ
our Redeemer. Amen and Amen.
                    —Improvement Era, Vol. 26, No. 12, October, 1923, p. 1075.

Physical and Historical Description

On June 3, 1887, there arrived at Lees Creek, Alberta, now
the site of the town of Cardston, a company of immigrants from
Utah. The land at that time being unsurveyed, save the south
boundary of the Blood Indian Reservation, they "squatted" on
the open prairies on and near the present location of the town,
the latter being then the homestead and pre-emption of Charles
Ora Card, the leader of the Colony. This he divided into eight-
acre squares and on the highest elevation within a half-mile, an
eight-acre block was given to the Church of Jesus Christ of Latter-day Saints by this loyal pioneer, who called it Tabernacle
Square, and evidently intended that on it the main Church for
the town and district some day should be built. Soon others settled in what was then termed "Card Ward" but which was soon
changed to "Cardston," and in 1889 some two hundred to three
hundred people had found here a new home. Among the settlers
was an Apostle of the Church, John W. Taylor. To this little
pioneer band, then living on the cattle range of the West, he
made a prophetic utterance: "This land will yet become a bread-
basket to the world; and in this land a Temple shall be reared
to the worship of Almighty God." * * *

On July 27, 1913, in the presence of probably 1,500 members and friends, Joseph F. Smith, President of the Church,
dedicated this Tabernacle Square as the Temple site.

On November 9th of the same year, a large number of
people gathered to witness the breaking of ground as the beginning of the erection of this building. Daniel Kent Greene, of
Glenwoodville, turned the first furrow of sod. Work was immediately commenced, and by September 19, 1915, the laying
of the cornerstone ceremony was conducted by David O. Mc-
Kay of the Council of Twelve Apostles. Under the draped
Union Jack and amid bunting and flag decorations, an impressive service was held despite rain and sleet which was inter-

mittently falling. Within the hollowed stone and a copper-seal-ed box were placed various coins, a complete set of Church books, a history of Cardston, and several photographs and auto-graphs of importance.

The capstone laying took place on the 23rd of September, 1917, the service being in charge of President Edward J. Wood of Cardston; the dedicatory prayer being offered by Patriarch Henry L. Hinman. For this occasion a temporary auditorium was erected in the middle part of the unfinished structure. Some 1,500 to 2,000 people were in attendance and saw the stone placed in position by President Heber S. Allen of Raymond, Alberta. The edifice was completed during the summer of 1921.

This Temple was dedicated on August 26, 1923 by Presi-dent Heber J. Grant. Hyrum C. Pope and Harold W. Burton were the Architects. William Baxter was the Supervisor of Con-struction. Extensive alterations and additions were made to the Temple in 1955. Harold W. Burton served as the Architect for this project. These alterations and additions are incorpor-ated in this write-up (1965).

Approaching the town of Cardston from any direction, the large white straight lines of the Temple are the first things that greet and attract the eye. Impressive and unique, it occupies a distinctive place of its own in the historic field of architecture. It has the Grecian massiveness, a Peruvan touch, and is similar only to the ancient temples of the Aztecs and other aborigines of Central and South America, ruins of which have been dis-covered in recent years. The optic impression is that of the pyramid or the huge pile effect.

The site of the Temple is on a pronounced elevation, around which a cluster of dwellings is grouped, housing the inhabitants of the prairie town of Cardston.

The plan arrangement of the Temple proper is octagonal in shape, similar in outline to a Maltese Cross, and is 100 feet by 100 feet over its main dimensions. The Temple sets on a stylobate 165 feet by 165 feet, ten feet in height from its sur-rounding grade to the top of its coping. The tip to the capstone is 92 feet above the finished street grade on the west side of the Temple. Viewed from a distance and from any angle, the outline of the building gives the impression of a "great pile" of white granite inclining from the four main sides and the four lesser sides to the topmost point. The roof over the central part of the building is pryamidical in form, thirty feet square at its base and is roofed with 81 huge granite slabs which interlock together making this stone roof thoroughly waterproof. The capstone which sets at the apex of the pyramid weighs 3200 pounds.

A striking feature of the Temple's exterior is a sculptured panel thirty-three feet wide and six feet in height setting at the east end of the forecourt. The sculpture depicts Jesus of Nazareth with "The Samaritan woman at the well," showing the Savior in the attitude of saying He would give the woman of "living water." This sculpture is the work of Torlief Knaphus.

The Temple Bureau of Information is at the extreme west end of the forecourt. This forecourt is 92 feet wide from north to south and 100 feet long from east to west, through which all temple patrons pass before entering the Temple Annex. This court is beautifully landscaped with lawns, flower beds and ornamental shrubbery.

The Temple proper technically faces east, the first Ordinance Room occupying the east bay of the building.

The exterior walls of the Temple and the walk of the Stylobate are faced with an off-white slightly gray granite, crystalline in structure with large quartz crystals which reflect the sun's rays. This granite was quarried and cut at Nelson, B.C., and shipped by rail to Cardston. The frame of the Temple is of structural steel including supporting columns, beams and girders. The foundations, floors, roofs and the backing of the granite faced walls are of reinforced concrete. All of the exterior walls are lined with hollow burned clay tile, which provides the necessary insulation against a rigorous climate. The building is provided with a modern air conditioning system, automatically controlled. A separate building housing the Heating and Electrical lighting plants connects with an underground tunnel with the sub-basement of the Temple.

The principal rooms in the Temple are panelled from floor to the ceiling with rare hardwoods and with painted murals framed into the panelling. The murals occur in the Creation, Garden and World Rooms and in the Temple Chapel and Baptistery. The Creation Room is finished in American rift-grained oak inlaid with ebony and boxwood. The Garden Room is in birdseye maple; the World Room in American Walnut; the Terrestrial Room in South American mahogany inlaid with ebony and boxwood. The Celestial Room is panelled from the top of a marble wainscot up to the ceiling, twenty-five feet in height, with African mahogany, inlaid with vermillion, rosewood, ebony and other rare woods. The wainscot in this room is three feet high and is of golden travis marble quarried in Utah. There are three Sealing Rooms: one panelled in American walnut, one in Circassian walnut, and one in ribbon-grained Tobascan mahogany. All of the furniture in these foregoing rooms was specially designed by the Architects and were executed in woods exactly matching the room in which the furniture occurs.

The walls, column casings, and floor of the Baptistery are of light gray Tennessee marble. The walls of the Initiatory rooms and other rooms throughout the Temple are of the same marble with ceramic tile floors. In the exact center of the Baptistery is the baptismal font, a large sculptured basin supported on the backs of twelve life-sized sculptured oxen, supposedly symbolic of the twelve tribes of Israel. The oxen appear to be emerging from reeded foilage. They are typical of the oxen used by the early Mormon pioneers, but subtlely stylized after the manner of ancient animal sculptures. The font was designed by the Architects after the description in holy writ of the font in Solomon's Temple. The sculpturing is the work of Torlief Knaphus.

President Edward J. Wood was set apart as the first President of the Temple by President Heber J. Grant on the day of its dedication.

By Harold W. Burton, *Architect*

Prophetic Gift Made Manifest
By Nellie T. Taylor

It was one of those rare Canadian mornings in October. The busy pioneers were in the best of spirits. Only the day before, Sunday, October 7, 1888, the Church officials had presided at the first conference held in their new meeting house—20x20½ —completed the previous January. A branch had been organized and named "Cardston" in honor of the man who had blazed the trail two years before and who had decided on the location. There were not enough present to make a full and complete organization, but as each person stepped forward in response to the call and was set apart under the hands of the presiding priesthood, the spirit of expansion seemed to rest upon them. They were not only willing but qualified to assume a double duty of work. The Spirit of the Lord bore testimony to that which was being done and all rejoiced under its influence.

Monday morning had been filled with council meetings, affairs of the Church and of the Dominion. At 10 a.m. when Charles O. Card guided his team up the hill to the west, explaining to his six passengers the survey of the town as he had drawn it, from stake to stake, their eyes beheld the expanse of green, the titanic mass of Rockies lined against the curtain of the sky, the grand "Old Chief" mountain whose summit has not yet been reached by man, towered before them as a bulwark of safety more assuring than an army. The coming of our fathers only a few short decades before to the "strength of the hills" must have inspired that which followed.

Turning again to the east, the white top was drawn to the summit of the elevation overlooking Lees Creek, among the wooded banks of which nestled the few homes in evidence of life and habitation. That was half a century ago.

President Francis M. Lyman, the senior Apostle, informed those present that they had been invited to come on "this morning trip that they might participate in the sacred service of dedicating that land to the habitation of the Saints." He then moved forward until impressed to stop, taking his place facing the east. He said to Apostle John W. Taylor: "You will please stand at my right, your wife Nellie next, President Charles O. Card at my left, his wife Zina Y. next, Bishop John A. Wolf and wife (Mary Hyde) facing me." Thus was a perfect circle formed by seven men and women. At this point he called upon Apostle John W. Taylor to be mouth in the dedicatory prayer. The outpouring of the Spirit of the Lord during the conference the previous day had warmed the hearts of all present but now the Spirit was of a pentecostal nature, accompanied by a divine light. Everything seemed hushed as those present listened to the inspirational words of the prayer. Then there came a pause: "I now speak by the power of prophecy and say that upon this very spot shall be erected a Temple to the name of Israel's God and nations shall come from far and near and praise His high and holy name." It was with mellowed heart and silent lips that those favored few reluctantly moved away from that hallowed spot.

It was during the administration of President Joseph F. Smith that Bishop Charles W. Nibley was dispatched to Canada to consider the advisability of erecting a Temple and of selecting the best locations. Four pictures were taken of suggested locations. While making this report, the four pictures were laid before the President who thoughtfully observed them at a distance. Then lightly touching one, he said: "I feel strongly impressed that this is the one."

The same Spirit was directing the same Priesthood in the fulfillment of the prophecy uttered many years ago.

Loved Ones Looking This Way
By Edward J. Wood, President of Alberta Temple

For several years the Northwestern States Mission Caravan have visited our Alberta Temple in two divisions. The Western division included the States of the Mission such as Washington, Oregon, Vancouver, B.C., and some parts of Idaho; the Eastern division included parts of Idaho and Montana. One division would stay a week in June; the other division would stay a week in July. They called themselves the Northwestern States Mission Caravan. Each Caravan included the Mission President and his wife (President William R. Sloan and Sister Sloan), and the Missionaries laboring in each division. Each family rode in their own car and had their own camping equipment, stopping at tourist camps enroute, and holding outdoor meetings at places where they were given a welcome. The trip usually took two or three days. They aimed to arrive in Cardston on Monday afternoon, and would hold an outdoor street meeting on the main street in Cardston, which was always attended by thousands. On Tuesday they would bring their children to the Temple to do baptismal work—some for their own baptisms and others for the dead. These good Caravan people would always bring names on their own lines to be officiated for and many were present to go through the Temple for the first time for themselves and then have their children sealed to them.

It was during one of the Caravan visits that the following incident happened: Quite an elderly lady (a member of the

Caravan) was in the Temple to do the work for herself and to have the work performed for her husband, and then to be sealed to her husband and their children sealed to them. One of the Elders was acting as proxy for the dead husband and father, and two brethren who were members of the branch to which the old lady belonged were kneeling at the altar as proxy for the dead children—two sons as reported by the old lady.

The sealing room was filled with neighbors and friends who wished to do the old lady honor. As I held the sheet in my hand to seal the two sons whose birth and death, etc., were duly filled out by the old lady (their mother), I was impressed to ask her if these two sons were the only children she had, and she said: "Yes." I then proceeded to seal these sons, when I heard a voice behind me, as I thought, saying: "I am her child." I then stopped and asked again: "Are you sure you never had any other children?" She answered as before, but with some hesitation: "Yes, Brother Wood, the record is right." But I felt sure there was a feeling of doubt in the room, and as I was again about to proceed, the voice again spoke to me with greater emphasis, saying, "I am her daughter." I looked around and into the faces of all who witnessed this wonderful manifestation and then I spoke as kindly as possible to the old lady, saying, "Surely, grandmother, you had a daughter, didn't you?" She then broke into tears and asked that all be seated and said she hoped we would forgive her, as she had a little girl in her early married life, and then a lapse of several years before she had the two boys in their order, and that in her great anxiety to have her work and that of her husband and making of the sheet, to have her children sealed while on this, her first visit to a Temple, she had overlooked recording the name of the little girl. She then asked that she might meet and relate this experience in our devotional exercise the next morning and ask forgiveness of all the Caravan company. In the morning she asked to come to the stand and as she was about to speak she turned to me and asked how I knew she had another child. I then told her what I had heard in the sealing room. She stood in silence and wept for joy as the vast audience did also, as she bore testimony of the nearness of those whom we officiate for in the Temple when the sealing ordinance is being performed for them. The record was then completed and in the afternoon the three children were sealed by proxy at the altar and all witnesses were again in tears and the room seemed filled with an influence most divine.

President Heber J. Grant

President Heber J. Grant was born in Salt Lake City on November 22, 1856, being the son of Jedediah Morgan Grant and Rachel Ridgeway Ivins Grant. His father had passed through all the trying experiences in Missouri and Nauvoo, in the exodus and in the pioneering of Utah up to the time of his death which occurred when Heber was but nine days old, being only forty years of age at the time of his demise.

President Grant was set apart as President of the Church by the Quorum of the Twelve Apostles on November 22, 1918, in the Salt Lake Temple, he being sixty-two years of age at the time. At the Special General Conference of the Church held on June 1, 1919, he was sustained as President of the Church, and as Prophet, Seer and Revelator.

The Hawaiian, Canadian and Arizona Temples were dedicated by him; the Idaho Falls Temple was erected and sites for the Los Angeles and Oakland Temples were purchased by the Church during his administration. He labored early and late for the advancement of the work of the Lord, in doing Temple work himself, in exhorting the Saints both by word of mouth and by pen, to "Keep the Commandments of God," which counsel is the epitome of all instruction—the same as the Redeemer gave two thousand years ago, namely: "Thou shalt love the Lord thy God with all thy mind, might and strength." During his Presidency, the number of wards increased from 839 in 1918 to 1,273 at the present time (1945), the stakes from 75 to 151 and the Missions from 22 to 39. He died on May 14, 1945.

Presidents of Alberta Temple:

Edward J. Wood, 1923-1948

Willard L. Smith, 1948-1955.

Octave W. Ursenbach, 1956—Present Incumbent.

Chapter IX

THE ARIZONA TEMPLE

DEDICATORY PRAYER

By

President Heber J. Grant

(October 23, 1927)

O God, the Eternal Father, we, Thy servants and handmaidens, come to Thee with hearts overflowing with gratitude and in the name of Jesus Christ, Thy Well-Beloved Son, we thank Thee that we are privileged this day to dedicate unto Thy Most Holy Name, a temple of the Living God.

We thank Thee, O God, the Eternal Father, that Thou and Thy Son, Jesus Christ, did visit Joseph Smith, Jr., in his youth, and that he was instructed by Thee and by Thy Beloved Son.

We thank Thee that Thou didst send Thy servant, John the Baptist, and that he did lay his hands upon Joseph Smith and Oliver Cowdery and ordain them to the Aaronic, or Lesser Priesthood.

We thank Thee for sending Thy servants Peter, James and John, Apostles of the Lord Jesus Christ, who ministered with the Savior in the flesh and after His crucifixion, and that they did ordain Thy servants Joseph Smith and Oliver Cowdery, Apostles of the Lord Jesus Christ, and bestow upon them the Holy Melchizedek Priesthood, by which, authority and apostleship we do dedicate unto Thee, this day, this holy edifice.

We thank Thee for sending Thy servant Moroni to deliver the plates from which the Book of Mormon was translated by the gift and power of God. We rejoice before Thee in the influence for good that the Book of Mormon has had in the world, and that it is indeed a new witness for Christ, confirming His teachings as recorded in the Holy Bible. We thank Thee that thousands and hundreds of thousands of Thy children have proved the truth of the testimony of Thy servant Moroni, which he left on record in the book itself: "And when ye shall receive these things, I would exhort you that ye would ask God the Eternal Father, in the name of Christ, if these things are not true, and if ye shall ask with a sincere heart, with real intent, having faith in Christ, he will manifest the truth of it unto you, by the power of the Holy Ghost. And by the power of the Holy Ghost ye may know the truth of all things." Grant, we pray Thee, that the Book of Mormon may have an ever-widening influence in the world and that many more of Thy children may receive the conviction of its truth in their

ARIZONA TEMPLE

Site Dedicated on November 28, 1921. Temple Dedicated on October 23, 1927, by President Heber J. Grant.

hearts. We rejoice that after the lapse of an hundred years, in spite of all the attacks that have been made against its divine authenticity, it still stands unimpeached as the Word of God, and that the evidences brought forth from archaeological and other sources only tend to confirm its truth.

We thank Thee for the integrity and the devotion of Thy servants, the Prophet and Patriarch, Joseph Smith and Hyrum Smith. We thank Thee that they labored in Thy cause all the days of their lives, from the time of the restoration of the Gospel of Jesus Christ until the day of their martyrdom, and that they were faithful even to the sealing of their testimony with their blood.

We thank Thee for Thy servants, who have stood at the head of Thy Church since the martyrdom of Thy servant Joseph Smith, who have led and directed Thy people by the inspiration of the Holy Spirit, and who have sent forth representatives to proclaim an everlasting gospel in nearly every land and clime.

We thank Thee for each and all of the faithful men who have ministered as general authorities of the Church in this last dispensation.

O God, our Eternal Father, we pray Thee to bless the Presidency of Thy Church—Thy servants Heber J. Grant, Anthony W. Ivins and Charles W. Nibley. May they be guided by the unerring counsels of Thy Holy Spirit, day by day. May they be even as a three-fold cord that cannot be broken. May they see eye to eye in all matters for the upbuilding of the Church of Jesus Christ upon the earth.

Bless, O Father, in like manner, each and all of the Apostles, the Presiding Patriarch, the First Council of the Seventy, and the Presiding Bishopric.

Bless, we beseech Thee, those who preside in all the stakes of Zion, and in all the wards and branches of the Church, and over the various quorums of the Priesthood, whether of the Melchizedek or of the Aaronic Priesthood.

Bless those who preside over the missions of the Church throughout the world, together with all Thy servants and hand-maidens who have gone forth to proclaim to the peoples of the world the restoration to the earth of the plan of life and salvation. Be graciously pleased to give the success in their ministry, and grant that every barrier now standing in the way of the proclamation of the gospel may be removed, and liberty of conscience accorded to all peoples.

Bless, O Father in Heaven, all Thy servants and hand-maidens who hold responsible positions in the various auxiliary organizations of Thy Church, whether as general, stake, or ward officers: in the Relief Societies, in the Sunday Schools, in the Mutual Improvement associations, in the Primary associations, Genealogical associations and in the Religion Class organizations. Bless each and every one who is laboring for the benefit of the members, as well as the members themselves, in these associations. Bless likewise those who preside and who labor in the Church schools and seminaries.

Bless those, O Father, who have been called to preside and labor in this temple and also in other temples that have been erected to Thy Holy Name. We thank Thee for all of the temples that have been erected in this last dispensation, and we pray Thee choice blessings to be and abide with all those who minister therein. We pray that the same sweet spirit which is present in all of the temples that have heretofore been erected may abide with all those who shall labor in this holy house.

We pray that Thy blessings may be upon kings and rulers in all nations, that they may minister in justice and righteousness and give liberty and freedom to the peoples over whom they rule.

We thank Thee for this land of liberty in which we dwell, which Thou hast said is "a land choice above all other lands." We are grateful that Thou didst inspire the noble men who framed the Constitution of our beloved country, and we beseech Thee that the principles of that wonderful document may ever be maintained; that contention and bitterness may cease, and that peace and patriotism, love and loyalty, may prevail.

We pray Thee to bless the President of the United States. May he find favor in Thy sight and be governed in all his administration by the principles of righteousness. May Thy blessings also be upon the vice-president, the members of the cabinet, the senators and congressmen, and upon all the officers in every state and territory of the nation.

We beseech Thee, O God in Heaven, that the people of the United States of America may ever seek to Thee for guidance and direction, that Thy declaration and promise that this is a land choice above all other lands, and shall be protected against all foes, provided the people serve Thee, may be realized and fulfilled, and that the people may grow in power and strength and dominion, and, above all, in a love of Thy truth.

We now pray for the State of Arizona, in which this temple has been erected. We thank Thee for the splendid men and women who were pioneers of this land. We thank Thee for their courage and indomitable purpose, and their lofty ideals which sustained them mid hardships and privations. We are grateful that Thou didst bless the land in answer to their toil, and that the desert has been made to blossom as the rose. We thank Thee for the kind and generous treatment that has ever been accorded Thy people who have settled in this state, by the officers thereof. We pray Thee to bless the governor of the state and all who are charged with the administration of the affairs thereof. And may the people who dwell here be blessed and prospered of Thee in righteousness.

We beseech Thee, O Lord, that Thou wilt stay the hand of the destroyer among the descendants of Lehi who reside in this land and give unto them increasing virility and more abundant health, that they may not perish as a people but that from this time forth they may increase in numbers and in strength and in influence, that all the great and glorious promises made concerning the descendants of Lehi may be fulfilled in them; that they may grow in vigor of body and of mind, and above all in love for Thee and Thy Son, and increase in diligence and in faithfulness in keeping the commandments which have come to them through the gospel of Jesus Christ, and that many of them may have the privilege of entering this holy house and receiving ordinances for themselves and their departed ancestors.

We thank Thee, O God, our Eternal Father, that the land of Palestine, the land where our Savior and Redeemer ministered in the flesh, where He gave to the world the plan of life and salvation, is now redeemed from the thralldom of the unbeliever, and is under the fostering care of the great, enlightened, and liberty-loving empire of Great Britain. We acknowledge Thy hand, O God, in the wonderful events which led to the partial redemption of that land, and we now renew the supplication made unto Thee in behalf of Thy covenant people at the dedication of the Salt Lake Temple: "O God of Israel, turn Thy face, we pray Thee, in loving kindness toward Thy stricken people of the House of Judah. Deliver them from those that oppress them. Heal up their wounds, comfort their hearts, strengthen their feet, and give them ministers after Thine own heart who shall lead them, as of old, in Thy way. May the days of their tribulation soon cease, and they be planted by Thee in the valleys and plains of their ancient home; and may Jerusalem rejoice and Judea be glad for the multitude of her sons and daughters, for the sweet voices of children in her streets, and the rich outpouring of Thy saving mercies upon them. May Israel no more bow the head, or bend the neck to the oppressor, but may his feet be made strong on the everlasting hills, never more, by violence, to be banished therefrom, and the praise and the glory shall be Thine."

We remember before Thee Thy people in all parts of the world. May their hearts be turned unto Thee and to the keeping of Thy commandments, that Thy Name may be glorified in the whole earth.

We pray for Thy Saints in distant lands. May they enjoy the companionship of Thy Spirit, and be blessed with increasing faith and power for good. Continue to remember, we pray Thee, Thy Saints in the valleys of the mountains, whereunto they were led by Thy servant Brigham Young and his associates, under divine guidance, and where the greatest of all temples in this dispensation has been erected, and where Thou has blessed and prospred Thy people even beyond all that could have been expected.

We especially pray Thee, O Father in Heaven, to bless the youth of Thy people in Zion and in all the world. Shield them from the adversary and from wicked and designing men. Keep the youth of Thy people in the straight and narrow path that leads to Thee; preserve them from the pitfalls and snares that are laid for their feet. O Father, may our children grow up in the nurture and admonition of the Lord Jesus Christ. Protect them from infidelity and unbelief, and give unto them a testimony of the divinity of this work as Thou hast given it unto us. Preserve them in purity and truth, and lead them in the way of salvation.

We thank Thee, O God, that Thy Son, our Redeemer, after having been crucified, laying down His life for the sins of the world, did open the prison doors and proclaim the gospel of repentance unto those who had been disobedient in the days of Noah, and that He subsequently came to the land of America, where He established His Church and chose disciples to guide the same.

We thank Thee for restoring again to the earth the ordinances of the gospel of Thy Son Jesus Christ, whereby men and women can be, in very deed, saviors upon Mount Zion, and where they can enter into Thy holy temples and perform the ordinances necessary for the salvation of those who died without a knowledge of the gospel.

We thank Thee, O Father, above all things, for the gospel of Thy Son Jesus Christ, and for the Priesthood of the Living God, and that we have been made partakers of the same, and have an abiding knowledge of the divinity of the work in which we are engaged.

We thank Thee for the words of Thy Son Jesus Christ to the Prophet Joseph Smith and Sidney Rigdon: "This is the gospel, the glad tidings which the voice out of the heavens bore record unto us, that He came into the world, even Jesus, to be crucified for the world, and to bear the sins of the world, and to sanctify the world, and to cleanse it from all unrighteousness, that through Him all might be saved whom the Father had put into His power and made by Him, who glorifies the Father, and saves all the works of His hands."

We thank Thee, O Father, that thou didst send Thy Son Jesus Christ, to visit Thy servants Joseph Smith and Oliver Cowdery in the Kirtland Temple. We thank Thee for the words of our Redeemer spoken in that temple:

"I am the first and the last, I am He who liveth, I am He who was slain. I am your advocate with the Father. Behold, your sins are forgiven you, you are clean before me, therefore lift up your heads and rejoice, and let the hearts of all my people rejoice, who have with their might built this house to my Name, for behold, I have accepted this house, and my Name shall be here, and I will manifest myself to my people in mercy in this house."

We thank Thee, O God, that by the testimony of Thy Holy Spirit Thou hast manifested Thine acceptance of all the temples that have been erected from the days of Kirtland until this present time.

We also thank Thee for sending Thy servants, Moses and Elias, and Elijah, to the Kirtland temple, to confer upon Thy servants, Joseph and Oliver, the keys of every dispensation of the gospel of Jesus Christ from the days of Father Adam down to the present dispensation, which is the dispensation of the fulness of times.

We thank Thee, that through the visitation of Elijah the prophecy of Thy servant Malachi—that the hearts of the fathers should be turned to the children, and the hearts of the children to the fathers, lest the earth be smitten with a curse—has been fulfilled in our day, and that our hearts in very deed go out to our fathers; and we rejoice beyond our ability to express that we can, through the ordinances of the gospel of Jesus Christ, become saviors of our ancestors.

We thank Thee, O God, our Eternal Father, with all our hearts for the testimony of Thy servants Joseph Smith and Sidney Rigdon: "And now, after the many testimonies which have been given of him, this is the testimony last of all, which we give of Him, that He lives; for we saw Him, even on the right hand of God, and we heard the voice bearing record that He is the Only Begotten of the Father—that by Him and through Him, and of Him the worlds are and were created, and the inhabitants thereof are begotten sons and daughters unto God."

We thank Thee, O Father, for the knowledge which we possess, that Thou dost live, and that Thy Son Jesus Christ is our Redeemer, and our Savior, and that Thy servant, Joseph Smith, Jr., was and is a prophet of the true and living God. And, O Father, may we ever be true and faithful to the gospel of Thy Son Jesus Christ, revealed through Thy servant Joseph.

We now thank Thee, O God, our Eternal Father, for this beautiful temple and the ground upon which it stands, and we dedicate the ground, and the building, with all the furnishings and fittings thereof, and everything pertaining thereunto, from the foundation to the roof, to Thee, our Father and our God. And we humbly pray Thee, Father, to accept of it and sanctify it, and to consecrate it through Thy Spirit to the holy purposes for which it has been erected.

We beseech Thee to enable us to guard this house that no unclean thing shall enter here. May Thy Spirit ever dwell in this holy house and rest upon all who shall labor as officers and workers herein, as well as upon all who shall come here to perform ordinances for the living or for the dead.

May Thy peace ever abide in this holy building, that all who come here may partake of the spirit of peace, and of the sweet and heavenly influence that Thy Saints have experienced in other temples, may all who come upon the grounds which surround this temple, whether members of the Church of Christ or not, feel the sweet and peaceful influence of this blessed and hallowed spot. And may this building be sacred unto Thee and protected from the elments of destruction.

O God, our Heavenly and Eternal Father, sanctify the words which we have spoken, and accept the dedication of this house, and these grounds, which we have dedicated unto Thee by virtue of the Priesthood of the Living God which we hold, and we most earnestly pray that this sacred building may be a place in which Thy Son may see fit to manifest Himself and to instruct Thy servants, and in which Thou shall delight to dwell.

All this we ask and do in the authority of the Holy Priesthood and in the name of Thine Only Begotten Son, Jesus Christ, our Redeemer. Amen and Amen.

Liahona, Vol. 25:245.

Physical and Historical Description

The site for the Arizona Temple was chosen by President Heber J. Grant, Apostles David O. McKay and George F. Richards and the church architect, Willard Young. It contains twenty acres of land which belonged to the Kimball tract which adjoins Mesa on the east, and was purchased for $20,000. Immediately adjacent on the north of this tract passes the paved ocean-to-ocean highway which is here called the Apache Trail. William Kimball, the former owner, was a son of Heber C. Kimball.

As one approaches the Temple from the west, broad granite flagstones arranged in walks with green grass in the open spaces between, greet the eye. These lead by a large mirror pool in which is reflected the brilliant outlines of the Temple beyond. The Temple door is approached by a series of wide steps of granite which were quarried in Massachusetts. Over the door to the entrance of the building are the words, in large, gilt letters: "The House of the Lord, Erected by the Church of Jesus Christ of Latter-day Saints."

The temple site was dedicated on November 28, 1921, by President Heber J. Grant. The first ground was broken on April 25, 1923. The exterior dimensions, including the annex, are 128 feet north and south, 184 feet east and west. The foundation footings of the main building on the north are 10 feet, 4 inches; on the east and west, 10 feet, 11 inches; on the south, 12 feet, 6 inches. On this foundation to the level of the first floor the walls are four feet thick. All concrete is laid with steel, about 130 tons of steel being used in the building. From the wall to the roof concrete pillars sustain the building. From these are tied the concrete floors and roof, and around them is constructed a brick wall faced with burned fire-clay blocks having an eggshell glaze which is attained by spraying each block before it is placed in the kiln. The height of the building is 55 feet. The structure is surrounded by terrace built up four feet high, which together with the one-story annex gives the Temple a terraced appearance similar to the Temple of Herod as well as the temples found on the American continent of ancient origin.

Surrounding the roof and as a finish to the walls of the building is a parapet about four feet high, which forms the background for a sculptural frieze work which decorates the apex of the Temple wall on all four sides. The roof gradually slopes from the parapet toward the center, where is constructed an immense skylight which from its four sides allows the light of heaven to shower the sunshine below, illuminating the giant stairway and grand hall extending from the Celestial Room to the front entrance.

The heating and cooling system cost approximately $37,-500. The heating plant is located 350 feet south of the Temple. It contains two large boilers in which fuel oil is fed. These boilers supply steam heat to the basement of the Temple along a concrete underground tunnel. At a point 120 feet south of the Temple is placed the fresh air intake, a small building 6'x9', from which the air is forced into the Temple and distributed to each room by the latest scientific air-conditioning methods.

The Arizona Temple, like the Hawaiian and Canadian Temples, is devoid of spires and towers. It is colonial in appearance, though not of any one period. Its style of architecture is really an American adaptation of the classic architecture. The building faces both east and west, though the entrance is from the west. On the north, south and east the annexes are separated by open colonnades or courts. These inclosed areas are beautified by flowers, shrubbery and grasses, and open above to the canopy of heaven. The landscape gardening extends thirty-five feet out from the building and is on the level with the open courts. This terrace is four feet above the level of the surrounding ground.

A floodlighting system is arranged for night illumination of the exterior, by means of large lights being placed on tall pillars which shed a soft white glow over the beautiful building and grounds, reflecting into the mirror pool an almost perfect replica of the Temple. The total cost of the Temple was approximately $300,000. It was dedicated on October 23, 1927, by President Heber J. Grant and is the ninth temple to be dedicated in sequence of time in this Dispensation.

Presidents of the Arizona Temple:
>
> David K. Udall, 1927-1934.
>
> Charles R. Jones, 1934-1940.
>
> Charles Pugh, 1940-1944.
>
> Harry L. Payne, 1944-1953.
>
> Orwell L. Pierce, 1953-1960.
>
> J. Robert Price, 1960-1963.
>
> Jesse M. Smith, 1963—Present Incumbent.

A Remarkable Confirmation of An Authentic Pedigree History

By F. T. Pomeroy, of Mesa, Arizona

In the Pomeroy History, a footnote listed Richimir II as a descendant of Antenor, the King of the Cimmerians, who lived on the Black Sea, so in setting them down in my Temple Record, I left several lines between the two names and records, and the baptisms had been done for each on the 18th day of September, 1923.

Continuing my research, I wrote a second letter to Elisha Loomis, a professor of mathematics in the High School at Cleveland, Ohio, who was also a genealogist of national fame, and who had compiled and published the Loomis Genealogy, and had assisted in compiling the Pomeroy Ancestral Chart. I submitted to him some genealogy I had compiled, with some queries. On the back of one of the large sheets I had sent him, he wrote the following: "This will interest you."

He then set down my lines of ancestry, beginning with the father of Richimir II, Clodimir III who was my 49th gr. gr. parent, and continuing back with the parent, and sometimes parents, in each generation, giving the date of death where available, or living date of each name for 34 generations, to "Antenor, the King of the Cimmarians, who lived on the Black Sea, and who died 443 B.C."

He wrote he had discovered the line while doing some research work in the Harvard Library of the Harvard University earlier in the summer, in a volume by Professor James Anderson, much prized and now rare book "Royal Genealogies, 2nd Edition, 1776," of which I made a copy, and which I am now sending you."

I immediately transferred the names to my Temple Record and after some verifications by the Genealogical Society of Utah, which also had recently obtained a copy of this work, and sent them to the Salt Lake Temple, where they were baptized for on the 9th day of April, 1927. The baptisms for this royal ancestral line were performed in the Salt Lake Temple, about the same time as the completion of the Arizona Temple in April, 1927.

When the Arizona Temple was dedicated, I was called to the honorable position of Door Keeper, and was set apart with my wife, as officiators in the temple service. My brother, Talma E. Pomeroy, and his wife, were also called to the same labor. This gave us a wonderful opportunity to carry on the ordinance work for our extended and long ancestral line, most of them having been baptized for in the other temples of the church.

The Pomeroy family responded nobly to the temple ordinance work, and by November 2, 1927, we were ready for the sealing for time and all eternity as husband and wife, Richimir II and his wife, Nastilla.

Long lines of pedigreed ancestry with proven identifying data, necessary before the work could be done in the Temples, were rare in the Church; in fact, this line to Richimir II, and back to Antenor, who died in 443 B.C., was the most extended ancestral line yet presented to the temple. Naturally, many questioned its accuracy, and it was the subject of many wise-cracks, "there was no way of knowing these were real people or just simply a list of names." I was satisfied in my own mind, since the authorities were given in the Pomeroy Ancestral Chart for every name back to 350 A.D. But now we had added an ancestral line running back 793 years farther, with Richimir II as the "key man."

I had been praying that in some way a confirmation, or otherwise, might be manifested, that I might be assured that the work done in this line, and to be done, would not be in vain.

I was officiating that day and was not prepared to act as proxy, and Brother Samuel Weston of Logan, Utah, and Sister Hayne of Douglas, Arizona, volunteered to stand as proxy for the royal couple. President James W. LeSueur officiated. I sat in a chair facing the door of the sealing room, acting as one of the witnesses.

When the ceremony commenced my head was bowed in prayer. Suddenly I received the impression that something extraordinary was happening. I looked up and to my surprise and joy, I visualized standing just inside the door and gazing directly at me the dim form and smiling countenance of a personage. He was tall and brawny. He had piercing eyes, and heavy eyebrows, and rather high cheek bones. The lower part of his face was covered by a gray beard which hung well down upon his breast. I was impressed that he was the personage for whom the ceremony was being performed. I was nearly overcome, but said nothing about it at the time. After the ceremony Brother Weston asked for information concerning Richimir II, and I gave him such information as I had.

I thought over and treasured the visitation, as one given to me, and intended to say nothing about it. The next morning Brother Weston came to me and said: "Brother Pomeroy, I expect you are wondering why I was so anxious to obtain information concerning the man for whom I stood as proxy yesterday. I wanted to write about him in my diary, for they were present and witnessed the ceremony, for I felt their presence." "I am glad to hear you say that," I replied, "as I also know they were there, for I visualized his countenance and will know him when I meet him on the other side." Sister Hayne testified to the same thing and President LaSueur also testified he was impressed with their presence while the ceremony was in progress. This manifestation cleared up all of my misgivings and fears concerning this ancestral line, and since we have completed all of the ordinances of the Gospel for the entire line of 83 generations back, including the father and mother of Antenor Aesyeges and Cleomaestra, his wife.

The Genealogical and Historical Magazine, Mesa, Arizona, July, 1935, pp. 29-30.

Manifestations in Arizona Temple: At the time when the first excursion came to the Arizona Temple from the St. Johns Stake, Brother Charlie Watson was Bishop's counselor of Kimball Ward, this excursion going to the Temple two years after its construction, 1929. At that time I was taking the part of Peter in all of the sessions. Brother Watson came down to the desk after the session was through and said: "Brother Nash, I saw President Kimball today." (Brother Kimball having died in 1924). "Well," I said, "couldn't you have been mistaken?" He said: "I have seen President Kimball a thousand times and I would know him anywhere. I was sitting in a seat in the terrestrial room, waiting for my turn at the veil and I looked up and saw President Kimball standing on the rostrum, with his arms folded, looking over the congregation. My first thought was President Kimball's mantle had fallen on you because you were so closely associated with him, but I saw you working at the veil. Brother Kimball was standing just as he used to stand in life, with arms folded, and he had such a pleasant expression on his face. I looked around to see if anyone was noticing but no one seemed to be paying any attention, and when I looked back President Kimball was gone."

The following occurrence happened a few weeks later: This incident was told to me by Brother William Follett. He said: "Brother Nash, I was sitting in the Creation Room today and there were two old men who were sitting beside me who began to talk very loud. I reached my hand over and touched one on the knee and at the same time I turned my eyes toward the rostrum, and there stood a Lamanite, a splendid specimen of manhood, clothed only with a loin cloth. He seemed to be looking over the congregation and the room in general. I wondered what it could mean. I looked to see if anybody else saw the same thing and when I looked back he was gone."

"What do you think it meant, Brother Nash?" "Well," I said, "it might possibly be this: This Temple is the Lamanite Temple. We have all the Lamanite records here and it has been built especially for the purpose of Lamanites receiving their endowments here, whenever they are ready, and it might be possible that he was sent ahead to look over the building and see how he would like the building and the services that were being performed." "Well," he said, "Brother Nash, I believe you are right."

On April 4, 1940, Brother Charlie Angel came to the Temple and stated that he had just lost his wife. He said: "Brother Nash, my wife did a lot of work for her people before she died, and I got the sealing record work ready and Brother Jones, a lady friend, and I went up into the sealing room and while we were sealing and I was acting as proxy, I looked in the corner of the room and there stood my wife, with the most beautiful expression on her face that I ever saw on a human being. I can scarcely hold back the tears when I think of it, and I told Brother Jones my experience and he said: 'Your wife is perfectly satisfied with the work that you have done.' "

By Patriarch John F. Nash.

Chapter X

IDAHO FALLS TEMPLE

DEDICATORY PRAYER

By. Pres. George Albert Smith

(September 23, 1945)

O Thou great and eternal God, Father of our spirits, Creator of the heavens, the earth and all things therein; before whom all things are present, whether past or yet to come; full of mercy and love, guided by wisdom, judgment and justice in their perfection; in humility and with thanksgiving and with our hearts filled with gratitude unto Thee, we approach Thee through Thy Beloved Son, Jesus Christ, our elder Brother, who, through the great and exquisite sacrifice wrought out for us magnanimous beyond our comprehension, made it possible that we might approach Thee in humility on this great occasion, with our petitions and supplications, in this House which we have built to Thy most holy name.

We pray Thee that Thou wilt cause our hearts to be purified in Thy sight and our faith in Thee to be multiplied and increased so that our petitions may reach Thy holy habitation and be answered in our behalf in accordance with Thy infinite wisdom and love, and grant that the blessings we here seek may be fully realized to Thy name's honor and glory.

PRES. GEORGE ALBERT SMITH

We thank Thee for having raised up Thy servant, Joseph Smith, and that Thou didst endow him and inspire him and reveal unto him Thy great purposes, and that Thou didst manifest Thyself and Thy Beloved Son unto him, and didst cause holy resurrected beings to minister unto him and to confer upon him the Holy Priesthood after the order of Thine Only Begotten Son, and its appendage, the Aaronic Priesthood; that Thou didst cause to be preserved on gold plates, that they might withstand the ravages of time, an abridgement of the political and ecclesiastical history of Thy ancient peoples who occupied this western hemisphere, and of the inspired writings and sayings of their prophets; and that Thou didst prepare Joseph Smith to receive and translate these sacred records and make them available to all mankind, that thereby man in our time might have a witness to the divine mission of Thine Only Begotten Son, Jesus Christ, in addition to the Holy Bible, and thereby be left without excuse on the last day when all shall be judged of their works and accordingly be rewarded by a kind and loving though just and merciful parent.

We thank Thee for the restoration of the gospel in its fulness in these latter days, and that Joseph Smith was directed to organize the Church of Jesus Christ of Latter-day Saints, and that Thou didst reveal unto him the proper order thereof, including apostles, prophets, pastors, teachers, evangelists, etc. We thank Thee that Thou didst restore in these latter days through the Prophet Joseph Smith the keys of each of the former dispensations of the gospel of Thy beloved Son by those to whom they had been committed, from Adam down to the present time, through Thine ancient prophets, Elias, Moses, Elijah and Moroni. We thank Thee for the many revelations Thou didst give to Thy servant, Joseph Smith, and didst cause to be published for the benefit and guidance of Thy saints, as well as for all mankind who would believe and follow them; and that Thou didst see fit to covenant with Thy servant, Joseph Smith, that the Keys of the Kingdom which Thou didst bestow upon him should not be taken from him in this world nor in the world to come, and that Thou didst make provision for his successors and their authority to carry forward Thy great work. We refer to Presidents Brigham Young, John Taylor, Wilford Woodruff, Lorenzo Snow, Joseph F. Smith and Heber J. Grant. We are all grateful for their ministries and for the marvelous accomplishments each in his time was able to achieve under Thy divine guidance.

We are grateful unto Thee for those who now preside over Thy Church. We pray that Thy servant, George Albert Smith, may be endowed of Thee with a vigorous body and mind, with health and strength, and with the spirit of prophecy, seership, revelation and of presidency, and with the ability to magnify Thy great and holy name. Bless his faithful counselors, Joshua Reuben Clark, Jr., and David Oman McKay, whom Thou hast given to advise him and assist him, that they may possess great wisdom and excellent judgment in all matters pertaining to Thy Church. Grant that perfect love and confidence may exist in this Thy Presidency that they may be united as one in all things pertaining to Thy work.

We do thank Thee for the labors of all faithful men, the Apostles and Assistants, Patriarch, Seventies, Presiding Bishopric, and all those whom Thou hast called to labor as General Authorities

IDAHO FALLS TEMPLE

Temple dedicated on September 23, 1945, by President George Albert Smith.

(East or front view)

in Thy vineyard in this last gospel dispensation, as well as those of all former dispensations. We pray that Thou wilt sanctify their labors to the everlasting good of all peoples everywhere, and to Thy name's honor and glory.

We thank Thee for Thy plan of salvation, for its magnitude and comprehensiveness, and pray that Thy saints may live to be worthy to learn of Thy desires concerning them until they come to a complete knowledge of the truth. We pray that Thou wilt hasten the day when righteousness shall cover the earth as the waters cover the mighty deep, and all men walk in Thy paths and delight to do Thy holy will.

We thank Thee for the various offices in Thy Holy Priesthood, for High Priests, Seventies, Elders, Priests, Teachers and Deacons. Wilt Thou inspire these, in whatsoever office to which they may be called, to function to the everlasting benefit of all to whom they may minister. We pray that Thou wilt bless Zion with all of her interests, in all her Stakes, Wards and Branches. May her borders be extended until Zion shall be fully redeemed and her inhabitants glorify Thy holy name.

Confer upon Thy people, and especially upon Thy leaders, in all of their various callings, Thy precious gifts of love, wisdom and judgment, knowledge and understanding, faith and the spirit of testimony, light, intelligence and capacity, and every attribute, blessing, gift and qualification either necessary or desirable for them to have and to enjoy in order that Thy great and important work may go forward to consummate its glorious purpose. Father, wilt Thou preserve Thy saints in the unity of the faith, in the way of truth, in the bonds of peace, and holiness of life. We pray that the weak may be strengthened and Thy Holy Spirit be imparted to all.

We pray for the youth everywhere, and all organizations calculated to develop their character and spirituality, and all which Thou hast caused to be established for their blessing and instruction, including the Primary Association, Sunday Schools, Young Men's and Young Women's Mutual Improvement Associations, the Church educational system, including the seminaries and institutes, and all the quorums of the Priesthood that have to do with the teaching and instruction of the youth. May Thy Holy Spirit be richly imparted to Thy young sons and daughters, that their faith may be enlarged, that they may walk righteously and circumspectly before Thee. We seek Thy blessings for all those who in any way devote their time in teaching the youth of Zion, that they may exercise great wisdom and judgment. May they be inspired in their guidance of Thy precious little ones to lead them into paths of truth and righteousness, that thereby the youth may lay a foundation upon which to establish righteous character and become useful in developing Thy Church and Kingdom in the earth.

We pray for the daughters of Zion. May they be preserved in virtue, chastity and purity of life, be blessed with vigorous bodies and minds, and with great faith. May they develop into true womanhood and receive choice companions under the new and everlasting covenant for time and for all eternity in Thy temples provided for this priceless privilege and purpose. May they too be privileged to enjoy as the fruits of their union a noble posterity which, we pray Thee, may be taught at their mother's knee to believe in Thee and in the divine mission of Thy Beloved Son.

We thank Thee, O our Father, that Thou didst restore that grand and glorious principle of marriage for eternity, and didst bestow upon Thy servant the power to seal on earth and have it recognized in the heavens. We acknowledge this privilege as one of Thy most marvelous gifts to us. May all the youth of Thy Church come to know of its beauty and of its eternal importance to them, and to take advantage of it when they marry. May they, our Father, on the other hand, realize fully that the glorious opportunity for eternal companionship of husband and wife, and the power of eternal increase, may be forfeited by them if they fail, through negligence or indifference, to conform to Thy requirements, or if having taken advantage thereof, they may still through improper conduct lose their blessings.

Wilt Thou, O Father in heaven, remember the Relief Society throughout the length and breadth of the Church. May those who engage therein, either as officers or teachers, be abundantly rewarded for their unselfish sacrifices, for the services they render, for their acts of mercy and kindness, and for their ministrations to the sick, the needy, and the unfortunate. We pray Thee that in their homes and in their responsibilities they may enjoy the rich companionship of Thy Holy Spirit.

Thou, O Father, hast commanded mankind to subdue the earth, and also to earn his bread by the sweat of his brow. Nevertheless there are those among us who because of misfortune that overtakes them are not able to keep fully these great commandments at all times. We are most grateful unto Thee that Thou didst inspire Thy servants to institute the Welfare Program of the Church through which it is made possible that the poor and unfortunate might be provided for without the forfeiture of self-respect. May Thy servants continue in Thy favor that they may thereby merit Thy inspiration in developing the Welfare Program until it becomes perfect in all respects to the care and blessing of Thy people.

Our Father which art in heaven, hallowed by Thy name. Thy kingdom come, Thy will be done in earth as it is in heaven. With deep gratitude in our hearts we thank Thee that the nations have ceased their warfare and the destruction of human life. We thank Thee that peace temporarily is established in the earth. We do pray that all people everywhere will now take cognizance of the horrors of war, and repent of their sins and follies and with contrite spirits turn unto Thee, the God of love and peace; that they may be inclined to follow the admonitions of Thy servants that thereby the peace now enjoyed by them may be made permanent, and the day of the coming of Thy Beloved Son hastened. We do most fervently pray that hate may lose its place in the hearts of men and that Thy peace and love may enter and abide therein. We also pray that Thy sons and daughters who have been required to participate in the great conflict to preserve liberty, may return to their homes and engage in wholesome and useful pursuits, and contribute to the building up of Thy Kingdom in the earth. May they whose release from the armed services, for any reason, may be delayed, be abundantly blessed of Thee and comforted, and be preserved in health and strength and righteousness, and may the day of their union with loved ones at home come as speedily as possible.

Wilt Thou, O Lord, have remembrance the promises made by Thee to Judah in his stricken and scattered condition. Hasten the time when he shall be restored to the land of his inheritance. Remove from him Thy displeasure, and may the days of his tribulation soon cease, and Jerusalem rejoice and Judah be made glad for the multitude of her sons and daughters, for the sweet voices of children in her streets, and for the manifold blessings Thou wilt pour out upon them.

Remember, O Lord, Thy promises to Israel, whom Thou didst cause to be taken captive and scattered among the heathen and to be dispersed throughout all countries, that Thou wouldst again gather them from among the nations whither they had been scattered. Wilt Thou, O gracious Father, in Thy wisdom and mercy, speedily fulfill Thy promises unto Israel and cause that they may again be gathered and hearken unto the voice of Thy servants, the prophets, and thereby merit the rich blessings Thou hast promised them when they acknowledge Jesus Christ, Thy Beloved Son, as their Redeemer.

O Father, remember Thy promises made unto Thy holy prophets regarding the remnants of those whom Thou didst lead unto this western hemisphere, that they should not be utterly destroyed but that a remnant should be preserved which would turn from their wickedness, repent of their sins, and eventually become a white and delightsome people. May the day speedily come when those promises will be fulfilled.

We thank Thee, O God, for the choice land upon which we reside, and for the marvelous promises Thou hast made concerning America, that it should be free from bondage, and from captivity, and from all other nations under Heaven so long as the inhabitants of the land should worship the God of the land who is

Jesus Christ. Thou hast revealed unto us that in the great controversy which took place in Heaven that the cornerstone of Thy
plan of salvation was the free agency of man, and that Lucifer,
who was an angel in authority in Thy Holy presence, proposed a
different way; that Lucifer's plan was rejected because the effect
of its application would be to deprive Thy children of their free
agency. When Lucifer's plan was rejected by Thee he rebelled
against Thee; there was war in Heaven and he and his followers
were cast out. We thank Thee that Thou hast warned us by revelation that Satan would deceive the nations in our time. Thou hast
said: "I will give you a pattern in all things, that ye may not be
deceived, for Satan is abroad in the land, and he goeth forth deceiving the nations." As we look about in the world among the
various countries we find philosophies and forms of government
the effect of which is to deprive men of their free agency, but by
reason of Thy timely warning to us, we know that they are not
approved of Thee. Since the God of this choice land is Jesus Christ,
we know that His philosophy of free agency should prevail here.
Thou didst amply demonstrate this great principle to us by raising
up wise men for the very purpose of giving us our Constitutional
form of government, concerning which Thou hast said: "I have
suffered to be established, and should be maintained for the rights
and protection of all flesh, according to just and holy principles;
that every man may act in doctrine and principle pertaining to
futurity, according to the moral agency which I have given unto
him, that every man may be accountable for his own sins in the
day of judgment. Therefore, it is not right that any man should be
in bondage one to another. And for this purpose have I established
the Constitution of this land, by the hands of wise men whom I
raised up into this very purpose." There are those, our Heavenly
Father, both within and without our borders who would destroy
the Constitutional form of government which Thou hast so mag-
nanimously given us, and would replace it with a form that would
curtail if not altogether deprive man of his free agency. We pray
Thee, therefore, that in all these matters Thou wilt help us to conform our lives to Thy desires, and that Thou wilt sustain us in
our resolve so to do. We pray Thee that Thou wilt inspire good
and just men everywhere to be willing to sacrifice for, support
and uphold the Constitution and the government set up under it
and thereby preserve for man his agency.

We thank Thee that Thou hast revealed to us that those who
gave us our Constitutional form of government were men wise
in Thy sight and that Thou didst raise them up for the very purpose of putting forth that sacred document.

Wilt Thou, O our Father, bless the Chief Executive of this
land that his heart and will may be to preserve for us and our posterity the free institutions Thy Constitution has provided. Wilt

Thou too bless the Legislative and Judicial branches of our government as well as the Executive, that all may function fully and courageously in their respective branches completely independent of each other to the preservation of our Constitutional form of government forever.

We pray that kings and rulers and the peoples of all nations under heaven may be persuaded of the blessings enjoyed by the people of this land by reason of their freedom under Thy guidance and be constrained to adopt similar governmental systems, thus to fulfill the ancient prophecy of Isaiah that "out of Zion shall go forth the law and the word of the Lord from Jerusalem."

We pray that the barriers which have blocked the pathway to the preaching of the Gospel to the inhabitants of many of the nations may be broken down or swept aside so that Thy servants, the missionaries, may carry the gospel of peace and good will to the honest in heart in every nation under heaven.

Our hearts are filled with gratitude towards Thee, O God our Eternal Father, that Thou didst cause Thy Spirit to move upon our forebears and inspire them to come to this goodly land, declared by Thee to be choice above all other lands, where they might worship Thee untrammeled; that Thou didst promise, "The wilderness and solitary place shall be glad for them; and the desert shall rejoice, and blossom as the rose. It shall blossom abundantly, and rejoice even with joy and singing . . . And the parched ground shall become a pool, and the thirsty land springs of water." For the fertility of this land which, once most undesirable and forbidding, now produces in rich abundance delicious grain, fruits and vegetables, we are most grateful. We too express to Thee our joy in beholding great mountains towering majestically toward the sky to inspire Thy children to look up as well as around them that they might enjoy Thy handiwork.

We thank Thee, O God, for sending Elijah, the ancient prophet, to whom was "committed the keys of power of turning the hearts of the fathers to the children, and the hearts of the children to the fathers, that the whole earth may not be smitten with a curse." We thank Thee that he was sent to Thy servant Joseph Smith, to confer the keys of authority of the work for the dead, and to reveal that the plan of salvation embraces the whole of the human family; that the gospel is universal in scope, and that Thou art no respecter of persons, having provided for the preaching of the gospel of salvation to both the living and the dead. We are most grateful unto Thee that salvation is provided for all who desire to be saved in Thy kingdom. May it be pleasing to Thy people to search out the genealogy of their forebears that they may become saviors on Mt. Zion by officiating in Thy temples for their kindred dead. We pray also that the spirit of Elijah may rest mightily upon all peoples everywhere that they may be moved upon to gather and make available the genealogy of their ancestors; and that Thy faithful children may utilize Thy holy temples in which to perform on behalf of the dead all ordinances pertaining to their eternal exaltation.

Bless all those who shall be workers in this Temple, whether they be officers, ordinance workers or caretakers. May they fulfill the functions of their respective callings in accordance with the spirit and purpose of it. May all ordinances to be performed in this House, including baptisms, confirmations, washings, anointings, sealings, endowments, and all that is done, be acceptable unto Thee. Bless, we pray Thee, those who make and copy records that their work may be accurate and acceptable unto Thee; and also those who have labored in the erection of this Thy Holy House, or who have contributed of their means or time toward its completion. May their reward be sure and their joy complete.

We are grateful, Heavenly Father, that we have been permitted to rear this Temple on this beautiful spot upon the bank of one of Thy majestic rivers, the waters of which have made it possible for Thy faithful Saints residing here to subdue the land and establish delightful homes. We thank Thee for the means that Thou hast placed in our hands that has been utilized in constructing this edifice and preparing it for holy purposes.

We now present ourselves before Thee in humble gratitude and with hearts filled with praise and thanksgiving that Thou hast seen fit to permit us to complete this sacred building, which is now finished and ready to be dedicated to Thee and to Thy most holy name. And today we here and now dedicate this Temple unto Thee with all that pertains unto it that it may be holy in Thy sight; that it may be a house of prayer, a house of praise and of worship, that Thy glory may rest upon it and Thy holy presence be continually in it; and that it may be an acceptable abode for Thy Well-Beloved Son, Jesus Christ, our Savior; that it may be both sanctified and consecrated in all its parts sacred unto Thee. And we pray that all those who may cross the threshold of this Thine House may be impressed with the holiness of it, and deport themselves herein with righteous conduct, and may no uncleanliness ever pass its portals.

We pray now that Thou wilt accept this Temple as a freewill offering from Thy children, that it will be sacred unto Thee. We pray that all that has been accomplished here may be pleasing in Thy sight and that Thou wilt be mindful of this structure at all times that it may be preserved from the fury of the elements and wilt Thou, our Heavenly Father, let Thy presence be felt here always, that all who assemble here may realize that they are Thy guests and that this is Thy House.

In the authority of Thy Holy Priesthood, we dedicate unto Thee these grounds, this building in all its parts, from foundation to capstone, together with all that appertains thereunto, including furnishings and equipment and all facilities, and we pray that accepting this our offering Thou wilt preserve the same from decay and the ravages of time. We now present this precious Temple unto Thee, Holy Father, with all that pertains to it, inside and out, with our love and gratitude, and pray that Thou wilt accept of our offering, and unto Thee we ascribe all honor, glory and praise forever through Thy Beloved Son, Jesus Christ. Amen.

—Deseret News, September 29, 1945.
—Also Improvement Era, October, 1945.

Physical Description

By John Fetzer
(Member Board of Temple Architects)

In the beautiful city of Idaho Falls, Idaho, is located one of the most notable and impressive church edifices in the West. It is the recently completed Temple of the Church of Jesus Christ of Latter-day Saints, which was dedicated on September 23, 1945, the Dedicatory Services being repeated on the 24th and 25th.

Surrounded by broad and spacious grounds with the clear placid waters of the Snake River flowing by it on the west, it is a most monumental structure of shining warm white, which rises with deep setbacks and strikingly impressive bladed pilasters, to a final central shaft, capped with stainless steel. The main body of the building is symmetrical in plan and at any hour of the day is characterized by brilliant high-lights and strongly contrasting shadows. Its architecture is distinctly modern and of the 20th Century. Set in its wide, green valley, with distant mountains fringing the horizons, this Temple is visible for many miles and its towering, tapering mass, pointing skyward, seems to tell of eternal values, to symbolize the aspiration and strength of the human spirit, rising above material things.

In the construction of this building, only materials of the finest and most enduring quality were employed. The structural frame is of concrete heavily reinforced, the walls are of reinforced concrete. The exterior walls are 16 inches in total thickness and are faced with 2-inch slabs made of selected aggregates, tooled and finished. These facing slabs, with metal ties and anchors projecting from their interior surfaces, were set and held in position and the remainder of the concrete was poured against them, thereby creating a practically monolithic construction. All copings and window sills are flashed with copper, the sash is aluminum, the great entrance doors are bronze. The foundations rest upon the valley's volcanic lava bedrock. It is a building for the centuries.

The aim of the exterior design has been to give an impression of strength through the use of the simple basic reinforced concrete masses by depending for effect entirely on their intrinsic proportions, texture and color, avoiding stoically the addition of ornament. The same character of simplicity, so much in keeping with the Gospel spirit, has been continued in the interior. For more "honesty" in design the wall and ceiling surfaces will not be "inflicted" with the addition of ornament. The desired effect and "atmosphere" in the important rooms of the Temple will be achieved solely through the natural means of the room proportions, the lighting and the intrinsic texture and color of the various surface materials used. For richness, several varieties of foreign and local marbles have been used in the Entry and on the Grand Stair and the Altars in the Ordinance Rooms. The Terrestrial Room is enriched by the use of wall height drapes completely covering all walls. In the chaste setting of very light colored plaster walls and terrazzo floor the white Bronze Oxen of the Font are another note of richness. Floor materials have been carefully chosen and include such as rubber, tile, and terrazzo generally and carpet in the Ordinance Rooms. Special mention should be made of the lighting. The aim in design has been to suffuse the rooms with soft indirect light of the special colors desired in such a way that the occupants will not be conscious of the light source. To achieve this the ceilings of the Ordinance Rooms form immense light reflecting surfaces for concealed fluorescent tubes. Tempered or cooled air from inconspicuous ceiling outlets assures comfort the year around.

The Temple is designed to accommodate a company of 150 people for each session. Special thought has been given by the Board of Temple Architects to plan so as to save time and effort for those going through the Temple to the end that all may be done with the utmost dispatch. The annex contains the President's Room, the spacious Annex Lobby, Recorders' Room with accompanying typing and record Photographing Departments, linen, Matron's and Children's Rooms and also Dining Room and Kitchen with the Record Vault, Laundry and Kitchen Storage Rooms in the basement. The clerestory lighted Assembly Room with its two hallways (separated only by draped openings and with full height windows onto the Temple gardens) form the connecting link between the annex and the Temple proper.

The first floor of the Temple proper contains in one half the Men's Dressing and Wash Rooms, Workers' Rooms and a Groom Room, in the other half similar rooms for the Women. In the basement are located the Font Room with accompanying large Font Lobby and Dressing Rooms. In keeping with its importance the Baptismal Font Room extends through two stories in height and is located in the exact center of the Temple proper in the base of the tower and immediately below the Celestial Room.

The Ordinance Rooms, namely, the Creation, Garden, Telestial or World Room, Terrestrial and Celestial Rooms are located on the second floor as are also the Sealing Rooms and the Grand Stair Lobby. The Celestial Room is near the center of the plan. The remaining Ordinance Rooms are arranged to encircle this Final Room, each increasing in color, light and richness in their order to the climax in the Celestial Room in the tower.

The Temple dimensions are as follows: The one story Annex east of the Temple proper is 173 feet by 34 feet and includes an entrance 37½ feet by 10 feet. This Annex is connected to the Temple proper by corridors and an Assembly Hall 36 feet by 53 feet. The Temple proper, which is two storied, measures 95 feet by 131 feet. The tower, at the center of the Temple proper, measures 127 feet above the main floor, and with the additional 23 feet to the sub-basement floor has a total height of about 150 feet. The cost of $700,000 includes the building, furnishings, and landscaping. The Temple approach is through a columned porch, flanked at each end with a small attendant office and a bureau of information.

Three reflecting pools with planting boxes on either side lead to the main entrance of the Temple. A similar but simpler approach is to the west of the Temple from the Riverside Memorial Drive. The outer gardens are surrounded by a low wall and hedge. The inner garden is surrounded by a higher wall to give quiet and sacredness.

Within the Temple are a series of beautifully furnished rooms whose walls are decorated with great murals. An impressive sight is the Baptismal Font, a great bronze pool, borne upon the backs of twelve silver bronze oxen of full natural size.

The building is completely air-conditioned, has a loudspeaker system and its heating and ventilating equipment is of the best quality. There has been an extensive use of beautiful drapes and upholstered furniture, and rich, heavy carpets with which all floors are covered. Mention should also be made of the beautiful garden of wide lawns and marginal flowers and shrubbery that surrounds the building on three sides. Without the garden walls are green sloping lawns.

The Temple was designed by the Board of Temple Architects which consists of Edward O. Anderson, John Fetzer, Ramm Hansen, Hyrum C. Pope, Lorenzo S. Young of Salt Lake City, Georgius Y. Cannon of Pasadena, California, and Arthur Price of Salt Lake City, Advisor. The Contractor was Bird Finlayson of Pocatello, Idaho.

Historical Description

Decision of the First Presidency of the Church of Jesus Christ of Latter-day Saints to build a Temple in Idaho was first made public in March, 1937. By the fall of 1939 plans for the new edifice were finished and approved. On December 19, 1939, at 10 a.m., amid a big program and celebration, ground was broken and the work of excavation began. President David Smith of the North Idaho Falls Stake, who was later set apart as President of the Temple, removed the first shovelful of soil. The plan for the new structure called for an 18-foot excavation, and just at that depth a solid bed of lava rock was encountered which provided a most ideal foundation. Fifty-six test holes were drilled to a considerable depth and the footing was found to be firm. Bishop Bird Finlayson of Pocatello was awarded the contract for construction of the building and actual work on the foundation was begun on August 5, 1940. On October 19, 1940, the cornerstone was laid at the southeast corner by President David O. McKay, at which time appropriate services were had, which were presided over by President J. Reuben Clark, Jr., and attended by many of the General Authorities of the Church as well as many thousand members and friends from far and near. On August 19, 1941, a stainless steel plate and the capstone were laid on top of the tower, the scaffolding was removed and to outward appearance the building seemed completed.

The Temple is entirely fireproof, being constructed of reinforced concrete of which it required 6,168 cubic yards and 271 tons of steel. Some of the marble used in its construction came from Utah but most of it was imported from France, Italy and Sweden. Upon the temple block are now growing over 1,600 evergreens and many other trees, shrubs and hedges. The streets and walks around the block are wide, and uniform rows of maple shade trees are planted and growing in the parkings. A complete and up-to-date sprinkling system has been installed and the latest methods of keeping the grounds in perfect shape are used. While sufficient city water is available, the system is also supplied with water through a pump from the river which flows along by the boulevard on the west of the Temple. While the spotless white Temple presents a very attractive view from four sides, the most costly front is toward the east. Here leading up to the main entrance between wide cement walks inlaid with blocks of native stone of different colors are three ponds or lagoons built of concrete. A stream of clear, sparkling water flows continuously from one to the other, thus creating three picturesque waterfalls which add nature's music to the grandeur of the scene. (For additional data see Deseret News of October 26, 1940, September 1, 1945, and September 29, 1945, the last reference giving the full account of the Dedicatory Services. See also Improvement Era, 43:720 and Vol. 48, No. 10.)

Presidents of the Idaho Falls Temple:

David Smith—1943-1949.

William L. Killpack—1949— Present Incumbent.

The Swiss Temple

Site Dedicated on August 5, 1953
Temple Dedicated on September 11, 1955 by President David O. McKay

Chapter XI

Acquisition of Property of the Swiss Temple

By Samuel E. Bringhurst, President, Swiss Temple

Favorable action on the erection of a temple of the Church of Jesus Christ of Latter-day Saints in Europe was taken by the First Presidency and Council of the Twelve on April 17, 1952. President David O. McKay was authorized to go to Switzerland to select a site.

On June 26, 1952, President and Mrs. McKay arrived at the Mission Home in Basel. We went into conference immediately. Those attending were President McKay, David Lawrence McKay, President Stayner Richards of the British Mission, President Golden Woolf of the French Mission, the writer and his first counselor, William Zimmer of the Swiss-Austrian Mission.

President McKay informed us of the decision that the first European Temple should be built in Switzerland. It was the unanimous opinion that the location should be in, or near as possible, the capital city of Bern.

Next morning, June 27, 1952, we drove to Bern and inspected several sites, deciding on one, in the southeastern part of the city. President McKay and his party left in the afternoon for Holland, authorizing me to proceed with the negotiations to acquire the selected site.

I learned that the property we were interested in had just been transferred to the City of Bern, to be used for a teacher's college. I informed President McKay by telephone. He advised that he would return to Switzerland in a few days and requested that we have some properties ready for his inspection.

He returned July 5, and approved a site which was in an estate. Investigation disclosed that there were five groups of heirs, totaling 30 in all, who were widely scattered. The main heir, a banker in Bern, said he would exchange his equity for income property and use his influence with the others. It was necessary to get the written consent from each of them.

After several months of corresponding and contacting, we had the written consent of all heirs and delivered them to the banker in Bern, who promised immediate action, but he demurred, and for several weeks we waited for word from him. It was now the beginning of October, 1952, and President McKay wished to make a definite announcement at October Conference.

All during the negotiating period we had prayed that the Lord would remove the obstacles and make possible the acquisition of the property. Finally, during a sleepless night in October the thought occurred that perhaps there was a reason for the delay, and that we should pray for a decision, and leave the matter with the Lord.

The next morning being Friday, we telephoned the district presidents, asking them to contact all missionaries and request that they fast and pray the following Monday and Tuesday, that we might receive a decision concerning the proposed temple site.

Wednesday, shortly after noon, Mr. Herman Schulthess, the real estate man through whom we were working in Bern, telephoned, stating that at 11 a.m. that day he received a call from the banker, informing him that they were withdrawing from the market the property we were seeking and that it was no longer available. He said he was so shocked and disappointed that he could not muster courage to call sooner. This answer so quickly, while a little disappointing, was a wonderful testimony to all of us. We advised Mr. Schulthess that we would go immediately to Bern and spend the balance of the week with him looking for a new site.

Before leaving, I sent an air mail letter to President McKay telling him what had happened and suggesting he call over long distance telephone upon receipt of our letter and we would have some information on a new site.

We met Mr. Schulthess in Bern and inspected a number of properties that had recently come on the market. After due investigation we reduced them to three suitable properties, and returned to Basel. The following morning Mr. Schulthess called, saying that one of the considered properties had been sold and that we could only get a two-day option on the others.

I prayed earnestly for guidance, and accompanied by Mrs. Bringhurst, drove back to decide between the remaining two properties. The one considered choice number two the day before, now seemed to be more desirable. We left again for Basel, when a short distance out, we turned around, drove back to the site, and as we walked over it, all doubt seemed to leave and we felt certain we were on the site the Lord wished for the first European temple.

It contains seven acres, prominently situated above most of the surrounding area. To the south is the beautiful Aare River, the capital city of Bern and the Alps. On the north and west is a well kept national forest. It is located in the town of Munchenbuchsee, about three miles north of Bern, only a four-minute walk from the railroad station and street car terminal in Zollikofen.

Upon my return to Basel, President McKay called on the phone. I related to him what had happened and recommended the new site. During his last visit we had shown him properties in the area, but the new site was not then available. He said he would confer with the brethren and call back in time to exercise our option, if they deemed it advisable.

Within a few hours President McKay called again, authorized the purchase, and said a check was on the way with which to consummate the transaction, and we were able to exercise our option within the time limit.

At this time we learned why the Lord did not allow us to purchase the first site. It was on a slope, with the highest part facing a narrow 20-foot street on the south, a super state highway was planned on the west, and they took 100 feet of the highest part of the site on the south for an access road, which would have necessitated placing the temple on low filled ground.

Plans for the new temple were prepared by Edward O. Anderson, temple architect.

On April 3, 1953, I was called to return to Switzerland to obtain the building permit, have a dedicated street closed that ran through the property and check available building materials. I left by plane, April 14, 1953, and at the request of President McKay, spent a few days in London assisting President A. Hamer Reiser with the acquisition of the British Temple site.

Arriving in Basel, April 22, 1953, I made a contract with

Brother William Zimmer, of Bercher and Zimmer, Architects, to redraw the plans in German and supervise construction. A contract was also made with Hans Jordi, contractor of Bern, to do the construction work. The plans were completed within a week and applications were filed for the building permit and to close the street.

A 21-day advertising period was required by law, during which the plans were placed on public exhibition in the City Hall.

At the first meeting of the City Commission, after the first run of the notice in the newspaper, the leading protestant minister of the town, with three of his members, appeared and protested granting of the building permit. Mayor Walter Rauber informed us of the protests. Our investigation disclosed that none of the protestors owned property contiguous to or in the area of the temple site.

We were able to answer their objections to the entire satisfaction of the mayor and other officials, so the building permit was granted, contingent upon the permission from the federal authorities in Bern to close the street through the site. After further negotiating, permission was granted on condition that consent also be obtained from the Military Affairs Commission, because of the National Forest adjoining the temple site in the rear. This required more time and the help of several outside people. We gratefully recognized the help of the Lord in guiding our efforts and influencing those with whom we dealt.

By July 1, 1953, all permits were in our hands and the assignment given to me by the First Presidency was completed. President McKay was notified and the site dedication and ground breaking was set.

On Aug. 4, 1953 President and Mrs. McKay, Architect Anderson and President Reiser, arrived at the Basel Airport. We drove to mission headquarters in Basel and reviewed the program for the following day.

It having rained in Switzerland for more than a month, we fasted and prayed for clear skies and sunshine for Aug. 5. President McKay asked what we would do if the weather were bad, as the ceremony had to be held in the open. We assured him it would be good weather on Aug. 5.

The next morning as we left, the skies were clear and the sun shining brightly. After a most enjoyable two hour ride we arrived at the temple site. It was a glorious morning, with the majestic Alps in clear view. President McKay was elated with the site and surroundings.

After a program the group marched to the southeast corner of the temple lot for the ground breaking. President McKay removed the first shovel of dirt, the writer the second, then followed President Perschon, President Zimmer, Dr. Llewelyn McKay, President Reiser, Mayor Walter Rauber, Mr. Ernest Schneider and Mr. Albert Bodmer.

After a very enjoyable day we returned to Basel, and the rain came again during the night.

Construction was started October 1, 1953, and Elder Kurt Liggenstorfer of Thun, Switzerland, was employed as supervising architect, to assist Elder Zimmer.

The structure is reinforced concrete with an attractive terra cotta facing. The Swiss Temple is the first of a new type. It is a 2-story building, with all offices and work rooms on the first floor. The ordinance work will be done in one room on the second floor, with changes of scenery projected on a screen.

On November 1, 1954, President Stephen L Richards was appointed to lay the cornerstone. His party arrived in Basel, Nov. 12, 1954 and drove to the Temple the following morning; and at 2 p.m. he had laid the cornerstone.

The following nine missions will use the Temple: Swiss-Austrian, East German, West German, French, Holland, Danish, Swedish, Norwegian and Finnish.

Samuel E. Bringhurst was set apart as the first President of the Swiss Temple on July 30, 1955, by President David O. McKay.

Dedicatory Exercises

The Dedicatory Exercises were held in the Celestial Room on September 7, 1958. The touring Salt Lake Tabernacle Choir members were seated in a circle around this room, and in the main assembly room President McKay presided and conducted the meeting. In addition to the 600 persons with the Tabernacle Choir, hundreds of Church members, missionaries and servicemen from all parts of Europe, several hundred Church members from Utah, Idaho, California and various other parts of the world, were in Bern for the dedicatory services. Representing the Council of the Twelve were Elders Spencer W. Kimball, Ezra Taft Benson, Henry D. Moyle and Richard L. Evans. President David O. McKay gave the Dedicatory Prayer.

The Salt Lake Tabernacle Choir opened the services by singing "The Morning Breaks, the Shadows Flee."

The schedule of dedicatory services for the week was as follows: Monday morning, Swiss-Austrian Mission; afternoon, West German; Tuesday morning, East German; afternoon, East German; Wednesday morning, Netherlands; afternoon, Danish and Norwegian; Thursday morning, Swedish and Finnish; afternoon, French. Each dedicatory service was spoken in the language of those attending. President McKay gave the dedicatory prayer each time in English and a phrase-by-phrase translation was made by one of the mission officials.

Presidents of the Swiss Temple:

Samuel E. Bringhurst, 1955-1958.

Walter E. Trauffer, 1958—Present Incumbent.

Chapter XII

THE LOS ANGELES TEMPLE

By Edward O. Anderson
Temple Architect

" . . . in the process of time the shores of the Pacific may yet be overlooked from the temple of the Lord."

This message, which contains a note of prophecy, was part of an inspiring and encouraging epistle sent from Brigham Young and Willard Richards from the Salt Lake Valley in August 1847, to the Saints in California.

One hundred years later, as the Los Angeles Temple nears completion, the Saints on "the shores of the Pacific" have every reason for rejoicing. Their prayers have been answered. Their labors have been rewarded. Their sacrifices have borne fruit.

Situated on a prominent hill near Westwood Village, Los Angeles, California, just five miles from the ocean, the temple has already become a landmark. Because of its location and height (the spire is 257 feet above the first floor) it can be seen from such distant points as San Pedro, Catalina Island, and from ships twenty-five miles out to sea.

City officials, architects, builders, local residents, and tourists have been loud in their prase of the excellence of the structure and the striking beauty of the building and the grounds.

The prayer of the architect from the beginning has been that the same spirit that guided the builders of the temples and the Salt Lake Tabernacle in the early days of the Church be imparted to this project and that this temple might express in appearance the spiritual work to be carried on within it and at the same time be arranged so as to give comfort and ease of operation.

Title to the property which includes 24.23 acres, was obtained by the Church in March 1937, from Harold Lloyd of motion picture fame. The temple site now includes thirteen acres of the original plot. The rest of the ground is occupied

LOS ANGELES TEMPLE
Site dedicated on September 22, 1951. Temple dedicated on March 11, 1956
by President David O. McKay.

by a Bureau of Information, a heating plant, the California Mission home, and the Westwood Ward Chapel.

As much time was required to build the structure on paper as was needed to build it with concrete and stone. The former board of temple architects began making sketches the same year that the property was purchased for a building which would accommodate a company of two hundred persons. Before plans were completed, the work was stopped by World War II. After the war, zoning problems caused further delays. Then, in January 1949, the Church architect was notified by the First Presidency that he had been appointed sole architect to the temple. He was instructed to prepare plans for a larger temple, one which would accommodate a company of three hundred persons, equal to the Salt Lake Temple in size, and to add an assembly room on the top floor.

Ground-breaking ceremonies were held on September 22, 1951 at midday. Exercises were directed by President David O. McKay. Appropriate remarks were made by President McKay, his counselors, Stephen L Richards and J. Reuben Clark, Jr., President Joseph Fielding Smith representing the Council of the Twelve Apostles; Presiding Bishop LeGrand Richards, and Mayor Fletcher Bowron of the City of Los Angeles.

Following the ceremony President McKay offered the prayer, dedicating the ground in the name of the Lord as a place upon which a temple should stand.

By July 7, 1952 plans and specifications had been fully prepared, a permit to build the temple had been issued by the Los Angeles building department, and construction work was ready to begin.

Soren N. Jacobsen was called by the Church to supervise the construction, and his workmanship has brought great praise from many sources.

The Saints in the temple area meanwhile had not been idle. The task of raising a million dollars seemed like a tremendous project, but the people never hesitated. On February 1, 1952, stake presidencies, high council members, patriarchs, and bishoprics, and their wives, along with representatives of the California Mission, met in the South Los Angeles Stake Center at Huntington Park to launch the campaign. Each stake president made a pledge for his stake, and throughout the area ward and stake leaders showed the way by being the first to make contributions and pledges.

People were asked to contribute what they considered to be their fair share of the total. The response was immediate and overwhelming. At April conference in 1952, stake presidents reported to the First Presidency that they had received money and pledges, not for $1,000,000, but for $1,648,613.17!

Stories of sacrifices and devotion beyond the call of duty are legion. Small children drained their savings banks and gave up their allowances so they could help build the temple. Teen-agers by the thousands gave generously, often going without things they wanted and needed. Some families put off home improvements; others decided to drive the old car a few more years; still others contributed their vacation money to the cause.

By early August of 1955 the stakes and mission had given to the Church in excess of $1,300,000.00 with the promise that before the temple is dedicated they would contribute the full amount of their pledge. Stake presidents have reported that the project has been faith-promoting and testimony-building, an ex-perience that none who has participated will forget. Peace and happiness have come to all as a result of having the opportunity to help build the house of the Lord.

It was a joyous day in August 1952 when heavy equipment moved onto the site, and excavation was begun. An idea of the size of the undertaking can be had from the following figures:

The temple is 364 feet wide and 241 feet deep and con-tains 190,614 square feet of floor space, or approximately four and one half acres. Some 90,258 sacks of cement were used in the project, and 16,050 cubic yards of concrete were poured. The depth of the concrete foundations is 24 feet, and the over-all height of the building including the tower is 257 feet 8½ inches. The tower extends 151 feet 8½ inches above the roof.

The temple contains ninety rooms. Each of the ordinance rooms, which are on the second floor, has a capacity of 300 persons. The chapel in the southwest wing seats 380, while the dining room in the southeast wing will accommodate 300. The largest room in the building is the assembly room, which occupies most of the third floor. It is 257 feet long, 76 feet 7 inches wide, 34 feet high, and will seat 2,600 persons.

The electrical capacity of the temple is sufficient to light 1,000 five-room residences. There are in the building approximately 16,500 feet (nearly three and one-half miles) of fluorescent tubing, with 38 miles of cable and wire, and 52 lighting panels.

Built of reinforced concrete and structural steel, the building is fireproof and quake-resistant. The exterior is covered with 146,000 square feet of Mo-Sai stone facing of crushed quartz and white Portland cement quarried in Utah and Nevada. Each stone is eight by seven feet in size and 2¼ inches thick, weighing approximately 1600 pounds. The stones are fastened to the concrete wall with bolts and concrete grout. The wainscot around the exterior of the temple is of Rockville granite from Cold Springs, Minnesota. Exterior stair treads are solid granite.

The building exterior was designed to withstand the wear and tear of the elements. The quartz of the cast stone and the quartz in the granite are in harmony and each gives the same life to the wall surface in daylight; they sparkle in the sunshine, and glow in the floodlights at night. The surface is also self-cleaning.

The statue of the Angel Moroni which surmounts the tower is the creation of Millard F. Malin. The cast aluminum statue, which weighs 2100 pounds and is 15 feet 5½ inches tall is covered with gold leaf. The trumpet in the hands of the angel is eight feet long. While the building itself faces southeast, the statue faces east.

The stone grilles over the windows not only add to the beauty of the building but also serve to cut down the direct rays of the sun, at the same time emitting a maximum amount of light.

All materials used have been selected to withstand wear and to cut down cost of maintenance. Eight types of marble, quarried in Vermont, Tennessee, Italy, and France, adorn the inside the building. High-grade carpets and tile are used on the floors. Vinylized fabric and mosaic tile cover many of the walls.

The baptismal font, which is supported by twelve bronze

oxen modeled by Sculptor Millard F. Malin, is a fine piece of workmanship in stainless steel. A mural on the wall of the baptistry depicting the baptism of the Savior by John the Baptist in the River Jordan with the Mount of Temptation in the background was painted by Joseph Gibby of Los Angeles (formerly of Ogden, Utah).

The murals in the ordinance rooms, are brilliantly executed, and startling in their effect. Artist Harris Weberg of Ogden who has painted murals in the Idaho Falls Temple depicts the creation of the earth in the oval creation room. Edward Grigware, of Cody, Wyoming has created unbelievably beautiful scenes on the walls of the garden room. Here planting areas filled with potted flowers and plants, along with marble trim throughout, blend harmoniously with the murals.

The world room shows Adam and Eve leaving the Garden of Eden entering the lone and dreary world. The artist, Robert L. Shepherd, formerly bishop of Winder Ward in Salt Lake City, has indeed captured the stark but enchanting beauty of the deserts in his paintings. He has also done work in the Idaho Falls and Manti temples.

The terrestrial room has been planned for peace and comfort with subdued colors and furnishings. This arrangement helps to accent further the lovely brilliance of the celestial room where the walls were decorated by Alfred Lippold and his workers under the direction of Edward Grigware. As elsewhere in the temple, the furnishings for the room were fashioned by th architect, and the carpets, draperies, and upholstery material were especially designed or selected for the room, and blend into a symphony of indescribable beauty. The sealing rooms are equally lovely. The story of the landscaping of the temple grounds is intriguing, but can be told only briefly here. Long before the building itself was completed approximately four acres of lawn was put in, some twelve species of trees (several dozen individual trees in all) were transplanted, and ornamental plants and shrubs and flowers were placed. It is difficult to believe that many of the trees, some of which extend 80 feet into the air, have not been growing on the grounds for many years.

Twenty-two Specimen Olive trees line the two walks leading up to the building from Santa Monica Boulevard. This is a favorite shade and ornamental tree in Southern California and was selected because of its interesting multiple branching and because it is easily adapted to domestic use. These trees (which are 35 to 45 feet wide and 35 feet tall) were secured in the La Mirada area, thirty miles from the temple, and hauled in at night under special permits because of the great width.

About two dozen Canary Island Pine trees also adorn the grounds. Two of the largest are seventy feet tall. One of these was boxed in a nine foot box about one-half mile from the temple and left for three months to become established before it was moved to the temple grounds. The tree and soil weighed about 17 tons.

Also planted on the grounds are three varieties of palm trees, Bird of Paradise trees, fern trees, coast Redwoods, Liquid Amber trees, Coral trees and maidenhair trees, and two very rare Chinese Ginkgo trees.

Two rock gardens, a reflection pool, a rose garden (Mia Maid roses contributed by Mutual girls of the area) and two fountains, add to the beauty of the grounds. Shrubs planted in large boxes on top of the wings of the building draw much comment. More than two carloads of peat moss, and over 600 tons of fertilizer were used in preparing the grounds.

The reaction of men who have worked on the project is worthy of note. Each day's work was started with prayer, and in spite of all the activity of construction a spirit of peace seemed to permeate the grounds.

Families of at least three of the men who worked on the building have joined the Church, and a number of families of other workmen are seriously investigating. One non-member sent his son on a mission after he started working on the building. When the son returned he baptized his father into the Church.

Improvement Era, November, 1955.

Physical and Historical Description

Millard F. Malin designed and cast the oxen supporting the baptismal font, assisted by Morris Brooks and Carl Quilter. The temple font is a perfect circle, the fonts for the Swiss and London temples will be constructed in oval shape. Each of the six oxen on one side of the font differ in appearance and position, as is also the case on the other side of the font. The oxen are first modeled in clay, after which plaster casts are made and are then cast in aluminum or bronze in a foundry in New York. Types of the Ranger Spanish fighting bulls with curving horns were used instead of the modern developed beef cattle, as the former are more artistic.

With the removal of much of the scaffolding and beautiful stone work, named Mo-Sai, has added vitality and living essence to the huge monolithic structure. The installation of the Mo-Sai is complete on the wings, the four sides and two ends of the temple. Only sections at the center, now almost completed, and the tower, are yet to be covered with this sparkling veneer.

The Mo-Sai, manufactured by the Otto Buehner Company, has been cast in over 2,500 separate pieces to overlay the 126,000 square feet of surface of the Temple, enough to cover an area slightly larger than three football fields. It is to the credit of the makers that of 2,500 pieces cast, all are of the same texture and the same color.

The Mo-Sai is made of crushed and graded quartz aggregate mixed in white Portland cement. Each stone is 2½ inches thick and reinforced throughout with a steel four-inch mesh. Each unit has a compressive strength of not less than 6,000 pounds per square inch. Because of the extreme hardness of the aggregate and the fine quality of cement used, the Mo-Sai stones should last for hundreds of years.

Most of the Mo-Sai blocks are six by seven feet and weigh in excess of 1,600 pounds. The delicate patterns of grille and simple decoration are likewise of Mo-Sai and are among the largest pieces of cast stone ever made. Those surrounding the front courtyard are 14 feet high, seven feet wide and weigh nearly two tons each.

To fasten the blocks to the 15,053 cubic yards of poured concrete, some 60,000 holes were formed in the walls. All the holes were matched to the blocks of stone so that bolts can hold each stone in place. These bolts are then cemented into place by pouring a thin concrete, called grout, behind each stone and into the bolt holes.

The surface of each piece has been etched with acid to expose the facets of aggregate. When sunshine strikes the stone work, it glistens and sparkles and reflects the light.

From the careful and expert skill of Stanley N. Child, masonry supervisor, every piece of stone is put into place straight and true, not varying as much as 1/100 of an inch. Not even a slight warp in a single stone is allowed to remain. When fastened into place the stones are tightened against the concrete wall making them as flat as the proverbial Kansas Prairie. A slight crack is left between each stone to allow for any expansion or contraction which might result from extremes in temperatures. A pliable plastic putty which will never harden is filled or "pointed" between the stones.

Deseret News, May 8, 1954.

The cornerstone for this, the eleventh and largest temple to be built by the Church of Jesus Christ of Latter-day Saints, was laid on Friday, December 11, 1953, with most of the General authorities of the Church in attendance, with President David O. McKay presiding. Some ten thousand members and interested friends, who gathered on the temple lot are said to have constituted the largest number of Latter-day Saints ever to come together in California on one occasion. Many distinguished guests and public officials were also present. President Stephen L. Richards laid the cornerstone.

The temple is located on a hill overlooking a vast area of Los Angeles. It is at Santa Monica Boulevard and Selby Avenue in west Los Angeles, approximately five miles from the ocean front.

The cost of the Los Angeles Temple itself was around $4,000,000.00 and with other buildings and properties connected with the Temple will bring the valuation plant to about $6,000,000.00, said President David O. McKay.

Elder Benjamin L. Bowring was named Temple president, and A Merlin Steed was chosen as President of the Los Angeles Temple Mission, with Raymond A. Summers as first counselor of that Mission.

A. Bent Petersen, second counselor in the Manti Temple presidency, was appointed recorder of the Los Angeles Temple.

The Los Angeles Temple was dedicated on March 11, 1958, by President David O. McKay.

General Authorities present at the dedication — All members of the First Presidency: David O. McKay, Stephen L. Richards, J. Reuben Clark. Presiding Patriarch: Eldred G. Smith.

All members of the Council of Twelve Apostles: Joseph Fielding Smith, Mark E. Petersen, LeGrand Richards, Harold B. Lee, Henry D. Moyle, Adam S. Bennion, Spencer W. Kimball, Delbert L. Stapley, Richard L. Evans, Ezra Taft Benson, Marion G. Romney, George Q. Morris. All Assistants to the Twelve: ElRay Christiansen, Thomas E. McKay, John Longdon, Clifford E. Young, Hugh B. Brown, Alma Sonne, Stirling W. Sill.

All members of the First Council of Seventy: Levi Edgar Young, Milton R. Hunter, Antoine R. Ivins, Bruce R. McConkie, Oscar A. Kirkham, Marion T. Hanks, S. Dilworth Young.

THOUSANDS TOUR THE LOS ANGELES TEMPLE

— Before its dedication, on March 11, 1956, visitors were permitted to see the Temple for a period from December 19, 1955 to Feb. 18, 1956. During that time 662,336 persons had the privilege of making this tour. During the final week 25,000 persons entered the temple each day. This photograph shows 3,500 persons (four abreast, one-half mile long) waiting to go through the temple on the Monday morning of the last week it was open to the public. On this day 120 persons made the tour on wheel chairs.

Chapter XIII

NEW ZEALAND TEMPLE
Site Selected by Inspiration

The story of a temple to be erected by the Church of Jesus Christ of Latter-day Saints in the far off South Pacific islands began when President David O. McKay assigned President Wendell B. Mendenhall of the San Joaquin Stake to a special mission, that of investigating possible temple sites in the lands of the South Seas. President Mendenhall accepted this confidential appointment. He investigated available lands in Auckland, New Zealand, where mission headquarters are located. But the satisfaction of obtaining the proper place for the temple was not experienced as yet.

"Then one day I felt I should go to Hamilton to visit the college," (eighty miles southeast of Auckland), President Mendenhall related to the writer. "While in the car on the way, the whole thing came to me in an instant. The temple should be there by the college. The Church facilities for construction were already there, and that was the center of the population of the mission. Then, in my mind, I could see the area even before I arrived, and I could envision the hill where the temple should stand. As soon as I arrived at the college and drove over the top of the hill, my whole vision was confirmed. In my heart I felt that the Lord had especially made this hill for his temple, everything, about it was so majestic and beautiful."

Without discussing the matter of a temple site with anyone, President Mendenhall investigated the possibility of purchasing this land for an addition to the Church property but received a negative response. This was the only strip of property separating the college grounds from the extensive Church farm lands; if the property could be acquired, it would join the land together into one choice whole.

Two weeks later, President McKay arrived late one evening. Being travel weary, he retired at once, and it was not until

THE NEW ZEALAND TEMPLE

Site dedicated on December 21, 1955, by Ariel S. Ballif.
The Temple was dedicated on April 20, 1958, by President David O. McKay.

early the next morning that President Mendenhall greeted him while in the company of three other brethren. Consequently, there could be no mention of a site for the temple. President McKay, President Mendenhall, and the other three brethren drove out to look over the college construction and the farm lands.

"As we drove up the road, there was that noble hill," continued President Mendenhall. "We directed our travel around the back of it to the farm lands. After we stepped from the car and were looking around, President McKay called me to one side. By the way he was looking at the hill, I could tell immediately what was on his mind. I had not said a word to him. He asked, "What do you think?" I knew what his question implied, and I simply asked in return, "What do you think, President McKay?" And then in an almost prophetic tone he pronounced 'This is the place to build the temple.' "

The Lord had again revealed his will unto his servant, a prophet of God.

". . . Then a week later President McKay came to this beautiful spot," President Mendenhall related, "and I bear witness to you, . . . that I saw the prophet of this Church in the spirit of vision, and when he walked away from that hill, he knew the house of the Lord was to be erected upon that particular spot."

President Mendenhall had found that the Murray family, the property owners — three brothers, their mother and a sister — were not willing to sell. But the day President McKay returned to the hill, the three brothers watched as he walked around it. Then as the brethren went to get in the car to leave the hill, one of the three approached President Mendenhall and said they did not want to sell the property, but suggested they discuss the matter after President McKay had finished his tour. As the car drove away, President McKay said in a tone of reassuring confidence, "They will sell it; they will sell it."

Accordingly, the day President McKay left, President Mendenhall and Elder George Biesinger, supervisor of Church construction in New Zealand, went to see the Murray brothers. That morning they sat upon the hill itself as they discussed the property, and by eleven o'clock the owners had agreed to see an attorney about the sale. There were two of the brothers present at the morning meeting, so they called the other brother, who was fishing, the sister from another community, and their mother, and all went into town. At three o'clock that afternoon the Murray family had definitely decided to sell the property.

"Elder Biesinger and I previously had gone over the property very thoroughly and had put a valuation on it by breaking it down into various lots and acres," President Mendenhall reported. "When we met with the attorney, we found the sellers had over-priced the property considerably. After debating the matter for about an hour, the attorney said, 'Would you be willing to consider this purchase if I break the property down my way and arrive at its valuation?' We told him we would."

After working a while, he passed his figures to President Mendenhall and Elder Biesinger. As they looked at it, the figures were difficult to believe — the proposal was, to the penny, the evaluation they had computed.

By late afternoon the Church had a signed agreement from the owners to sell. A family of five all decided in a few hours against their negative decision of the week before. "And today," President Mendenhall explains, "they can't understand why they ever sold the land."

But this was not the only marvel in the acquisition of the land. The purchase naturally had to be approved by the New Zealand Land Aggregation Court. The day the local court turned it down, Mr. Corbett, the National Minister of Lands, went with President Mendenhall to look over the property. He did not know of the local denial. As he drove past the Church construction, he was impressed by the college and by the Church belief of developing the Maori people to the highest standard. Genuinely pleased, he turned to President Mendenhall and asked him to take this dictation: "Received personal assurance this day from the Minister of Lands and Maori Affairs that the New Zealand Government will not oppose the acquisition of this property."

The Spirit of the Lord had moved: The property was now owned by the Church; the temple would arise from the spot pronounced by a latter-day prophet as the place where the house of the Lord should be built.

The hill from which the temple will rise is 170 feet high and makes, in President Mendenhall's opinion, "The most beautiful temple site in the Church."

Members of the Church in New Zealand indeed deserve to be called Saints because of their ingenuous spirit, childlike faith, and consecration to the things of the Lord. Their humility was once again evidenced the day the plans to build the temple were announced. The annual *hui tau*, the all mission conference, was in progress with four thousand members in attendance. A telephone call was placed from Salt Lake City so the announcement could be made on that occasion. Returning to the conference with this humbling yet thrilling telephone message, Elder Biesinger related that the First Presidency desired a temple to be built and that it be completed two years from the date of ground breaking. It was to be built, as was the college, entirely through volunteer missionary labor.

The joy in the hearts of these people was exceedingly great. All four thousand of them raised their hands and solemnly, with tears of joy in their eyes, sustained the proposal. Perhaps this will be the most remembered *hui tau* of New Zealand. Today the members of the mission are supporting two hundred labor missionaries. What little they have, they are giving in support of their sustaining vote at that eventful conference.

As some of the pioneers in the Salt Lake Valley learned their crafts while working on the Assembly Hall before applying their skills to the building of the Salt Lake Temple, a similar story is being written in New Zealand. The unskilled native missionary volunteers have been assisting with the college construction there. When work on the college commenced in 1949, in that area there were no transportation permits or available building materials — lumber, gravel, or concrete. Today, with nothing but a purpose for a beginning, a rock quarry has been acquired, and four thousand acres of timberland furnish the lumber which is cut and then sawed in a mill now owned by the Church. While serving the Lord, men and boys have learned their trades. Today they are ". . . working in sawmills, in the rock crushers, in the lime pits, in the cement plant, in the planing mill, in the timber, and some are laying brick. You have never seen such a pioneer organization in your life, . . ." They have learned to use machinery and materials with such adeptness that they are prepared for the construction of the temple. They have indeed sought first the kingdom of God and other things are being added unto them. When the construction is completed, they will be trained for specialized occupations.

The temple was designed by Church architect, Elder Edward O. Anderson, and the blueprints were mailed from Salt Lake City, September 1, 1955. After the plans are approved by the New Zealand government and after the dedication and ground-breaking services are held, all will be in readiness for work on the temple to commence. It is expected that this edifice will be completed within two years. The construction will be a special type of concrete brick. The outward appearance will resemble the recently dedicated Swiss Temple, and the floor plan will be similar.

The New Zealand Temple will serve a Church membership of over 40,000. Thirteen thousand are from New Zealand, and the rest from the Tongan, Tahitian, Samoan, and Australian missions. The Saints there have pledged their readiness and willingness to give their money or labor or both to this house of the Lord in the South Pacific.

Last May, President Mendenhall was set apart by the First Presidency to perform a "special service pertaining particularly to the erection and completion of the college in New Zealand and of the temple that is to be erected." This service is also to include the development of the farm lands, from which the college will eventually receive some financial support. Since that time, President Mendenhall has been appointed chairman of the Church building committee, but the special New Zealand assignment stands.

While in New Zealand in January 1955, President McKay assigned Elder George Biesinger, who was supervisor of all Church construction in New Zealand, the additional task of supervising construction of the temple.

With the construction of the college, the development of the farm lands, and the acquisition of the temple site, there are three to four hundred people visiting the grounds each Sunday. This is proving to be the "Temple Hill" mission of New Zealand, for there are forty native missionary guides there to explain the Church program, the great gospel plan, and to leave their testimonies written upon the hearts of the visitors. In this sense, the people of New Zealand are flocking unto the hill of the Lord.

In every deed, this temple in the South Pacific will stand as a beacon light upon a hill, and with the spirit of the Saints there, others will be led to the blessings and power to be received therein.

Improvement Era, November, 1955

Location of Temple Site

The temple site and college property in New Zealand is located about three miles south of Hamilton, which is approximately twenty-five miles south of the New Zealand Mission headquarters in Auckland. It comprises a tract of land aggregating 1,300 acres. Approval for building the temple was given in a meeting of the First Presidency and the Council of the Twelve on Thursday, February 17, 1955, after which the decision was publicly given.

The site embodies the mission Hui Tau Hall, a large joinery or workshop, faculty and administration residence, girls' dormitories, five classroom buildings, an administrative building, a large gymnasium, auditorium, swimming pool and cafeteria, five boys' dormitories, native workers' homes, and situated on this site is a beautiful lake owned by the Church and a future ball field. The buildings above mentioned have either been erected or will be erected.

Most of the land surrounding the college and temple site will be operated by the Church as a model farm. It is adjacent to a 17,000 acre tract of land owned by the New Zealand government which is under course of reclamation.

Ground-Breaking Historical Data

On December 21, 1955, ground-breaking services were held, signifying the commencement of construction of the temple, also the David O. McKay Auditorium Building and the Matthew Cowley Memorial Administration Building.

Presided over by Ariel S. Ballif, New Zealand Mission president, the exercises began at 2 p.m. on Temple Hill, which overlooks the college campus. In spite of inclement weather for several days before, the day was clear, calm and warm. The countryside from the hilltop was picturesque, with the white college buildings dotted against the landscape of low green rolling hills and evergreen shrubs.

Over 600 people, representing all the districts of the mission, and with district presidents of 15 of the 16 districts, were seated in the area on which the actual structure of the temple will be erected. The united and enthusiastic spirit of those present added to the spiritual event.

Adding a beautiful touch, the music was furnished by a well-balanced combined choir, composed mainly of the Auckland District Choir, assisted by members from nearly every district. Directed by Elder Kelly Harris, their lovely rendition of "Let the Mountains Shout for Joy" and "I Walked Today Where Jesus Walked" were inspirational and touched the hearts of all.

A prayer of dedication invoking the blessings of the Lord to attend building program and workmen in erecting the college structures and temple, that they might be speedily completed and properly used for the development of the lives of the people here, was offered by President Ballif, after which he, with Elder Mendenhall and Elder Biesinger, turned the first sod.

Construction of New Zealand Temple

The temple contains 75 rooms on three levels, the basement floor containing the baptistry, offices, dressing rooms, dining rooms, kitchen, laundry, and the baptismal font.

This font, cast in bronze in Italy, is oval in shape and is supported on the shoulders of twelve oxen. A mural of Jesus Christ being baptized by John the Baptist adorns one wall. It is the work of artist Paul P. Forster.

On the main floor are 24 rooms including the chapel, lounges, entries, foyers, and general offices. The upper floor consists of ten rooms including the lecture room, the Celestial room, four sealing rooms and rest rooms.

During a twenty-three day "open house," 112,500 persons toured the temple's interior, prior to its dedication, after which only faithful Church members may participate in the sacred ceremonies for which the temple was built.

The cornerstone for this temple was laid on December 22, 1956, by Elder Hugh B. Brown.

President David O. McKay dedicated the New Zealand Temple on April 20, 1958.

Presidents of the New Zealand Temple:

E. Albert Rosenvall, 1958-1961.
John B. Hawkes, 1961-1964.
Heber G. Jensen, 1964—Present Incumbent.

THE LONDON TEMPLE

Site dedicated on August 10, 1953, by President David O. McKay.
This Temple was dedicated on September 7, 1958,
by President David O. McKay.

Chapter XIV

THE LONDON TEMPLE

The site for the erection of a temple in London was approved by President David O. McKay when visiting England in 1952. The exact spot where the Temple will be erected was chosen by him in association with Edward O. Anderson, architect of the Los Angeles, London and Swiss temples. This temple is in the vicinity where twenty millions of people live. The temple site was dedicated by President McKay on August 10, 1953. Nearby this property is the little hamlet of New Chapel, which is named for the Baronial Hall.

The estate purchased by the Church includes several buildings, the most important being the big mansion, referred to as "The Hall." This stately mansion will lend itself to holding services, as well as housing a temple president, caretaker and providing sleeping rooms for people coming long distances to attend the temple. This mansion with oak finish, overlooks the gardens and is a source of delight and inspiration to those who have the privilege of exploring it. It is a three-story country home of forty spacious and comfortable rooms, a small-ballroom with orchestra balcony, two large kitchens, two dining rooms, fifteen bedrooms and eight large modern bathrooms. Other buildings — garages, laundry, fuel sheds, servants' lodges, power plant, are shielded from the gardens by a row of tall evergreens. All buildings will be put to proper use; all are in good repair.

Beyond the buildings and formal gardens (which comprise about ten acres) are two hayfields, and across the highway but a part of the estate are two more hayfields. This 32-acre estate is located twenty-four miles south of London, near East Grinstead, in Surrey.

When President David O. McKay broke ground for the British Temple on Saturday, August 27, 1955, at Newchapel, Surrey, England, about twenty-five miles south of London, the dream of the British members of the Church for a house of the Lord in their homeland moved a step closer to realization.

The services were conducted under a cove of trees in the garden until it was time for President McKay to walk to the point for the southeast corner of the temple. The program included:

"The Morning Breaks," Salt Lake Tabernacle Choir; Invocation, Elder J. Spencer Cornwall, conductor of the Choir; "The Lord's Prayer," Tabernacle Choir; Address, President A. Hamer Reiser of the British Mission; Address, Elder Edward O. Anderson, Church Temple Architect; Address, Sir Thomas Bennett, supervising architect for the British Temple; Address, President David O. McKay followed by the ground breaking; "O My Father," male chorus of the Tabernacle Choir; Benediction, Elder Richard L. Evans of the Council of the Twelve.

The sun shone until the breaking of the ground, and then rain fell during the closing hymn and prayer. Later there was sunshine again as the visitors toured the temple grounds.

The story of Newchapel, the site of the London Temple, is a fascinating one. The earliest record appears to be found in William the Conqueror's *Doomsday Book*. The lands surrounding the temple site are inventoried there, and the documents formed the basis for the division of the land to William's loyal followers and the establishment of the feudal system.

Newchapel was an old Elizabethan farm, and the remains of the old farmhouse can be seen in the present house which stands on the estate.

Much later the property was acquired by a British inventor who undertook to develop the farm into a country estate. He sold the property to an American who made the largest investment in the property, developing the gardens and the home. Again the property was sold, this time to Mr. and Mrs. Pears of the Pears Soap Company.

During his 1952 European tour, President McKay examined several sites in Great Britain that might be suitable for a temple. Late in this exploration, he and the late Elder Stayner Richards, who was then an Assistant to the Council of the Twelve and president of the British Mission, found Newchapel but discovered that it was not for sale. President Richards completed his mission, and President Reiser assumed his duties, one of which was to find a site for the temple. About six months after President McKay and President Richards had seen the New chapel property, the owners were again approached. This time they consented to sell to the Church. It took several months to close the negotiations, but when President

McKay returned to Europe in 1953, he dedicated this site for a temple.

The home on the property, although Elizabethan in style, is only about thirty years old.

A branch of the Church has been established at New-chapel, and the genealogical offices of the British Mission have been moved to a remodeled building on the grounds. President Charles Beckingham of the Newchapel Branch has been appointed caretaker of the grounds and building, and Brother Albert Stephenson has been appointed gardener. The beautiful formal gardens occupy about one-third of the property. It is a site of natural beauty the year around.

Improvement Era, November, 1955

Construction Data on the London Temple

The cornerstone of the London Temple was laid on May 11, 1957, by Elder Richard L. Evans, a member of the Council of the Twelve.

The Temple covers 13,000 square feet and incorporates 34,000 square feet of floor space in its four floors. It is faced with white Portland stone, roofed in copper and surmounted by a Portland stone tower with a spire covered in lead-coated copper, the tip of which rises 160 feet above the ground.

President David O. McKay dedicated the London Temple on September 7, 1958. At the dedication services only 600 people could be accommodated in the main temple auditorium where the speakers could be seen. An additional 1,400 were crowded into the other rooms of the building where they heard the speeches and prayer over a public address system.

Some 76,000 people had visited the temple during the public viewing held August 16 to September 3. Only 50,000 had been anticipated, and the viewing period had to be extended three days to accommodate the crowds.

At the dedication services, in addition to President McKay, there were present of the General Authorities of the Church President Joseph Fielding Smith, Elder Henry D. Moyle, Elder Richard L. Evans and Elder Hugh B. Brown of the Council of the Twelve. Elder ElRay L. Christiansen and Elder Gordon B. Hinckley represented the Assistants to the Council of the Twelve. Bishop Thorpe B. Isaacson represented the Presiding Bishopric. Mrs. Belle S. Spafford represented the Relief Society and Mrs. Emily H. Bennett represented the YWMIA presidency.

Elder Selvoy J. Boyer was set apart as the first president of this Temple on August 12, 1958, by President David O. McKay.

Chapter XV

THE ENDOWMENT HOUSE

HISTORICAL SKETCH

PRES. HEBER C. KIMBALL

When the Saints had arrived in the Great Salt Lake Valley, it was readily apparent that unless some temporary building should be constructed in which to do ordinance work for the living and the dead, pending the completion of the Salt Lake Temple, the necessary ordinances for their salvation could not be performed. It was therefore decided to construct such a building and in April of 1854 the site for this building was laid out in the northwest corner of the Temple Block in Salt Lake City. This building was being plastered in February of 1855 and was completed in April following. This two-story adobe building was known first as the Endowment Rooms and later as the Endowment House. It was dedicated on May 5, 1855, by President Heber C. Kimball, who also conducted the services for many years in this building which President Young called "The House of the Lord." On the day of its dedication eight people received their endowments and in the years that followed as many as sixty persons would receive their endowments in one day. In addition to endowment work, prayer circles were held here and outgoing missionaries received instructions and were set apart before leaving for their missions. In 1856 an addition was built on the south side of the building because of the lack of room for the increased attendance, for the work therein conducted. The spirit of prophecy[1 and 2] and other gifts of the Spirit were enjoyed abundantly in this building in accordance with the statement made by President Brigham Young at the time of its dedication: "The Spirit of the Lord would be in it, for no one will be permitted to go into it to pollute it." In the spring of 1889, President Wilford Woodruff gave orders that this building be taken down, it having served for thirty-four years; the Saints being privileged to do work for the salvation of the living and dead in the St. George, Logan, and Manti Temples, besides anticipating that privilege in the Salt Lake Temple which was fast being completed at the time the Endowment House was razed.

[1]*Statement by Bishop James Watson:* "On the morning of the 15th day of April, 1865, my wife and I were going through the Temple block towards the Endowment House, as we had been previously requested by our Bishop to go and get our endowments. I was in a very thoughful mood and prayed silently in my own mind that the Lord would give me grace to always adhere to the truth and have my mind quickened by the Holy Ghost, so that I might always be able to decide between truth and error and to have courage to defend the principles of the Gospel of our Lord and Savior Jesus Christ.

"We overtook President H. C. Kimball and were walking leisurely along, when Willard G. Smith overtook us and said to President Kimball, 'Have you heard the news? President Lincoln was assassinated last night while at the theatre in Washington. See the flags are at half-mast.' After some little conversation we entered the Endowment House. The thought of the sad death of President Lincoln weighed heavily on my mind, and made a deep impression on me. In going through the House, Brother Kimball gave me a very impressive lecture. Fixing his eyes on me, he said:

"'Do you know that you will yet be called upon to stand in front of the enemy?' Then he paused for a reply.

"After studying a few seconds, I answered, 'No, sir.'

"Giving me a piercing look, he said: 'Don't you believe it?" I answered, 'No, sir.'

"Gazing at me intently, he said, 'Don't you believe what I say?' I answered, 'How can I believe when I have no evidence or knowledge of it?' 'You foolish man,' he said, 'If you had a knowledge of it you would not require anv belief.'

"Pointing at me again, he said, 'You will yet be called upon to stand in front of the enemy, while bullets will fly around as thick as hail. Yet not a hair of your head shall be hurt. Do you believe that?'

"After a little study, I answered, 'No, sir.' He seemed a little perplexed at my obstinacy and asked, 'Why don't you believe it?' I said, 'Because I have been in a hailstorm, and I know that it is impossible to be in a hail-storm without being hit, and if the bullets are to fly around me as thick as hail, I am sure I will be hit.' He said, 'Don't you think if you saw them coming you could duck them?' I said I thought I could. 'But,' said he, 'they come so quick you cannot do it.'

"Then fixing his eyes on me, he said: 'The day will come when you will stand in the front rank in face of the enemy, but if you will live pure and keep your garments clean, not one hair of your head will be hurt. Do you believe that?'

"I said, 'Brother Kimball, I believe what you say.' "

ENDOWMENT HOUSE

Site laid out in April, 1854. Building dedicated on May 5, 1855, by President Heber C. Kimball. This building was razed in the spring of 1889.

²*Statement by Elder Edward Stevenson:* "I cheerfully contribute the following, concerning one of the greatest prophets of the nineteenth century—Heber C. Kimball. In 1856 a little group of friends convened in the House of the Lord were engaged in pleasant conversation on the isolated condition of the Latter-day Saints.

" 'Yes,' said Brother Heber (by which name he was so familiarly known), 'we think we are secure here in the chambers of the everlasting hills, where we can close those few doors of the canyons against mobs and persecutors, the wicked and the vile, who have always beset us with violence and robbery, but I want to say to you, my brethren, the time is coming when we will be mixed up in these now peaceful valleys to that extent that it will be difficult to tell the face of a Saint from the face of an enemy to the people of God. Then, brethren, look out for the great sieve, for there will be a great sifting time, and many will fall; for I say unto you there is a test, a test coming, and who will be able to stand?'

"The emphasis with which those words were spoken I shall never forget."

Life of Heber C. Kimball, by Orson F. Whitney, pp. 455-7.

Impression Given of the Spirit Verified

By Heber C. Kimball

(From Discourse given on April 4, 1866, in Salt Lake Tabernacle)

Under President Young I have presided over the giving of endowments for the last fifteen years. Last Saturday there were over twenty persons in the house to receive their endowments. They came well recommended by their bishops as being worthy, good, and faithful members of the Church of Jesus Christ of Latter-day Saints. I had previously had an impression that many of the people were becoming lukewarm, and even cold, in the performance of some of their duties. After the company had gone through, I gave them a lecture, and it came to me by the Spirit of God to try, if my impression was correct or not. After instructing them that they must not lie, steal nor bear false witness, etc., I asked them how many of them prayed in their families, and it transpired that there were many who neglected their duties in this respect; yet they were all recommended by their bishops as good, faithful members of the Church of Christ.

J. D., Vol. 11:210.

Chapter XVI

THE INDEPENDENCE TEMPLE SITE

Designation and Dedication of Temple Site
By Joseph the Prophet

And thus saith the Lord your God, if you will receive wisdom here is wisdom. Behold, the place which is now called Independence is the center place; and the spot for the temple is lying westward, upon a lot which is not far from the court-house.
Doctrine and Covenants, Sec. 57:3. Revelation given in July, 1831.

On the third day of August, I proceeded to dedicate the spot for the Temple, a little west of Independence, and there were also present Sidney Rigdon, Edward Partridge, W. W. Phelps, Oliver Cowdery, Martin Harris, Joseph Coe and Newel Knight.

The 87th Psalm was read. The scene was solemn and impressive.
D. H. C., Vol. 1:199.

Verily this is the word of the Lord that the city New Jerusalem shall be built by the gathering of the saints, beginning at this place, even the place of the temple, which temple shall be reared in this generation.

For verily *this generation shall not all pass away until an house shall be built unto the Lord,* and a cloud shall rest upon it, which cloud shall be even the glory of the Lord, which shall fill the house.
Doctrine and Covenants, Sec. 84:4-5. Sept. 22, 1832.

Jackson County Courthouse, erected in 1827. The building referred to in Doc. and Cov., Sec. 57:3.
(Courtesy of R. W. Pope, Independence, Mo.)

Sacred Records to be Deposited in Great Temple
By Orson Pratt

The Hill Cumorah is situated in western New York, between the villages of Palmyra and Canandaigua, about four miles from the former. It is celebrated as the ancient depository of the sacred gold plates from which the Book of Mormon was translated. Cumorah was the name by which the hill was designated in the days of the Prophet Moroni, who deposited the plates about four hundred and twenty years after the birth of Christ. The Prophet Mormon, the father of Moroni, had been entrusted with all the sacred records of his forefathers, engraved on metallic plates. New plates were made by Mormon, on which he wrote, from the more ancient books, an abridged history of the nation, incorporating therewith many revelations, prophecies, the Gospel, etc. These new plates were given to Moroni on which to finish the history. All the ancient plates Mormon deposited in Cumorah, about three hundred and eighty-four years after Christ. When Moroni, about thirty-six years after, made the deposit of the book entrusted to him, he was, without doubt, inspired to select a department of the hill separate from the great sacred depository of the numerous volumes hid up by his father. The particular place on the hill, where Moroni secreted the book, was revealed, by the angel, to the Prophet Joseph Smith, to whom the volume was delivered in September, A. D. 1827. But the grand depository of all the numerous records of the ancient nations of the western continent was located in another department of the hill, *and its contents under the charge of holy angels, until the day should come for them to be transferred to the sacred temple of Zion.*

Millennial Star, 28:417:19.

(See also "Assorted Gems of Priceless Value," pp. 295-6.)

Hill Cumorah, the depository of sacred records which will be
transferred to the Great Temple when erected.

INDEPENDENCE TEMPLE SITE. BUILDING TO THE RIGHT IS THE
HEDRICKITE OR CHURCH OF CHRIST CHAPEL.

This Temple Site was dedicated on August 3, 1831, by Joseph Smith the
Prophet, in the presence of Sidney Rigdon, Edward Partridge, W. W. Phelps,
Aliver Cowdery, Martin Harris, Joseph Coe, and Newel Knight.

Temple to be Reared in This Generation

(Excerpt from a sermon delivered by Orson Pratt on April 9, 1871.)

"The sons of Moses and the sons of Aaron shall offer an acceptable offering and
sacrifice in the house of the Lord, which house shall be established in this generation
upon the consecrated spot, as I have appointed; and the sons of Moses and of Aaron
shall be filled with the glory of God upon Mount Zion in the Lord's house, whose
sons are ye, and also many whom I have called and sent forth to build up my church;
for whosoever is faithful to the obtaining of these Priesthoods of which I have spoken,
and the magnifying of their calling are sanctified by the spirit unto the renewing of
their bodies, that they become the sons of Moses and of Aaron and the seed of Abraham and the church and kingdom and the elect of God."

Here then we see a prediction, and we believe it. Yes! The Latter-day Saints have as firm faith and rely upon this promise as much as they rely upon the promise of forgiveness of sins when they comply with the first principles of the Gospel. We just as much expect that a city will be built, called Zion, in the place and on the land which has been appointed by the Lord our God, and that a temple will be reared on the spot that has been selected, and the cornerstone of which has been laid, in the generation when this revelation was given; we just as much expect this as we expect the sun to rise in the morning and set in the evening; or as much as we expect to see the fulfillment of any of the purposes of the Lord our God, pertaining to the works of His hands. But, says the objector, "thirty-nine years have passed away." What of that? The generation has not passed away; [1, 2, 3, 4] all the people that were living thirty-nine years ago, have not passed away; but before they do pass away this will be fulfilled."

Journal of Discourses, Vol. 14, p. 275.

[1] "This generation shall not all pass away, etc. This is a promise that some living at the time when it was made, in 1832, would still be on earth in the flesh, when the house of the Lord would begin to lift its lofty spires toward the sky on that consecrated ground. A generation does not pass away in one hundred years, and every generation has a few who live over a hundred years."—Doctrine and Covenants Commentary, 1923 Edition, by Hyrum M. Smith and Janne M. Sjodahl.

(It does not say those still living in this generation shall be Saints—Why not Lamanites, Armenians, etc.?)

[2] MOSCOW, April 20 (UP)—The newspaper Socialist Agriculture said Saturday that the oldest man in the Soviet Union and probably in the world is Vaisly Nikiforovich Ivanov, who is described as 142 years old Ivanov is a Siberian peasant living at Minusinsk, near Krasnoyarsk, according to the newspaper. He was born near Minsk and migrated to Siberia when he was 90 years old. The newspaper said that he had survived six czars, six wars, four revolutions, and still claims to have a good memory. He remembers the Napoleonic invasion of Russia, the dispatch said. Ivanov now lives on a state pension. He is practically hairless and toothless, but is healthy and walks two miles a day.—Salt Lake Tribune, Sunday morning, April 21, 1940.

[3] Death came to Kasper Kerkorian as to all men—but to him it came after 115 years of active life. The gnarled Armenian, who farmed his own land until 1928, died Sunday at Rancho Los Amigos. Since the death of the 115-year-old Evan Stall last year he had been the eldest among the rancho's patriarchs. Kerkorian, who, according to records, was born in Armenia in 1825, came to this country 50 years ago to continue the rural life he loved. When asked about his age in recent years, he would smile and recount that his mother lived to be 145. For 42 years Kerkorian lived in California, much of the time near Reedley. His body will be sent there for funeral services. He leaves a son, A. Kerkorian, who resides at 5626 Blackwelder St. The son is 51.—Los Angeles Times, Wednesday morning, Feb. 14, 1940.

Present Conditions of the Land Where Eden Was

By B. H. Roberts

Note: Owing to the doubtful authenticity of the stones, the picture of which was inserted on page 200 of former printings, that illustration is omitted from the present edition of this book, and the subject matter below given is inserted in its place.

Jackson County, where is to be built the Center Stake of Zion, is in 94 West Longitude, and 39 North Latitude, being nearly equally distant from the northern boundary of the United States and the Gulf of Mexico; also about midway between the Atlantic and Pacific Oceans. The climate is delightful, being mild three-fourths of the year, though the summers are warmer and its winters colder than are the same seasons in Salt Lake Valley.

The soil is a rich black loam, in places intermingled with sand and clay, and is from two to ten feet in depth, with a subsoil of a fine quality of clay. Both climate and soil are favorable to the production of all the fruits and vegetables of the warm temperate climate; not only the hardy cereals such as oats, barley, wheat, rye, buck-wheat, corn, etc., but also tobacco, cotton, flax, sweet potatoes, and all other common vegetables, also apples, pears, apricots, persimmons, plums of many varieties, the luscious peach, the delicious grape, and a great many kinds of berries . . .

Though the supply of timber useful for lumbering purposes is nearly exhausted, you still find luxuriant growth of hickory, some black walnut, a variety of oaks, plenty of elm, cherry, honey-locust, mulberry, basswood, and box elder, huge sycamore and cottonwood in the river bottoms, also hard and soft maple. Formerly many wild animals roamed over the prairies, or lived in the woods, such as the buffalo, elk, deer, bear, wolf, beaver, and many smaller animals, together with wild turkeys, geese, quail, and a variety of singing birds. In short, it was once the hunter's paradise. Civilization, however, has driven away nearly all these animals, especially the larger ones; but they are replaced by the domestic species so useful to man, both for food and clothing, as well as rendering him valuable assistance in his labors.

The clay, of which there is unlimited quantities, makes a fine quality of brick, and at no very great distances are stone quarries which supply a good quality of light-colored sandstone, so that substantial building material may be said to be plentiful. Such is the land of Zion as I found it — a land with resources well nigh unlimited — a land yielding an abundance of all useful products, though but indifferently cultivated by the husbandmen who possess it — a land of surpassing loveliness, though its beauties are marred rather than increased by those who inhabit it.

The land being thus bountiful in its products when it is defiled under the inhabitants thereof, the mind naturally inquires, what will it be when the curse shall be removed — when it shall be possessed by the Saints of the Most High, who will consecrate liberally of their substance for the building of Zion; and all their exertions will be to glorify God, and benefit mankind—when covetousness is subdued and virtue and righteousness shall reign in every heart—and when under the blessings of Jehovah the land shall yield in its strength? When the glory of Lebanon shall be brought to Zion, the fir tree, the pine tree, and the box tree together; when for brass will be brought gold; and for iron, silver; for wood, brass; and for stones, iron; to glorify the place of God's Sanctuary! Surely when this shall come to pass, the land of Zion shall be the perfection of beauty!—*Contributor*, Vol 7:4.

Temple in Jackson County Described

By Orson Pratt

(From Discourse delivered in Tabernacle, October 26, 1879.)

"We went there because the Lord told us to go. We settled upon the very spot where the Lord commanded us. We commenced to lay the foundation of a temple about three-quarters of a mile from Independence, Jackson County, Missouri. It was then a wilderness, with large trees on the temple block. I visited that place forty-seven years afterwards, namely, a year ago last September, and not a tree was to be found on that temple block —not so much as a stump—everything seemed to be cleared off, and one would scarcely know, unless very well acquainted with the ground, where the temple site was located. There, however, we expect to build a temple different from all other temples in some respects. It will be built much larger, cover a larger area of ground, far larger than this Tabernacle covers, and this Tabernacle will accommodate from 12,000 to 15,000 people. We expect to build a temple much larger, very much larger, according to the revelation God gave to us forty years ago in regard to that temple. But you may ask in what form will it be built? Will it be built in one large room, like this Tabernacle! No; there will be twenty-four different compartments in the Temple that will be built in Jackson County. The names of these compartments were given to us some forty-five or forty-six years ago; the names we still have, and when we build these twenty-four rooms, in a circular form and arched over the center, we shall give the names to all these different compartments just as the Lord specified through Joseph Smith. Now, our enemies do not believe one word of this. They think we are enthusiastic, they think that this is all nonsense, and I do not know but there may be some of the Latter-day Saints that begin to partake of the same spirit, owing to their assimilating themselves so much to the fashion of the world, that they have lost their strong and powerful faith in that which God has predicted by the mouth of his servants. Perhaps you may ask for what purpose these twenty-four compartments are to be built. I answer not to assemble the outside world in, nor to assemble the Saints all in one place, but these buildings will be built with a special view to the different orders, or in other words, the different quorums or councils of the two Priesthoods that God has ordained on the earth That is the object of having twenty-four rooms so that each of these different quorums whether they be High Priests or Seventies, or Elders, or Bishops, or lesser Priesthood, or Teachers, or Deacons, or Patriarchs, or Apostles, or High Councils, or whatever may be the duties that are assigned to them, they will have rooms in the Temple of the Most High God adapted, set apart, constructed, and dedicated for this special purpose. Now, I have not only told you that we shall have these rooms, but I have told you the object of these rooms in short, not in full. But will there be any other buildings, excepting those twenty-four rooms that are all joined together in a circular form and arched over the center —are there any other rooms that will be built—detached from the Temple. Yes. There will be tabernacles, there will be meeting houses for the assembling of the people on the Sabbath day. There will be various places of meeting so that the people may gather together; but the Temple will be dedicated to the Priesthood of the Most High God, and for most sacred and holy purposes. Then you see that, notwithstanding all these Temples that are now building in this Territory, and those that have been built before we came here, in Kirtland and Nauvoo, the Lord is not confined to an exact pattern in relation to these Temple buildings in the different Stakes any more than He is confined in the creation of worlds to make them all of the same size. He does not make them all of one size, nor does He set them rolling on their axis in the same plane, nor does He construct any in many respects alike; there is variation as much as there is in the human form. Take men and women. There are general outlines that are common to all, but did you ever see two faces alike among all the millions of the human family? What a great variety, and yet all are constructed in general outline alike—after the image of God. So in regard to the building of Temples. The Lord will not confine Himself to any one special method to be so many feet long, so many feet wide, and so many places for the Priesthood to stand, but He will construct His Temples in a great variety of ways, and by and by, when the more perfect order shall exist we shall construct them, through the aid of revelation, in accordance with the Temples that exist in yonder heaven. And when I speak of yonder heaven I do not refer to that kind of heaven, the sectarian world sings about, beyond the bounds of time and space. I have no reference to any heaven beyond space, but I have reference to the heaven that the Lord has sanctified and made heaven in other worlds that he has created, consisting of all kinds of materials the same as our world is, and when this world passes through its various ordeals, it, too, by and by, will pass away and die like the body of man and be resuscitated again, a new heaven and a new earth, eternal in its nature. The new worlds that are thus constructed and quickened by the fullness of the celestial glory will be the heavens where the Gods will dwell, or in other words, those that are made like unto God, when their bodies are changed in all respects like unto His glorious body, changed from materiality and cleansed from sin and redeemed, they will then be immortal and dwell in a heavenly world. Now, in this world there will be Temples, and these Temples will be constructed according to the most perfect law of the celestial kingdom, for the world in which they are built or in which they stand will be a celestial body. This last Temple that I am speaking of, or this last one to be built in Jackson County, Missouri, will be constructed after that heavenly pattern in all particulars. Why? Because it will never perish, it will exist forever. "What! Do you mean to say," says one, "that the materials of that temple will not wear?" "Do you mean to say," some of you may inquire in your hearts, "that age will have no effect upon the walls and the materials of that temple?" This is what I mean—I mean to say that not only the Temple, but all the buildings that shall be built round about that Temple, and the city that will be built round about it, which will be called the New Jerusalem, will be built of materials that never will decay. "But," says one, "that will be contrary to the laws of nature." You may cite me to some of the buildings that existed before Christ that were built out of the most durable materials that could be found, and yet when the storms of hail, rain and snow came, these buildings began to waste away until they could scarcely be recognized. Well, I do not ask you to think that this Temple and the city round about it will defy the rough hand of time and the work of the elements of our globe, and exist forever, so far as natural laws are concerned; but there is a principle higher than these natural laws. Did you never think of it—a higher principle, a higher kingdom that governs all these laws of nature, such as you and I have been accustomed to understand ever since our youth. I say there is a higher law, a controlling power over all the laws of nature, that will prevent these buildings from decaying; and I wish while dwelling upon this subject to say a little about another subject; that is, the building up of Palestine with the New Jerusalem. It will be the old Jerusalem rebuilt upon its former site. Now, will that city ever be destroyed; will it ever decay? Will the Temple to be built in Palestine ever be thrown down or ever be furrowed with hail, rain, snow and frost—will these ever have any effect upon it? No, not in the least. Why? Because God will be there. So He will be in the temple of Zion on this continent, and by His power, by His laws —which are superior to all those grosser laws of nature—He will preserve both of these cities, one on the western hemisphere, and one on the eastern hemisphere, from any decay whatever. Now, we have it recorded here in this book, in the 31st chapter of Jeremiah, that this city on the eastern continent shall not be thrown down any more forever. It seems, therefore, to be an eternal city, never to be destroyed. "But," says one, "I cannot believe that; I cannot believe but what these cities will be subject, just as much as anything else, to decay." Do you believe this good book—the Bible? If you do, you are obliged to believe that such things are possible. Do you want to know some of them? I will mention one instance. You will recollect that Moses commanded Aaron to take a pot of manna and lay it before the Lord, to be kept for their generations. Now it was a noted fact that if the children of Israel gathered more manna than would last them until after the next morning, it would decay, but on the last day before the Sabbath they gathered manna for two days, and they found that on the Sabbath day it was preserved. Who preserved it? Why did it last two days instead of one? Because God counteracted those lesser laws, or laws of nature, by His divine power, which is greater than them all and He therefore preserved for two days that which would not last longer on the other days of the week than twenty-four hours. Well, we find that the Lord ordered the manna to be placed in the tabernacle to be kept for their generations, that they might see the bread wherewith He had fed them in the wilderness when He brought them forth from the land of Egypt. Did that manna decay? No, it remained fresh and pure in the tabernacle. Why? Because God was there; His divine power was there; a miracle was wrought to counteract the general laws of nature such as we generally understand them to be, and this manna was preserved from generation to generation. Now the Being that could produce this effect upon a small quantity of substance—on a pot of manna, could He not do the

same in regard to whole buildings, or is His arm so limited that
He has to work in a little narrow corner and preserve a little
handful of manna from spoiling through decay? I would say
that the same Being that could perform this, which we might
term a lesser miracle, could extend the same power to stone,
wood, and to all kinds of metal and material that might enter
into the construction of a Temple. Shall I limit that power to
the preserving of a Temple! No. The same Being could preserve
the city round about the Temple, hence it is a city that shall
never be destroyed nor thrown down from that time henceforth
and forever. God will be in the city. He will take care that the
building materials suffer nothing from the laws of nature. He
will take care that the city is illuminated by His divine power,
and especially the Temple, the most sacred of all the Temples,
where He will have His throne, where the Twelve Apostles will
have their thrones, as the judges of the twelve tribes of Israel;
He will take care that there is nothing in that Temple that shall
decay in the least degree. So it will be in the New Jerusalem.
Zion upon this great western hemisphere will have a city called
the New Jerusalem (because it has never been built before)
and God will preserve it by His divine power."

J. D. Vol. 24, pp. 24-27.

The Great Temple Seen in Vision

Diary of Joseph Lee Robinson

We had adopted the rule of attending to our family prayers
at precisely six o'clock in the evening. At this time the Saints
were in their deepest trouble. On a Sunday evening, after reading a portion of the scriptures as usual, we knelt down to attend
to our secret prayers. After addressing the Throne of Grace and
saying a few words, we commenced to pray for the Saints of
Zion, when a heavenly vision opened to my view. A light, a
beautiful light, was present before my eyes. It was in the shape
and color of a rainbow, only the bow was turned down. It was
perfect in shape and moved as a pendulum of a clock, back and
forth, with prefect exactness. I gazed upon it for a length of
time as it grew brigther until it was the purest and brightest
light I ever had seen. Then as quick as thought, a very large
building was present before my eyes. It was far enough away
for me to have a good view. I gazed with wonder and astonish-

ment upon a large and very beautiful house built of hewn gray stone, gray rock polished in with white joints, with large and beautiful windows and door sills and caps. It was altogether the largest, most impressing and beautiful building I had ever seen.

As soon as the house appeared this extraordinary light was out of my sight. Presently the voice of the Good Shepherd said to me: "This house you see is the temple of the Living God that shall be built in this generation by the hands of the Latter-day Saints, upon the consecrated spot in Jackson County, Missouri." Presently, after this and as quick as thought, I found myself in a room of that house. To me it was a heavenly place. In front of me, in the other end of the room, there was a stand, a large and beautiful stand with drapes and curtains. Over this stand this marvelous light that had led me to Zion was waving magnificently. Then the same voice said: "This is the Temple of the Living God that shall be built by the hands of the Latter-day Saints in this generation upon the consecrated spot in Jackson County, Missouri, and the pure in heart shall see the face of the Father and live. For the light you see is the glory of God that shall fill the house." Again, as quick as thought, I was removed to my former position where I gazed with wonder and admiration upon the wonderful house of God. While I was able to see the exterior of the house, the wonderful light was not visible, and I gazed again in admiration but when the house disappeared the light was visible again, waving in perfect motion until it gradually vanished from my sight and the vision closed.

I arose from my knees, my face wet with tears. "Glory to God in the highest," I exclaimed, "I have seen the Temple of the living God." My wife said after I started to pray I remained quiet for some length of time. I know and have testified many times that I know that whatever might befall the Saints, the Temple of the living God will be built by the Saints — the Latter-day Saints — in this generation.

The Great Temple and City to be Eternal

By Orson Pratt

(Excerpts from Sermon delivered in Logan, Utah, November 1, 1879.)

Now there will be this difference between that city and the cities and Temples which are being built. The cities and temples which we are now engaged in building, we expect to decay; we expect the rock and the various building materials will in time waste away, according to natural laws. But when we build that great central city, the New Jerusalem, there will be no such thing as the word decay associated with it; it will not decay any more than the pot of manna which was gathered by the children of Israel and put into a sacred place in the ark of the covenant. It was preserved from year to year by the power of God; so will He preserve the city of New Jerusalem, the dwelling houses, the tabernacles, the Temples, etc., from the effects of storms and time. It is intended that it will be taken up to heaven, when the earth passes away. It is intended to be one of those choice and holy places where the Lord will dwell, when He shall visit from time to time, in the midst of the great latter-day Zion, after it shall be connected with the City of Enoch. That, then, is the difference.

The Lord our God will command His servants to build that Temple in the most perfect order, differing very much from the Temples that are now being built. You are engaged in building Temples after a certain order, approximating only to a celestial order; you are doing this in Salt Lake City. One already has been erected in St. George, after a pattern in part of a celestial order. But by and by, when we build a Temple that is never to be destroyed, it will be constructed, after the most perfect order of the celestial worlds. And when God shall take it up into heaven, it will be found to be just as perfect as the cities of more ancient, celestial worlds which have been made pure and holy and immortal. So it will be with other Temples. And we, in order to build a Temple, after a celestial order in the fulness of perfection, will need revelators and prophets in our midst, who will receive the word of the Lord; who will have the whole pattern thereof given by revelation, just as much as everything was given by revelation pertaining to the tabernacle erected in the wilderness by Moses. Indeed, before we can go back to inherit this land in all its fulness of perfection, God has promised that He would raise up a man like Moses. Who this man will be I do not know; it may be a person with whom we are entirely unacquainted; it may be one of our infant children; it may be some person not yet born; it may be someone of middle age. But suffice it to say, that God will raise up such a man, and He will show forth His power through him, and through the people that he will lead forth to inherit that country, as He did through our fathers in the wilderness. Did He then display His power by dividing the waters? Yes. Did the mountains and land shake under His power? Yes. Did He speak to the people by his own voice? Yes. Did He converse with Moses face to face? Yes. Did He show Him His glory? Yes. Did He unfold to him in one moment more than all our schools and academies, and universities could give us in ten thousand years? Yes. God will assuredly raise up a man, like unto ·Moses, and redeem His people, with an outstretched arm, as their fathers were redeemed, at the first, going before them with His own presence, and will also surround them by His angels. I expect, when that time comes, that man will understand all the particulars in regard to the Temple to be built in Jackson County. Indeed we have already a part of the plan revealed, and also the plat explaining how the city of Zion is to be laid off, which may be found commencing on page 438, Volume 14 of the Millennial Star. From what has been revealed of this Temple to be erected, we can readily perceive that it will differ from anything that we have had. It will differ in regard to the number of rooms; it will differ very much in its outward and also in its inward form; and it will differ in regard to the duties to be performed in each of its rooms to be occupied by the respective departments of priesthood. This house will be reared then, according to a certain plan, which God is to make known to His servant whom He will, in His own due time, raise up. And He will have to give more revelation on other things equally as important, for we shall need instructions how to build up Zion; how to establish the center city; how to lay off the streets; the kind of ornamental trees to adorn the sidewalks, as well as everything else by way of beautifying it, and making it a city of perfection, as David prophetically calls it.

And then God will come and visit it; it will be a place where He will have His throne, where He will sit occasionally as King of Kings and Lord of Lords, and reign over His people who will occupy the great western continent; the same as He will have His throne at Jerusalem. "Beautiful for situation, the joy of the whole earth is Mount Zion, on the sides of the north, the city of the great King." And again He says: "Out of Zion, the perfection of beauty, God hath shined." Does the Psalmist mean that God will shine literally out of Zion? Yes, shine with light that will be seen by the righteous and the wicked also.

For fear of taking up too much of the time, I will bring my remarks to a close. I will say, however, I desire greatly that the Lord will bless the Latter-day Saints, and bless His servants that some, at least, may have the pleasure of entering into all the perfection of this glory, here in this temporal life; while the more aged, the gray haired and gray bearded like myself, will perhaps pass away, if the Lord requires it. And that our sons may rise up after us, being filled with the power and Spirit of God, to carry out His great and righteous purposes, even to completion.

I pray God to bless the inhabitants of Logan and those of the towns round about in this valley, and throughout all our mountain regions; and that His peculiar blessings and favor may continue to attend us while we sojourn in these mountains, and go with us when Zion shall be redeemed in all its fulness. Amen.

J. D., Vol. 21:153-4.

Temple to be Built Before Second Coming

By Orson Pratt

(Excerpts from Discourse delivered in Tabernacle, Salt Lake City, May 20, 1855.)

A great work has to be brought about; how many years, or scores of years, it will be, I know not, but from the scenes we behold among the people, the breaking up of the nations, and the signs of the times, and the present aspects of the European war, and from the shutting up and closing up of the proclamation of the Gospel in many lands, the coming of Christ seems to be near at hand, yet Zion must be redeemed before that day, the temple must be built upon the consecrated spot, the cloud and glory of the Lord rest upon it, and the Lamanites; many of them, brought in, and they must build up the New Jerusalem! It is true, so says the Book of Mormon, "that inasmuch as the Gentiles receive the Gospel, they shall assist my people the remnant of Jacob, saith the Lord, to build the New Jerusalem." And when they have it built, then we are told that they shall assist my people who are of Jacob to be gathered in unto the New Jerusalem. Only a few thousand or hundreds of thousands, then, are to be engaged in this work, and then, after it is done, we are to assist the Lamanites to gather in; and then shall the powers of heaven be in your midst; and then is the coming of Christ.

J. D., 3-17-18.

Many of You Will Assist in Building the Temple

By President Lorenzo Snow

(Remarks made at a reunion of the authorities of the Priesthood in the Weber Stake, held on June 12, 1901, in the Fifth Ward Assembly Hall.)

Many of you will be living in Jackson County and there you will be assisting in building the Temple; and if you will not have seen the Lord Jesus at that time you may expect Him very soon, to see Him, to eat and drink with Him, to shake hands with Him and to invite Him to your houses as He was invited when He was here before. I am saying things to you now which I know something of the truth of them. I feel with all my heart to say God bless you from the President down to the Counselors of the Bishops and all of you. God has blessed you with light and knowledge; and all those within the sound of my voice who have not received a perfect understanding of their prospects and what they may reach in the next life, I want you to so live and to so exercise your faith that you may go into the Temple and receive your higher blessing, and have there unfolded to your view the glorious prospects for which the Latter-day Saints have struggled and suffered and for which they have been driven and driven until they finally located here. I suppose I am talking to some who have had worry and trouble and heart burnings and persecution, and have at times been caused to think that they never expected to endure quite so much. But for everything you have suffered, for everything that has occurred to you which you thought an evil at that time, you will receive four-fold, and that suffering will have a tendency to make you better and stronger and to feel that you have been blessed. When you look back over your experiences you will then see that you have advanced far ahead and have gone up several rounds of the ladder toward exaltation and glory.   Deseret News, June 15, 1901.

Are We Prepared to Build the New Jerusalem?
By President Brigham Young

Suppose the word should come, "Return and build up the centre stake of Zion," are we ready for it? No. I have often alluded to our mechanics. We have not a mechanic that would know how to lay the first stone for the foundation of the wall around the New Jerusalem, to say nothing about the Temples of our God. Are you prepared for the day of vengeance to come, when the Lord will consume the wicked by the brightness of His coming? No. Then do not be too anxious for the Lord to hasten His work. Let our anxiety be centered upon this one thing, the sanctification of our own hearts, the purifying of our own affections, the preparing of ourselves for the approach of the events that are hastening upon us. This should be our concern, this should be our study, this should be our daily prayer and not to be in a hurry to see the overthrow of the wicked. Be careful, for if they were all to be overthrown at once, how many would there be left that are called Saints? Not as many as I would have remain; not as many as you would like to have remain. We are prepared for the day that is approaching, let us then prepare ourselves for the presence of our Master—for the coming of the Son of Man.

The Deseret News, Vol. 11, No. 9, May 1, 1861.

Cornerstone of Great Temple Laid in 1831

By Orson Pratt

We will build a great city in Missouri. We will also build a great temple unto the Lord our God, in that city, and the temple block and place where it is to stand is already known. It was laid out in the year 1831, and *the cornerstone laid,* and we will build a temple there, and build it after the pattern that the Lord gave to his servant Joseph the Prophet, and also according to the pattern that he shall hereafter show, if the pattern is not already given in full. I will tell you another thing that will happen in our promised land, after that temple is built; there will be a cloud of glory rest upon that temple by day, the same as the cloud rested upon the tabernacle of Moses, that was carried in the wilderness. Not only that, but also a flaming fire will rest upon the temple by night, covering the whole temple; and if you go inside the temple, the glory of God will be seen there as it was anciently; for the Lord will not only be a glory and a defense on the outside of that wonderful building, but he will also be a glory and a power in the inside thereof, and it shall come to pass that every man and every woman who is pure in heart, who shall go inside of that temple, will see the Lord. Now, how great a blessing it will be to see the Lord of Hosts as we see one another in the flesh. That will take place, but not till after the temple is built. Moreover, you will not only be favored with this great privilege, but Isaiah tells us that "the Lord will create upon every dwelling place of Mount Zion, and upon her assemblies, a cloud and smoke by day, and the shining of a flaming fire by night." When you hold your meetings in the day time, you shall be sheltered by a cloud, and when you hold your meetings in the night time, instead of lighting up your lamps with common oil, or with gas, or anything of this kind, you will have no need of any artificial light, for the Lord God will be the light thereof, and his glory will be there and you will see it and you will hear his voice. Have you not read in this book called the Bible, about the Lord suddenly coming into his temple? Read the 3rd chapter of Malachi: "Behold, I will send my messenger, and he shall prepare the way before me; and the Lord whom ye seek shall come to his temple * * * And he shall sit as a refiner and purifier of silver; and he shall purify the sons of Levi and purge them as gold and silver, that they may offer unto the Lord an offering in righteousness." That same fire will rest upon the abodes of those that come into that temple, and they will be filled with fire and the Holy Ghost. They will be purged of all iniquity, and every ordinance that will be administered in that temple will be administered by holy hands, and you will understand and know the meaning thereof. The Lord will reveal these things in their day; he will reveal everything that is needful, so that the knowledge of God may rest upon you, and that there may be no darkness with you. Amen.   J. D., Vol. 21:330-31.

Chapter XVII

THE FAR WEST TEMPLE SITE

Dedicatory Services of the Far West Temple Site

July 4 (1838) * * * The cornerstones of the House of the Lord, agreeable to the commandments of the Lord unto us, given April 26, 1838,[1] were laid.

Joseph Smith, Junior, was president of the day; Hyrum Smith, vice-president; Sidney Rigdon, orator; Reynolds Cahoon, chief marshall; George M. Hinckle and J. Hunt, assistant marshals, and George W. Robinson, clerk.

The order of the day was splendid. The procession commenced forming at 10 o'clock a.m., in the following order: First, the infantry (militia); second, the Patriarchs of the Church; the president, vice-president, and orator; the Twelve Apostles, presidents of the stakes, and High Council; Bishop and counselors; architects, ladies and gentlemen. The calvary brought up the rear of the large procession, which marched to music, and formed a circle with the ladies in front, round the excavation. The southeast cornerstone of the Lord's House in Far West, Missouri, was then laid by the presidents of the stake assisted by twelve men. The southwest corner, by the presidents of the Elders, assisted by twelve men. The northwest corner by the Bishop, assisted by twelve men. The northeast corner by the president of the Teachers, assisted by twelve men. This house is to be one hundred and ten feet long, and eighty feet broad.

The oration was delivered by President Rigdon, at the close of which was a shout of Hosanna, and a song, composed for the occasion by Levi W. Hancock, was sung by Solomon Hancock. The most perfect order prevailed throughout the day.

Documentary History of Church, Vol. 3:41-2.

(For History of Events between July 4, 1838, and April 26, 1839, see footnote 2.)

SOUTHWEST CORNERSTONE OF THE FAR WEST TEMPLE SITE.
The site was dedicated on July 4, 1838, by Brigham Young.
(To the left, Wilford C. Wood; to the right, Samuel O. Bennion)

The Far West Temple Site Re-Dedicated

Friday, April 26 (1839): Early this morning, soon after midnight, the brethren arrived at Far West, and proceeded to transact the business of their mission according to the following minutes. * * *

Elder Alpheus Cutler, the master workman of the house, then re-commenced laying the foundation of the Lord's House, agreeable to revelation, by rolling up a large stone near the southeast corner. The following of the Twelve were present: Brigham Young, Heber C. Kimball, Orson Pratt, John E. Page and John Taylor, who proceeded to ordain Wilford Woodruff and George A. Smith (who had been previously nominated by the First Presidency, accepted by the Twelve and acknowledged by the Church), to the office of Apostles and members of the quorum of the Twelve, to fill the places of those who are fallen. Darwin Chase and Norman Shearer (who had just been liberated from the Richmond prison, where they had been confined for the cause of Jesus Christ), were then ordained to the office of the Seventies.

The Twelve then offered up vocal prayer in the following order: Brigham Young, Heber C. Kimball, Orson Pratt, John E. Page, John Taylor, Wilford Woodruff and George A. Smith. After which we sang Adam-ondi-Ahman, and then the Twelve took their leave of the following saints, agreeable to the revelation.* * *

Elder Alpheus Cutler then placed the stone before alluded to in its regular position, after which, in consequence of the peculiar situation of the Saints, he thought it wisdom to adjourn until some future time, when the Lord shall open the way; expressing his determination then to proceed with the building; whereupon the conference adjourned.

Brigham Young, President.

John Taylor, Clerk.

Thus was fulfilled a revelation of July 8, 1838,[1a] which our enemies had said could not be fulfilled, as no "Mormon" would be permitted to be in the state.[2,3]   D. H. C., Vol. 3:336-9.

---

[1] *Revelation, given through Joseph, the Seer, at Far West, Missouri, April 26, 1838, making known the will of God concerning the building up of this place, and of the Lord's House.*

For thus shall my church be called in the last day, even the Church of Jesus Christ of Latter-day Saints.

Verily I say unto you all, Arise and shine forth, that thy light may be a standard for the nations.

And that the gathering together upon the land of Zion, and upon her Stakes, may be for a defence, and for a refuge from the storm, and from wrath when it shall be poured out without mixture upon the whole earth.

Let the city, Far West, be a holy and consecrated land unto me, and it shall be called most holy, for the ground upon which thou standest is holy;

Therefore I command you to build unto me, for the gathering together of my saints, that they may worship me;

And let there be a beginning of this work, and a foundation, and a preparatory work, this following summer;

And let the beginning be made on the 4th day of July next, and from that time forth let my people labor diligently to build an house unto my name.

And in one year from this day let them re-commence laying the foundation of my house;

Thus let them from that time forth labor diligently until it shall be finished, from the cornerstone thereof unto the top thereof, until there shall not anything remain that is not finished.

Verily I say unto you, let not my servant Joseph, neither my servant Sidney, neither my servant Hyrum, get in debt any more for the building of an house unto my name;

But let an house be built unto my name according to the pattern which I will show unto them.

And if my people build it not according to the pattern which I shall show unto their Presidency, I will not accept it at their hands;

But if my people do build it according to the pattern which I shall show unto their Presidency, even my servant Joseph and his counselors, then I will accept it at the hands of my people.

And again, verily I say unto you, it is my will that the city of Far West should be built up speedily by the gathering of my saints,

And also that other places should be appointed for Stakes in the regions round about, as they shall be manifest unto my servant Joseph from time to time;

For behold, I will be with him, and I will sanctify him before the people, for unto him have I given the keys of this kingdom and ministry. Even so. Amen.

Doc. & Cov., Sec. 115:4-19.

[1a]*Revelation, given through Joseph, the Seer, at Far West, Missouri, July 8, 1836, in answer to the question, "Show us thy will, O Lord, concerning the Twelve?"*

Verily, thus saith the Lord, let a conference be held immediately, let the Twelve be organized, and let men be appointed to supply the place of those who are fallen.

Let my servant Thomas remain for a season in the land of Zion, to publish my word.

Let the residue continue to preach from that hour, and if they will do this in all lowliness of heart, in meekness and humility, and long suffering, I, the Lord, give unto them a promise that I will provide for their families, and an effectual door shall be opened for them, from henceforth;

And next spring let them depart to go over the great waters, and there promulgate my gospel, the fulness thereof, and bear record of my name.

Let them take leave of my saints in the city of Far West, on the 26th day of April next, on the building spot of my house, saith the Lord.

Let my servant John Taylor, and also my servant John E. Page, and also my servant Wilford Woodruff, and also my servant Willard Richards, be appointed to fill the places of those who have fallen, and be officially notified of their appointment.

Doc. & Cov., Sec. 118.

² *Narration by George Q. Cannon:* A great many have wondered how it is that the Latter-day Saints are so anxious to have temples built. We built a temple in Kirtland, and after we had built it we were compelled to leave it and flee to Missouri. We laid the foundations of two in Missouri, one in Jackson County, the other in Caldwell County. That in Caldwell was not laid until after we were driven from there. A revelation was given through Joseph Smith, I think, on the 11th day of July, 1838, that on the succeeding 26th day of April, the foundation stone of the temple should be laid in Far West; and the Twelve Apostles should take their departure from that cornerstone, and cross the ocean to preach the gospel in Europe. Now, said the mob, "There being a date fixed to this revelation, if Joseph Smith never was a false prophet before, we will make him one now." And they turned and drove the Latter-day Saints from Missouri, and made it worth a man's life to go back there if he was a Mormon. They drove every one out of Missouri, under a ban of extermination, in the winter previous to the time set for the fulfillment of this revelation. That was in the winter of 1838-9; and there were but very few left, and they were in peril of their lives all the time. Joseph, Hyrum and several of the leading Elders were in prison, and it seemed as though the words of Joseph would fall to the ground that time, at any rate. President Young was then President of the Twelve Apostles; he with others had to flee to Quincy, and he proposed to his fellow Apostles that they should go up to Missouri, to fulfill that revelation. Father Joseph Smith, father of the Prophet, thought that the Lord would take the will for the deed, and it would not be necessary. He felt as though there would be great danger in the undertaking, and that the brethren's lives would be in peril. A good many of the Elders felt the same, but the Spirit rested upon President Young and his brother Apostles, and they determined to go, and they did go, and, according to the revelation, they laid the cornerstone in the town of Far West. They laid it in the midst of their enemies; they sang their songs, ordained two of the Twelve, and if I recollect right, two of the Seventies, and then shook hands with the Saints there, bade them adieu, and took their departure for Europe, thus fulfilling the word of God given nearly a year previously through the Prophet Joseph, and which the enemies of the Kingdom of God said should never be fulfilled.

J. D., 14:319-20.

³ *Narration by President John Taylor:* Well, the Twelve were told to go to Far West, some 200 miles distant from Quincy, Illinois, where many of the Saints were then staying. We did not have railroads then whereby we could travel as we do now. We had to go with our teams, and we had to go among a people that would kill every one of us as quick as they would rattlesnakes. We were told to go and lay the foundation stone of the Temple, and thus fulfill the revelation that had been given on the subject. Arrived at the spot, we prayed and sang hymns. We had with us a man that was appointed by revelation for that work — Alpheus Cutler, Bishop A. A. Kimball's grandfather. The stone was duly laid according to the order which was designed after which right upon the foundation stone, Wilford Woodruff and George A. Smith were ordained into the Quorum of the Twelve, and Norman Shearer and Darwin Chase into the Seventies. Chase apostatized, and was afterwards with the soldiers under Colonel Connor's command who had a fight with the Indians on Bear River a number of years ago, where he was mortally wounded. Many

people declared that this revelation would never be fulfilled. But it was fulfilled; and we took our departure for Europe.

Now, it was not a nice thing, after being pillaged, robbed, and driven from our homes, to leave our families and proceed on a mission to Europe. But the Twelve had to do it, and they did do it. There were two that did not go—John E. Page and William Smith, and both of them apostatized. The wrench[a] that the Prophet Joseph spake about was too much for them. But the rest went. They felt it was an honor to go on that mission even under such unpropitious circumstances.

([a] *I heard the Prophet say, in speaking to the Twelve on one occasion: "You will have all kinds of trials to pass through. And it is quite necessary for you to be tried as it was for Abraham and other men of God, and (said he) God will feel after you, and He will take hold of you and wrench your very heart strings, and if you cannot stand it you will not be fit for an inheritance in the Celestial Kingdom of God.")* J. D., Vol. 24:197.

The Rise and Fall of Far West

The first settlement of the Saints in the vicinity of Far West was made in October, 1836. By July following about one hundred buildings had been erected, eight of which were stores. Some non-members of the Church expressed a desire to establish saloons in the growing town, and endeavored to induce some of the brethren to sell intoxicants on commission for them, but the High Council resolved not to sustain any persons as members of the Church who would become retailers of spirituous liquors. A general conference of the Church was held at Far West in October, 1837, at which difficulties were adjusted, covenants renewed, and all things set in order. It was voted to enlarge the town plat so that it would contain four sections—two miles square. The conference voted not to support any store or shops selling spirituous liquors, tea, coffee or tobacco.

In 1836, Caldwell county, of which Far West was the county seat, was a wilderness. By the spring of 1838 the population was more than 5,000, of which more than 4,900 were Latter-day Saints, composed of sturdy pioneers, craftsmen, skilled mechanics, artisans. During the year 1838 persecution and mobocracy grew by leaps and bounds against the Saints, encouraged by the extermination order of Gov. Lilburn W. Boggs of Missouri, which was dated Oct. 27, 1838. Joseph Smith, with others, had been taken as hostages and prisoners and were compelled to listen to the filthy obscenity of those who watched them, and hear them relate their deeds of rapine and murder. The arms were taken from the citizens of Far West, and under pretext of searching for arms, the mobocrats ransacked every house, tore up the floors, upset haystacks, destroyed property, shot down cattle for mere sport, and the people, robbed of their most valuable property, were insulted and whipped. The chastity of women was defiled by force; some were strapped to benches and repeatedly ravished by brutes until they died from the effects of this treatment. Joseph Smith and others were courtmartialed to be shot, this court being composed of the traitor Hinkle and about twenty sectarian priests of various denominations, with Judge Austin A. King and Attorney Thomas Burch participating. The order of this courtmartial was that the prisoners should be shot on the public square of Far West in the morning, at 9 o'clock. *General Donophan's reply to the order of execution read: "It is cold-blooded murder. I will not obey your order. My brigade shall march for Liberty tomorrow morning at 8 o'clock; and if you execute these men, I will hold you responsible before an earthly tribunal, so help me God."

————————

For more complete information on the burning of homes, killing and expulsion of the Saints from Far West, consult Vol. 1, *Comprehensive History of the Church*, by Elder B. H. Roberts; also Elder Roberts' book, *Missouri Persecutions*. 236 *Contributor*, Vol. 7; *Times and Seasons*, 4:247-251; D.H.C., 3:322-326.

*On the statue erected by the State of Missouri, at Richmond, in honor of this great man, the following is inscribed: "Col. Alexander William Donophan: Col. Donophan was of immense stature, noble appearance, brilliant parts, fearless, of great moral courage, sanguine, faithful, just, patriotic, poetic in temperament, the champion of the downtrodden, eloquent beyond description, and without doubt entitled to be classed among the greatest orators and lawyers that ever lived."

Chapter XVIII

PALESTINE DEDICATED FOR THE RETURN OF JUDAH
By Orson Hyde

O Thou! who are from everlasting to everlasting, eternally and unchangeable the same, even the God who rules in the heavens above, and controls the destinies of men on the earth, wilt Thou not condescend, through Thine infinite goodness and royal favor, to listen to the prayer of Thy servant which he this day offers up unto Thee in the name of Thy holy child Jesus, upon this land, where the Sun of Righteousness set in blood, and thine Anointed One expired.

ORSON HYDE

Be pleased, O Lord, to forgive all the follies, weaknesses, vanities, and sins of Thy servant, and strengthen him to resist all future temptations. Give him prudence and discernment that he may avoid the evil, and a heart to choose the good; give him fortitude to bear up under trying and adverse circumstances, and grace to endure all things for Thy name's sake, until the end shall come, when all the Saints shall rest in peace.

Now, O Lord! Thy servant has been obedient to the heavenly vision* which Thou gavest him in his native land; and under the shadow of Thine outstretched arm, he has safely arrived in this

---

*In the early part of March last (1840), I retired to my bed one evening as usual, and while contemplating and inquiring out, in my own mind, the field of my ministerial labors for the then coming season, the vision of the Lord, like clouds of light, burst upon my view. The cities of London, Amsterdam, Constantinople, and Jerusalem all appeared in succession before me; and the Spirit said unto me, "Here are many of the children of Abraham whom I will gather to the land that I gave to their fathers, and here also is the field of your labors.

"A strict observance of the movements of the Jews, and a careful examination of their faith relative to their expected Messiah—the setting up of His kingdom among them, and the overthrow of the present kingdoms and governments of the Gentiles, will serve to open the eyes of many of the uncircumcised, when faithfully laid before them, that the great day of the Lord comes not upon them unawares as a thief.

place to dedicate and consecrate this land unto Thee, for the gathering together of Judah's scattered remnants, according to the predictions of the Holy Prophets—for the building up of Jerusalem again after it has been trodden down by the Gentiles so long, and for rearing a Temple in honor of Thy name. Everlasting thanks be ascribed unto Thee, O Father, Lord of heaven and earth, that Thou hast preserved Thy servant from the dangers of the seas, and from the plague and pestilence which have caused the land to mourn. The violence of many has also been restrained, and Thy providential care by night and by day has been exercised over Thine unworthy servant. Accept, therefore, O Lord, the tribute of a grateful heart for all past favors, and be pleased to continue Thy kindness and mercy towards a needy worm of the dust.

O Thou, Who didst covenant with Abraham, Thy friend, and Who didst renew that covenant with Isaac, and confirm the same with Jacob with an oath, that Thou wouldst not only give them this land for an everlasting inheritance, but that Thou wouldst also remember their seed forever. Abraham, Isaac, and Jacob have long since closed their eyes in death, and made the grave their mansion. Their children are scattered and dispersed abroad among the nations of the Gentiles like sheep that have no shepherd, and are still looking forward for the fulfillment of those promises which Thou didst make concerning them; and even this land, which once poured forth nature's richest bounty, and flowed, as it were, with milk and honey, has, to a certain extent, been smitten with barrenness and sterility since it drank from murderous hands the blood of Him who never sinned.

Grant, therefore, O Lord, in the name of Thy well-beloved

"Take, therefore, proper credentials from My People, your brethren, and also from the Governor of your State, with the seal of authority thereon, and go ye forth to the cities which have been shown unto you, and declare these words unto Judah, and say:

"Blow ye the trumpet in the land; cry, gather together; and say, assemble yourselves, and let us go into the defended cities. Let the standard be reared towards Zion. Retire! stay not; for I will bring evil from the north and a great destruction. The lion is come up from his thicket, and the destroyer of the Gentiles is on his way, he is gone forth from his place to make thy land desolate, and thy cities shall be laid waste without inhabitant. Speak ye comfortably to Jerusalem, and cry unto her that her warfare is accomplished—that her iniquity is pardoned, for she has received at the Lord's hand double for all her sins. Let your warning voice be heard among the Gentiles as you pass, and call ye upon them in my name for aid and for assistance. With you it mattereth not whether it be little or much; but to me it belongeth to show favor unto them who show favor unto you. Murmur not, therefore, neither be ye sorrowful that the people are slow to hear your petition; but do as has been told you. All things shall work together for your good if you are humble and keep My commandments; for it must needs be that all men be left without excuse, that a righteous retribution may be awarded to all."
—Historical Sketch of Orson Hyde, by Jos. S. Hyde, p. 5.

"The vision continued open about six hours, that I did not close my eyes in sleep. In this time many things were shown unto me which I have never written; neither shall I write them until they are fulfilled in Jerusalem."
—Course of Study for Deacons, 1913, p. 89.

Son Jesus Christ, to remove the barrenness and sterility of this land, and let springs of living water break forth to water its thirsty soil. Let the vine and olive produce in their strength, and the fig-tree bloom and flourish. Let the land become abundantly fruitful when possessed by its rightful heirs; let it again flow with plenty to feed the returning prodigals who come home with a spirit of grace and supplication upon it; let the clouds distil virtue and rich-ness, and let the fields smile with plenty. Let the flocks and the herds greatly increase and multiply upon the mountains and the hills; and let Thy great kindness conquer and subdue the unbelief of Thy people. Do Thou take from them their stony heart, and give them a heart of flesh; and may the Sun of Thy favor dispel the cold mists of darkness which have beclouded their atmosphere. Incline them to gather in upon this land according to Thy word. Let them come like clouds and like doves to their windows. Let the large ships of the nations bring them from the distant isles; and let kings become their nursing fathers, and queens with motherly fondness wipe the tear of sorrow from their eyes.

Thou, O Lord, did once move upon the heart of Cyrus to show favor unto Jerusalem and her children. Do Thou now also be pleased to inspire the hearts of kings and the powers of the earth to look with a friendly eye towards this place, and with a desire to see Thy righteous purposes executed in relation thereto. Let them know that it is Thy good pleasure to restore the kingdom unto Israel—raise up Jerusalem as its capital, and constitute her people a distinct nation and government with David Thy servant, even a descendant from the loins of ancient David to be their king.

Let that nation or that people who shall take an active part in behalf of Abraham's children, and in the raising up of Jerusalem, find favor in Thy sight. Let not their enemies prevail against them, neither let pestilence or famine overcome them, but let the glory of Israel overshadow them, and the power of the Highest protect them; while that nation or kingdom that will not serve Thee in this glorious work must perish, according to Thy word—"Yea, those nations shall be utterly wasted."

Though Thy servant is now far from his home, and from the land bedewed with his earliest fear, yet he remembers, O Lord, his friends who are there, and family, whom for Thy sake he has left. Though poverty and privation be our earthly lot, yet ah! do Thou richly endow us with an inheritance where moth and rust do not corrupt, and where thieves do not break through and steal.

The hands that have fed, clothed, or shown favor unto the family of Thy servant in his absence, or that shall hereafter do so, let them not lose their reward, but let a special blessing rest upon them, and in Thy kingdom let them have an inheritance when Thou shalt come to be glorified in this society.

Do Thou also look with favor upon all those through whose liberality I have been enabled to come to this land; and in the day

when Thou shalt reward all people according to their works; let
these also not be passed by or forgotten, but in time let them be
in readiness to enjoy the glory of those mansions which Jesus has
gone to prepare. Particularly do Thou bless the stranger in Philadelphia,** whom I never saw, but who sent me gold, with a request that I should pray for him in Jerusalem. Now, O Lord, let
blessings come upon him from an unexpected quarter, and let his
basket be filled, and his storehouse abound with plenty, and let
not the good things of the earth be his only portion, but let him be

---

    **The footnotes on pages 301-2 of Nephi L. Morris' excellent contribu-
tion: "Prophecies of Joseph Smith and Their Fulfillment," are here quoted
in full:
    Orson Hyde and his companion, John E. Page, departed upon their mis-
sion to the Holy Land. This latter had sufficient means to take him to his destination. The former, however, traveled literally "without purse or scrip" as
was the practice for the most part among the missionaries of the Church in
those days. At Philadelphia, while addressing a gathering of people in the capacity of a preacher of the Gospel, and a missionary on the way to his appointed field of labor, it would appear that he announced the conditions under which he was performing this mission. At the close of the meeting a
stranger handed him a purse of gold, with but one request, which was that the
Elder remember him in the prayer when he stood upon the Mount of Olives.
    In the dedicatory prayer, Orson Hyde remembered the stranger who gave
him the gold in Philadelphia: "Do Thou, O Lord, bless him in his basket and
his store. May he never lack for the necessities of life, and also Lord, bless
him with the riches of eternity."
    In Septembr, 1924, the author, in a discourse delivered in the Salt Lake
Tabernacle, spoke of the mission of Orson Hyde to the Holy Land, and of the
part which he played in dedicating the land of Palestine to the re-gathering
of the Jews unto the land of their fathers. Allusion was made to the stranger
in Philadelphia who rendered financial aid to Elder Hyde by handing him a
purse of gold. The annals of the Church did not contain a single reference to
this stranger, except as contained in this narrative. To the surprise of the
author, and the enlightenment of the Church upon this interesting but rather
obscure incident, the author received a few days afer the discourse was delivered, a letter from a gentleman named John F. Beck, who disclosed the very
interesting fact that he was a son of the man who befriended Orson Hyde with
monetary aid while on his way to Palestine. The following letter is self-explan-
atory and is of sufficient interest to warrant its permanent preservation in
printed form:

November 22nd, 1924.

    My father, Joseph Ellison Beck, born 1810, was the man who sent the
purse of gold to Elder Orson Hyde, with which to bear his expenses on his
mission to Palestine. He did not have much to say about it, but all our family
knew very well that he did that generous deed. He was a humble farmer of
moderate means, living in New Jersey where there was a small branch of the
Church. Father was no preacher, but he always had prayers in his family,
and always paid his tithing. Our family came to Utah in 1850 and after
residing in the Ninth Ward, Salt Lake City, eighteen months, we settled in
Spanish Fork where we continued to live until father died at the age of ninety-
three, having enjoyed good health until within three days of his death. He
had fourteen children. They all lived in peace together, and all the children,
eight sons and six daughters, grew up and married. I do not know of an
apostate among any of father's posterity. He always had plenty for his family
and loaned breadstuffs to scores who were in want. He did not become rich,
but always had money laid aside for a time of need. I have heard the prayer
of Elder Hyde offered up in his behalf, and am a witness that every feature
of it was wonderfully fulfilled. (Signed) John F. Beck.

found among those to whom it shall be said: "Thou hast been faithful over a few things, and I will make thee ruler over many."

O my Father in heaven! I now ask Thee in the name of Jesus to remember Zion, with all her Stakes, and with all her assemblies. She has been grievously afflicted and smitten; she has mourned; she has wept; her enemies have triumphed, and have said, "Ah, where is thy God?" Her Priests and Prophets have groaned in chains and fetters within the gloomy walls of prisons, while many were slain, and now sleep in the arms of death. How long, O Lord, shall iniquity triumph, and sin go unpunished?

Do Thou arise in the majesty of Thy strength, and make bare Thine arm in behalf of Thy people. Redress their wrongs, and turn their sorrow into joy. Pour the spirit of light and knowledge, grace and wisdom, into the hearts of her Prophets, and clothe her Priests with salvation. Let light and knowledge march forth through the empire of darkness, and may the honest in heart flow to their standard, and join in the march to go forth to meet the Bridegroom.

Let a peculiar blessing rest upon the Presidency of Thy Church, for at them are the arrows of the enemy directed. Be Thou to them a sun and a shield, their strong tower and hiding-place; and in the time of distress or danger be Thou near to deliver. Also the quorum of the Twelve, do Thou be pleased to stand by them for Thou knowest the obstacles which they have to encounter, the temptations to which they are exposed, and the privations which they must suffer. Give us (the Twelve) therefore, strength according to our day, and help us to bear a faithful testimony of Jesus and His Gospel, to finish with fidelity and honor the work which Thou hast given us to do, and then give us a place in Thy glorious kingdom. And let this blessing rest upon every faithful officer and member in Thy Church. And all the glory and honor will we ascribe unto God and the Lamb forever and ever. Amen.

On the top of Mount Olives I erected a pile of stones as a witness according to ancient custom. On what was anciently called Mount Zion (Moriah?) where the Temple stood, I erected another, and used the rod according to the prediction upon my head.—D. H. C. Vol. 4, pp. 456-9.

Chapter XIX

ANCIENT RECORDS BRING FORTH LIGHT

Historical Sketch of the Mummies and the Papyrus Found With Them

(For a detailed account, see *History of the Church*, Vol. 2, pages 236, 238, 286, 349-50; also Josiah Quincy's book, *Figures of the Past*, page 367.)

In 1828, Antonio Sebolo, the celebrated French traveler, received permission from Mehomet Ali then Viceroy of Egypt, under the protection of Chevalier Drevetti, the French Consul, to explore the catacombs in the vicinity of the ancient city of Thebes. With the aid of 433 Egyptian or Turkish soldiers, and after laboring four months, he entered the catacomb on June 7, 1831, and obtained eleven mummies from among about one hundred that had been embalmed after the first order, there also being two or three hundred that were embalmed after the second and third orders which were in a bad state of decay, as were all of the first order except the eleven he took from the catacomb. On his way from Alexandria to Paris, he put in at Trieste and after ten days' illness, expired (1832). By his will he left the mummies to his nephew, Michael H. Chandler who lived in Philadelphia, but who he thought was in Dublin, to which latter city they were shipped, and upon arriving at Dublin they were reshipped to New York City. Mr. Chandler paid the duty on them and upon opening the coffins for the first time, he discovered that in connection with "*two of the bodies* was something rolled up with the same kind of linen and saturated with the same bitumen. *Two or three other small pieces of papyrus with astronomical calculations, epitaphs, etc., were found with others of the mummies.*" He was told while yet in the custom house (1833), by a *stranger*, that there was no man in New York City who could translate his rolls but was referred by the same person to Mr. Joseph Smith who, continued he, "possessed some kind of power or gifts by which he had previously translated similar characters." Mr. Chandler took his collection to Philadelphia and other cities and thence to Kirtland, at which place he met Joseph Smith, the Prophet, for the first time. Before arriving at Kirtland he apparently had disposed of all the mummies except four. The Prophet Joseph made the following notations in his diary respecting this matter:

"On the 3rd of July (1835), Michael H. Chandler came to Kirtland to exhibit some Egyptian mummies. There were four human figures, together with some *two or more rolls of papyrus* covered with hieroglyphic figures and devices. As Mr. Chandler had been told I could translate them, he brought me some of the characters, and I gave him the interpretation.

"Sunday, July 5: Soon after this, some of the Saints at Kirtland purchased the mummies and papyrus, a description of which will appear hereafter, and with W. W. Phelps and Oliver

Facsimile of Egyptian Plate

EXPLANATION OF CUT SHOWN ON PAGE 242

Fig. 1. Kolob, signifying the first creation, nearest to the celestial, or the residence of God. First in government, the last pertaining to the measurement of time. The measurement according to celestial time, which celestial time signifies one day to a cubit. One day in Kolob is equal to a thousand years, according to the measurement of this earth, which is called by the Egyptians Jah-oh-eh.

Fig. 2. Stands next to Kolob, called by the Egyptians Obliblish, which is the next grand governing creation, near to the celestial or the place where God resides; holding the key of power also, pertaining to other planets; as revealed from God to Abraham, as he offered sacrifice upon an altar, which he had built unto the Lord.

Fig. 3. Is made to represent God, sitting upon his throne, clothed with power and authority; with a crown of eternal light upon his head; representing, also, the grand Key-Words of the Holy Priesthood, as revealed to Adam in the Garden of Eden, as also to Seth, Noah, Melchizedek, Abraham, and all to whom the priesthood was revealed.

Fig. 4. Answers to the Hebrew word raukeeyang, signifying expanse or the firmament of the heavens; also a numerical figure, in Egyptian, signifying one thousand; answering to the measuring of the time of Obliblish, which is equal with Kolob in its revolution and in its measuring of time.

Fig. 5. Is called in Egyptian Enish-go-on-dosh. This is one of the governing planets also, and is said by the Egyptians to be the Sun, and to borrow its light from Kolob through the medium of Kae-evanrash, which is the grand Key, or, in other words, the governing power, which governs fifteen other fixed planets or stars, as also Floeese or the Moon, the Earth and the Sun in their annual revolutions. This planet receives its power through the medium of Kli-flos-is-es-, or Hah-ko-kau-beam, the Stars represented by numbers 22 and 23, receiving light from the revolutions of Kolob.

Fig. 6. Represents the earth in its four quarters.

Fig. 7. Represents God sitting upon His throne revealing through the heavens, the grand Key-Words of the priesthood; as, also, the sign of the Holy Ghost unto Abraham, in the form of a dove.

Fig. 8. Contains writing that cannot be revealed unto the world; but is to be had in the Holy Temple of God.

Fig. 9. Ought not to be revealed at the present time.

Fig. 10. Also.

Fig. 11. Also. If the world can find out these numbers, so let it be. Amen.

Figs. 12, 13, 14, 15, 16, 17, 18, 19, and 20, will be given in the own due time of the Lord.

The above translation is given as far as we have any right to give, at the present time.

Cowdery as scribes, I commenced the translation of some of the characters or hieroglyphics, and much to our joy found that *one* of the rolls contained the writings of Abraham, *another* the writings of Joseph of Egypt, etc., a more full account of which will appear in its place as I proceed to examine or unfold them. Truly we can say, the Lord is beginning to reveal the abundance of peace and truth.

"July 20, 1835: The remainder of this month I was continually engaged in *translating an alphabet* to the Book of Abraham, and arranging a *grammar of the Egyptian language as practiced by the ancients.*

"October 1, 1835: This afternoon I labored on the Egyptian alphabet, in company with Brothers Oliver Cowdery and W. W. Phelps, and during the research, *the principles of astronomy as understood by Father Abraham and the ancients,* unfolded to our understanding, the particulars of which will appear hereafter.

"December 31, 1835: * * * The record of Abraham and Joseph, found with the mummies, is beautifully written on papyrus, with black, and a small part red ink or paint, in perfect preservation. The characters are such as you find upon the coffins of mummies—hieroglyphics, etc., which many characters of letters like the present (though probably not quite so square) form the Hebrew without points."

The Prophet Joseph translated only a portion of the hieroglyphics found on the papyrus as before related, which portion is now called the Book of Abraham, incorporated in the book called the Pearl of Great Price. This Book of Abraham was first published in the Times and Seasons, Vol. 3, in Nauvoo, Illinois, in 1842.

Lucy Smith, the mother of the Prophet, exhibited these mummies and papyrus, charging the small sum of twenty-five cents. (See Josiah Quincy's book entitled: "Figures of the Past," page 387.) Elder B. H. Roberts told the compiler of this book, that after the death of Lucy Smith, the mummies and papyrus were held in the custody of William Smith, the brother of the Prophet. Later on, to settle some difficulties between William Smith and Isaac Sheen (who later became the Editor of "True Saints Herald," the organ of the Reorganized Church of Latter-day Saints) William Smith transferred the ownership of these to Isaac Sheen. Isaac Sheen in turn transferred them to the Chicago Museum which burned to the ground in the Chicago fire of 1871.

Josiah Quincy visited the Prophet Joseph in Nauvoo but a few months prior to the martyrdom, and in his book entitled *Figures of the Past* (pages 385-7), the following interesting item is given (*by permission*):

"And now come with me," said the Prophet, "and I will show you the curiosities." So saying, he led the way to a lower room, where sat a venerable and respectable-looking lady. "This is my mother, gentlemen. The curiosities we shall see belong to her. They were purchased with her own money, at a cost of six thousand dollars," and then, with deep feeling, were added the words, "And that woman was turned out upon the prairie in the dead of night by a mob." There were some pine presses fixed against the wall of the room. These receptacles Smith opened, and disclosed four human bodies, shrunken and black with age. "These are mummies," said the exhibitor. "I want you to look at that little runt of a fellow over there. He was a great man in his day. Why, that was Pharaoh Necho, King of Egypt!" Some parchments inscribed with hieroglyphics were then offered us. They were preserved under glass and handled with great respect. "That is the handwriting of Abraham, the Father of the Faithful," said the prophet. "This is the autograph of Moses, and these lines were written by his brother Aaron. Here we have the earliest account of the Creation, from which Moses composed the First Book of Genesis." The parchment last referred to showed a rude drawing of a man and woman, and a serpent walking upon a pair of legs. I ventured to doubt the propriety of providing the reptile in question with this unusual means of locomotion. "Why, that's as plain as a pikestaff," was the rejoinder. "Before the Fall snakes always went about on legs, just like chickens. They were deprived of them in punishment for their agency in the ruin of man." We were further assured that the prophet was the only mortal who could translate these mysterious writings, and that his power was given by direct inspiration."

In a letter written by W. W. Phelps (who, it will be noted, assisted the Prophet as a scribe in translating the hieroglyphics) to William Smith, dated Nauvoo, Illinois, December 25, 1844, and published in the *Times and Seasons,* Vol. 5, pp. 757-761, the following item occurs:

"Eternity, agreeably to the records found in the catacombs of Egypt, has been going on in this system (not this world) almost two thousand five hundred and fifty-five millions of years."

It will be noted that none of the writings of Joseph of Egypt were translated. Nothing is known concerning *"an alphabet to the Book of Abraham;"* nothing is known concerning a *"grammar of the Egyptian language as practiced by the ancients;"* and but a small part is known of *"the principles of astronomy as understood by Father Abraham and the ancients,"* and that small part is given in the Book of Abraham. What wonderful information was hidden in those records and not translated! And such carelessness exhibited in not preserving these priceless jewels! Do you suppose that the Lord would permit these wonderful records to be destroyed in that Chicago fire? The compiler says, No. And again, who was that "stranger" that gave Mr. Chandler the information before mentioned? Is it not significant that this "stranger" appeared on the scene at about the right time? These are queries and thoughts that may not be totally groundless.

Again, what wonderful mysteries are hidden in those portions of the Facsimile Cut reproduced in this chapter which are designated as Explanations to Figures 7 to 20! What wonderful depth of knowledge was revealed to the Prophet Joseph in 1835 when he first came in contact with these hieroglyphics, as he translated them; and this was long before he joined the Masonic order.[1]

Other Items of Interest

"Father Crosby also related that among other writings found on the mummies were the books of Moses, Enoch, and Abraham; also the book of Jacob which gave an account of the Ten Lost Tribes, their journeyings, present location, their return and manner of their coming to Zion."

"Everlasting covenant was made between three personages

("Sayings of the Prophet Joseph," as gathered by the compiler of this book when visiting St. George, Utah, in 1936.)

before the organization of this earth, and relates to their dispensation of things to men on the earth; these personages, according
to *Abraham's record,* are called God the first, the Creator; God
the second, the Redeemer; and God the third, the witness, or
Testator."   Compendium, 1884 Ed., page 289.

---

[1] *Orson Pratt's Account of the Mummies and Papyrus:* These are not the only
revelations given through this great modern Prophet. The Lord brought to light
sacred records from the Catacombs of Egypt. After several hundred men had wrought
and toiled for many months in digging down one of these vast structures, they entered into its interior; they found a great number of mummies—the bodies of persons that had been preserved since the catacomb was built, and some eleven of these
mummies, well preserved, were taken out by these men, and they finally fell into
the hands of a person named M. H. Chandler. They were sent from Egypt to Ireland,
where it was supposed he resided, but learning that he resided in America, they
were sent to him. After receiving the mummies, he began to take off some of the
ancient covering or wrapping, and to his astonishment he found upon the breast
of one of these mummies a record written upon ancient papyrus in plain characters,
written both in black and red inks, or stains, or colors. And the mummies and the
records were exhibited by Mr. Chandler in New York, Philadelphia, and many of
the Eastern States of our Union; and thousands of people saw them, and among
them many learned men; and these characters were presented to them, and not
infrequently was Mr. Chandler referred to "Jo" Smith as they used to term him,
who, they said, pretended to have translated some records that he found in the
western part of New York, and that if Mr. Chandler would go and see him perhaps
he would translate those ancient characters. Many of these references were made
with the intention of ridiculing Mr. Smith; but it so happened that in traveling
through the country, he visited Kirtland, Ohio, where the Prophet Joseph Smith
resided, bringing the mummies and the ancient papyrus writings with him. Mr.
Chandler had also obtained from learned men the best translation he could of some
few characters, which, however, was not a translation, but more in the shape of
their ideas with regard to it, their acquaintance with the language not being sufficient to enable them to translate it literally. After some conversation with the Prophet
Joseph, Mr. Chandler presented to him the ancient characters, asking him if he
could translate them. The Prophet took them and repaired to his room and' inquired of the Lord concerning them. The Lord told him they were sacred records,
containing the inspired writings of Abraham when he was in Egypt, and also of
Joseph while he was in Egypt; and they had been deposited, with those mummies,
which had been exhumed. And he also inquired of the Lord concerning some few
characters which Mr. Chandler gave him by way of a test, to see if he could translate
them. The Prophet Joseph translated these characters and returned them, with the
translation, to Mr. Chandler; and who, in comparing it with the translation of the
same few characters by learned men, that he had before obtained, found the two to
agree. The Prophet Joseph having learned the value of these ancient writings, was
very anxious to obtain them, and expressed himself wishful to purchase them. But
Mr. Chandler told him that he would not sell the writings, unless he could sell the
mummies, for it would detract from the curiosity of his exhibition. Mr. Smith inquired of him the price, which was a considerable sum, and finally purchased the

Additional Information

Note: While employed in the U.S. Forest Service (1910-16) in Bozeman, Montana, a news item from Clyde Park, Montana, appeared in the Bozeman *Daily Chronicle*, under date of January 3, 1915, which stated that a Mrs. Sylvia Whitmar had just celebrated her one hundredth natal anniversary. It stated she knew Joseph Smith, the Mormon Prophet, etc. The compiler of this book wrote her under date of January 8, 1915, asking for detailed information as to this acquaintance. Under date of January 18, 1913, her granddaughter, Miss Evalina Gurule, made reply as dictated by Mrs. Whitmar, and among the things mentioned she wrote:

"The three mummies that he (Joseph Smith) found, the two men had dark hair, the woman had yellow hair, and were very good looking people. They were preserved in some kind of liquid. These people lived some ages ago."

This item is of interest in showing that one of the three mummies was a woman. For an excellent detailed account of the mummies, the papyrus found with them, and the Book of Abraham, consult the 1938-39 Adult Department M.I.A. Manual, entitled *"Ancient Records Testify in Papyrus and Stone,"* by Dr. Sidney B. Sperry.

Robert Horne Saw Papyrus and Mummies

"Oh, here is the Pearl of Great Price," said Brother Horne, picking up that book. "I've seen these records with my own eyes," referring to the Book of Abraham, "and handled them with these hands. Mother Lucy (Joseph's Mother) showed them to me. You know Joseph had purchased four mummies. They were one of the Egyptian Pharaohs, his wife, sister and daughter. I took hold of the breastbone of one of them. The records which I saw were some kind of parchment or papyrus, and it contained writing in red and black. Mother Lucy told me that one was the writings of Abraham and the other the writngs of Joseph, who was sold in Egypt."

Millennial Star, 55:584

mummies and the writings, all of which he retained in his possession for many years; and they were seen by all the Church that saw proper to visit the house of the Prophet Joseph and also by hundreds of strangers. The Prophet translated the part of these writings which, as I have said, is contained in the Pearl of Great Price, and known as the Book of Abraham. Journal of Discourses, Vol. 20:64-5.

JOSEPH THE PROPHET'S STORE ON WATER STREET, IN WHICH ON MAY 4, 1842, THE PROPHET FIRST INTRODUCED THE ENDOWMENTS FOR THE LIVING AND THE DEAD.

Here also the Relief Society was organized by him on March 17, 1842. To the right may be seen the Mississippi River.

Chapter XX

THE BEGINNING OF CEREMONIAL ENDOWMENTS IN THIS DISPENSATION

Revealing of Endowments

Wednesday, May 4, 1842: I spent the day in the upper part of the store, that is in my private office (so called because in that room I keep my sacred writings, translate ancient records, and receive revelations) and in my general business office, or lodge room (that is where the Masonic fraternity meet occasionally, for want of a better place) in council with General James Adams, of Springfield, Patriarch Hyrum Smith, Bishops Newel K. Whitney and George Miller, and President Brigham Young, and Elders Heber C. Kimball and Willard Richards, instructing them in the principles and order of the Priesthood, attending to washings, anointings, endowments and the communication of keys pertaining to the Aaronic Priesthood, and so on to the highest order of the Melchisedek Priesthood, setting forth the order pertaining to the Ancient of Days, and all those plans and principles by which any one is enabled to secure the fullness of those blessings which have been prepared for the Church of the First Born, and come up and abide in the presence of the Eloheim in the eternal worlds. In this council was instituted the ancient order of things for the first time in these last days. And the communications I made to this council were of things spiritual, and to be received only by the spiritual minded; and there was nothing made known to these men but what will be made known to all the Saints of the last days, so soon as they are prepared to receive, and a proper place is prepared to communicate them, even to the weakest of the Saints; therefore, let the Saints be diligent in building the Temple, and all houses which they have been, or shall hereafter be, commanded of God to build; and wait their time with patience in all meekness, faith, perseverance unto the end, knowing assuredly that all things referred to in this council are always governed by the principle of revelation.

Thursday, May 5. General Adams started for Springfield, and the remainder of the council of yesterday continued their meeting at the same place, and myself and Brother Hyrum received in turn from the others, the same that I had communicated to them the day previous.[1, 2, 3, 4, 5]

Documentary History of Church, Vol. 5, pp. 1-3.

---

[1] *The Prophet Joseph Gives the Endowment to the Twelve:* Before I went east on the 4th of April, last, we were in council with Brother Joseph almost every day for weeks. Says Brother Joseph, in one of those councils, "There is something going to happen; I don't know what it is, but the Lord bids me to hasten, and give you your endowment before the temple is finished." He conducted us through every ordinance of the holy priesthood, and when he had gone through with all the ordinances he rejoiced very much and said, "Now if they kill me you have got all the keys, and all the ordinances, and you can confer them upon others, and the hosts of Satan will not be able to tear down the kingdom as fast as you will be able to build it up; and now," said he, "on your shoulders will rest the responsibility of leading this people for the Lord is going to let me rest awhile." Now why did he say to the Twelve "on your shoulders will this responsibility rest"?—why did he not mention Brother Hyrum? The Spirit knew that Hyrum would be taken with him, and hence he did not mention his name; Elder Rigdon's name was not mentioned, although he was there all the time, but he did not attend our councils.

Trial of Sidney Rigdon, by Orson Hyde, Millennial Star, Vol. 5:104. (Dec. 1844.)

[2] *By Wilford Woodruff:* Has the Prophet Joseph found Elder Rigdon in his councils, when he organized the quorum of the Twelve a few months before his death, to prepare them for the endowment? And when they *received their endowment, and actually received the keys of the Kingdom of God, and oracles of God, keys of revelation, and the pattern of heavenly things:* and thus addressing the Twelve, exclaimed: "Upon your shoulders the kingdom rests, and you must round up your shoulders and bear it, for I have had to do it until now. But now the responsibility rests upon you. It mattereth not what becomes of me." But I say, has this been the case with Elder Rigdon in any wise?

Trial of Sidney Rigdon, Millennial Star, Vol. 5:109. (Dec. 1844.)

[3] *Pattern of Endowments Revealed from Heaven:* This great and good man was led, before his death, to call the Twelve together from time to time and to instruct them in all things pertaining to the kingdom, ordinances and government of God. He often observed that he was laying the foundation, but it would remain for the Twelve to complete the building. Said he, "I know not why; but for some reason I am constrained to hasten my preparations, and to confer upon the Twelve all the ordinances, keys, covenants, endowments, and sealing ordinances of the priesthood, and so set before them a pattern in all things pertaining to the sanctuary and the endowment therein."

Having done this, he rejoiced exceedingly; "for," said he, "the Lord is about to lay the burden on your shoulders and let me rest awhile; and if they kill me," continued he, "the Kingdom of God will roll on, as I have now finished the work which was laid upon me, by committing to you all things for the building up of the kingdom *according to the heavenly vision, and the pattern shown me from heaven.*" With many conversations like this, he comforted the minds of the Twelve, and prepared them for what was soon to follow.

He proceeded to confer on Elder Young, the President of the Twelve, the keys of the sealing power, as conferred in the last days by the spirit and power of Elijah, in order to seal the hearts of the fathers to the children, and the hearts of the children to the fathers, lest the whole earth should be smitten with a curse.

This last key of the priesthood is the most sacred of all, and pertains exclusively to the first presidency of the church, without whose sanction, and approval or authority, no sealing blessing shall be administered pertaining to things of the resurrection and the life to come.

After giving them a very short charge to do all things according to the pattern, he quietly surrendered his liberty and his life into the hands of his blood-thirsty enemies, and all this to save the people for whom he had so long labored from threatened vengeance.

By Parley P. Pratt, Millennial Star, Vol. 5:151.

⁴*Endowments Given in Nauvoo by Joseph the Prophet*: Joseph Smith, before his death, was much exercised about the completion of the Temple in Nauvoo, and the administering of ordinances therein. In his anxiety and for fear he should not live to see the Temple completed, he prepared a place over what was known as the brick-store—which many of you who lived in Nauvoo will recollect—where to a chosen few he administered those ordinances that we now have today associated with Endowments, so that if anything should happen to him—which he evidently contemplated—he would feel that he had then fulfilled his mission, that he had conferred upon others all the keys *given to him by the manifestations of the power of God.*

By President John Taylor, Journal of Discourses, Vol. 25:183.

⁵*Second Anointing Also Given by the Prophet.* In the evening the best and indeed the crowning feature of the whole excursion was enjoyed. President Snow announced that the evening would be occupied by the Temple workers as a Testimony meeting, and it was so done. Most of the brethren workers bore strong and grateful testimonies, not only of their delight and joy in the work of the Temple, but testified also of their happiness and of their gratitude to the Saints in Box Elder Stake, who had made it possible for them to enjoy such a rare treat.

Three of the sisters, Sister Zina D. Young, who is the President of the sisters in the Temple, with Sister Bathsheba W. Smith and Minnie J. Snow, her two counselors, spoke briefly of their joy in the work. Aunt Bathsheba mentioned the fact that she had received her blessings in Nauvoo under the hands of the Prophet Joseph Smith, she being now the only living woman who has received these blessings.

President Woodruff spoke afterwards on the same subject, and bore testimony to the receiving of the same blessings in the same manner, he being the only living man at present who has thus received his endowments. This, then, should be recorded in the mind, and in the private journal of everyone, that President Woodruff and Sister Bathsheba W. Smith were endowed and received their blessings of sealing and anointings under the hands of the Prophet Joseph Smith. There were many more who likewise had this great privilege, but they are all dead, leaving only these two living witnesses.* * *

We are having many men come to us with pretended revelations, Josephites and Strangites and other men. One man came to me and said he had revelations to lead this Church; I am willing to leave all these things in the hands of God. Where has the power of God been since the death of Joseph? With this people. They say, these apostates, that Brigham Young organized the endowments and originated the principle of plural marriage. They're liars, every one of them, and the truth is not in them in so far as this matter is concerned. There's Sister Bathsheba Smith; she and I both had our endowments under the hands of the Prophet Joseph Smith. I had my second anointing and sealings under his hands. There is not a single principle in this Church that he did not lay the foundation for. He called the Twelve together the last time he spoke to us, and his face shone like amber. And upon our shoulders he rolled the burden of the Kingdom, and he gave us all the keys and powers and gifts to carry on this great and mighty work. He told us that he had received every key, every power and every gift for the salvation of the living and the dead, and he said: "Upon the Twelve I seal these gifts and powers and keys from henceforth and forever. No matter what may come to me. And I lay this work upon your shoulders. Take it and bear it off, and if you don't you'll be damned." I don't feel justified in contending with these apostates and such men. There is too much work to be done. And these things are true, and if such men don't find it out here, they will hereafter.

There is an anxiety in the spirit world concerning this people. The angels of God are with us, and they will assist us in this work. God bless you and all this people. I felt that I had finished my work when that Temple was finished; and doctors said I could not live. But my life was spared because this people were putting up petitions in my behalf continually before God. I feel to bless you, my brethren and sisters. May He help us all to do our duty, and be prepared for the great events coming upon this earth. Amen.

(Report written by Susa Young Gates of the Temple Workers' Excursion, Young Woman's Journal, August, 1894, Vol. 5, No. 11.)

Endowments Same Now as in Nauvoo

By *Bathsheba W. Smith:*

I was a resident of Nauvoo, State of Illinois, from 1840 to 1846, I was married to George A. Smith July 25, 1841, Elder Don Carlos Smith performing the ceremony. Near the close of the year 1843, or in the beginning of the year 1844, I received the ordinance of anointing in a room in Sister Emma Smith's house in Nauvoo, and the same day, in company with my husband, I received my endowment in the upper room over the Prophet Joseph Smith's store. The endowments were given under the direction of the Prophet Joseph Smith, who afterwards gave us lectures or instructions in regard to the endowment ceremonies. There has been no change, to my certain knowledge, in these ceremonies. They are the same today as they were then. A short time after I received my anointing, I was sealed to my husband, George A. Smith, for time and eternity, by President Brigham Young, in the latter's house, according to the plan taught, to my knowledge, by the Prophet Joseph Smith. When I was married in 1841, I was married for time, and not for eternity.

Blood Atonement and the Origin of Plural Marriage. Discussion between R. C. Evans and Elder Joseph Fielding Smith, p. 87.

Chapter XXI

EFFICACY AND SACREDNESS OF TEMPLE ORDINANCES

Significance of the Endowment

By President Brigham Young
(Sermon delivered in the Tabernacle, April 6, 1853.)

"Soon after, the Church, through our beloved Prophet Joseph, was commanded to build a Temple to the Most High in Kirtland, Ohio, and this was the next House of the Lord we hear of on the earth, since the days of Solomon's Temple. Joseph not only received revelation and commandment to build a temple, but he received a pattern also, as did Moses for the Tabernacle, and Solomon for his Temple; for without a pattern, he could not know what was wanting, having never seen one, and not having experienced its use.

"Without revelation, Joseph could not know what was wanting, any more than any other man, and, without command-ment, the Church were too few in numbers, too weak in faith, and too poor in purse, to attempt such a mighty enterprise. But by means of all these stimulants, a mere handful of men, living on air, and a little hominy and milk, and often salt or no salt when milk could not be had; the great Prophet Joseph, in the stone quarry, quarrying rock with his own hands; and the few men in the Church, following his example of obedience and dili-gence wherever most needed; with laborers on the walls, holding the sword in one hand to protect themselves from the mob, while they placed the stone and moved the trowel with the other, the Kirtland Temple, the second House of the Lord that we have any published record of on the earth, was so far com-pleted as to be dedicated. And those first Elders who helped to build it, received a portion of their first endowments, or we might say more clearly, some of the first, or introductory, or initiatory ordinances preparatory to an endowment.

"The preparatory ordinances there administered, though accompanied by the ministration of angels, and the presence of the Lord Jesus, were but a faint similitude of the ordinances of the House of the Lord in their fullness; yet many, through the instigation of the devil, thought they had received all, and knew as much as God; they have apostatized, and gone to hell. But be assured, brethren, there are but few, very few of the Elders of Israel, now on earth, who know the meaning of the word endowment. To know, they must experience; and to experience, a Temple must be built.

"Let me give you the definition in brief. Your endowment is to receive all those ordinances in the House of the Lord, which are necessary for you, after you have departed this life, to enable you to walk back to the presence of the Father, passing the angels who stand as sentinels, being enabled to give them the key words, the signs and tokens, pertaining to the Holy Priesthood, and gain your eternal exaltation in spite of earth and hell.

"Who has received and understands such an endowment in this assembly? You need not answer. Your voices would be few and far between, yet the keys to these endowments are among you, and thousands have received them, so that the devil, with all his aids, need not suppose he can again destroy the Holy Priesthood from the earth, by killing a few, for he cannot do it. God has set His hand, for the last time, to redeem His people, the honest in heart, and Lucifer cannot hinder Him.

"Before these endowments could be given at Kirtland, the Saints had to flee before mobocracy. And, by toil and daily labor, they found places in Missouri, where they laid the corner-stones of Temples, in Zion and her stakes, and then had to retreat to Illinois, to save the lives of those who could get away alive from Missouri, where fell the Apostle David W. Patten, with many like associates, and where they were imprisoned in loathsome dungeons, and fed on human flesh, Joseph and Hyrum, and many others. But before this had transpired, the Temple at Kirtland had fallen into the hands of wicked men, and by them been polluted, like the Temple at Jerusalem, and consequently it was disowned by the Father and the Son.

J. D., Vol. 2, pp. 31-2.

Latter-day Saints, What Does This Mean to You?

Remember therefore how thou hast received and heard, and hold fast, and repent. If therefore thou shalt not watch, I will come on thee as a thief, and thou shalt not know what hour I will come upon thee.

Thou hast a few names even in Sardis which have not *defiled their garments*; and they shall walk with me in white; for they are worthy.

He that shall overcome, shall thus be *clothed in white garments,* and I will not blot out his name out of the book of life, and I will confess his name before my Father, and before his angels. Rev. 3:3-5.

I counsel thee to buy of me gold fire tried, that thou mayest be made rich; and mayest be *clothed in white garments,* and that the shame of thy nakedness may not appear; and *anoint thy eyes with eyesalve, that thou mayest see.* Rev. 3:18.

Behold, I come as a thief. Blessed is he that watcheth, and *keepeth his garments,* lest he walk naked, and they see his shame. Rev. 16:15.

And to her was granted that she *should be arrayed in fine linen, clean and white for the fine linen is the righteousness of saints.* Rev. 19:8.

Good Advice for the Present Day
By President Joseph F. Smith

We entered into covenants with the Lord that we will keep ourselves pure and unspotted from the world. We have agreed before God, angels and witnesses, in sacred places, that we will not commit adultery, will not lie, that we will not steal or bear false witness against our neighbor, or take advantage of the weak, that we will help and sustain our fellow men in the right, and take such a course as will prove most effectual in helping the weak to overcome their weaknesses and bring themselves into subjection to the requirements of heaven. We cannot neglect, slight, or depart from the spirit, meaning, intent and purpose, of these covenants and agreements, that we have entered into with our Father in heaven, without shearing ourselves of our glory, strength, right and title to His blessings, and to the gifts and manifestations of His Spirit.

The Lord has given unto us garments of the holy priesthood, and you know what that means. And yet there are those of us who mutilate them, in order that we may follow the foolish, vain and (permit me to say) indecent practices of the world. In order that such people may imitate the fashions, they will not hesitate to mutilate that which should be held by them the most sacred of all things in the world, next to their own virtue, next to their own purity of life. They should hold these things that God has given unto them sacred, unchanged and unaltered from the very pattern in which God gave them. Let us have the moral courage to stand against the opinions of fashion, and especially where fashion compels us to break a covenant and so commit a grievous sin.　　　　　　The Improvement Era, Vol. 9:813.

What is Meant by Keys, Power and Calling of Elijah?

On April 3, 1836, one week after the dedication of the Kirtland Temple, the ancient Prophet Elijah appeared to Joseph Smith and Oliver Cowdery, thereby fulfilling the prediction made by Malachi. He bestowed upon the Prophet Joseph and upon Oliver the same keys and blessings which he had bestowed upon the heads of Peter, James, and John, on the Mount of Transfiguration. What were these powers held by Elijah? Answer:

By Elder Joseph Fielding Smith: The keys that Elijah held were the keys of the everlasting priesthood, the keys of the sealing power, which the Lord gave unto him, and that included a ministry of sealing for the living as well as the dead — and it is not confined to the living and it is not confined to the dead, but includes them both.

Elijah was the last of the old prophets who held the fulness of the priesthood, the sealing power of the priesthood; and being the last of the prophets, it was his place to come — but in order that the binding power should come which is recognized in the heavens, and by which we pass by the angels and the Gods to exaltation, had to come from Elijah, who held that power upon the face of the earth, for the Lord had given it to him, and so he came to Joseph Smith and Oliver Cowdery on the 3rd day of April, and bestowed upon them the keys of this priesthood.

By the Prophet Joseph Smith: Now for Elijah. The spirit, power, and calling of Elijah is, that he have power to hold the keys of the revelation, ordinances, oracles, powers and endowments of the fulness of the Melchizedek Priesthood and to receive, obtain, perform, all the ordinances pertaining to the kingdom of God.

The Improvement Era, November, 1955.

Adjustment of sealings during Millennium: Children who are legally adopted may, under proper circumstances, be sealed into the families who adopted them. It is not possible, however, to rob the dead of their children, if they are entitled to them, even if they are adopted by others.

If a man or a woman who has been sealed in the temple for time and eternity should sin and lose the right to receive the exaltation in the celestial kingdom, he or she could not retard the progress of the injured companion who had been faithful. Everyone will be judged according to his works, and there would be no justice in condemning the innocent for the sins of the guilty.

We may be sure that the Lord is not going to permit any ordinance which we perform incorrectly, through our lack of understanding, to be left binding forever without correction. During the millennium there will be a great deal of adjusting where we, for lack of proper knowledge, have performed sealings ignorantly, but according to our best judgment.

Doctrines of Salvation, pp. 177-178.

Millennium: Great Era of Salvation for the Dead: Some people may think that it is impossible for us to do this work for the dead because we have not the names of people who lived in ancient times. We have not the records, we do not know how to reach them from anything we have in this life, and there have been millions of people who no doubt were honest, and did the best they knew, but died without a knowledge of the gospel, whose names it is impossible for us to obtain. How are they going to be saved?

It is our duty to go to the temple and take our records and work for the dead of our own lineage as far back as we can go, but what about these others? I will tell you. The great work of the millennium, of one thousand years, will be for the salvation of these souls.

Now let us keep it clearly in our minds that we do not enter into exaltation until after the resurrection. We do not enter into exaltation in the spirit world. We have privileges there, of course, based upon faithfulness and obedience to the gospel, but during the millennium — and that is the great purpose of the millennium — we will go into the temples.

Those who will be living here will be in daily communication with those who have passed through the resurrection, and they will come with this information, this knowledge that we do not have and will give it to those who are in mortality, saying, "Now go into the temples and do this work; when you get this done, we will bring you other names." And in that way every soul who is entitled to a place in the celestial kingdom of God will be ferreted out, and not one soul shall be overlooked.

The Lord has not overlooked these things. He has seen the end from the beginning. Every name is recorded. Bless your soul, when the Lord says that a sparrow cannot fall without the notice of the Father, do you think he will overlook the people who lived upon this earth, who have tried to the best of their ability to live righteously, but never had the privilege of receiving the gospel? He will give unto them these privileges of salvation and the right, through their obedience of the gospel which shall come unto them, of receiving exaltation in his kingdom.

To think anything less than this would be an evil thought. God is just. He is merciful, and while mercy cannot rob justice, yet in the wisdom of our Father in heaven every soul shall receive blessings according to his merits and according to the mercies of our Heavenly Father, and he will do for the people the best he can."

Doctrines of Salvation, 2:166-168.

Sacred Ordinances for the Dead

Sealing power continues family in eternity: The doctrine of salvation for the dead, of temple work, holds out to us the glorious prospect of the continuance of the family relation. Through it we learn that family ties are not to be broken, that husbands and wives will eternally have a claim upon each other and upon their children to the latest generation. However, in order to receive privileges, the sealing ordinances in the temple of our God must be obtained.

All contracts, bonds, obligations and agreements made by men shall come to an end, but the obligations and agreements entered into in the house of the Lord if faithfully kept, will last forever. This doctrine gives us a clearer concept of the purposes of the Lord toward his children. It shows his abundant and unlimited mercy and love to all who obey him, aye, even to those who are rebellious, for in his goodness he will grant great blessings even unto them. Doctrines of Salvation, Vol. 2, p. 173.

No blessing will be denied the faithful: Those who have been faithful members of the Church and could not reach a temple while living will have the work done for them after they are dead.

We have the assurance that the Lord will reward every soul according to his or her works. He will judge each of us by the intent of the heart. If any worthy person is denied in this life the blessings which so readily come to others, and yet lives faithfully and to the best of his or her ability in striving to keep the commandments of the Lord, then nothing will be lost to him. Such a person will be given all the blessings that can be given. The Lord will make up to him the fulness after this life is ended and the full life has come. The Lord will not overlook a single soul who is worthy, but will grant to him all that can be given which those, apparently more fortunate, received in this life. Ibid., p. 177.

No Match-making for the dead: We never make matches for the dead in the temples. The Lord will bless all who are worthy of the blessings, and they will lose nothing. The work of the millennium will be largely work for the dead who did not have an opportunity when living to obtain the blessings;

but who would have accepted the blessings if they had lived. Justice demands this. We need not worry, therefore, because young men or young women die without being married. All who are worthy will be blessed just the same as if they had lived and obtained the blessings. Where, however, a couple is engaged and the woman dies, she may be sealed to her intended husband. *Ibid., p. 177.*

By President Joseph Fielding Smith

The Power to Receive Revelation and to Be Sealed to God

Who believes Joseph Smith to be a prophet? These my brethren and sisters who are now sitting before me. They entertain no doubts on this subject. They may sometimes be tempted and tried, and neglect their prayers, until they hardly know whether "Mormonism" is true or untrue. The cares of the world, we know very well, flood in upon them; but let me tell you one thing—and I want you to seriously remember it—if you are in darkness, and have not the spirit of prayer, still do not neglect your prayers in your families in the morning. You, fathers and husbands, get down upon your knees, and when the cares of this world intrude themselves upon your devotions, let them wait while you remain on your knees and finish your prayer. Brother Daniel D. Hunt's blessings over a dinner in Missouri, when he and Benjamin Clapp first met, is a very good prayer for us all. It was: "O Lord, save us from error." If you can say no more than this very short but comprehensive prayer, go down upon your knees and say it. When you have labored faithfully for years you will learn this simple fact—that if your hearts are right, and you still continue to be obedient, continue to serve God, continue to pray, the spirit of revelation will be in you like a well of water springing up to everlasting life. Let no person give up prayer because he has not the spirit of prayer, neither let any earthly circumstance hurry you while in the performance of this important duty. By bowing down before the Lord to ask Him to bless you, you will simply find this result—God will multiply blessings on you temporally and spiritually. Let a merchant, a farmer, a mechanic, any person in business, live his religion faithfully, and he need never lose one minute's sleep by thinking about his business; he need not worry in the least, but trust in God, go to sleep and rest. I say to this people—pray, and if you cannot do anything else, read a prayer aloud that your family may hear it, until you get a worshipping spirit, and are full of the riches of eternity, then you will be prepared at any time to lay hands on the sick, or to officiate in any of the ordinances of this religion. I do not recollect that I have seen five minutes since I was baptized that I have not been ready to preach a funeral sermon, lay hands on the sick, or to pray in private or in public. I will tell you the secret of this. In all your business transactions, words, and communications, if you commit an overt act, repent of that immediately, and call upon God to deliver you from evil and give you the light of His spirit. Never do a thing that your conscience, and the light within you, tells you is wrong. Never do a wrong, but do all the good you possibly can. Never do a thing to mar the peaceable influence of the Holy Spirit in you; then whatever you are engaged in—whether in business, in the dance, or in the pulpit, you are ready to officiate at any time in any of the ordinances of the House of God. If I commit an overt act, the Lord knows the integrity of my heart, and, through sincere repentance, He forgives me. Before Joseph's death he had a revelation concerning myself and others, which signified that we had passed the ordeal, and that we should never apostatize from the faith of the holy gospel; "and," said Joseph, "if there is any danger of your doing this, the Lord will take you to Himself forthwith, for you cannot stray from the truth." When men and women have traveled to a certain point in their labors in this life, God sets a seal upon them that they never can forsake their God in His kingdom; for, rather than they should do this, He will at once take them to Himself. Probably this is so with many of the elders who are taken from us, and over whom many ignorantly mourn. I say, to God give thanks, for who knows but that had they lived there might have been trials to pass through which they could not overcome. It is all right, blessed be the name of the Lord."

Brigham Young, J. D., Vol. 12:102-3.

The Efficacy of the Sealing Ordinance

The men who were in his bosom, shared his confidence, and professed to be his warmest and best friends, were the men to treacherously shed his blood. Why? Because He had revealed one additional principle of the law of redemption, that is, that the man is not without the woman, nor the woman without the man, in the Lord; that if a man went to the eternal world without obeying the law of sealing, he would remain forever alone, forever a servant, and could never have any increase; that if a woman entered the celestial world without having complied with the law of sealing as, entrusted by the Savior to His Apostles, she would remain forever alone, and without any increase; and if either man or woman should reject the principles of that law, they would forever lament and mourn that they might have been exalted to an eternal increase, and an everlasting dominion, but they would not have it.   By George A. Smith, J. D., Vol. 2:217-18.

Instructions to Adam and to Saints

By Heber C. Kimball

Father Adam was instructed to multiply and replenish the earth to make it beautiful and glorious, to make it, in short, like unto the garden from which the seeds were brought to plant the Garden of Eden. I might say much more on this subject, but I will ask, has it not been imitated before you in your holy endowments that you might understand how things were in the beginning of creation and cultivation of this earth? God the Father made Adam the Lord of this creation in the beginning, and if we are the Lords of this creation under Adam, ought we not to take a course to imitate our Father in Heaven? Is not all this exhibited to us in our endowments? The earth made glorious and beautiful to look upon, representing everything which the Lord caused to be prepared and placed to adorn the earth. The Prophet Joseph frequently spoke of these things in the revelations which he gave, but the people generally did not understand them, but to those who did they were cheering, they had a tendency to gladden the heart and enlighten the mind. By faith and works we shall subdue the earth and make it glorious. We can plant vineyards and eat the fruit thereof; we possess this power within ourselves.   J. D., Vol. 10:235.

Revelation Necessary to Know Endowments

To many of the Latter-day Saints the endowment has been of great significance. The instructions imparted, both by beautiful paintings and by word of mouth, are most ennobling and uplifting. To the impure these endowments mean nothing. From the Creation Room to the Celestial Room, the instructions imparted, the obligations taken and the responsibilities assumed are of the highest character. The progressive course of instruction gives the events of the creation, the fall of Adam and Eve through disobedience, their expulsion from Eden, their condition in a dreary world after their banishment, the plan of redemption offered them, the restoration of the Gospel with all of its keys, powers and blessings, and the final exaltation that comes to those who live in strict obedience to the Gospel. Sacred obligations and covenants are taken which require one to be virtuous, charitable, benevolent, tolerant and pure, and require the living of the highest ideals embodied in the law of God.

To acquire the meaning of these symbolic rituals, one must be in tune with the Almighty. No person having impure thoughts or motives can ever receive the meaning of the symbols given in the endowment. The instructions given by the Prophet Joseph are full of meaning and should be read and re-read:

"The communications I made to this council (See Chapter XVI) were things spiritual, and to be received ONLY BY THE SPIRITUALLY MINDED; and there was nothing made known to these men but what WILL BE MADE KNOWN TO ALL SAINTS OF THE LAST DAYS, AS SOON AS THEY ARE PREPARED TO RECEIVE, and a proper place is prepared to communicate them, even to the weakest of the Saints; therefore, let the Saints be diligent in building the Temple and all houses which they have been, or shall hereafter be, commanded of God to build; and wait their time with patience in all meekness, faith, perseverance unto the end, KNOWING ASSUREDLY THAT ALL THESE THINGS REFERRED TO IN THIS COUNCIL ARE ALWAYS GOVERNED BY THE PRINCIPLE OF REVELATION." The reader is also referred to Explanations Nos. 7 and 20 of the Facsimile of Egyptian Plate in Chapter XV—Ancient Records Bring Forth Light.

What is Meant by the
Fullness of the Priesthood?

By the Prophet Joseph Smith: "If a man gets the fulness of the Priesthood of God, he has to get it in the same way that Jesus Christ obtained it, and that was by keeping all the commandments and obeying all the ordinances of the house of the Lord."

Teachings of the Prophet Joseph Smith, p. 17

By Pres. Joseph Fielding Smith: If you want salvation in the fullest, that is exaltation in the kingdom of God, so that you may become his sons and his daughters, you have got to go to the temple of the Lord and receive these holy ordinances which belong to that house, which cannot be had elsewhere. No man shall receive fulness in eternity of exaltation alone; no one shall receive that blessing alone; but man and wife when they receive the sealing power in the temple of the Lord, shall pass on to exaltation and shall continue and be like the Lord and that is the destiny of man, that is what the Lord desires for his children.

Ibid., pp. 19-20.

If we want to receive the fulness of the priesthood of God then we must receive the fulness of the ordinances of the house of the Lord and keep his commandments. This idea that we can put off our salvation because of some weakness of the flesh until the end and then our children will go and do the work for us in the temple of the Lord when we are dead will get us nowhere. Salvation for the dead is for those who die without a knowledge of the gospel so far as celestial glory is concerned and those who have rejected the truth and who fought the truth, who would not have it, are not destined to receive celestial glory.

Ibid., p. 17.

The Fullness of the Priesthood

By Daniel Tyler

The Lord informed the prophet that the temples were the places to receive "the fullness of the priesthood." He said, "for a baptismal font there is not upon the earth, that my Saints may be baptized for those who are dead; for this ordinance belongeth to my house." (a temple) "and cannot be acceptable to me, only in the days of your poverty, wherein ye are not able to build a house unto me."

These additional powers include all of the keys that belong to the holy priesthood on the earth, or were ever revealed to man in any dispensation, and which admit men and women within the veil. They enable them to pass by the angels and the gods, until they get into the presence of the Father and the Son. They make of them kings and priests, queens and priestesses to God, to rule and reign as such over their posterity and those who may be given them by adoption, in the great jubilee of rest which is near at hand. It gives them the right to the tree of life and the "seal of the living God in their foreheads," spoken of by John the revelator. No marvel, then, that the Lord requires sacred places for such great and glorious things — "the fullness of the holy priesthood" to be restored.

Juvenile Instructor, vol. 15.

Chapter XXII

PRE-MORTAL, MORTAL AND POST-MORTAL EXISTENCE AND INTELLIGENCE OF SPIRITS

PURPOSE OF THIS CHAPTER

The purpose of this chapter is to prove the existence and intelligence of spirits; that they are living entities; that they have their free agency to accept or reject truth or error as they themselves will; and they therefore can accept or reject the Gospel after death; that there is a devil with his agencies and that they are continually persuading mankind to do evil; that these evil dis-embodied and un-embodied spirits are not intangible, non-entities, merely an essence or condition of the mind as some modern sects proclaim; that the spirits of all beings endure beyond what is called death which is the separation of the mortal body from the spirit or soul as some designate it; and are entities and not mere air as others teach. This doctrine is no doubt pleasing to Satan, the prince of devils. It is mentioned in the Book of Mormon wherein it states in the latter days people would say: "There is no devil." This doctrine to the Latter-day Saints is as absurd as the doctrine held by some that the spirit is not material, which is effectually answered by Orson Pratt on pages 282-4 of this book. Equally absurd is the doctrine held by countless thousands that man as well as the earth, sun, moon and stars were made of nothing. The teachings of the Prophet Joseph Smith and such eminent scientists and philosophers as Rev. Baden Powell, Herbert Spencer, Robert Kennedy Duncan, Fiske, and others, are given on pages 21-25 of THE VISION.

The teachings of the Prophet Joseph on these points were:

"Now, I ask all who hear me why the learned men who are preaching salvation, say that God created the heavens and the earth out of nothing? The reason is, that they are unlearned in the things of God, and have not the gift of the Holy Ghost; they account it blasphemy in any one to contradict their idea. If you tell them that God made the world out of something, they will call you a fool. * * * You ask the learned doctors why they say the world was made out of nothing, and they will answer, "Doesn't the Bible say he created the world?" And they infer, from the word *create*, that it must have been made out of nothing. Now the word *create* came from the word *baurau*, which does not mean to create out of nothing; it means to organize; the same as a man would organize materials and build a ship. Hence we infer that God had materials to organize the world out of chaos—chaotic matter, which is element, and in which dwells all the glory. Element had an existence from the time He had. The pure principles of element are principles which can never be destroyed; and they may be organized and reorganized, but not destroyed. They had no beginning, and can have no end.

"I have another subject to dwell upon, which is calculated to exalt man; but it is impossible for me to say much on this subject; I shall therefore just touch upon it, for time will not permit me to say all. It is associated with the subject of the resurrection of the dead—namely, the soul—the mind of man—the immortal spirit. Where did it come from? All learned men and doctors of divinity say that God created it in the beginning; but it is not so; the very idea lessens man in my estimation. I do not believe the doctrine; I know better. Hear it, all ye ends of the world; for God has told me so; and if you don't believe me, it will not make the truth without effect. I will make a man appear a fool before I get through if he does not believe it. I am going to tell of things more noble.

"We say that God himself is a self-existent being. Who told you so? It is correct enough; but how did it get into your heads? Who told you that man did not exist in like manner upon the same principles? Man does exist upon the same principles. God made a tabernacle and put a spirit into it, and it became a living soul. How does it read in the Hebrew? (Refers to the old Bible.) It does not say in Hebrew that God created the spirit of man. It says: "God made man out of earth and put into him Adam's spirit, and so became a living body." * * *

"I am dwelling on the immortality of the spirit of man. Is is logical to say that the intelligence of spirits is immortal, and yet that it had a beginning? The intelligence of spirits had no beginning, neither will it have an end. That is good logic. That which has a beginning may have an end. There never was a time when there were not spirits. * * *

"I want to reason more on the spirit of man; for I am dwelling on the body and spirit of man—on the subject of the dead. I take my ring from my finger and liken it unto the mind of man—the immortal part, because it has no beginning. Suppose you cut it in two; then it has a beginning and an end; but join it again and it continues one eternal round. So with the spirit of man. As the Lord liveth, if it had a beginning, it will have an end. All the fools and learned and wise men from the beginning of creation, who say that the spirit of man had a beginning, prove that it must have an end; and if that doctrine is true, then the doctrine of annihilation would be true. But if I am right, I might with boldness proclaim from the housetops that God never had the power to create the spirit of man at all. God himself could not create himself. Intelligence is eternal and exists upon a self-existent principle. It is a spirit from age to age, and there is no creation about it. All the minds and spirits that God ever sent into the world are susceptible of enlargement."

In opposition to the scientific views held by Joseph the Prophet and the eminent authorities referred to but not quoted, the following doctrines are held by countless thousands who claim to be intelligent:

"In the beginning God created the heavens and the earth." What did He make them out of? Nothing, absolutely nothing. When the earth was made, what did He hang it on? Nothing. Pretty satisfactory earth to be made of nothing, eh? Remember, not a scrap of anything was used to make it. "He * * * hangeth the earth upon nothing." It hangs all right, doesn't it? Very well, then a God who can make an earth, a sun, a moon and stars out of nothing and keep them hanging on nothing can supply all one needs whether He had anything to begin to work with or not. Wonderful, isn't it? Trust Him and He will see you through though He has to make your supplies out of nothing. Read this over and over again. It will mean more to you each time."

Excerpt from tract published by the "Free Tract Society," of Los Angeles, California, 746 Crocker Street.

"That God created the soul of Adam out of nothing and personally fashioned his body, becomes still clear from Gen. 2:7: 'And the Lord God formed man of the slime of the earth, and breathed into his face the breath of life, and man became a living soul.' These words, taken in their natural and obvious sense, represent the creative act of God as one, though divided into two moments, viz., formation and breathing.

"That the universe was created out of nothing is one of the fundamental articles of the Catholic faith. Dogmatic theology demonstrates it from holy scripture, defends it against opposing heresies of Dualism and Pantheism clears up certain supplementary and explanatory notions that centre about the dogma, e.g., the liberty of the divine act of Creation, the simultaneous beginning of the world and of time, the incommunicability of creative power.

"Catholic Philosophy, in accord with ecclesiastical tradition, defines Creation as the 'production of a thing from or out of, nothing.' In this definition, 'production' expresses the proximate genus, while 'out of nothing' gives the specific difference by which Creation is marked off from all other modes of production as a singular operation peculiar to God."

"God—The Author of Nature and the Supernatural," by Rt. Rev. Msgr. Joseph Pohle, Ph.D., D.D. pp 4-5.

What follows, therefore, in this Chapter, is in har-mony with scientific truth and the revealed word of God. Important Messages from the Spirit World

By President Wilford Woodruff

(Delivered at General Conference, Salt Lake City, October 10, 1880.)

I will here make a remark concerning my own feelings. After the death of Joseph Smith I saw and conversed with him many times in my dreams in the night season. On one occasion he and his brother Hyrum, met me when on the sea, going on a mission to England. I had Dan Jones with me. He received his mission from Joseph before his death; and the prophet talked freely to me about the mission I was then going to perform. And he also talked to me with regard to the mission of the Twelve Apostles in the flesh, and he laid before me the work they had to perform; and he also spoke of the reward they would receive after death. And there were many other things he laid before me in his interview on that occasion. And when I awoke many of the things he had told me were taken from me, I could not comprehend them. I have had many interviews with Brother Joseph until the last 15 or 20 years of my life; I have not seen him for that length of time. But during my travels in the south-ern country last winter I had many interviews with President Young, and with Heber C. Kimball, and George A. Smith, and Jedediah M. Grant, and many others who are dead. They at-tended our conference, they attended our meetings. And on one occasion, I saw Brother Brigham and Brother Heber ride in the carriage ahead of the carriage in which I rode when I was on my way to attend conference; and they were dressed in the most priestly robes. When we arrived at our destination I asked Pres-ident Young if he would preach to us. He said, "No, I have finished my testimony in the flesh; I shall not talk to this people any more. But," (said he), "I have come to see you; I have come to watch over you, and to see what the people are doing. Then," (said he), "I want you to teach the people—and I want you to follow this counsel yourself—that they must labor and so live as to obtain the Holy Spirit, for without this you cannot build up the kingdom; without the Spirit of God you are in danger of walking in the dark, and in danger of failing to accomplish your calling as apostles and as elders in the church and kingdom of

God. And," (said he), "Brother Joseph taught me this principle." And I will here say, I have heard him refer to that while
he was living. But what I was going to say is this: The thought
came to me that Brother Joseph had left the work of watching
over this church and kingdom to others, and that he had gone
ahead, and that he had left this work to men who have lived
and labored with us since he left us. This idea manifested itself
to me, that such men advance in the spirit world. And I believe
myself that these men who have died and gone into the spirit
world had this mission left with them, that is, a certain portion
of them, to watch over the Latter-day Saints.

J. D. Vol. 21:317-18.

Elder Orson Pratt, an Apostle Paul to This Age

It is with great satisfaction that the likeness is produced of
one whose discourses and writings are generously quoted in this
book—Orson Pratt. He was a great leader, a pioneer, a writer,
a great expounder of the Gospel, a philosopher and thinker. He
was always in the vanguard of all pro-
gressive undertakings in the history of
the church and state. It would be impossible, as President Wilford Woodruff stated at his funeral services, "to
give the history of that great man, or to
depict the glory that awaits him. It
would take the trumpet of the sixth
angel to do that. * * * Brother Pratt
had lived longer in this Church, traveled more miles and preached more sermons than any man in it. He had
baptized thousands, and fulfilled the
revelation given to him through the
Prophet Joseph Smith, November 4, 1830. His garments were
clear from the blood of this generation. He had studied and
written more upon the Gospel and upon science than any man
in the Church." (Contributor XII:460-1.) His contributions
in this volume demonstrate his greatness. He was nobility and

humility personified. He lived and died as he himself expressed:

"It is a great satisfaction to me to have the privilege of being numbered with this people, and to have my name enrolled among those who profess to be Latter-day Saints. With them is safety; with them are joy, peace, and satisfaction. And I feel to say, as one said in old times—that with this people I desire to live, and if it is necessary to die, I desire to have the privilege of dying with them. But I do not know whether it will be necessary for all of us to die, perhaps there may be some who will escape this curse in some measure, and who may meet with a change equivalent to that of death."

J. D. 12:84.

The Existence and Duration of the Spirit
By Orson Pratt.

There are two classes of Atheists in the world. One class denies the existence of God in the most positive language; the other denies his existence in duration or space. One says, "There is no God;" the other says, "God is not here or there, any more than He exists now and then." The infidel says, God does not exist anywhere. The Immaterialist says, "He exists Nowhere." The infidel says, There is no such substance as God. The Immaterialist says, There is such a substance as God, but it is "*without parts*." The Atheist says, There is no such substance as Spirit. The Immaterialist says, "A Spirit, though he lives and acts, occupies no room, and fills no space, in the same way and after the same manner as matter, not even so much as does the minutest grain of sand." The Atheist does not seek to hide his infidelity; but the Immaterialist, whose declared belief amounts to the same thing as the Atheist's, endeavours to hide his infidelity under the shallow covering of a few words. * * *

That which is "not extended and not divisible" and "without parts," cannot be anything else than nothing. Take away these qualities and conditions, and no power of language can give us the least idea of existence. The very idea conveyed by the term existence is something extended, divisible, and with parts. Take these away, and you take away existence itself. It cannot be so much as the negative of space, or, what is generally called, an indivisible point, for that has a relation to the surrounding spaces. It cannot be so much as the negative of duration, or, what is generally called, an indivisible instant, for that has a relation to the past and future. Therefore, it must be the negative of all existence, or what is called absolutely nothing. Nothing, and nothing only, is a representative of that which has no relation to space or time—that is, unextended, indivisible, and without parts. Therefore, the Immaterialist is a religious Atheist; he only differs from the other classes of Atheists, by clothing an indivisible, unextended NOTHING with the powers of a god. One class believes in no God; the other class believes that NOTHING IS god, and worships it as such. There is no twisting away from this. The most profound philosopher in all the ranks of modern Christianity cannot extricate the Immaterialists from atheism. He cannot show the least difference between the idea represented by the word *nothing*, and the idea represented by that which is unextended, indivisible, and without parts, having no relation to space or time. All the philosophers of the universe could not give a better or more correct definition of NOTHING. And yet this is the god worshipped by the Church of England—the Methodists—and millions of other atheistical idolators, according to their own definitions, as recorded in their respective articles of faith. An open atheist is not so dangerous as the Atheist who couches his atheistical doctrines under the head of "Articles of Religion." The first stands out with open colors and boldly avows his infidelity; the latter, under the sacred garb of religion, draws into his yawning vortex, the unhappy millions who are persuaded to believe in, and worship an unextended, indivisible NOTHING without parts, deified into a god. A pious Atheist is much more serviceable in building up the kingdom of darkness than one who openly, and without any deception, avows his infidelity.

No wonder that this modern god has wrought no miracles and given no revelation since his followers invented their "articles of religion." A being without parts must be entirely powerless, and can perform no miracles. Nothing can be communicated from such a being; for, if nothing give nothing, nothing will be received. If, at death, his followers are to be made like him, they will enjoy, with some of the modern Pagans, all the beauties of annihilation. To be made like him! Admirable thought! How transcendently sublime, to behold an innumerable multitude of unextended nothings, casting their crowns at the feet of the great unextended, infinite NOTHING, filling all space, and yet "without parts!" There will be no danger of quarreling for want of room; for the Rev. David James says, "Ten thousand spirits might be brought together into the smallest compass imaginable, and there exist without any inconveniences for want of room. As materiality," continues he, "forms no property of a spirit, the space which is sufficient for one must be amply sufficient for myriads, yea, for all that exist." According to this, all the spirits that exist, "could be brought together into the smallest compass imaginable," or, in other words, into no compass at all; for, he says, a spirit occupies "no room, and fills no space." What an admirable description of NOTHING! NOTHING "occupies no room, and fills no space!" If myriads of NOTHINGS were "brought together into the smallest compass imaginable," they would "there exist without any inconvenience for want of room." Everything which the Immaterialist says, of the existence of SPIRIT, will apply, without any variation, to the existence of NOTHING. If he says that his god cannot exist "Here" or "There," the same is true of NOTHING. If he affirms that he cannot exist "Here"· and "Then," the same can, in all truth, be affirmed of NOTHING. If he declared, that he is "unextended," so is NOTHING. If he asserts that he is "indivisible" and "without parts," so is NOTHING. If he declared that a spirit "occupies no room and fills no space," neither does NOTHING. If he says a spirit is "Nowhere," so is NOTHING. All that he affirms of the one, can in like manner, and, with equal truth be affirmed of the other. Indeed, they are only two words, each of which express precisely the same idea. There is no more absurdity in calling NOTHING a substance, and clothing it with Almighty powers than there is in making a substance out of that which is precisely like nothing, and imagining it to have Almighty powers. Therefore, an immaterial god is deified NOTHING, and all his worshippers are atheistical idolators.***

That spirit or mind has a relation to duration is manifest in the act of remembering. Through the memory, the mind perceives itself to be the same conscious being *now*, that it was an hour, day, a year ago; it perceives that itself has existed through a certain period of duration. There is as much certainty of its own relations to duration as there is of any such relation in any other substance whatever. If there is no certainty that mind has a relation to duration, there is no certainty that any other substance has such a relation; hence all would be uncertainty, even our own existence.   Absurdities of Immaterialism, pp. 11, 12, 13.

Pre-Mortal and Post-Mortal Intelligence of Spirits
By Orson Pratt

The word of the Lord, through Joseph, the Prophet, to Martin Harris, reads thus: "I command you to repent—repent, lest I smite you by the rod of my mouth, and by my wrath, and by my anger, and your sufferings be sore—how sore you know not! how exquisite you know not! yea, how hard to bear you know not! For behold, I, God, have suffered these things for all, that they might not suffer if they would repent; but if they would not repent, they must suffer even as I, which suffering caused myself, even God, the greatest of all, to tremble because of pain, and to bleed at every pore, and to suffer both body and spirit; and would that I might not drink the bitter cup and shrink, nevertheless, glory be to the Father, and I partook and finished my preparations unto the children of men." (Doc. and Cov. Sec. 44). Jesus suffered, not only in body, but also in spirit. By the sufferings of His body He atoned for the sins of men committed in and by the body; by the sufferings of His spirit, He atoned for the sins committed by the spirit; hence, the atonement redeems both body and spirit. It is reasonable, therefore, to suppose that if spirits in the first estate sinned, they might be forgiven through their faith and repentance, by virtue of the future sufferings of Christ.

That the spirits of men did receive promises and gifts before the world began, is clearly manifest in many parts of Scripture. The Apostle Paul writes as follows: "In hope of eternal life, which God, that cannot lie, promised before the world began." (Titus 1:2). God "promised" "eternal life." When was this promise made? It was made "before the world began." To whom was it made? It was made to the spirits of men, who existed before the world began. We were comforted with the promises of God when we dwelt in His presence. We could then look upon the face of the First Born and consider Him as already slain, or as Peter says, that He 'verily was fore-ordained before the foundation of the world.' (I Peter 1:20). When we were in our spiritual state, all the grace or mercy we received, was because of Christ. Paul, in speaking of God, says, "Who hath saved us, and called us with an holy calling, not according to our works, but according to His own purpose and grace, which was given us in Christ Jesus before the world began." (2 Tim. 1:9). According to this passage, and the preceding ones, Paul, Timothy, Titus, and others, existed before the world began, and in that anterior existence, God made promises unto them of eternal life, and also give them grace in "Christ Jesus." The Apostle Paul also says: "Blessed be the God and Father of our Lord Jesus Christ, who hath blessed us with all spiritual blessings in heavenly places in Christ: according as He hath chosen us in Him before the foundation of the world." (Eph. 1:3-4). Now if the Apostles and others were called "with an holy calling," and "chosen in Christ before the foundation of the world," and actually received grace in Christ, and had the promise of "Eternal Life" made to them "before the world began," then why should it be thought incredible, that in and through Christ they also received forgiveness of the sins which they may have committed in that pre-existent state?

If all the two-thirds who kept their first estate were equally valiant in the war and equally faithful, why should some of them be called and chosen in their spiritual state to hold responsible stations and offices in this world, while others were not? If there were none of those spirits who sinned, why were the Apostles, when they existed in their previous state, chosen to be blessed "with all spiritual blessings in heavenly places in Christ?" All these passages seem to convey an idea, that there were callings, choosings, ordinances, promises, predestinations, elections, and appointments, made before the world began. The same idea is also conveyed in the quotation which we have already made from the Book of Abraham. "Now the Lord has shewn unto me, Abraham, the intelligences that were organized before the world was; and among all these there were many of the noble and great ones; and God saw these souls that were good, and He stood in the midst of them, and He said, these I will make My rulers; for He stood among those that were spirits, and He saw that

they were good; and He said unto me, Abraham, thou art one
of them, thou wast chosen before thou wast born." Now is there
not reason to believe, that the nobility or greatness which many
of these spirits possessed, was obtained by faithfulness to the
cause of God? Was it not because of their righteousness that
they were appointed to be the Lord's rulers? How did Abraham
become one of the noble and great spirits? How came the Lord
to choose Abraham before he was born; If we had an answer
to these questions we should very probably find that Abraham
stood up valiantly for the Son of God at the time the rebellion
broke out; and that because of his integrity and righteousness,
the Lord chose him before he was born to hold authority and
power in his second estate, to become the father of the faithful,
and to be a blessing to all nations.

All the spirits when they come here are innocent, that is, if
they have ever committed sins, they have repented and obtained
forgiveness through faith in the future sacrifice of the Lamb. So
far as innocency is concerned, they enter this world alike; but
so far as circumstances are concerned, they are not alike. One
class of spirits are permitted to come into the world in an age
when the Priesthood and Kingdom of God are on the earth, and
they hear and receive the Gospel; others enter the world in an
age of darkness, and are educated in foolish and erroneous doctrines. Some are born among the people of God and are brought
up in the right way; others are born among the heathen, and
taught to worship idols. Some spirits take bodies in the lineage
of the chosen seed, through whom the Priesthood is transferred,
others receive bodies among the African negroes, or in the lineage
of Canaan, whose descendants were cursed, pertaining to the
Priesthood. Now if all the spirits were equally faithful in their
first estate in keeping the laws thereof, why are they placed in
such dissimilar circumstances in their second estate? Why are
some placed in circumstances where they are taught of God, become rulers, kings, and priests, and finally are exalted to all the
fulness of Celestial glory; while others are taught in all kinds of
wickedness, and never hear the Gospel, till they hear it in prison
after death, and in the resurrection receive not a Celestial glory,
but a Terrestrial? If rewards and punishments are the results
of good and evil actions, then it would seem that the good and
evil circumstances under which the spirits enter this world, must
depend upon the good and evil actions which they had done

in the previous world. Our condition when we enter the next world will depend upon our conduct here. By analogy, then, does not our condition when we enter this world depend upon our conduct before we were born? Does not the question which the Apostles put to the Savior, respecting the man who was born blind, show that they considered it possible for a man to sin before he was born? They considered it reasonable that a person should be born blind as a penalty for the sins which he had committed before he was born. Though the spirits are all innocent when they come here, may it not be possible that they are forgiven and made innocent on condition that they shall enter this world under circumstances either favorable or unfavorable, according to the nature of their sins? Do not the inhabitants of our world, who are raised from the dead, differ in glory as one star differs from another? Is it not necessary that they should be forgiven of all their sins and made innocent, before they can receive the Holy Ghost or any degree of glory? And do not the differences of their condition in the resurrection depend upon the nature of their actions in this life? If then they must be forgiven, and become innocent, before they can even enter a kingdom of glory; and if, when they do enter there, it is under a great variety of circumstances depending on their actions here, then we may, from analogy, reason that the spirits must be forgiven and become innocent before they can even come here, and that when they do come, it will be under a great variety of conditions depending on their actions in a previous state.

Orson Pratt, The Seer, pp. 55-57.

Comforted While in Confinement in a
Missouri Dungeon

By Parley P. Pratt

To be tried without friends or witnesses, or even with them, by a set of "Gadianton robbers" and murderers, who could drive out and murder women and children, was but to be condemned and executed; to tarry there and drag out a miserable life, while our wives and children wandered abroad in a land of strangers, without the protection of husbands and fathers, was worse than to die ten thousand deaths.

Under these circumstances, and half way between hope and despair, I spent several days in fasting and prayer, during which one deep and all absorbing inquiry, one only thought, seemed to hold possession of my mind. It seemed to me that if there was a God in Heaven who ever spake to man on earth I would know from Him the truth of this one question. It was not how long shall I suffer; it was not when or by what means I should be delivered; but it was simply this: Shall I ever at any time, however distant it may be, or whatever I may suffer first; shall I ever be free again in this life, and enjoy the society of my dear wife and children, and walk abroad at liberty, dwell in society and preach the gospel, as I have in bygone years?

Let me be sure of this and I care not what I suffer. To circumnavigate the globe, to traverse the deserts of Arabia, to wander amid the wild scenes of the Rocky Mountains to accomplish so desirable an object, would seem like a mere trifle if I could only be sure at last. After some days of prayer and fasting, and seeking the Lord on the subject, I retired to my bed in my lonely chamber at an early hour, and while the other prisoners and the guard were chatting and beguiling the lonesome hours in the upper apartment of the prison, I lay in silence, seeking and expecting an answer to my prayer, when suddenly I seemed carried away in the spirit, and no longer sensible to outward objects with which I was surrounded. A heaven of peace and calmness pervaded my bosom; a personage from the world of spirits stood before me with a smile of compassion in every look, and pity mingled with the tenderest love and sympathy in every expression of the countenance. A soft hand seemed placed within my own, and a glowing cheek was laid in tenderness and warmth upon mine. A well known voice saluted me, which I readily recognized as that of the wife of my youth, who had for near two years been sweetly sleeping where the wicked cease from troubling and the weary are at rest. I was made to realize that she was sent to commune with me, and answer my question.

Knowing this, I said to her in a most earnest and inquiring tone: Shall I ever be at liberty again in this life and enjoy the society of my family and the Saints, and preach the gospel as I have done? She answered definitely and unhesitatingly: "Yes!" I then recollected that I had agreed to be satisfied with the knowledge of that one fact, but now I wanted more.

Said I: Can you tell me how, or by what means, or when I shall escape? She replied: "That thing is not made known to me yet." I instantly felt that I had gone beyond my agreement and my faith in asking this last question, and that I must be contented at present with the answer to the first.

Her gentle spirit then saluted me and withdrew. I came to myself. The doleful noise of the guards, and the wrangling and angry words of the old apostate again grated on my ears, but Heaven and hope were in my soul.

Autobiography of Parley P. Pratt, 1874 Ed., pp. 206-7.

The Increased Powers and Faculties of Mind in a Future State

By Orson Pratt

(Excerpts of Discourse Delivered in the Tabernacle, Salt Lake City, Oct. 15, 1854.)

We are told in the Book of Mormon that the spirits of all men, as soon as they leave this mortal body, and return home to that God who gave them life, whether they be wicked or whether they be righteous, go back to where they once were; they return to their former state, to their former location and residence; they appear in the presence of the Being that gave them life.

What further are we told on the subject? That after we get back into the presence of God, and return home again, then it shall come to pass that the spirits of the righteous, those who have done good, those who have wrought the works of righteousness here upon the earth, shall be received into a state of rest, a state of happiness, of peace, a state of joy, where they will remain until the time of the resurrection. We are also told that another portion of spirits, another class of them that return home to God, after leaving this mortal tabernacle, are cast out, are sent off again, and are not permitted to stay at home, but are cast out into outer darkness where there is weeping and wailing and gnashing of teeth. Now there must be some intense suffering, some intense misery in connection with the wicked class of spirits in order to cause them to weep and wail.

We might now inquire, what is the cause of this intense suffering and misery? Is it the action of the elements upon the spirit? Is it the materials of nature, operating from without upon it, that causes this distress, this weeping, wailing, mourning and lamentation? It may be in some measure; it may help to produce the misery and the wretchedness; but there is something connected with the spirit itself that no doubt produces this weeping, wailing, and mourning. What is this something? It is memory, and remorse of conscience; a memory of what they have once done, a memory of their disobedience. Do you not suppose the spirits can have power to remember in that world as well as in this? Yes, they certainly can. Have you never read in the Book of Mormon, where it informs us, that every act of our lives will be fresh upon the memory, and we shall have a clear consciousness of all our doings in this life? Yes; we have read in the Book of Mormon—"a clear consciousness."

We read or learn a thing by observation yesterday and today or tomorrow it is gone, unless it be something that impresses us distinctly, that makes a vivid impression upon the mind, that we can remember it perhaps for days, months, and years; but common information and knowledge are constantly coming into our minds, and as constantly being forgotten. And some of the knowledge we receive here at one time becomes so completely obliterated, through the weakness of the animal system, that we cannot call it to mind, no association of ideas will again suggest it to our minds; it is gone, erased, eradicated from the tablet of our memories. This is not owing to the want of capacity in the spirit; no, but the spirit has a full capacity to remember; for do you suppose that God in begetting spirits in the eternal world would beget an imperfect thing, that he had no capacities? No. The Being, who is full of intelligence, knowledge, and wisdom, and acting upon the great principles that are ordained for the generation of living beings, spiritual beings, brings them forth with capacities capable of being enlarged or extended wider and wider; consequently it is not the want of capacity in the spirit of man that causes him to forget the knowledge he may have learned yesterday; but it is because of the imperfection of the tabernacle in which the spirit dwells; because there is imperfection in the organization of the flesh and bones, and in things pertaining to the tabernacle; it is this that erases from our memory many things that would be useful; we cannot retain them in our minds, they are gone into oblivion. It is not so with the spirit when it is released from this tabernacle.

I might refer to the words of many of the Prophets upon this subject, but every person on reflection and observation knows that the imperfection of the tabernacle does have a bearing upon the memory, as well upon other faculties and powers of man. It has been proved that when the skull has been depressed by accident, or in the way of experiment, every particle of the knowledge that the person has possessed has been entirely suspended. Relieving the skull from the pressure, things come fresh again into the mind; this shows that the spirit has not lost its capacity for memory, but it is the organization of the tabernacle that prevents it from remembering. Wait until these mortal bodies are laid in the tomb; when we return home to God who gave us life; then is the time we shall have the most vivid knowledge of all the past acts of our lives during our probationary state; then is the time that we will find that this being we call man—this spirit that dwells within the tabernacle, is a being that has capacity sufficient to retain all its past doings, whether they be good or bad.

It is, then, this memory that will produce the suffering and the pains upon that class of spirits whose works have been wicked and abominable in the sight of God. A spirit, then, will remember, that "at such a time in yonder world, and at such a place, I disobeyed the commandments of God; I did not hearken to the counsel of those whom God had appointed to be my counsellors; I did not give heed to the man of God; no, but I rejected his sayings; good counsel was imparted to me, but I did not heed it." In this life, things that may have been erased from your memory for years will be presented before you with all the vividness as if they had just taken place. This will be like a worm upon the conscience; it will prey upon the spirit and produce unhappiness, wretchedness and misery. This will cause you to lament, and mourn, and weep after you are cast out from the presence of God—from the home to which you have returned.

I am speaking now of the wicked. What is it that produces the opposite principle. There is an opposition in all things! it is the reflection of the memory that produces joy; that is one of the elements by which joy and happiness are produced upon the spirit of man in the future state; we remember the acts of our past lives that they have been good; we perceive by our memories that we have been obedient to counsel; we perceive that when we have erred through our weakness we have repented of that error; when we have been told of a fault we have forsaken it. When we look back upon acquaintances and neighbors we perceive that we have observed the golden rule to do unto others as we would that others should do unto us. We look back upon our past lives, and we perceive we have never spoken evil against a brother or sister, that we have never striven to stir up family broils, and that we have never desired to injure any of the children of men, male or female. What do these reflections produce? They produce joy, satisfaction, peace, consolation, and this joy is a hundred fold more intense than what the spirit is capable of perceiving or enjoying in this life. Why? Because just in proportion to the vividness of the conscience, or the memory, so will be the joy. This you may have knowledge of by every-day experience; just in proportion to the vividness of your ideas, and of the truth set before your minds, and of the good things that are imparted to you, the more intense is your happiness here; how much more intense would it be hereafter, when this mortal clog with all its imperfections has been laid down in the grave! The fact is, our spirits then will be happy, far more happy than what we are capable even of conceiving, or having the least idea of in this world.

Our happiness here is regulated in a great measure by external objects, by the organization of the mortal tabernacle; they are not permitted to rise very high, or to become very great; on the other hand it seems to be a kind of limit to our joys and pleasures, sufferings, and pains, and this is because of the imperfection of the tabernacle in which we dwell; and of those things with which we are surrounded; but in that life everything will appear in its true colors; in my estimation not a single thought of the heart, that has ever passed through the mind, not a single act of an individual, from the earliest period of its memory till the time it comes into the presence of God, will escape the notice of the memory when it appears there, unclogged from this tabernacle.

Are there any other circumstances that will produce pain or joy, besides that which is connected with the spirit—besides its own conscience or memory. Yes, a great deal will depend upon the place of the residence of these spirits. Suppose you were a righteous spirit, and you were cast out to dwell a certain time, not cast out, but sent out, on a mission to the abodes of darkness, or to those who are not righteous as yourselves; though you might have peace of conscience and happiness dwelling within your own bosoms in reflecting upon your past conduct, yet the society with which you are compelled to mingle for a short period, in order to import knowledge and wisdom and such information as is calculated to benefit them, is, in a measure, disagreeable; you are compelled, for a season, to mingle with those who are inferior to yourself in their capacities. When you go and associate with them there is something disagreeable in the nature of this association; you feel to pity them in their ignorance, in their condition and circumstances; their conversation is not agreeable to you as that of your own associates in the presence of God. There is something that is calculated to render their society disagreeable to themselves, which increases as the degradation of the society is increased. Then a wicked man entering into the company of such beings has not only a hell within himself—a conscience gnawing like a worm, but he sees misery and wretchedness; and they cleave one to another in their wickedness, and in their conversation, and acts, and doings, and intercourse with each other; all these things are calculated in their nature to produce misery and wretchedness, as well as their own consciences. It should then be our constant study to escape this order of things. We are free and independent; it is all in our hands whether to escape this order of wretchedness and misery, and the abodes of the wicked in the spiritual world; we can dwell in the society of the righteous, or in the society of the wicked, just as we choose. As the revelation states, all intelligence and all truth is independent in that sphere in which God has placed it to act for itself, consequently, you and I are the ones to make ourselves happy by taking the course pointed out by our superiors, by those who have a right to teach, control, and direct us. It is for us to create a heaven within our own minds. It is for us to choose the place of our abode, either among the spirits of the just or the spirits of the damned.

We have spoken of the memory of spirits in the future state; the same principle will apply to many other faculties of the mind of man, as well as memory; knowledge for instance. How limited, how very limited, in its nature is the knowledge of man in this life. Why is it that our knowledge is so limited? I say limited compared with that which is to be known, and which will be known. The reason is, God has seen proper in His infinite wisdom to place us in circumstances where we can learn the very first elements of knowledge, and act upon them in the first place. Instead of having the whole of the rich treasures of knowledge and wisdom unfolded to us at once, He begins to feed us little by little, the same as you would feed a weakly, sickly infant with food prepared and adapted to its taste, and to the weakness of its system. The Lord brings us in this state under similar circumstances, endowed with certain senses by which we can gain, by little and little, knowledge and information but it takes a long time to get a little into our minds. It seems that our spirits, that once stood in the presence of God, clothed with power, capacities, wisdom, and knowledge, forget what they once knew—forget that which was once fresh in their minds.

But, inquires one, "Do you have an idea we had once much information and knowledge in the spirit world?" Yes, we had a great deal of knowledge and information, but to what extent I know not; suffice to say we had much knowledge, we were capable, when the morning stars sang together for joy, when the foundations of this earth were laid, of lifting up our voices and shouting aloud for joy. What produced this joy? The contemplation of a world on which we were to receive our probation, and have tabernacles of flesh and bones, and obtain our redemption. All these things were known to us in our anterior state, but we have forgotten them all. We knew then about the Redeemer—about Christ, but we forgot it in our infantile moments.

As soon as our spirits were enclosed in this tabernacle all our former knowledge vanished away—the knowledge of our former acts was lost, what we did then we know not; we had laws to govern us; how obedient to them we were we know not; how faithful we were we know not; we had a contest with the one third part of the hosts of heaven, and we overcame them; and then the Lord made an earth where we might have a second probation, and forget all we once knew concerning the battles we had fought, before we came here, against Lucifer the son of the morning. We forget about the laws that were given to govern us in that spiritual state. Why all this? If we came here with all the knowledge we formerly possessed, could we be again tried as those who possess only the first principles of knowledge? We must begin at the alphabet of knowledge; and when once we begin to gain knowledge and information the Lord tries us to see if we will comply with that, and if we do, He gives us more, in this probationary state; but after we have gained all we can here, it is nothing compared with that immense fullness, which it is the privilege of the children of men to obtain in the future state of existence.

Our knowledge here is, comparatively speaking, nothing; it can hardly be reckoned the elements of knowledge. What few glimmering ideas, the wisest of us get, we obtain by experience, through the medium of our senses, and the reflecting powers of the mind.

Some people suppose that we do not acquire scarcely any knowledge, only what we get by seeing, hearing, tasting, smelling, and feeling; we may not, in one sense of the word, but in another sense, there is a vast amount of knowledge which we gain by reflection; the solving of mathematical problems from beginning to end is not brought about by seeing, hearing, tasting, smelling, or feeling, unless the mind can feel them; we reason from one step to another until we solve the proposition. There is a vast field of knowledge, pertaining to this state, that mankind can gain through the medium of their reflecting or reasoning powers; and then there is another vast field that they can explore through the medium of their senses. I am now speaking of temporal knowledge.

We became acquainted with light and color through the organization of our bodies. In other words, the Lord has constructed the mortal eye and framed it in such a manner that it is capable of being acted upon by one of the elements of nature, called light; and that gives us a great variety of knowledge. A blind man knows nothing about light, as we were told here the other day by our President, the blind man knows nothing about light if he were born blind. You cannot, by talking with him for a thousand years, instill into his mind an idea what red, yellow, white, black, green, blue are like; they are ideas that have never entered his mind. Why? Because the little inlet to this kind of knowledge is closed up, and there is no other part of the spirit exposed to the light. It is only a small place by which the spirit can converse with light and its colors. Just so in regard to many other ideas.

Take a man who is perfectly deaf, who was born deaf, so that no sound has ever entered his ears; what does he know about music? About the various sounds that are so beautiful to the mind of man? He knows nothing at all about it, neither can it be described to him.

A man that has always been deprived of the organ of smell, has no other inlet of knowledge by which he can know and understand the nature of smell; he cannot see a smell, or hear a smell; it can only be perceived by this little organ called the nose; that is the only way these ideas can get to the spirit. If he ever knew them before he came here, he has forgotten them, which is the same as if he had never known them; and if he wishes to gain an idea of the sensations produced by the elements of nature, he must learn them anew by these media. If a man be devoid of taste what can he know about sweet and sour? You might as well talk to him about the bounds of time and space, and get him to comprehend a heaven located beyond their limits, as to comprehend what sweet and bitter are, or tell the difference between a piece of sugar and vinegar, so far as its taste is concerned.

So with regard to touch. There are many things we cannot feel, yet we have knowledge of them; we cannot feel the sun, moon, stars, and comets, and many other things; and if it were not for some senses that give a knowledge of them we should be wrapped in total ignorance concerning them. How do we know, when this spirit is freed from this mortal tabernacle, but that all these senses will be greatly enlarged? If we, by looking through these little eyes of ours, can see objects some thousands of millions of miles distant; if we can see objects that are existing at that immense distance through the medium of these little inlets; suppose that the whole spirit were uncovered and exposed to all the rays of light, can it be supposed that light would not affect the spirit if it were thus unshielded, uncovered and un-clothed? Do you suppose that it would not be susceptible of any impressions made by the elements of light? The spirit is inherently capable of experiencing the sensations of light; if it were not so, we could not see. You might form as fine an eye as ever was made but if the spirit, in and of itself, were not capable of being acted upon by the rays of light, an eye could be of no benefit. Then unclothe the spirit, and instead of exposing a small portion of it about the size of a pea to the action of the rays of light, the whole of it would be exposed. I think we could then see in different directions at once, instead of looking in one particular direction. We could then look all around us in the same instant. We can see this verified, in some small degree, by bringing to our aid artificial means. Look at the telescopes in-vented, of what advantage are they? Why they bring a greater number of rays of light together, and concentrate them upon the retina of the eye. The glasses within the telescope are so con-structed as to bring the rays of light to a focus; and when they are placed properly in that instrument it brings a larger number of rays upon the eye, so that it brings objects we cannot see with the natural eye within the power of our vision, thus we are enabled to see how many glorious objects in the heavens, that the natural eye could never have gazed upon.

Let the spirit itself be a telescope; or in other words, let there be a million of times more of the surface of the spirit exposed to the rays of light, than is now exposed through the medium of the eyes, or were this body of flesh and bones taken off, and the whole spirit exposed to the rays of light; would not these rays produce an effect upon the spirit? Yes; inasmuch as it is inherently capable of such effects, independent of flesh and bones. Then there would be a vast field opened to the view of the spirit, and this would be opened not in one direction only, but in all directions; we should then have the advantage of the telescope, though it were as large as Lord Ross's, whose object glass is six feet in diameter. What great improvement it would be if a telescope could be invented to bring the rays of light on other parts of the spirit, besides the eye. Such will be the case when this tabernacle is taken off; we shall look, not in one direction only, but in every direction. This will be calculated to give us new ideas, concerning the immensity of the creations of God, concerning worlds that may be far beyond the reach of the most powerful instruments that have been called to the aid of man. This will give us information and knowledge we never can know as long as we dwell in this mortal tabernacle. This tabernacle, although it is good in its place, is something like the scaffolding you see round about a new building that is going up; it is only a help, and aid in this imperfect situation; but when we get into another condition, we shall find that these imperfect aids will not be particularly wanted; we shall have other sources of gaining knowledge, besides these inlets, called senses.

In relation to this matter, touching the extension of our knowledge year after year, some people have thought that we should have to learn everything by study. I do not believe it; there are a great many ways of learning things without reasoning or studying them out; without obtaining them through the medium of the five senses. Man will be endowed, after he leaves this tabernacle, with powers and faculties which he, now, has no knowledge of, by which he may learn what is round about him. In order to prove this, let me refer you to some things in some of the revelations which God has given. What is said about the brother of Jared? It is said that the Lord showed him all the children of men previous to his day and all that were on earth at the time he lived, and all that would be to the end of time. How do you suppose he beheld them? Did he look at them with his natural eyes? How long do you suppose it would take a man to see all that are now living, if he only employed one second to look at each individual? It would take him a long time; it would take him over thirty years. In order to see them all he must place his eye upon them all. If a man look at one individual in this assembly, though he may indistinctly perceive, on each side of that individual, a vast variety of faces, yet there is only one person that he sees distinctly; the rest only produce very indistinct images upon his vision. So with the brother of Jared: if he had looked at each individual of all the generations for one second successively, it would have taken him over three thousand years to have beheld them all.

There must be some faculty or power natural to God and to superior beings, that man, in this life, is not in possession of in any great degree, by which they can look at a great variety of objects at once. The brother of Jared could look upon past, present, and future generations; they all came before him, and he gazed upon them all; there was not a soul that he did not behold.

Moses also had a similar view; he, at a certain time, was clothed upon with the glory of God; and while he was thus clothed upon, he was enabled to behold many things; and seeing some things that looked very glorious he wanted to see more; but the Lord said unto him: "No man can behold all My works, except he behold all My glory; and no man can behold all My glory and afterwards remain in the flesh;" that is, it would consume him; the sight would be so overwhelming that the mortal tabernacle would melt away. Should a mortal man be permitted to gaze upon all the works of God, which include all His glory, mortality could not endure it. But the Lord did condescend to give him, in measure, the same principle that He Himself is in possession of; for the Lord beholds all His works. He says, "Mine eye can pierce them all," after telling us that the number of worlds were greater than the number of particles in millions of earths like this. Jesus says that he "looked forth upon the wide expanse of eternity," and that "all things are present before mine eyes."

Now, the Lord imparted a portion of this principle to Moses. Let us see how it operated on his vision. As soon as Moses got this new principle, not natural to man, what did he behold? He looked upon that which mankind never can look upon in this natural state without the aid of the same principle; he beheld every particle of the earth, or, as the new revelation says, and there was not a particle of it that he did not behold, discerning it by the Spirit of God. What an excellent telescope! Did the Spirit of God impress it by the rays of light upon the retina of the eye only? No. The vision was exhibited to the mind, independent of the natural eye. Instead of acting upon the mere eye, every part of the human spirit could behold and discern, through the medium of that all-powerful substance, the Spirit of God, every particle of this earth. How long would it have taken Moses to have gazed at each particle separately, with the natural eye? While he was gazing with the eye at one, he could not be looking directly at another. It would have taken him a great many millions of years to have gazed directly and distinctly upon every particle of the earth, as we naturally see things in succession. But, instead of this, we find him, in a short space of time, perhaps the interval was only a few minutes or hours, gazing upon every particle of it. Here was something new, and independent of the natural vision, showing him things beneath the surface of the earth. Men look at things above the surface by the natural eye; but here is a man who, by the power of heaven, is enabled to penetrate that which the natural eye could never behold. Suppose that the spirit of man were unclogged from this mortal tabernacle, the Lord could show him the particles of millions on millions of worlds, in the same way, and with the same ease that he showed Moses the particles of one.

By the same power and principle that Moses beheld every particle of this earth, he could have looked at the moon, and beheld every particle of it; and the same power could have shown him every particle of the sun, planets, comets, and fixed stars.

Here, then, is a new faculty of knowledge, very extended in its nature, that is calculated to throw a vast amount of information upon the mind of man, almost in the twinkling of an eye. How long a time would it take a man in the next world, if he had to gain knowledge as we do here, to find out the simplest things in nature? He might reason, and reason for thousands of years, and then hardly have got started. But when this Spirit of God, this great telescope that is used in the celestial heaven, is given to man, and he, through the aid of it, gazes upon eternal things, what does he behold? Not one object at a time, but a vast multitude of objects rush before his vision, and are present before his mind, filling him in a moment with the knowledge of worlds more numerous than the sands of the sea shore. Will he be able to bear it? Yes, his mind is strengthened in proportion to the amount of information imparted. It is this tabernacle, in its present condition, that prevents us from a more enlarged understanding. Moses understood all he saw, so far as the Lord pleased to show him; and if the Lord showed him all the properties, qualities and connections of those particles, he would have understood it.

There is faculty mentioned in the word of God, which we are not in possession of here, but we shall possess it hereafter;

that is not only to see a vast number of things in the same moment, looking in all directions by the aid of the Spirit, but also to obtain a vast number of ideas at the same instant. Here, we have to confine ourselves in a little, narrow, contracted space, and we can hardly think of two things at a time; if we do, our minds are distracted, and we cannot think distinctly. Some, by habit, it is true, are able to think of two or three little things at once, or at least the interval between the successive thoughts is so small as to be inappreciable. Some people play on an instrument of music, and may go through a very difficult performance, while their minds are thinking of something else; and by habit, they hardly perceive the working of the musical instrument.

I believe we shall be freed, in the next world, in a great measure, from these narrow, contracted methods of thinking. Instead of thinking in one channel, and following up one certain course of reasoning to find a certain truth, knowledge will rush in from all quarters; it will come in like the light which flows from the sun, penetrating every part, informing the spirit, and giving understanding concerning ten thousand things at the same time; and the mind will be capable of receiving and retaining all. * * *

When I speak of the future state of man, and the situation of our spirits between death and the resurrection, I long for the experience and knowledge to be gained in that state, as well as this. We shall learn many more things there; we need not suppose our five senses connect us with all the things of heaven, and earth, and eternity, and space; we need not think that we are conversant with all the elements of nature, through the medium of the senses God has given us here. Suppose He should give us a sixth sense, a seventh, an eighth, a ninth sense, or a fiftieth? All these different senses would convey to us new ideas, as much so as the senses of tasting, smelling, or seeing communicate different ideas from that of hearing.

Do we suppose the five senses of man converse with all the elements of nature? No. There is a principle called magnetism; we see its effects, but the name of the thing does not give us a knowledge of its nature, or of the manner in which the effects are produced. We know not why a piece of iron will turn towards a magnet this way or that. Now, suppose we had a sixth sense that was so adapted as to perceive this very thing, we should learn some new ideas, connected with the elements of nature, besides those we have learned by the five senses we already possess. I believe there are ten thousand things with which we are surrounded, that we know nothing about by our present natural senses. When the Lord imparts to us a principle by which we can look upon the past and future, as well as the present, by which we can look upon many intricate objects of nature which are now hidden from our view, we shall find our capacity for obtaining and retaining knowledge to be greatly enlarged.

We already have the capacity, and all it wants is to bring things into a situation to act upon it. The capacity is here; and when the Lord sees fit, it will be instructed and taught, and things will be revealed, even the things of God, and the laws that have been hidden concerning the celestial, terrestrial, and telestial worlds, and concerning all the variety of things that are organized in the immensity of space, so far as the Lord sees proper to unfold them; and we shall learn more and more of them until the perfect day, as the Lord places us in circumstances to become acquainted with them.

I have dwelt upon this subject in order that we may be looking forward with joyful anticipations to the future. I am constantly looking to the future, as well as to the present, and trying to frame my present course of conduct in such a way as shall enable me to attain to that which is in the future for the faithful. If I had no knowledge or understanding of the future, it would be like a person pursuing a phantom that he did not know was of any worth; but the more knowledge we get of the future, the more we impress it upon our minds and in our thoughts, the more we will be stirred up in our exertions to do that which concerns us at the present moment, knowing that it has an all-important bearing upon the future.

J. D., Vol. 2:238-248.

Council Meetings Held Behind the Vail

By Wilford Woodruff

(Excerpts of Discourse delivered in Salt Lake City, Oct. 8, 1881.)

The same Priesthood exists on the other side of the vail. Every man who is faithful in his quorum here will join his quorum there. When a man dies and his body is laid in the tomb, he does not lose his position. The Prophet Joseph Smith held the keys of this dispensation on this side of the vail, and he will hold them throughout the countless ages of eternity. He went into the spirit world to unlock the prison doors and to preach the Gospel to the millions of spirits who are in darkness, and every Apostle, every Seventy, every Elder, etc., who has died in the faith, as soon as he passes to the other side of the vail, enters into the work of the ministry, and there are a thousand times more to preach to there than there are here. I have felt of late as if our brethren on the other side of the vail had held a council and that they had said to this one, and that one, "Cease thy work on earth, come hence, we need help," and they have called this man and that man. It has appeared so to me in seeing the many men who have been called from our midst lately. Perhaps I may be permitted to relate a circumstance with which I am acquainted in relation to Bishop Roskelley, of Smithfield, Cache County. On one occasion he was suddenly taken very sick, near to death's door. While he lay in this condition, President Peter Maughan, who was dead, came to him and said: "Brother Roskelley, we held a council on the other side of the vail. I have had a great deal to do, and I have the privilege of coming here to appoint one man to come and help. I have had three names given to me in council, and you are one of them. I want to inquire into your circumstances." The Bishop told him what he had to do, and they conversed together as one man would converse with another. President Maughan then said to him: "I think I will not call you. I think you are wanted here more than perhaps one of the others." Bishop Roskelley got well from that hour. Very soon after, the second man was taken sick, but not being able to exercise sufficient faith, Brother Roskelley did not go to him. By and by this man recovered, and on meeting Brother Roskelley he said: "Brother Maughan came to me the other night and told me he was sent to call one man from the ward," and he named two men as had been done to Brother Roskelley. A few days afterwards the third man was taken sick and died. Now, I name this to show a principle. They have work on the other side of the vail; and they want men, and they call them. And that was my view in regard to Brother George A. Smith. When he was almost at death's door, Brother Cannon administered to him, and in thirty minutes he was up and ate breakfast with his family. We labored with him in this way, but ultimately, as you know, he died. But it taught me a lesson. I felt that man was wanted behind the vail. We labored also with Brother Pratt; he, too, was wanted behind the vail.

Now, my brethren and sisters, those of us who are left here, have a great work to do. We have been raised up of the Lord to take this kingdom and bear it off. This is our duty; but if we neglect our duty and set our hearts upon the things of this world, we will be sorry for it. We ought to understand the responsibility that rests upon us. We should gird up our loins and put on the whole armor of God. We should rear temples to the name of the Most High God, that we may redeem the dead.

I feel to bear my testimony to this work. It is the work of God. Joseph Smith was appointed by the Lord before he was born as much as Jeremiah was. The Lord told Jeremiah: "Before I formed thee in the belly I knew thee; and before thou camest forth out of the womb I sanctified thee, and I ordained thee a Prophet unto the nations." He was commanded to warn the inhabitants of Jerusalem of their wickedness. He felt it a hard task, but ultimately he did as he was commanded. So I say with regard to Joseph Smith: He received his appointment from before the foundation of the world, and he came forth in the due time of the Lord to establish this work on the earth. And so it is the case with tens of thousands of the Elders of Israel. The Lord Almighty has conferred upon you the Holy Priesthood and made you the instrument in His hands to build up this kingdom. Do we contemplate these things as fully as we ought? Do we realize that the eyes of all the heavenly hosts are over us? Then let us do our duty. Let us keep the commandments of God, let us be faithful to the end, so that when we go into the spirit world, and look back upon our history, we may be satisfied. The Lord Almighty has set His hand to establish His kingdom never more to be thrown down or given to another people, and, therefore, all the powers of earth and hell combined will never be able to stay the progress of this work. The Lord has said He will break in pieces every weapon that is raised against Zion, and the nations of the earth, the Kings and Emperors, Presidents and Governors have got to learn this fact. It is a fearful thing to fall into the hands of the Lord. It is a fearful thing to shed the blood of the Lord's anointed. It has cost the Jews 1800 years of persecution, and this generation have also a bill to pay in this respect.

I bear testimony to these things. The Bible, the Book of Mormon, the Book of Doctrine and Covenants, contain the words of eternal life unto this generation, and they will rise in judgment against those who reject them. May God bless this people and help us to magnify our calling, for Jesus' sake. Amen.

J. D., Vol. 22:333-5.

My Father Rewards Me

By Solomon F. Kimball

After the Saints had driven West, and had established themselves in these valleys, among the first things that the leaders of the Church did was to get their historical records together. They realized that Church history would be dependent upon these records to a great extent. The Lord through the Prophet Joseph had instructed them to keep a record of all principal events of their lives, which made it doubly important. I well remember the interest manifest by my father in relation to such matters. He had been an apostle for twelve years, and one of the First Presidency for twenty. During the drivings and mobbings of the Saints, he had lost the part of his journal that contained an account of his second mission to England. This he felt keenly, as it made a break into one of the most important periods of his life. When time permitted, he would have Brother Bullock come to his house, and they sometimes spent a week or two straightening out these records and compiling his history. In order to do this they had to wade through hundreds of pages of blurred and dingy journals, and package after package of old, musty letters. Father would then let this work rest a year or two, or until the spirit came upon him again. He would then get Brother Robert Campbell, or some other competent man, to assist him. He continued in this way as long as he lived. After his death, there was nothing more done with his history until the fall of 1876. I was living with my sister Helen at the time. We were in possession of all of father's letters, journals and manuscripts. We knew that he had prophesied that Edward W. Tullidge would write his history, so I visited Mr. Tullidge several times in relation to this matter. He finally agreed to write the history and publish three thousand volumes of it for three thousand dollars. He was present when father made the prediction concerning him, and knew about the lost records.

With this fact in view, and while writing the history of the Prophet Joseph and President Young, he made a note of any historical facts bearing upon this part of father's life. This advantage enabled him to write the history in about six months. In the meantime, I had taken up a labor with my father's family, and found the majority of them not in sympathy with this movement. However, I managed to collect thirteen hundred dollars in cash, and five hundred dollars in real estate. This I turned over to Mr. Tullidge, and from then on it seemed like fate was against us and we were forced to let this work rest here. That summer I went to Arizona, where I remained nine years. After I returned, I spent several weeks visiting the family. The history spirit came upon me again stronger than ever. I was quite successful in uniting the family upon this subject. I was out of means, and went to Mayor Armstrong to see if I could get employment. He told me that the jailor had just broken his arm, and that I could come to work the next morning. Soon after I had commenced work, it seemed to me at times as though I was in the very presence of my father. I could plainly feel his spirit working with me. It became so strong that I could not rest until we had called the representative members of the family together and laid this subject before them. At that meeting a committee of five was chosen, and we decided to employ Bishop Orson F. Whitney to write the history over again. He was our father's grandson; while, on the other hand, Mr. Tullidge had publicly declared himself to be an apostate. We had a settlement with him, and he was allowed thirteen hundred dollars for his work. He deeded the real estate back to us and let Bishop Whitney have his manuscript of the history. The "boom" came soon after, and we sold a lot for just eighteen hundred dollars clear of expenses. Those of us who had contributed the eighteen hundred nine years before received back the exact sum that we gave, and this put the family on an equal footing. Before I went to Arizona the Kimball estate had been divided, and the administrators discharged. When I returned, we found four lots on the hill that had been overlooked, and which were almost worthless when I went away, but now had become valuable. We sold them for four thousand five hundred dollars, which was just enough to carry this enterprise through. This belonged to all of us, and we now were all in sympathy with the movement.

The day that the history was to be bound and placed upon the market, one of the most wonderful events of my life took place. As I was giving the prisoners their breakfast, imagine my joy and satisfaction when I heard the voice of my father's spirit saying to me that he had something more to go into the history, and would give it to me as a reward for my faithfulness in helping to bring that work forth. As soon as I could get the prisoners to work, I took a pencil and tab, and father's spirit told me what to write. Under his dictation, I wrote for about twenty minutes. I scribbled as fast as I could, and a minute or two before I had finished, several prisoners who were doing janitor work came into the room, and father's spirit left, I undertook to complete the unfinished part but was unable to do so. Then I began to feel uneasy, fearing that Bishop Whitney would reject the communication. I went into the old Council Chamber and prayed to the Lord to prepare his mind to receive it. When he came to work that morning, I told him that I had just received a visit from my father, and he had given me something more to go into the history. I handed him the communication. He read it over carefully and said "that is splendid." He completed the unfinished part, and corrected my mistakes. We decided to say nothing about it, and it went into the history in that form. This event was kept quiet until the spring of 1906, eighteen years later. At a High Priests meeting, held in the Brigham Young Memorial building at that time, I was called upon to speak. The moment I stood up it seemed to me as though my father was standing by my side. I was so filled with the Spirit of the Lord that I for the first time made this event public, Bishop Whitney being present at that time.

Improvement Era, Vol. II, p. 583.

Adminstration of Angels and Disembodied Spirits

(Excerpts from Discourse Delivered by President Wilford Woodruff, at the Weber Stake Conference, Ogden, Monday, October 19, 1896.)

After laboring in that part (Memphis, Tennessee) for a length of time, I received a letter from Joseph Smith and Oliver Cowdery, in which they requested me to stay in that country and take charge of the churches that we had built up there. The Prophet promised me many things, and said I should lose no blessings by tarrying in that country and doing as he wished me and letting the other brethren go and get their endowments. I was then at the house of Brother Abraham O. Smoot's mother. I received this about sundown. I went into a little room where there was a sofa to pray alone. I felt full of joy and rejoicing at the promises God had made to me through the Prophet. While I was upon my knees praying, my room was filled with light. I looked and a messenger stood by my side. I arose and this personage told me he had come to instruct me. He presented before me a panorama. He told me he wanted me to see with my eyes and understand with my mind what was coming to pass in the earth before the coming of the Son of Man. He commenced with what the revelations say about the sun being turned to darkness, the moon to blood, and the stars falling from heaven. Those things were all presented to me one after another, as they will be, I suppose, when they are manifest before the coming of the Son of Man. Then he showed me the resurrection of the dead— what is termed the first and second resurrections. In the first resurrection I saw no graves nor anyone raised from the grave. I saw legions of celestial beings, men and women who had received the Gospel all clothed in white robes. In the form they were presented to me, they had already been raised from the grave. After this he showed me what is termed the second resurrection. Vast fields of graves were before me, and the Spirit of God rested upon the earth like a shower of gentle rain, and when that fell upon the graves they were opened, and an immense host of human beings came forth. They were just as diversified in their dress as we are here, or as they were laid down. This personage taught me with regard to these things. Among other things he showed me, there were seven lions like burning brass placed in the heavens. I asked the messenger what they were for. He said they were representative of the different dispensations of the Gospel of Christ to men and they would all be seen in the heavens among the signs that would be shown. After this passed by me, he disappeared. Now, if I had been a painter, I could have drawn everything that I saw. It made an impression upon me that has never left me from that day to this. The next day we had a meeting in the academy. Brother Smoot and some others went with me; but I was a lost man. I hardly knew where I was, so enveloped was I in that which I had seen.

I refer to this as one of the visitations that was given me in my boyhood, so to speak, in the Gospel. I was a Priest at that time. Of course, there was a motive in this personage visiting me and teaching me these principles. He knew a great deal better than I did what lay before me in life. It was doubtless sent to me for the purpose of strengthening me and giving me encouragement in my labors.

The other instance I want to refer to is what I spoke about at the recent General Conference. I need not dwell particularly upon this now; but I had a motive in laying it before the people on that occasion. The history of Brother Kimball's operations with those evil spirits in England is before the Church. And while on this point I want to correct a mistake that I made in referring to this matter at our General Conference. I got the names of Brother Kimball and Brother Hyde confused in my mind, and made it appear that Brother Kimball rebuked those evil spirits from Brother Hyde, when in fact it was Brother Kimball who was afflicted with those spirits and Brother Hyde administered to him. As this is a matter of history I wish to state it correctly, and therefore make this explanation. When Brother Kimball, Brother George A. Smith and myself went to London, we encountered these evil spirits. They sought to destroy us. The very first house that was opened to us was filled with devils. They had gathered there for our destruction, so that we should not plant the Gospel in that great city. Brother Kimball went to Manchester on some business, and left Brother George A. Smith and myself there. One night we sat up till 11 o'clock, talking Mormonism, and then we went to bed. We had only just laid down when these spirits rested upon us, and we were in a very fair way of losing our lives. It was as if a strong man had me by the throat, trying to choke me to death. In the midst of this a spirit told me to pray. I did so, and while praying, the door opened, the room was filled with light and three messengers came in. Who they were I know not. They came and laid their hands upon us, and rebuked those powers, and thereby saved our lives. Not only so, but by the power they held they rebuked the whole army of devils that were in that great city, and bound them so they had never troubled any elder from that day to this. [1, 2, 3,]

---

[1]*Elder Heber C. Kimball's Narration of this incident:* "While thus engaged, I was struck with great force by some invisible power and fell senseless on the floor. The first thing I recollected was being supported by Elders Hyde and Richards, who were praying for me; Elder Richards having followed Russell up to my room. Elders Hyde and Richards then assisted me to get on the bed, but my agony was so great I could not endure it, and I arose, bowed my knees and prayed. I then arose and sat up on the bed, when a vision was opened to our minds, and we could distinctly see the evil spirits who foamed and gnashed their teeth at us. We gazed at them about an hour and a half (by Willard's watch). We were not looking towards the window, but towards the wall. Space appeared before us, and we saw the devils coming in legions, with their leaders, who came within a few feet of us. They came towards us like armies rushing to battle. They appeared to be men of full stature, possessing every form and feature of men in the flesh, who were angry and desperate; and I shall never forget the vindictive malignity depicted in their countenances as

they looked me in the eye; and any attempt to paint the scene which then presented itself, or portray the malice and enmity, would be vain. I perspired exceedingly, my clothes becoming as wet as if I had been taken out of the river. I felt excessive pain and was in the greatest distress for some time. I cannot even look back on the scene without feelings of horror; yet by it I learned the power of the adversary, his enmity against the servants of God, and got some understanding of the invisible world. We distinctly heard those spirits talk and express their wrath and hellish designs against us. However, the Lord delivered us from them, and blessed us exceedingly that day."

Elder Hyde's description of this event is as follows: "Every circumstance that occurred at that scene of devils is just as fresh in my recollection at this very moment as it was at the moment of its occurrence, and will ever remain so. After you were overcome by them and had fallen, their awful rush upon me with knives, threats, imprecations and hellish grins, amply convinced me that they were no friends of mine. While you were apparently senseless and lifeless on the floor and upon the bed (after we had laid you there), I stood between you and the devils and fought them and contended with them face to face, until they began to diminish in number and to retreat from the room. The last imp that left turned around to me as he was going out and said, as if to apologize, and appease my determined opposition to them, 'I never said anything against you!' I replied to him thus: 'It matters not to me whether you have or have not; you are a liar from the beginning! In the name of Jesus Christ, depart!' He immediately left, and the room was clear. That closed the scene of devils for that time."

Years later, narrating the experience of that awful morning to the Prophet Joseph, Heber asked him what it all meant, and whether there was anything wrong with him that he should have such a manifestation.

"No, Brother Heber," he replied, "at that time you were nigh unto the Lord; there was only a veil between you and Him, but you could not see Him. When I heard of it, it gave me great joy, for I then knew that the work of God had taken root in that land. It was this that caused the devil to make a struggle to kill you."

Joseph then related some of his own experiences, in many contests he had had with the evil one, and said: "The nearer a person approaches the Lord, a greater power will be manifested by the adversary to prevent the accomplishment of His purposes."

Life of Heber C. Kimball, by Orson F. Whitney, pp. 144-6.

[2]Where will those go that reject this gospel? Why, in reality they will not go anywhere. They will remain where they are, in hell, where my spirit was for a short time, when I was in England. Where was my body during that brief period? It was in Preston, on the corner of Wilford street, but my spirit could see and observe those evil spirits as plainly as it ever will after I die. Legions of disembodied evil spirits came against me, organized in companies, that they might have more power, but they had no power over me to any great extent because of the power that was in and sustaining me. I had the Priesthood and the power of it was upon me. I saw the invisible world of the condemned spirits, those who were opposed to me and to this work, and to the lifting up of the standard of Christ in that country. Did I at the same time see or have a vision of the angels of God, of His legions? No, I did not; though they were there and stood in defense of me and my brethren, and I knew it. And all this, not that there was any very great virtue in me but there was virtue in the Priesthood and Apostleship which I held, and God would and did defend; and the evil spirits were dispersed by the power of God. * * *

When I recovered I sat upon the bed, thinking and reflecting upon what had passed, and all at once my vision was opened and the walls of the building were no obstacle to my seeing and I saw nothing but the visions that presented themselves. Why did not the walls obstruct my view? Because my spirit could look through the walls of that house, and I looked with that spirit, element and power with which angels look; and as God sees all things, so were invisible things brought before me as the Lord would bring things before Joseph in the Urim and Thummim. It was upon that principle that the Lord showed things to the Prophet Joseph.

By Heber C. Kimball, J. D., 4:2.

Additional Information by Heber C. Kimball:

ᵃ "Some may think that the Almighty does not see their doings, but if He does not, the angels and ministering spirits do. They see you and your works, and I have no doubt but they occasionally communicate your conduct to the Father, or to the Son, or to Joseph, or to Peter, or to some one who holds the keys in connection with them. Perhaps there are some who do not believe in spirits, but I know that they exist and visit the earth, and I will tell you how and why I know it.

When I was in England, brother George D. Watt was the first man baptized, and his mother was baptized directly after he was. The night previous to my going forward to baptize Brother Watt and eight others, I had a vision, as old Father Baker used to say, "Of the infernal world." I saw legions of wicked spirits that night, as plain as I now see you, and they came as near to me as you now are, and company after company of them rushed towards me; and Brother Hyde and Brother Richards also saw them. It was near the break of day, and I looked upon them as I now look upon you. They came when I was laying hands upon Brother Russell. The wicked spirits got him to the door of the room. I did not see them till after that took place and soon afterwards I lay prostrate upon the floor. That was in England, pious England, in the little town of Preston, at the corner of Wilford Street, and they struggled and exerted all their power and influence. That was the first introduction of the Gospel into England, and I was shown those spirits as plainly as ever I saw anything. I was thinking of that circumstance while Brother Brigham was speaking this morning, and I was thinking that those spirits were just as much on hand to perplex this people as they were on hand there. I saw their hands, their eyes, and every feature of their faces, the hair on their heads, and their ears; in short, they had full-formed bodies.

If evil spirits could come to me, cannot ministering spirits and angels also come from God? Of course they can, and there are thousands of them, and I wish you to understand this, and that they can rush as an army going to battle, for the evil spirits came upon me and Brother Hyde in that way. There is one circumstance in the visit of those evil spirits, that I would not tell if Brother Hyde had not often told it himself: they spoke and said to Brother Hyde: "We have nothing against you." No, but I was the lad they were after. I mention this to show you that the devil is an enemy to me; he is also an enemy to Brother Brigham, to Brother Jedediah, to the Twelve, and to every righteous man. When Brother Benson goes to the old country he will find hosts of evil spirits, and he will know more about the devil than he ever did before. The spirits of the wicked, who have died thousands of years past, are at war with the Saints of God upon the earth. Do I ever pray that I may see them again? No, I do not. We had prayed all day and almost all night, that we might have power to establish the Gospel in England. Previous to this, Mr. Fielding, a clergyman, came and forbid my baptizing those persons who had come forward. Said I, "Sir, they are of age, and I shall baptize them, if they wish for it," and I baptized nine. The next morning I was so weak that I could scarcely stand, so great was the effect that those spirits had upon me. I wrote a few words to my wife about the matter and Brother Joseph called upon her for the letter and said: "It was a choice jewel, and a testimony that the Gospel was planted in a strange land."

When I returned home, I called upon Brother Joseph, and we walked down the bank of the river. He told me what contests he had had with the devil; he told me that he had contests with the devil, face to face. He also told me how he was handled, and afflicted by the devil, and said he had known circumstances where Elder Rigdon was pulled out of bed three times in one night. After all this some persons will say to me, that there are no evil spirits. I tell you they are thicker than the "Mormons" are in this country, but the Lord has said that there are more for us than there can be against us. "Who are they?" says one. Righteous men who have been upon the earth. But do you suppose that angels will pay friendly visits to those who do not live up to their privileges? Would you? No, you would not like to visit with the persons who lie, and steal your goods, and borrow and never pay. Would not you forsake such persons? No. It is written that where the Holy Ghost takes up its abode the Father and Son will come and abide. That is the God whom I serve, one who has millions of angels at His command. Do you suppose that there are any angels here today? I would not wonder if there were ten times more angels here than people. We do not see them, but they are here watching us, and are anxious for our salvation. * * *

If men and women do not qualify themselves and become sanctified and purified in this life, they will go into a world of spirits where they will have a greater contest with the devils than ever you had with them here. It will not be fifty years, perhaps, before all of us here today will leave this state of existence, and then you will prove whether Brother Brigham and the rest of the brethren have told you truth or not. You know that the world has made a great deal of fuss, and told many lies about the devil pitching onto Joseph Smith when he went to get the plates, but they will get to a place where the devils will handle them worse than they did Joseph when he got the plates; if they do not embrace the Gospel it will be so. Let us repent and forsake our sins and turn our hearts to our God, every one of us. I have said a thousand times if I was to die today, I could not do better than I have done, still I have my weaknesses.

J. D., Vol. 3:227-30.

Now those messengers were sent to us because it was necessary. We would have lost our lives if somebody had not delivered us. We needed help, and we could not get it anywhere else.

This is all I want to say with regard to the administration of angels to myself. This apostle that I refer to told me he had prayed and prayed for the administration of angels. Well, if it had been necessary to save his life, as it was in my case, he would have had the administration of angels. But he had access to the gift of the Holy Ghost, as all of us have. And that, brethren and sisters, is what I want to talk to you about.

One morning, while we were at Winter Quarters, Brother Brigham Young said to me and the brethren that he had had a visitation the night previous from Joseph Smith. I asked him what he said to him. He replied that Joseph had told him to tell the people to labor to obtain the Spirit of God; that they needed that to sustain them and to give them power to go through their work in the earth.

Now I will give you a little of my experience in this line. Joseph Smith visited me a great deal after his death, and taught me many important principles. The last time he visited me was while I was in a storm at sea. I was going on my last mission to preside in England. My companions were Brother Leonard W. Hardy, Brother Milton Holmes, Brother Dan Jones, and another brother and my wife and two other women. We had been traveling three days and nights in a heavy gale and were being driven backwards. Finally I asked my companions to come into the cabin with me, and I told them to pray that the Lord would change the wind. I had no fears of being lost; but I did not like the idea of being driven back to New York, as I wanted to go on my journey. We all offered the same prayer, both men and women; and when we got through we stepped onto the deck and in less than a minute it was as though a man had taken a sword and cut that gale through, and you might have thrown a muslin handkerchief out and it would not have moved it. The night following this, Joseph and Hyrum visited me, and the Prophet laid before me a great many things. Among other things he told me to get the Spirit of God; that all of us needed it. He also told me what the Twelve Apostles would be called to go through on the earth before the coming of the Son of Man, and what the reward of their labors would be; but all that was taken from me for some reason. Nevertheless I know it was most glorious, although much would be required at our hands.

Joseph Smith continued visiting myself and others up to a certain time and then it stopped. The last time I saw him was in heaven. In the night vision I saw him at the door of the temple in heaven. He came and spoke to me. He said he could not stop to talk with me because he was in a hurry. The next man I met was Father Smith; he could not talk with me because he was in a hurry. I met a half dozen brethren who had held high positions on earth and none of them could stop and talk with me because they were in a hurry. I was very much astonished. By and by I saw the Prophet again, and I got the privilege to ask him a question. "Now," said I, "I want to know why you are in a hurry. I have been in a hurry all through my life but I expected my hurry would be over when I got into the kingdom of heaven, if I ever did." Joseph said, "I will tell you, Brother Woodruff, every dispensation that has had the Priesthood on the earth and has gone into the celestial kingdom, has had a certain amount of work to do to prepare to go to the earth with the Savior when He goes to reign on the earth. Each dispensation has had ample time to do this work. We have not. We are the last dispensation, and so much work has to be done and we need to be in a hurry in order to accomplish it." Of course, that was satisfactory with me, but it was new doctrine to me.

Brigham Young also visited me after his death. On one accasion he and Brother Heber C. Kimball came in a splendid chariot, with fine white horses, and accompanied me to a conference that I was going to attend. When I got there I asked Brother Brigham if he would take charge of the conference. "No," said he, "I have done my work here. I have come to see what you are doing and what you are teaching the people." And he told me what Joseph Smith had taught him in Winter Quarters, to teach the people to get the Spirit of God. He said, "I want you to teach the people to get the Spirit of God. You cannot build up a Kingdom of God without that."

That is what I want to say to the brethren and sisters here today. Every man and woman in this Church should labor to get that Spirit. We are surrounded by those evil spirits that are at war against God and against everything looking to the building up of the Kingdom of God; and we need this Holy Spirit to enable us to overcome these influences. I have had the Holy Ghost in my travels. Every man has that has gone out into the vineyard and labored faithfully for the cause of God. I have referred to the administration of angels to myself. What did those angels do? One of them taught me some things relating to the signs that should precede the coming of the Son of Man. Others came and saved my life. What then? They turned and left me. But how is it with the Holy Ghost? The Holy Ghost does not leave me if I do my duty. It does not leave any man who does his duty. We have known this all the way through. Joseph Smith told Brother John Taylor on one occasion to labor to get the Spirit of God, and to follow its dictation, and it would become a great principle of revelation within him. God has blessed me with that, and everything I have done since I have been in this Church has been done upon that principle. The Spirit of God has told me what to do, and I have had to follow that.

In the time of the apostasy in Kirtland, Joseph Smith hardly knew when he met a man, unless the Spirit of God revealed it to him, whether he was friend or foe. Most of the leading men were fighting him. Right in the midst of that darkness the Spirit of God said to me, "You choose a partner and go straight to Fox Islands." Well, I knew no more what was on Fox Islands than what was on Kolob. But the Lord told me to go and I went. I chose Jonathon H. Hale, and he went with me. I crossed Lake Ontario and went into Connecticut, and he went with me. We cast out some devils there, preached the Gospel and performed some miracles. I crossed Lake Ontario and went into Connecticut, where my father lived. I had not seen one of my relatives from the time I embraced the Gospel. I preached the Gospel there, and baptized my father, my stepmother and sister, and uncles and aunts, and organized a branch there. Every member of that branch was a relative of mine, excepting one, and he was a Methodist class leader who boarded at my father's house. This was all promised to me by Old Father Smith when he blessed me. I got to Fox Islands and did a good work there. Through the blessings of God I brought nearly a hundred from there up to Zion, at the time the Saints were driven out of Missouri into Illinois.

So it has been all through my life. If I have undertaken to do anything, and the Lord has wanted me to do something else, He has had to tell me. When we were sent to England, we were sent by revelation. I went into the Staffordshire potteries with Brother Alfred Cordon. We were doing a splendid work, baptizing almost every night, and I thought it was the finest mission I ever was on. I went into the town of Hanley one night, and attended meeting in a large hall, which was filled to overflowing. The spirit of the Lord came upon me and said that that was the last meeting I should be with them. After the meeting, they asked me where I was going. I told them I did not know. In the morning I asked the Lord what He wanted of me. He merely said, "Go to the south." I got into the stage and rode eighty miles. The first man's house I stopped at was John Benbow's in Herefordshire. In half an hour after I entered the house I knew exactly why the Lord had sent me. There was a people there who had been praying for the ancient order of things. They were awaiting for the Gospel as it was taught by Christ and His apostles. The consequences were, the first thirty days after I got there I baptized six hundred of those people. In eight months' labor in that country I brought eighteen hundred into the Church. Why? Because there was a people prepared for the Gospel, and the Lord sent me there to do that work. I have always had to give God the glory for everything good that has happened to me for I have realized by what power it came.

When I got back to Winter Quarters from the pioneer journey, President Young said to me, "Brother Woodruff, I want you to take your wife and children and go to Boston, and stay there until you can gather every Saint of God in New England and Canada and send them up to Zion." I did as he told me. It took me two years to gather everybody, and I brought up the rear with a company. When I got into Pittsburgh with this company it was dusk, and I saw a steamer just preparing to go out. I walked right up to the captain and asked if he was ready to go out. He said he was. "How many passengers have you?" "Two hundred fifty." "Can you take another hundred?" "I can." "Then," said I, "I would like to go aboard with you." The words were hardly out of my mouth when the Holy Ghost said to me, "Don't you nor your company go aboard that steamer." That was enough; I had learned the voice of the Spirit. I turned and told the captain that I had made up my mind not to go at present. That steamer started out. It was a dark night, and before the steamer had gone far she took afire, and all on board were lost. We should probably have shared the same fate had it not been for that monitor within me.

I refer to these things because I want you to get the same Spirit. All the Elders of Israel, whether abroad or at home, need that Spirit. When I was on my way east at one time. I drove into a man's yard in Indiana. Brother Orson Hyde had driven in and set his wagon in the dooryard and I set mine by the side of it. I turned my mules and tied them up to an oak tree. I had my wife and two children with me in my carriage. We went to lie down, and the Holy Spirit told me to get up and move my carriage. I got right up. My wife asked me what I was going to do. I said I was going to move the carriage. She wanted to know what for. I told her I did not know. I moved the carriage about fifteen rods, looked around, and then went to bed again. The Spirit told me to get up again and move my mules. I did so. In twenty minutes there came a whirlwind that blew that oak tree down and laid it right across where my carriage had been. By listening to that Spirit our lives were saved.

Now, it was not an angel that pointed out these things to me; it was the Holy Ghost. This is the Spirit that we must have to carry out the purposes of God on earth. We need that more than any other gift. I felt impressed yesterday to teach this principle to the Latter-day Saints. We are in the midst of enemies, in the midst of darkness and temptation, and we need to be guided by the Spirit of God. We should pray to the Lord until we get the Comforter. That is what is promised to us when we are baptized. It is the spirit of light, of truth and revelation, and can be with all of us at the same time.

Brethren and sisters, God bless you. I am glad to meet with you. There are very few of you as old as I am. How long I shall tarry in this country I do not know; but while I do stay I want to do what good I can. There are principles that have rested a great deal upon my mind. If we labor for this Spirit, we will have no quarreling and no difficulty, so long as that is dwelling within us. God bless you. Amen.

The Deseret Weekly News, Vol. 53, No. 21, November 7, 1896.

Offer of Salvation Made Either Now or in Spirit World

By Joseph Fielding Smith

The justice of the Lord is manifest in the right he grants to all men to hear the plan of salvation and receive it. Some have that privilege in this life; if they obey the gospel, well and good; if they reject it, then in the spirit world the same opportunities with the same fulness do not come to them.

If they die without that opportunity in this life, it will reach them in the world of spirits. The gospel will there be declared to them, and if they are willing to accept it, it is counted unto them just the same as if they had embraced it in mortality. In this way justice is meted out to every man; all are placed on an equality before the bar of God.

Those who have the opportunity here, those unto whom the message of salvation is declared, who are taught and who have this truth presented to them in this life — yet who deny it and refuse to receive it — shall not have a place in the kingdom of God. They will not be those who died without that knowledge and who yet accepted it in the spirit world.

Doctrines of Salvation, 2:182-3.

The Part Each Will Play at the Judgment Day
By John Taylor

Man sleeps the sleep of death but the spirit lives where the record of his deeds is kept—that does not die—man cannot kill it; there is no decay associated with it, and it still retains in all its vividness the remembrance of that which transpired before the separation by death of the body and the ever-living spirit. Man sleeps for a time in the grave, and by and by he rises again from the dead and goes to judgment; and then the secret thoughts of all men are revealed before Him with whom we have to do; we cannot hide them; it would be in vain for a man to say then: I did not do so-and-so; the command would be: Unravel and read the record which he has made himself, and let it testify in relation to these things, and all could gaze upon it. If a man has acted fraudulently against his neighbor—has committed murder, or adultery, or anything else, and wants to cover it up, that record will stare him in the face. He tells the story himself, and bears witness against himself. It is written that Jesus will judge not after the sight of the eye, or after the hearing of the ear, but with righteousness shall He judge the poor, and reprove with equity the meek of the earth. It is not because somebody has seen things, or heard anything by which a man will be judged and condemned, but it is because that record that is written that cannot lie—in the tablets of his own mind—that record that cannot lie—will in that day be unfolded before God and angels, and those who shall sit as judges. There will be some singular developments, I think. If this is to be the case, as was said formerly, "what manner of persons ought we to be in all holy conversation and godliness?" There is, in fact, something in this, that in a partial degree can be read even on this earth. There are men who profess to be phrenologists and physiologists who profess to read character, and perhaps some man, from a knowledge of human nature and from a study of the human mind can, upon natural principles, unfold a great many things. And there is associated with this Church such a gift as is called the discerning of spirits; but it is one of those things which we see in part and understand in part, etc.; "But when that which is in part is done away, and that which is perfect has come, then we shall see as we are seen, and know as we are known." That is only a part of what the other will be the perfection of. When we get into the eternal world, into the presence of God our Heavenly Father, His eye can penetrate every one of us, and our own record of our lives here shall develop all. I do not say that He will take trouble to read everybody. We read concerning the apostles in former times, that when Jesus should sit in judgment, they should be seated upon twelve thrones, judging the twelve tribes of Israel; and it is also written: "Know ye not that the Saints shall judge the world?" Who will be judges of the world in this generation? You, yourselves, who understand the laws of the Priesthood, must say: Now, then, if these things are so, it behooves us to consider and ponder well the paths of our feet; it behooves me to be careful what I do, what doctrines I advance, what principles I inculcate, and see to it that I do my duty before God, and the angels, and all men, for I cannot obliterate the record which is written here. If I am engaged in business transactions of any kind, it behooves me to know what I am doing; that I am dealing as I would wish men to deal with me; if I do not, the record is there. I think we read somewhere that if our conscience condemns us, God is greater than our conscience; "if our hearts condemn us, God is greater than our hearts." If I be a father and have charge of a family, it behooves me to know what kind of an example I set before them, and how I conduct myself; it behooves both fathers and mothers to know that they are making a record of their doings that they will not be ashamed of. It behooves children to know what kind of a course they take towards their parents, and towards the building up of the kingdom of God upon the earth. If I am an Elder in Israel, or whatever office I hold in the Church, it behooves me to comprehend my position, know myself, and act as a Saint of God in all things, which may the Lord help us to do in the name of Jesus Christ. Amen.   J. D., Vol. 11:78-80.

To Rebuke Evil Powers, We Must Have Power With God

It requires all the care and faithfulness which we can exercise in order to keep the faith of the Lord Jesus; for there are invisible agencies around us in sufficient numbers to encourage the slightest disposition they may discover in us to forsake the true way, and fan into a flame the slightest spark of discontent and unbelief. The spirits of the ancient Gadiantons are around us. You may see battlefield after battlefield, scattered over this American continent, where the wicked have slain the wicked. Their spirits are watching us continually for an opportunity to influence us to do evil, or to make us decline in the performance of our duties. And I will defy any man on earth to be more gentlemanly and bland in his manners than the master spirit of all evil. We call him the devil; a gentleman so smooth and so oily, that he can almost deceive the very elect. We have been baptized by men having the authority of the Holy Priesthood of the Son of God, and consequently we have power over him which the rest of the world do not possess, and all who possess the power of the Priesthood have the power and right to rebuke those evil spirits. When we rebuke those evil powers, and they obey not, it is because we do not live so as to have the power with God, which it is our privilege to have. If we do not live for this privilege and right, we are under condemnation.

Brigham Young, J. of D., Vol. 12:128.

Adminstration of Angels and of Good and Evil Spirits
By Parley P. Pratt

O what an unspeakable blessing is the ministry of angels to mortal man! What a pleasing thought, that many who minister to us, and watch over us, are our near kindred—our fathers who have died and risen again in former ages, and who watch over their descendants with all the parental care and solicitude which characterize affectionate fathers and mothers on the earth.

Thrice happy are they who have lawful claim on their guardianship, and whose conduct does not grieve them, and constrain them to depart from their precious charge.

Spirits are those who have departed this life, and have not yet been raised from the dead. These are of two kinds, viz., good and evil. These two kinds also include many grades of good and evil. The good spirits, in the superlative sense of the word, are they who, in this life, partook of the Holy Priesthood, and of the fullness of the Gospel. This class of spirits minister to the heirs of salvation, both in this world and in the world of spirits. They can appear unto men, who permitted; but not having a fleshly tabernacle, they cannot hide their glory. Hence an unembodied spirit, if it be a holy personage, will be surrounded with a halo of resplendent glory, of brightness, above the brightness of the sun.

Whereas, spirits not worthy to be glorified, will appear without this brilliant halo; and, although they often attempt to pass as angels of light, there is more or less of darkness about them. Many spirits of the departed, who are unhappy, linger in lonely wretchedness about the earth, and in the air, and especially about their ancient homesteads, and the places rendered dear to them by the memory of the former scenes. The more wicked of these are the kind spoken of in Scripture, as "foul spirits," "unclean spirits," spirits who afflict persons in the flesh, and engender diseases in the human system. They will sometimes enter human bodies, and will distract them, throw them into fits, cast them into the water, into the fire, etc. They will trouble them with dreams, nightmares, hysterics, fever, etc. They will also deform them in body and in features, by convulsions, cramps,

contortions, etc., and will sometimes compel them to utter blas-
phemies, horrible curses, and even words of other languages.
If permitted, they will often cause death. Some of these spirits
are adulterous, and suggest to the mind all manner of lascivious-
ness, all kinds of evil thoughts and temptations.

A person, on looking another in the eye, who is possessed
of an evil spirit, will feel a shock—a nervous feeling, which will,
as it were, make his hair stand on end; in short, a shock re-
sembling that produced in a nervous system by the sight of a
serpent.

Some of these foul spirits, when possessing a person, will
cause a disagreeable smell about the person thus possessed, which
will be plainly manifest to the senses of those about him, even
though the person thus afflicted should be washed and change
his clothes every few minutes. There are, in fact, most awful instances of the spirit of lust, and of bawdy and abominable words
and actions, inspired and uttered by persons possessed of such
spirits, even though the person were virtuous and modest so long
as they possessed their own agency. Some of these spirits cause
deafness, others dumbness, etc. We can suggest no remedy for
these multiplied evils, to which poor human nature is subject,
except a good life, while we are in possession of our faculties,
prayers and fastings of good and holy men, and the ministry of
those who have power given them to rebuke evil spirits, and cast
out devils, in the name of Jesus Christ.

Key to Theology, pp. 117-120.

Truth Told By One Who Knew

By Heber C. Kimball

God says, "My house is a house of order, and not of confusion." The Holy Ghost will not dwell where there is confusion. I do not ask you whether you know this or not, because every one knows that confusion does not come from the Father, nor from the Son. Does it come from the Holy Ghost. Every one of you will answer, "No." Where does it come from? It comes from the author of confusion, and is produced by those who rebel against God and against His authority. There were many who did this formerly, and they form part of that hell which Brother Wells was talking about. Although those men and women are dead, they have a good deal of power; their spirits have power over us when we render ourselves subject to them; their spirits are busy at work. They are diligent in performing the work of destruction and confusion; they go at that work the very moment their spirits leave their bodies.

On the other hand, when righteous persons die, their spirits also go into the spirit world, but they go to work with the servants of God to help to do good, and to bring about the purposes of the Almighty pertaining to this earth; while wicked spirits, those who have been wicked in this probation, take the opposite course, just the same as they did here. I have said a great many times, that the spirit which possesses us here will possess us when our spirits leave our bodies, and we shall there be very much the same as we are here.

If you are subject to rebellious spirits, or to a spirit of apostasy here, will you not have the same spirit beyond the vail that you had on this side? You will, and it will have power over you to lead you to do wrong, and it will control your spirit. If, then, you are opposed to the truth while you are here, you will be occupied in that opposition hereafter, for the spirit that is opposed to the work of God here, will be opposed to that work when beyond the vail. I do not guess at this, BECAUSE I HAVE BEEN AT THE OTHER SIDE OF THE VAIL, IN VISION, AND I HAVE SEEN A DEGREE OF ITS CONDITION WITH THE EYES THAT GOD GAVE ME. I HAVE SEEN IT AND HAVE SEEN THOSE THAT LIVED IN

THE FAITH AND HAD THE PRIVILEGE OF SEEING
JESUS, PETER, JAMES, AND THE REST OF THE AN-
CIENT APOSTLES, AND OF HEARING THEM PREACH
THE GOSPEL. I HAVE ALSO SEEN THOSE WHO RE-
BELLED AGAINST THEM, AND THEY STILL HAD A
REBELLIOUS SPIRIT, FIGHTING AGAINST GOD AND
HIS SERVANTS.   J. D., Vol. 4:273-4.

Wicked Spirits Hover Over Their Former Habitat

By George Q. Cannon

There are influences in the atmosphere that are invisible to
us that, while we are here upon the earth, we ought to resist with
all our might, mind and strength — influences which, if we
would be led by them, would lead us to destruction—influences
that are opposed to the Spirit of God—influences that would
bring upon us destruction here and hereafter, if we would yield
to them. These influences we have to resist. We have to resist
the spirit of adultery, the spirit of whoredom, the spirit of
drunkenness, the spirit of theft, and every other evil influence
and spirit, that we may continually overcome; and, when we
have finished our work on the earth, be prepared to govern and
control those influences, and exercise power over them, in the
presence of our Father and God. I have no doubt that many of
my brethren and sisters have sensibly felt in various places and
at various times evil influences around them. Brother Joseph
Smith gave an explanation of this. There are places in the Mississippi Valley where the influence or the presence of invisible
spirits are very perceptibly felt. He said that numbers had been
slain there in war, and that there were evil influences or spirits
which affect the spirits of those who have tabernacles on the
earth. I, myself, have felt those influences in other places besides
the continent of America; I have felt them in the old battle-
grounds on the Sandwich Islands. I have come to the conclusion
that if our eyes were open to see the spirit world around us, we

should feel differently on this subject than we do; we would not be so unguarded and careless, and so indifferent whether we had the spirit and power of God with us or not; but we would be continually watchful and prayerful to our Heavenly Father for His Holy Spirit and His holy angels to be around about us to strengthen us to overcome every evil influence.

When I see young men indulging in drunkenness and in stealing, I come to the conclusion that they are led captive by the evil spirits around them. We call it the spirit of the evil one; but he has numerous agencies at work, even as the Lord has numerous agencies to assist Him in bringing to pass the consummation of His great designs. The adversary has numerous agencies at his command, and he seeks to control and lead to destruction the inhabititants of the earth who will be subject to them. If we could see with our natural senses, we should be greatly shocked at the sight of the influences that prompt us to disobey the counsels of God or the Spirit of the Lord in our hearts. But we cannot see them, for they are spiritually discerned; and he who discerns the most, is the most fully impressed by the Spirit of God; he who does not discern, has not profited by the instructions given to him, and yields to those evil influences in an unguarded moment, and is taken captive in his blindness. He who is imbued with the Spirit of God is sensibly aware when the evil power approaches; but he does not welcome it to his bosom; he resists it with all the might and strength God has given unto him, and he obtains power over it, and it no more troubles him; if it does, its influence is more weakened than previously.

J. D., Vol. 11:30.

The Place of Wicked Spirits and of the Spirit World

By Brigham Young

(Excerpts of Discourse Delivered in the Bowery, Salt Lake City, June 22, 1856.)

I said a few words upon the principle of affection last Sabbath; now I wish to say a few words with regard to our lives hereafter. I will extend these remarks further than our existence here in the flesh.

We understand, for it has long been told us, that we had an existence before we came into the world. Our spirits came here pure to take these tabernacles; they came to occupy them as habitations, with the understanding that all that had passed previously to our coming here should be taken away from us, that we should not know anything about it.

We came here to live a few days, and then we are gone again. How long the starry heavens have been in existence we cannot say; how long they will continue to be we cannot say. How long there will be air, water, earth; how long the elements will endure, in their present combinations, is not for us to say. Our religion teaches us that there never was a time when they were not, and there never will be a time when they will cease to be; they are here, and will be here forever.

I will give you a figure that Brother Hyde had in a dream. He had been thinking a great deal about time and eternity; he wished to know the difference, but how to understand it he did not know. He asked the Lord to show him, and after he had prayed about it, the Lord gave him a dream, at least I presume He did, or permitted it so to be, at any rate he had a dream; his mind was opened so that he could understand time and eternity. He said that he thought he saw a stream issuing forth from a misty cloud which spread upon his right and upon his left, and that the stream ran past him and entered the cloud again. He was told that the stream was time, that it had no place where it commenced to run, neither was there any end to its running; and that the time which he was thinking about and talking about, what he could see between the two clouds, was a portion of or one with that which he could not perceive. So it is with you and I; here is time, where is eternity? It is here, just as much as anywhere in all the expanse of space; a measured space of time is only a part of eternity.

We have a short period of duration allotted to us, and we call it time. We exist here, we have life within us; let that life be taken away and the lungs will cease to heave, and the body will become lifeless. Is that life extinct? No, it continues to exist as much as it did when the lungs would heave, when the mortal body was invigorated with air, food and the elements in which it lived; it has only left the body. The life, the animating princi- pels, are still in existence, as much so as they were yesterday when the body was in good health. Here the inquiry will natural- ly arise, when our spirits leave our bodies, where do they go?

I will tell you. Will I locate them? Yes, if you wish me to. They do not pass out of the organization of this earth on which we live. You read in the Bible that when the spirit leaves the body it goes to God who gave it. Now tell me where God is not, if you please; you cannot. How far would you have to go in order to go to God, if your spirits were unclothed? Would you have to go out of this bowery to find God, if you were in the spirit? If God is not here, we had better reserve this place to gather the wicked into, for they will desire to be where God is not. The Lord Almighty is here by His Spirit, by His influence, by His presence. I am not in the north end of this bowery, my body is in the south end of it, but my influence and my voice extend to all parts of it; in like manner is the Lord here.

It reads that the spirit goes to God who gave it. Let me render this Scripture a little plainer: When the spirits leave their bodies they are in the presence of our Father and God; they are prepared then to see, hear and understand spiritual things. But where is the spirit world? It is incorporated within this celestial system. Can you see it with your natural eyes? No. Can you see spirits in this room? No. Suppose the Lord should touch your eyes that you might see; could you then see the spirits? Yes, as plainly as you now see bodies, as did the servant of Elijah. If the Lord would permit it, and it was His will that it should be done, you could see the spirits that have departed from this world as plainly as you now see bodies with your natural eyes; as plainly as Brothers Kimball and Hyde saw those wicked disembodied spirits in Preston, England. They saw devils there, as we see one another; they could hear them speak, and knew what they said. Could they hear them with the natural ear? No. Did they see those wicked spirits with their natural eyes? No. They could not see them the next morning, when they were not in the spirit; neither could they see them the day before, nor at any other time; their spiritual eyes were touched by the power of the Almighty.

They said they looked through their natural eyes, and I suppose they did. Brother Kimball saw them but I know not whether his natural eyes were open at the time or not; Brother Kimball said that he lay upon the floor part of the time, and I presume his eyes were shut, but he saw them as also did Brother Hyde, and they heard them speak.

We may inquire where the spirits dwell, that the devil has power over? They dwell anywhere, in Preston, as well as in other places in England. Do they dwell anywhere else? Yes, on this continent; it is full of them. If you could see and would walk over many parts of North America, you would see millions on millions of the spirits of those who were as good in the flesh as they knew how to be. Yes. Would you see the spirits of the wicked? Yes. Could you see the spirits of devils? Yes, and that is all there is of them. They have been deprived of bodies, and that constitutes their curse, that is to say, speaking after the manner of men, you shall be wanderers on the earth; you have got to live out of doors all the time you live.

That is the situation of the spirits that were sent to the earth, when the revolt took place in heaven, when Lucifer, the Son of the Morning, was cast out. Where did he go? He came here, and one-third part of the spirits in heaven came with him. Do you suppose that one-third part of all the beings that existed in eternity came with him? No, but one-third part of the spirits that were begotten and organized and brought forth to become tenants of fleshly bodies to dwell upon the earth. They forsook Jesus Christ, the rightful heir, and joined with Lucifer, the Son of the Morning, and came to this earth; they got here first. As soon as Mother Eve made her appearance in the Garden of Eden, the devil was on hand.

You cannot give any person their exaltation, unless they know what evil is, what sin, sorrow, and misery are, for no person could comprehend, appreciate, and enjoy an exaltation upon any other principle. The devil with one-third part of the spirits of our Father's Kingdom got here before us, and we tarried there with our friends, until the time came for us to come to the earth and take tabernacles; but those spirits that revolted were forbidden ever to have tabernacles of their own. You can now comprehend how it is that they are always trying to get possession of the bodies of human beings. We read of a man's being possessed of a legion, and Mary Magdalene had seven.

You may now see people with legions of evil spirits in and around them; there are men who walk our streets that have more than a hundred devils in them and round about them, prompting them to all manner of evil, and some too that profess to be Latter-day Saints, and if you were to take the devils out of them and from about them, you would leave them dead corpses; for I believe there would be nothing left of them.

I want you to understand these things; and if you should say or think that I know nothing about them, be pleased to find out and inform me. You can see the acts of these evil spirits in every place, the whole country is full of them, the whole earth is alive with them, and they are continually trying to get into the tabernacles of the human family, and are always on hand to prompt us to depart from the strict line of our duty.

You know that we sometimes need a prompter. If any of you were called by the Government of the United States to go to Germany, Italy, or any foreign nation, as an Ambassador, if you did not understand the language, somebody would have to interpret for you. Well, these evil spirits are ready to prompt you. Do they prompt us? Yes, and I could put my hands on a dozen of them while I have been on this stand; they are here on the stand. Could we do without these devils? No, we could not get along without them. They are here, and they suggest this, that, and the other.

When you lay down this tabernacle, where are you going? Into the spiritual world. Are you going into Abraham's bosom? No, not anywhere nigh there, but into the spirit world. Where is the spirit world? It is right here. Do the good and evil spirits go together? Yes, they do. Do they both inhabit one kingdom? Yes, they do. Do they go to the sun? No. Do they go beyond the boundaries of this organized earth? No, they do not. They are brought forth upon this earth, for the express purpose of inhabiting it to all eternity. Where else are you going? Nowhere else, only as you may be permitted.

When the spirits of mankind leave their bodies, no matter whether the individual was a Prophet or the meanest person that you could find, where do they go? To the spirit world. Where is it? I am telling you. The spirit of Joseph, I do not know that it is just now in this bowery, but I will assure you that it is close to the Latter-day Saints, is active in preaching to the spirits in prison and preparing the way to redeem the nations of the earth, those who lived in darkness previous to the introduction of the Gospel by himself in these days.

He has just as much labor on hand as I have; he has just as

much to do. Father Smith and Carlos and Brother Partridge, yes, and every other good Saint, are just as busy in the spirit world as you and I are here. They can see us, but we cannot see them unless our eyes were opened. What are they doing there? They are preaching, preaching all the time, and preparing the way for us to hasten our work in building temples here and elsewhere, and to go back to Jackson County and build the Great Temple of the Lord. They are hurrying to get ready by the time that we are ready, and we are all hurrying to get ready by the time our Elder Brother is ready.

The wicked spirits that leave here and go into the spirit world, are they wicked there? Yes. The spirits of people that have lived upon the earth according to the best light they had, who were as honest and sincere as men and women could be, if they lived on the earth without the privilege of the Gospel and the Priesthood and the keys thereof, are still under the power and control of evil spirits, to a certain extent. No matter where they lived on the face of the earth, all men and women that have died without the keys and power of the Priesthood, though they might have been honest and sincere and have done everything they could, are under the influence of the devil, more or less. Are they as much so as others? No, no. Take those that were wicked designedly, who knowingly lived without the Gospel when it was within their reach they are given up to the devil, they become tools to the devil and spirits of devils.

Go to the time when the Gospel came to the earth in the days of Joseph, take the wicked that have opposed this people and persecuted them to the death, and they are sent to hell. Where are they? They are in the spirit world, and are just as busy as they possibly can be to do everything they can against the Prophet and the Apostles, against Jesus and His Kingdom. They are just as wicked and malicious in their actions against the cause of truth, as they were while on the earth in their fleshly tabernacles. Joseph, also, goes there, but has the devil power over him? No, because he held the keys and powers of the eternal Priesthood here, and got the victory here in the flesh.

Before I proceed further I will give you an illustration. Send a man that is used to magnetizing people, and see if he can magnetize an Elder in Israel, one that is full of faith, or a faithful sister in the Church of God. Could LeRoy Sunderland, one of their greatest characters, magnetize one of the Latter-day Saints? No. He might as well try to magnetize the sun in the firmament. Why? Because the Priesthood is upon you, and he would try to magnetize you by another and lesser power.

The principle of animal magnetism is true, but wicked men use it to an evil purpose. I have never told you much about my belief in this magnetic principle. Speaking is a true gift, but I can speak to the glory of God, or to the injury of His cause and to my condemnation, as I please; and still the gift is of God. The gift of animal magnetism is a gift of God, but wicked men use it to promote the cause of the devil, and that is precisely the difference. You may travel through the world and make inquiries where the Elders have traveled, and you cannot find an instance where the devil has gained power over a good and faithful Elder through this power. He cannot do it, because the faithful Elder of this Church holds keys and power above that which is used by those who go around lecturing on magnetism and operating upon all who will become passive to their will. They have not the same power that the faithful Elders of Israel have, for those Elders have the eternal Priesthood upon them, which is above and presides over every other power.

When the faithful Elders, holding this Priesthood, go into the spirit world they carry with them the same power and Priesthood that they had while in the mortal tabernacle. They have got the victory over the power of the enemy here, consequently when they leave this world they have perfect control over those evil spirits, and they cannot be buffeted by Satan. But as long as they live in the flesh, no being on this earth, of the posterity of Adam, can be free from the power of the devil.

When this portion of the school is out, the one in which we descend below all things and commence upon this earth to learn the first lessons for an eternal exaltation, if you have been a faithful scholar, and have overcome, if you have brought the flesh into subjection by the powers of the Priesthood, if you have honored the body, when it crumbles to the earth and your spirit is freed from this home of clay, has the devil any power over it? Not one particle.

This is an advantage which the faithful will gain; but while they live on earth they are subject to the buffetings of Satan. Joseph and those who have died in the faith of the Gospel are free from this; if a mob should come upon Joseph now, he has power to disperse them with the motion of his hand, and to drive them where he pleases. But is Joseph glorified? No, he is preaching to the spirits in prison. He will get his resurrection the first of any one in this kingdom, for he was the first that God made choice to bring forth the work of the last days.

His office is not taken from him, he has only gone to labor in another department of the operations of the Almighty. He is still an Apostle, still a Prophet, and is doing the work of an Apostle and Prophet; he has gone one step beyond us and gained a victory that you and I have not gained, still he has not yet gone into the celestial kingdom, or if he has it has been by a direct command of the Almighty, and that, too, to return again so soon as the purpose has been accomplished.

No man can enter the celestial kingdom and be crowned with celestial glory, until he gets his resurrected body; but Joseph and the faithful who have died have gained a victory over the power of the devil, which you and I have not yet gained. So long as we live in these tabernacles, so long we will be subject to the temptations and power of the devil; but when we lay them down, if we have been faithful, we have gained the victory so far; but even then we are not so far advanced at once as to be beyond the neighborhood of evil spirits.

The third part of the hosts of heaven, that were cast out, have not been taken away, at least not that I have found out, and the other two-thirds have got to come and take bodies, all of them who have not, and have the opportunity of preparing for a glorious resurrection and exaltation, before we get through with this world; and those who are faithful in the flesh to the requirements of the Gospel will gain this victory over the spirits that are not allowed to take bodies, which class comprises one-third of the hosts of Heaven.

Those who have died without the Gospel are continually afflicted by those evil spirits, who say to them—"Do not go to hear that man Joseph Smith preach, or David Patten, or any of their associates for they are deceivers."

Spirits are just as familiar with spirits as bodies are with bodies, though spirits are composed of matter so refined as not to be tangible to this coarser organization. They walk, converse, and have their meetings; and the spirits of good men like Joseph and the Elders, who have left this Church on earth for a season to operate in another sphere, are rallying all their powers and going from place to place preaching the Gospel, and Joseph is directing them saying, go ahead, my brethren, and if they hedge up your way, walk up and command them to disperse. You have the Priesthood and can disperse them, but if any of them wish to hear the Gospel, preach to them.

Can they baptize them? No. What can they do? They can preach the Gospel, and when we have the privilege of building up Zion, the time will come for saviors to come up on Mount Zion. My brother Joseph spoke of this principle this forenoon. Some of those who are not in mortality will come along and say, "Here are a thousand names I wish you to attend to in this temple, and when you have got through with them I will give you another thousand;" and the Elders of Israel and their wives will go forth to officiate for their forefathers, the men for the men, and the women for the women.

A man is ordained and receives his washings, anointings, and endowments for the male portion of his and his wife's progenitors, and his wife for the female portion. Then in the spirit world they will say, "Do you not see somebody at work for you? The Lord remembers you and has revealed to His servants on the earth, what to do for you."

Is the spirit world here? It is not beyond the sun, but is on this earth that was organized for the people that have lived and that do and will live upon it. No other people can have it, and we can have no other kingdom until we are prepared to inhabit this eternally. In the spirit world those who have got the victory go on to prepare the way for those who live in the flesh, fulfilling the work of saviors on Mount Zion.

To accomplish this work there will have to be not only one temple but thousands of them, and thousands and tens of thousands of men and women will go into those temples and officiate for people who have lived as far back as the Lord shall reveal. If we are faithful enough to go back and build that great temple which Joseph has written about, and should the Lord acknowledge the labor of His servants, then watch, for you will see somebody whom you have not seen before, and many of you will see him whom you have not seen before, but you will know him as soon as you see him.

This privilege we cannot enjoy now, because the power of Satan is such that we cannot perform the labor that is necessary to enable us to obtain it.

When we commence again on the walls of the temple to be built on this Block, the news will fly from Maine to California. Who will tell them? These little devils that are around here, that are around this earth in the spirit world; there will be millions of them ready to communicate the news to devils in Missouri, Illinois, California, Mexico, and in all the world. And the question will be, "What is the news? There is some devilish thing going on among the 'Mormons' and I know it. Those 'Mormons' ought to be killed." They do not know what stirs them up to this feeling, it is those spirits that are continually near to them.

We all have got spirits to attend us; when the eyes of the servant of Elijah were opened he saw that those for them were more than those that were against them. There are two-thirds for us, and one-third against us; and there is not a son or daughter of Adam but what will be saved in some kingdom and receive a glory and an exaltation to a degree, except those who have had the privilege of the Gospel and rejected it and sinned against the Holy Ghost, they will become servants to devils.

How long will they exist? I do not know, neither do I care. Every one of this people, with the Saints that have lived before us, from the days of Adam until now, and those that may come after us, all say: "Build up the kingdom of God." What for? To save the inhabitants of the earth, to get them all back into some kind of a kingdom where they can be administered to, and not have this organized matter return again to its native element, for we wish this work to be preserved.

You know that when you make a farm you dislike to see it overrun with weeds, and it would hurt your feelings to see your houses, barns, and other property destroyed. True, you can make more, but how do you suppose the Lord feels, who is much more compassionate than we are, when He sees the devil gaining an advantage over His creatures to lead them away to destroy them? Do you not suppose that the bowels of His compassion yearn over this people, and that He is angry with the wicked? Do you not suppose that He often feels like saying: "O, my children, why do you not hearken to what I tell you and take hold of the principles of life, and cease pursuing a course that is calculated to destroy you? I have labored to bring forth this organization, and I do not wish to lose my labor, but I desire to have you hearken to the counsel I give to you and prepare yourselves to endure forever and come into my presence, and if you cannot do that and abide a celestial law, at least the law of a kingdom where I can send angels to you, and I will send and comfort you and administer unto you and will raise you up and make you glad and happy, and will fill you with joy and peace."

J. D., Vol. 3:367-73.

Results of Misuse of Priesthood

By President Wilford Woodruff

We have baptized a great many into this Church and kingdom—not many, certainly, when compared to the twelve hundred million inhabitants of the earth—but a great many have apostatized. What! Latter-day Saints apostatized? Yes. I tell you people will apostatize who have received the holy Priesthood and Gospel of Jesus Christ, if they do not honor God, if they do not keep His commandments, obey His laws, and humble themselves before the Lord; they are in danger every day of their lives. Look at the number of devils we have round about us! We have, I should say, one hundred to every man, woman and child. One-third part of the heavenly host was cast down to the earth with Lucifer, son of the morning, to war against us—which I suppose will number one hundred million devils—and they labor to overthrow all the Saints and the kingdom of God. They even tried to overthrow Jesus Christ; they overthrew Judas, and they have succeeded in overthrowing a good many Latter-day Saints who had a name and standing among us, who undertook to build themselves up instead of the Kingdom of God, and when men having this Priesthood—I do not care whether it was in the days of Adam, in the days of Moses, in the days of Joseph Smith, or in the days of Brigham Young, I care not what day they lived—if they bore this Priesthood and undertook to use it for any other purpose than the building up of the kingdom of God, then amen to the power and priesthood of such men.   J. D., Vol. 21:125-6.

A True Father's Desire

By Brigham Young

The Lord would like to see us take the course that leads unto the straight gate, that we might be crowned sons and daughters of God, for such are the only ones in the heavens who multiply and increase, and who frame and make and redeem worlds. The rest take an inferior kingdom, where the privilege is denied them. This the Lord has made known unto us through the Prophet Joseph; it is published and so plainly written, that we can read and understand for ourselves. It is for us to choose whether we will be sons and daughters, joint heirs with Jesus Christ, or whether we accept an inferior glory; or whether we sin against the Holy Ghost, which cannot be pardoned, or forgiven in this world, nor in the world to come; the penalty of which is to suffer the second death. What is that we call death, compared to the agonies of the second death? *If people could see it, as Joseph and Sidney saw it, they would pray that the vision be closed up; for they could not endure the sight. Neither could they endure the sight of the Father and the Son in their glory, for it would consume them.*

The Lord gives us little by little and is ever willing to give us more and more, even the fullness, when our hearts are prepared to receive all the truths of heaven. This is what the Lord desires, what He would delight in doing for His children. These are only a few reflections, when we take into consideration our Christian religion, for it incorporates every act of a person's life. We never should presume to do anything unless we can say: "Father, sanction this, and crown the same with success." If the Latter-day Saints live so, the victory is ours. There are a great many who want to live so, and I say God bless all such.

J. D., Vol. 18:216-7.

Divisions in the Spirit World
By Joseph Fielding Smith

All spirits of men after death return to the spirit world. There, as I understand it, the righteous — meaning those who have been baptized and who have been faithful — are gathered in one part and all the others in another part of the spirit world. This seems to be true from the vision given to President Joseph F. Smith and found in *Gospel Doctrine*.

What the Lord really said to the thief was that he would be with him in the world of spirits and there he would be taught the truth, as this seemed to be his desire while upon the cross.

I understand that the righteous may go among the other spirits, and there the gospel is being taught, but the spirits barred from the association of the righteous cannot go where the righteous are.

According to the story of Lazarus and the rich man, there was a gulf which separated the righteous from the unrighteous (which included all the spirits not baptized), and neither class could pass into the other until the Savior bridged the gulf, so those holding the priesthood then could cross over to teach the others.

Doctrines of Salvation, 2:230.

PRESIDENT JOSEPH F. SMITH

Born in the midst of great tribulation—at Far West, Missouri, in 1838; bereft of the love and care of his immortal and martyred father at the age of six years; driving two yoke of oxen one thousand miles across the plains and deserts in the greatest exodus of all time, when eight to ten years of age; going as a steerage passenger to the far-off Islands of Hawaii on a mission when but fifteen years of age, and being left an orphan but one year before starting on this mission, when his sainted mother departed this life to meet her beloved husband. With all of these experiences endured in his youth, he valiantly struggled, achieved and conquered in the battles of life. His life's voyage was not on a beautiful quiet calm of a peaceful sea, but among the mountainous waves that many times threatened destruction; but a life devoted to God and country.

He served as President of the Salt Lake Temple from 1898 to 1911; he dedicated the Alberta Tabernacle Square as the Temple site on July 27, 1913; he dedicated the Hawaiian Temple site on June 1, 1915. He lived and died beloved by the Saints of the Most High—a worthy goal for all who believe in the divinity of the great mission of his uncle, the Prophet Joseph Smith.

Communion With Spirits

By Parley P. Pratt

When the outward organs of thought, and perception are released from their activity, the nerves unstrung, and the whole of mortal humanity lies hushed in quiet slumbers, in order to renew its strength and vigor, it is then that the spiritual organs are at liberty, in a certain degree, to assume their wonted functions, to recall some faint outlines, some confused and half-defined recollections, of that heavenly world, and those endearing scenes of their former estate, from which they have descended in order to obtain and mature a tabernacle of flesh. Their kindred spirits, their guardian angels then hover about them with the fondest affection, the most anxious solicitude. Spirit communes with spirit, thought meets thought, soul blends with soul, in all the raptures of mutual, pure and eternal love.

In this situation, the spiritual organs are susceptible of converse with Deity, or of communion with angels, and the spirits of just men made perfect.

In this situation, we frequently hold communication with our departed father, mother, brother, sister, son or daughter; or with the former husband or wife of our bosom, whose affection for us being rooted and grounded in the eternal elements, or issuing from under the sanctuary of Love's eternal fountain, can never be lessened or diminished by death, distance of space, or length of years.

We may, perhaps, have had a friend of the other sex, whose pulse beat in unison with our own; whose every thought was big with aspirations, the hopes of a bright future in union with our own; whose happiness in time or in eternity, would never be fully consummated without that union. Such a one, snatched from time in the very bloom of youth, lives in the other sphere, with the same bright hope, watching our every footstep, in our meanderings through the rugged path of life, with longing desires for our eternal happiness and eager for our safe arrival in the same sphere.

With what tenderness of love, with what solicitude of affection will they watch over our slumbers, hang about our pillow, and seek, by means of the spiritual fluid, to communicate with our spirits, to warn us of dangers or temptation, to comfort and soothe our sorrow, or to ward off the ills which might befall us or perchance to give us some kind token of remembrance of undying love!

It is the pure in heart, the lovers of truth and virtue, that will appreciate these remarks, for they know, by at least a small degree of experience, that these things are so.

Those who are habitually given to vice, immorality and abomination; those who walk in the daily indulgence of unlawful lust; those who neither believe in Jesus Christ, nor seek to pray to Him, and keep His commandments; those who do not cultivate the pure, refined and holy joys of innocent and heavenly affection, but who would sacrifice every finer feeling at the shrine of lawless pleasure and brutal desires—those persons will not understand and appreciate these views, because their good angels, their kindred spirits have long since departed, and ceased to attend them, being grieved and disgusted with their conduct.

The Spirit of the Lord has also been grieved, and has left them to themselves, to struggle alone amid the dangers and sorrows of life; or to be the associates of demons and impure spirits. Such persons dream of adultery, gluttony, debauchery, and crimes of every kind. Such persons have the foreshadowings of a doleful death of darkness, and buffetings of fiends and malicious spirits.

But blessed are they who forfeit not their claims to the watchful care and protection of, and communion with, the heavenly powers, and pure and lovely spirits.

We can only advise the other classes of mankind, and entreat them, by the joys of love, by all the desires of life, by all the dread of death, darkness, and a dreary hereafter, yea, by the blood of Him who died, by the victory of Him who rose in triumph from the grave, by their regard for those whose kindred spirits which would gladly love them in worlds without end, to turn from their sinful course of life, to obey the ordinances and commandments of Jesus Christ, that the Spirit of God may return to them, and their good angels and spirits again return to their sacred charge.

Key to Theology, pp. 122-6.

A Temple Lot Dedicated at Adam-ondi-Ahman

After hearing of the mobbing, burning and robbing in Gallatin, Daviess County, and the region round about, the brethren of Caldwell went directly to Adam-ondi-Ahman, which is on the west fork of Grand River, Thomas B. Marsh, David W. Patten, Brigham Young, myself, Parley P. Pratt and John Taylor amongst the number. When we arrived there we found the Prophet Joseph Smith, Hyrum Smith and Sidney Rigdon, with hundreds of others of the Saints preparing to defend themselves from the mob, who were threatening the destruction of our people. Men, women, and children were fleeing to that place for safety from every direction; their houses and property were burned and they had to flee half naked, crying, and frightened nigh unto death, to save their lives.

While there we laid out a city on a high elevated piece of land, and set the stakes for the four corners of a temple block, which was dedicated, Brother Young being mouth; there were from three to five hundred men present on the occasion, under arms. This elevated spot was probably from two hundred and fifty to five hundred feet above the level of Grand River, so that one could look east, west, north or south, as far as the eye could reach; it was one of the most beautiful places I ever beheld.

Life of Heber C. Kimball, by Orson F. Whitney, pp. 221-2.

Angels and Ministering Spirits

By Joseph Smith

The difference between an angel and a ministering spirit; the one (the first) is a resurrected or translated body with its spirit ministering to embodied spirits; the other a disembodied spirit visiting and ministering to disembodied spirits.

Jesus Christ became a ministering spirit (while His body was lying in the sepulchre) to the spirits in prison, to fulfill an important part of His mission, without which He could not have perfected His work or entered into His rest. After His resurrection He appeared as an angel to His disciples.

Translated bodies cannot enter into rest until they have undergone a change equivalent to death.

Translated bodies are designed for future missions.

The angel which appeared to John on the Isle of Patmos was a translated or resurrected body.

Jesus Christ went in body after His resurrection to minister to translated and resurrected bodies.

It is no more incredible that God should save the dead than that He should raise the dead.

There is never a time when the spirit is too old to approach God.

All are within the reach of pardoning mercy, who have not committed the unpardonable sin, which hath no forgiveness, neither in this world, nor in the world to come. There is a way to release the spirit of the dead; that is by the power and authority of the Priesthood—by binding and loosing on earth. This doctrine appears glorious, inasmuch as it exhibits the greatness of divine compassion and benevolence in the extent of the plan of human salvation.

This glorious truth is well calculated to enlarge the understanding and to sustain the soul under troubles, difficulties, and distresses. For illustration, suppose the case of two men, brothers, equally intelligent, learned, virtuous and lovely, walking in uprightness and in good conscience, so far as they had been able to discern duty from the muddy stream of tradition, or from the blotted page of the book of nature. One dies and is buried, having never heard the Gospel of reconciliation; to the other the message of salvation is sent, he hears and embraces it, and is made heir of eternal life. Shall the one become a partaker of glory, and the other consigned to hopeless perdition? Is there no chance for his escape? Sectarianism answers none! none! none!! Such an idea is worse than atheism. The truth shall break down and dash in pieces all such bigoted Pharisaism; the sects shall be sifted, the honest in heart brought out, and their priests left in the midst of their corruption. * * *

This doctrine presents in a clear light the wisdom and mercy of God in preparing an ordinance for the salvation of the dead, being baptized by proxy, their names recorded in heaven, and they judged according to the deeds done in the body. This doctrine was the burden of the scriptures. Those Saints who neglect it, in behalf of their deceased relatives, do it at the peril of their own salvation. The dispensation of the fullness of times will bring to light the things that have been revealed in all former dispensations; also other things that have not been before revealed.

(Teachings Given at the October Conference, 1841, at Nauvoo, Illinois. Rise and Fall of Nauvoo, by B. H. Roberts, pp. 110-1.)

Other Worlds Than Ours and Their Redemption. Commenting on Revelation 5:13: "And every creature which is in heaven, and on the earth, and under the earth, and such as are in the sea, and all that are in them, heard I saying, Blessing, and honor, and glory, and power, be unto him that sitteth upon the throne, and unto the Lamb, forever and ever,"—the Prophet said:

I suppose John saw beings there of a thousand forms, that had been saved from ten thousand times ten thousand earths like this, strange beasts of which we have no conception; all might be seen in heaven. The grand secret was to show John what there was in heaven. John learned that God glorified Himself by saving all that His hands had made, whether beasts, fowls, fishes or men, and He will gratify Himself with them.

The World of Spirits. I will say something about the spirits in prison. There has been much said by modern divines about the words of Jesus (when on the cross) to the thief, saying, "This day shalt thou be with Me in paradise." King James' translation makes it out to say paradise. But what is paradise? It is a modern word, it does not answer at all to the original word that Jesus made use of. Find the original of the word paradise. You may as easily find a needle in a haymow. Here is a chance for battle, ye learned men. There is nothing in the original word in Greek from which this was taken that signifies paradise, but it was, "This day thou shalt be with me in the world of spirits; then I will teach you all about it and answer your inquiries." And Peter says he went out and preached to the world of spirits (spirits in prison, 1st Peter, 3:19), so that they who would receive it could have it answered by proxy by those who live on the earth. * * * Hades, the Greek, or Sheol, the Hebrew, these two significations mean a world of spirits. The righteous and the wicked will go to the same world of spirits until the resurrection. "I do not think so," says one. If you will go to my house at any time, I will take my lexicon and prove it to you. The great misery of departed spirits in the world of spirits, where they go after death, is to know that they come short of the glory that others enjoy, and that they might have enjoyed themselves, and they are their own accursers.

Rise and Fall of Nauvoo, by B. H. Roberts, pp. 213-216.

Chapter XXIII

CONCORDANCE AND REFERENCE ON TEMPLES, TEMPLE WORK AND KINDRED SUBJECTS

Concordance on Temples

Bible:

Herod's, Solomon's and Zerubabel's.
Temple: David desires to build, II; Sa. 7:3; I. Chr. 17:2; 28-2.
David forbidden to build, II. Sa. 7:5; I. Chr. 17:4; 28:3.
Solomon to build, II. Sa. 7:12; I. Chr. 17:11; 28.5.
Solomon builds, I. Ki. 6; II. Chr. 3:4.
Its solemn dedication, I. Ki. 8, 9; II. Chr. 6, 7.
Plundered by Shishak, king of Egypt, I. Ki. 14:25; II. Chr. 12:9.
Restored by Joash, II. Ki. 12:5, 12.
Cleansed by Hezekiah, II. Chr. 29:5.
Polluted by Manasseh, II. Chr. 33:7.
Repaired by Josiah, II. Chr. 34.
Spoiled by the Chaldeans, II. Ki. 25:9.
Decrees of Cyrus and Darius for rebuilding, Ezra 6:3, 13.
Finished and dedicated, Ezra 6:15, 16.
Christ drives out buyers and sellers, Mat. 21:12, Mar. 11:15; Lu. 19:45; John 2:14.
Christ foretells its destruction, Mat. 24:2; Mar. 13:2; Lu. 21:6.
Ezekiel's house of God, Ps. 65:4; Ec. 5:1; Heb. 10:21; I Pet. 4:17.
Symbolical of the body of Christ, John 2:19-21.
Of God and Holy Ghost, Christians are, II. Cor. 6:16.
He did hear my voice out of his t. II. Sa. 22:7; Ps. 18:6.
To enquire in his t. Ps. 27:4.
In His t. doth every one speak of His glory. Ps. 29:9.
His train filled the t. Isa. 6:1.
One greater than the t. Mat. 12:6.
Destroy this t. John 2:19.
T. made with hands, Ac. 7:48; 17:24.
Body is t. of Holy Ghost, I. Cor. 6:19.
Serve day and night in his t. Rev. 7:15.
Ezra, chapters 25, 26, 27 and 28, give a description of the Tabernacle constructed in the wilderness, with its appointments. This Tabernacle is frequently called a Temple, in the Old Testament as in I. Sam. 1:9.

I Kings, Chapters 6, 7 and 8, Temple of Solomon is described with the dedication ceremonies.

Ezra, Chapter 6. The rebuilding of Solomon's Temple by Syrus is given. The decree is found in Verse 3.

The final desolation of this Temple was foretold by Christ in Matt. 24:2. This terrible prophecy was fulfilled by the Romans under Titus about the year 70 of our Lord.

Bible:

1 Sam. 3:3	Lamp of God went out in temple
2 Sam. 22:7	Hear my voice out of temple
1 Ki. 6:3	Porch between temple and the house
2 Ki. 18:16	Cut gold from doors of temple
1 Chr. 6:10	Priest's office in temple
2 Chr. 37:7	Put vessels in temple at B.
Ex. 4:1	They builded temple unto Lord
Neh. 6:10	Let us shut doors of temple
Ps. 11:4	The Lord is in His holy temple

Isa. 6:1	And His train filled the temple
Jer. 7:4	Lying, saying, The temple of L.
Ezek. 41:1	He brought me to the temple and
Dan. 5:2	Nebuch. had ta. out of temple
Hos. 8:14	Forgot Maker, build temple
Joel 3:5	Into temple my goodly things
Am. 8:3	Songs of temple sh. be howlings
Jonah 2:4	Look toward thy holy temple
Mic. 1:2	Be witness fr. his holy temple
Hab. 2:20	The Lord is in His holy temple
Hag. 2:15	Laid upon sto. in temple
Zech. 6:12	He shall build temple of Lord
Mal. 3:1	Shall suddenly come to his temple
Mat. 4:5	Set. him on pinnacle of temple
Mat. 21:12	Jesus went into temple of God
Mark 11:11	Entered Jer. and into temple
Luke 2:17	He came by spirit into temple
Luke 19:47	He taught daily in temple
John 2:14	Found in temple th. sold oxen
John 7:28	Then cried Jesus in the temple
Acts 3:10	At beautiful gate of temple
Acts 26:21	Jews caught me in temple
I Cor. 3:10	Know ye are temple of God
I Cor. 3:17	For the temple of God is holy
2 Cor. 6:16	Ye are temple of living God
Eph. 2:21	Grow. Into temple in the Lord
2 Thes. 2:4	He as God sitteth in the temple
Rev. 3:12	I will make him a pillar in temple of
Rev. 21:22	God Almighty and Lamb are the temple
Judg. 4:21	Smote nail into his temples
S. of S. 4:3	Thy temples are like pomegranates

Book of Mormon:

2 Nephi 5:16	I, Nephi, did build a temple and I did construct it after the manner of the Temple of Solomon
2 Nephi 16:1	Lifted up, and his train filled the temple
Jacob 1:17	These words I taught them in the temple
Jacob 2:2	I came up into the temple this day, that I
Jacob 2:11	Get thou up into the temple on the morrow
Mosiah 1:18	To go up to the temple to hear the words
Mosiah 2:1	Might go up to the temple to hear the words
Mosiah 2:5	When they came up to the temple they pitched
Mosiah 2:6	Pitched their tents round about the temple
Mosiah 2:7	Teach them all within the walls of the temple
Mosiah 7:17	Might gather themselves together to the temple
Mosiah 11:10	Fine work within the walls of the temple
Mosiah 11:12	He built a tower near the temple
Mosiah 19:5	Got upon the tower which was near the temple
Alma 10:2	Writing which was upon the wall of the temple
Helaman 10:8	If ye shall say unto this temple, it shall be
3 Nephi 11:1	About the Temple which was in Bountiful
3 Nephi 24:1	Ye seek shall suddenly come to his temple
Mosiah 2:37	For he dwelleth not in unholy temples
Alma 7:21	And he doth not dwell in unholy temples
Alma 16:13	Repentance to the people in their temples
Alma 23:2	And also their temples and their sanctuaries
Alma 26:29	We have also entered into their temples

Alma 34:36   Said, He dwelleth not in unholy temples
Helaman 3:9   Timber to build their cities and their temples
Helaman 3:14   And their building of temples
Helaman 4:24   The Lord doth not dwell in unholy temples

Doctrine and Coverants:

36:8   I will suddenly come to my temple
42:36   In that day when I shall come to my temple
57:3   Place for temple in Independence designated
58:57   Sidney Rigdon to dedicate land for temple
84:3   New Jerusalem to be built beginning at temple lot
  4   Temple shall be reared in this generation
  5   Cloud of God's glory to rest upon temple
93:35   God will destroy defiled temple
  35   Man is tabernacle or temple of God
95:8   To endow those chosen with power from on high in house
  13   House to be built not after manner of world
  14   House to be built as I shall show
  15   Dimensions of temple revealed
97:15   House shall be built in name of the Lord
  15   Glory of God to rest upon it if not defiled
  16   Pure in heart shall see God in temple
  17   If temple defiled God will not come into it
101:23   When veil of temple is taken off, all flesh shall see Me
105:33   First elders to receive endowments in Kirtland temple
109:5   Temple erected through great tribulation
  5   Son of Man to manifest himself in temple
124:26   Precious things to be brought for temple
  27   Build house for Most High to dwell in
  28   Temple needed to restore fullness of Priesthood
  29   Baptism for dead to be performed in temple
  33   Temples instituted before foundation of world
  34   Keys of Priesthood ordained in temples
  37   Washings acceptable only in temple
  38   Moses' tabernacle built for temple ordinances
  39   Anointings, washings ordained by ordinance of temples
  40   Ordinances to be revealed in temples
  42   Priesthood to be shown to Joseph in temple
  47   If temple is built, ordinances must be performed in it
  51   Attempt to build temple accepted when hindered by enemies
  51   Jackson County temple not built but offering accepted
127:4   Work of my temple to be carried on
  9   Records to be put in archives in my holy temple
128:12   Baptism for dead in temple similitude of grave
  15   Temple ordinances essential to salvation of fathers
133:2   Lord shall suddenly come to His temple

References on Temple Work

(Exclusively from Utah Genealogical Magazine)

REFERENCES ON TEMPLES AND TEMPLE WORK
(From Improvement Era)

References on Translation of Book of Abraham
From Improvement Era, except (A) and (B)

Joseph Smith, Jr., As a Translator, by Rev. F. S. Spalding, D. D. (A)

The Book of Abraham, by Elder George Reynolds (B)

Condensed Basic Research Bibliography
"Baptism for the Dead"
By Ariel L. Crowley

The following bibliography, while not in any way exhaustive, is deemed substantially indicative of the primary sources of information on the historicity, degeneration and loss from the faith of the pristine doctrine of baptism for the dead, from the apostolic times to the middle ages. (Note: Abbreviations used below: With Bk. (Book) "c." indicates "chapter," otherwise it indicates "canon"; "v" indicates "verse"; "p." indicates "page"; "ch." indicates "Chapter"; "Ed." indicates "edition"; "e." indicates "epistle"; "pt." indicates "part". Citations 1:23:14 indicates Book, Chapter and Verse.)

ABOLITION OF ORDINANCES: Mant's Ed. (1822) Book of Common Prayer, p. xxviii.

ANCIENT AUTHORITIES AND SOURCE REFERENCES, ON BAPTISM FOR THE DEAD:
    Apocrypha: 2 Maccabees 12:43-46.
    Catholic Ency., Vol. II, p. 271.
    Boniface of Maintz, c. 20.
    Clement of Alexandria: Misc. Bk. 2, ch. 9.
    Cerinthus: See Epiph. Haer, ch. 28; Dummeloy Bible Comm. 771ff.
    Chrysostom of Constantinople, See 1 Smith Dict. 242.
    Cyprian, Ep. 66, p. 114 (Ed. Bened.)
    Councils and Synods of the Ancient Church. (See also Hefele, infra.)

Council at Hippi in Africa (393 A. D.) c. 4 and 32 in Second Series.
Third Council at Carthage (397 A. D.) c. 6.
Fourth Council at Carthage (398 A. D.) c. 79 and 95.
Synod at Orange (411 A. D.) c. 13.
Sixteenth Council at Carthage (418 A. D.) c. 3.
Synod at Vaison (443 A. D.) c. 2.
Synod at Arles (443 A. D.) c. 11.
Council at Auxerre (578 A. D.) c. 12.
Council of Trullo at Constantinople (A. D. 692) c. 83.

Epiphanius; haer, 27:3, 28.
Eusebius: H. E. Bk. 5, ch. 1; 4 ch. 22.
Emik: 17 Ency. Brit. (11) 692; Hastings Ency. R. & E. p. 388.
Five Books against Marcion (Anon.) Bk. 3, v. 385.
Gospel of Nicodemus 21:1-5; Second Gospel of Nicodemus c. 27.
Gregory Nazianzum, c. 40.
Hefele of Rottenburg: See H. of Councils, Oxenham.
Hermas (Rom. 16:14): Ninth Similitude.
Irenaeus: Adv. Haer. I, 26:1; e.: 2; I, 14:4.
Jewish Ency. Vol. 2, p. 499.
Marcion: See Tertullian, de Res. ch. 48; Adv. Mar. 1:9, 5:10; Schaff-Herzog Rel. Ency. Vol.
    8, p. 172; Fisher Hist. of Church 77; Smith, Sm. Dict. 242; Ency. Brit. (11) "Marcion."
Marcus: II Myth. of all Races 409.
Philastrius of Bracia: De Haer. ch. 2.
Talmud: Tan. Mezora, 6, ed. Buber, p. 46.
Westcott: Canon of N. T. Pt. 1, ch. 2, p. 194ff.

APOSTASY OF ANCIENT CHURCH: Book of Homilies of C. of E. "Perils of Idolatry." p. 3.

COMMENTARIES ON I COR. 15:29 CONCURRING.
Catholic: Catholic Ency. Vol. 4, p. 654.
Episcopal: Henry Alford, N. T. for Eng. Readers, ad. loc. Charles Gore, New Comm. on
    the Script p. 511.
Syriac: Murdock, marginal not, Trans. of Pesh. Version, on "hyper."
Unitarian: Thomas Rees, Int. Stand. Bible Ency. "Dead."
United Free Church: James Hastings, Ency. of R. and E., Vol. 2, p. 382 seq.

CONFUSION FROM LOSS OF MEANING:
Wisdom of Guatama: Chinese Trans. of Darmaraksha, record of Asvagahsha Bodhisattva,
    12th Buddhist Patriarch.

DEGENERACY AND LOSS OF DOCTRINES:
Milner: Church Hist. p. 817.
Pike: Irano-Aryan Faith, p. 100.
Osiris and the Egypt Res. Vol. II, p. 219.

MISCELLANEOUS:
Roberts: The Gospel, on I Cor. 15:29.
Talmage, James E.: House of the Lord, p. 92.
Times and Seasons: Quoted Hist. of Church, Vol. 4, 597.

MYTHOLOGY:
III Myth. of all Races, 253ff.

OUR DEBT TO THE DEAD:
Catholic: Cardinal Manning, Ridpath Lib. of Un. Lit. Vol. 1, p. 171.

VICARIOUS WORKS PARALLELING PROXY BAPTISMS:
Tibulus: I:1:43 on Cybele.
Lucian: Cyprian Priests.
Pope: Iliad 1:23-142 et seq.
Virgil: Aeneid 1:4:698 (Dryden).
Mariner: Tongan Islands.
Calmet: Lev. 19:28.

Ancient Temples in the Western Hemisphere

(References refer entirely to Volumes of the National Geographic Magazine.)

EXCAVATIONS AT QUIRIGUA, GUATEMALA. By Sylvanus Griswold Morley. Vol. 24, March, 1913.

MYSTERIOUS TEMPLES OF THE JUNGLES. The Prehistoric Ruins of Guatemala. By W. F. Sands. Vol. 24, March, 1913.

IN THE WONDERLAND OF PERU. The work accomplished by the Peruvian Expedition of 1912, under the auspices of Yale University and the National Geographic Society. By Hiram Bingham, Director of Expedition. Vol. 24, April, 1913.

THE HOME OF A FORGOTTEN RACE. Mysterious Chichen Itza, in Yucatan, Mexico. By Edward H. Thompson. Vol. 25, June, 1914.

FURTHER EXPLORATIONS IN THE LAND OF THE INCAS. The Peruvian Expedition of 1915 of the National Geographic Society and Yale University. By Hiram Bingham, Director of Expedition. Vol. 29, May, 1916.

STAIRCASE FARMS OF THE ANCIENTS. Astounding Farming Skill of Ancient Peruvians, Who Were Probably the Most Industrious and Highly Organized People in History. By O. F. Cook. Vol. 29, May, 1916.

SHATTERED CAPITALS OF CENTRAL AMERICA. By Herbert J. Spinder. Vol. 35, September, 1919.

ALONG OUR SIDE OF THE MEXICAN BORDER. By Frederick Simpich. Vol. 38, July, 1920.

RUINS OF CHACO CANYON, NEW MEXICO, Nature-Made Treasure-Chest of Aboriginal American History. Vol. 39, June, 1921.

THE FOREMOST INTELLECTUAL ACHIEVEMENTS OF ANCIENT AMERICA. The Hieroglyphic Inscriptions on the Monuments in the Ruined Cities of Mexico, Guatemala, and Honduras are Yielding the Secrets of the Maya Civilization. By Sylvanus Griswold Morley. Vol. 41, February, 1922.

THE PUEBLO BONITO EXPEDITION OF THE NATIONAL GEOGRAPHIC SOCIETY. By Neil M. Judd. Vol. 41, March, 1922.

PUEBLO BONITO, THE ANCIENT. The National Geographic Society's Third Expedition to the Southwest Seeks to Read in the Rings of Trees the Secret of the Age of Ruins. By Neil M. Judd. Vol. 44, July, 1923.

RUINS OF CUICUILCO MAY REVOLUTIONIZE OUR HISTORY OF ANCIENT AMERICA. Lofty Mound Sealed and Preserved by Great Lava Flow for Perhaps Seventy Centuries is Now Being Excavated in Mexico. By Byron Cummings. Vol. 44, August, 1923.

DISCOVERING THE OLDEST STATUES IN THE WORLD. A Daring Explorer Swims Through a Subterraneon River of the Pyrenees and Finds Rock Carvings Made 20,000 Years Ago. By Norbert Casteret. Vol. 46, Aug., 1924.

CHICHEN ITZA, AN ANCIENT AMERICAN MECCA. Recent Excavations in Yucatan are Bringing to Light the Temples, Palaces and Pyramids of America's Most Holy Native City. By Sylvanus Griswold Morley. Vol. 47, Jan., 1925.

EVERYDAY LIFE IN PUEBLO BONITO. As Disclosed by the National Geographic's Archeologic Exploration of the Chaco Canyon National Monument, New Mexico. By Neil M. Judd. Vol. 48, Sept., 1925.

EXPLORING IN THE CANYON OF DEATH. Remains of a People Who Dwelt in Our Southwest at Least 4,000 Years are Revealed. By Earl H. Morris. Vol. 48, Sept., 1925.

GUATEMALA: LAND OF VOLCANOES AND PROGRESS. Cradle of Ancient Mayan Civilization, Redolent With Its Later Spanish and Indian Ways, Now Reaping Prosperity from Bananas and Coffee. By Thomas F. Lee. Vol. 50, November, 1926.

ARCHAEOLOGY, THE MIRROR OF THE AGES. Our Debt to the Humble Delvers in the Ruins at Carchmish and Ur. By Leonard Woolley. Vol. 54, August, 1928.

THE SECRET OF THE SOUTHWEST SOLVED BY TALKATIVE TREE RINGS. Horizons of American History are Carried Back to A. D. 700 and a Calendar for 1,200 Years Established by National Geographic Society Expeditions. By Andrew Elliott Douglas. Vol. 56, December, 1929.

NORTH AMERICA'S OLDEST METROPOLIS. Through 600 Melodramatic Years, Mexico City has Grown in Splendor and Achievement. By Frederick Simpich. Vol. 58, July, 1930.

UNEARTHING AMERICA'S ANCIENT HISTORY. Investigations Suggest that the Maya May Have Designed the First Astronomical Observatory in the New World in Order to Cultivate Corn. By Sylvanus Griswold Morley. Vol. 60, July, 1931.

MONTE ALBAN, RICHEST ARCHAEOLOGICAL FIND IN AMERICA. A Tomb in Oaxaca, Mexico, Yields Treasures Which Reveal the Splendid Culture of the Mixtecs. By Alfonso Caso. Vol. 62, October, 1932.

AIR ADVENTURES IN PERU. Cruising Among Andean Peaks, Pilots and Cameramen Discover Wondrous Works of an Ancient People. By Robert Shippee. Vol. 63, January, 1933.

PRESERVING ANCIENT AMERICA'S FINEST SCULPTURES. By J. Alden Mason. Vol. 68, November, 1935.

AMERICA'S FIRST SETTLERS, THE INDIANS. By Matthew W. Stirling. Vol. 72, November, 1937.

YUCATAN, HOME OF THE GIFTED MAYA. Two Thousand Years Ago of History Reach Back to Early American Temple Buildings, Corn Cultivators, and Pioneers in Mathematics. By Sylvanus Griswold Morley. Vol. 70, November, 1936.

THE INCAS: EMPIRE BUILDERS OF THE ANDES. By Philip Ainsworth Means. Vol. 73, February, 1938.

DISCOVERING THE NEW WORLD'S OLDEST DATED WORKS OF MAN. A Maya Monument Inscribed 291 B.C. Is Unearthed Near a Huge Stone Head by a Geographic-Smithsonian Expedition in Mexico. By Matthew W. Stirling. Vol. 76, August, 1939.

STONE IDOLS OF THE ANDES REVEAL A VANISHED PEOPLE. Remarkable Relics of One of the Oldest Aboriginal Cultures of America are Unearthed in Colombia's San Agustin Region. By Hermann von Walde-Waldegg. Vol. 77, May, 1940.

GREAT STONE FACES OF THE MEXICAN JUNGLE. Five Colossal Heads and Numerous Other Monuments of Vanished Americans are Excavated by the Latest National Geographic-Smithsonian Expedition. By Matthew W. Stirling. Vol. 78, September, 1940.

A FORGOTTEN VALLEY OF PERU. Conquered by Incas, Scourged by Famine, Plagues, and Earthquakes, Colca Valley Shelters the Last Fragment of an Ancient Andean Tribe. By Robert Shippe. Vol. 65, No. 1, January, 1934.

A NEW ALPHABET OF THE ANCIENTS IS UNEARTHED. An Inconspicuous Mound in Northern Syria Yields Archeological Treasures of Far-reaching Significance. By A. F. Schaeffer. Vol. 58, No. 4, October, 1930.

THE LUSTER OF ANCIENT MEXICO. Abstract from "History of the Conquest ot Mexico," by William H. Prescott, Vol. 30, No. 1, July, 1916.

PETRA, ANCIENT CARAVAN STRONGHOLD. Mysterious Temples and Tombs Carved in Glowing Cliffs and Eroded Sandstone, are Remnants of City David Longed to Storm. By John D. Whiting. Vol. 67, No. 2, February, 1935.

GUATEMALA INTERLUDE. In the Land of the Quetzal a Modern Capital Contrasts with Primitive Indian Villages and the "Pompeii of America." By E. John Long. Vol. 70, No. 4, October, 1936.

NOTE: The National Geographic Magazine informed the Compiler of this book that photographs of ancient ruins and temples may be secured from: The Carnegie Institution of Washington, D. C.; Ewing Galloway, 420 Lexington Ave., New York City; and from New York Times Wide World Photos, 229 West 43rd Street, New York City.

Partial List of References on the Pre-mortal, Mortal and Post-mortal Existence and Intelligence of the Spirit

By Bion Tolman, Salt Lake City, Utah

Pre-mortal or Pre-existence of the Spirit:

(a) Our Father which art in Heaven ....Matt. 6-9
(b) For as much then as we are the offspring of God ....Acts 17:28-9
(c) Shall we not much rather be in subjection to the Father
    of our spirits and live? ....Heb. 12:9
(d) Which was the son of Adam, which was the son of God ....Luke 3:38
(e) When the foundations of the earth were laid, all the sons of
    God shouted for joy ....Job 38:3, 7
(f) Before thou camest forth from the womb, I sanctified thee
    and ordained thee to be a prophet ....Jer. 1:5
(g) Chosen before the foundations of the world ....Eph. 1:4, 5
(h) Hath determined the times before appointed, and the bounds
    of their habitation ....Acts 17:26
(i) Michael and his Angels fought, and Satan was cast out into the
    earth and his angels were cast out with him ....Rev. 12:7-9
(j) Master who did sin this man or his parents ....John 9:1-3

NOTE—We were all born spirit children to God (a) (b) (c) (d); these spirits could comprehend the events taking place and shouted for joy when the earth was created (e); they were all known to God and the great ones were chosen and set apart for missions (f); we were not only chosen by the Lord before the foundations of the earth were laid, but the time of earth life was set and the bounds of the habitations of the nations were before appointed (g) (h); we had the power of choice and could obey or disobey law (i) (j); in short—we were living, thinking, acting entities.

The Spirit a Living, Thinking, Intelligent Entity While in the Body:

(a) Why is thy spirit so sad that thou canst eat no bread ....I Kings 21:5
(b) Better is a handful with quietness than both hands full with
    travail and vexation of spirit ....Eccles. 4:6
(c) Now while Paul waited in Athens his spirit stirred within him ....Acts 17:16
(d) And my spirit has rejoiced in God my Savior ....Luke 1:47
(e) And the child grew and waxed strong in spirit ....Luke 1:80
(f) The spirit is willing; but the flesh is weak ....Matt. 26:48
(g) The spirit itself beareth witness with our spirit ....Rom. 8:16

NOTE—From the above the spirit may be sad (a); may be vexed (b); may be stirred (c); may rejoice (d); may be strong (e); may strive independently of the flesh (f); and may receive a witness of the truth (g); hence its intelligent existence while in the body.

When the Spirit Leaves the Body, the Body Dies—Death is the Separation of Body and Spirit:

(a) Father, into Thy hands I commend my spirit ....Luke 23:46

(b) Lord Jesus receive my spirit . . . and he fell asleep ....Acts 7:59, 60

(c) And when Jacob had made an end of commanding his sons . . .
he yielded up the ghost and was gathered to his fathers ....Gen. 49:33

(d) And Ananias hearing these words fell down and gave up the ghost ....Acts 5:5

(e) Yielded up the Ghost . . . and they found her dead ....Acts 5:10

(f) For as the body without the spirit is dead ....James 2:26

After Leaving the Body, the Spirit is Active and Intelligent:

(a) And the disciples saw him walking on the sea and they were
troubled, saying it is a spirit ....Matt. 14:26

(b) But they were terrified and affrighted, and supposed they
had seen a spirit ....Luke 24:37

(c) A spirit hath not flesh and bones as ye see me have ....Luke 24:39

(d) Then a spirit passed before my face ....Job 4:14, 15

(e) And I knew a man, whether in the body or out of the body
I cannot tell ....II Cor. 12:2-4

(f) And behold there talked with him two men—Moses and Elias ....Luke 9:30

(g) But quickened in the spirit by which also he went and preached
to the spirits in prison ....I Peter 3:18-19

(h) Gospel preached to the dead, that they might be judged according to men
in the flesh, but live according to God in the spirit ....I Peter 4:6

(i) Today thou shalt be with me in paradise ....Luke 23:43

(j) If in this life only we have hope in Christ, we are of all men
most miserable ....I Cor. 15:29

(k) Marvel not at this for the hour is coming when all that are
in the grave shall hear my voice ....John 5:25:28

(l) He that believeth in me though he were dead yet shall he live ....John 11:25

(m) Every knee shall bow, and every tongue confess ....Phil. 2:11

(n) What shall they do which are baptized for the dead, if the dead rise not ......I Cor. 15:29

NOTE—The spirit not only exists but it can be seen (a) (b); the Savior did not say it was impossible to see a spirit (c); if a spirit does not exist it could not have passed before Job (d); a spirit may be known and instructed out of the body (e); Moses had died (Deut. 34:4-6), his spirit appeared to Christ and the disciples before its resurrection, hence its existence before that event (f); the disembodied spirits of people who lived in Noah's day were shut up in prison, the spirit of Christ visited them and preached to them, hence they not only lived but were capable of hearing and comprehending him (g); the spirit can and does live in the spirit world, and is capable of accepting truth so that it may be judged by it (h); if the spirit did not exist after death it would be impossible for it to exist in paradise or anywhere else (i); if the spirit does not exist it could not exercise hope and could not be miserable or happy (j); if spirits shall hear his voice, they have organs with which to hear, and intelligence with which to comprehend, hence they exist and live (k); a spirit can believe whether in or out of the body (l); every tongue and every knee must include all mankind both living and dead or why the word *every* (m); the dead existed according to Paul's view or else why be baptized for a non-entity, a non-existent thing, a mere definition of nothing (n).

Objections Raised Against the Independent, Thinking Existence of the Spirit after Death:

(a) And his very thoughts perish ....Psalms 146:3-4

(b) Dead know anything—no wisdom, or knowledge, or learning in the grave ....Eccles. 9:3-10

Explanation of Objections:

(a) All passages such as the one quoted from the 146th Psalm merely emphasize the fact that "It is better to trust in the Lord, than to put confidence in man." ....Psalms 118:8

(b) Ecclesiastes was written or given as a sermon by Solomon ....Eccles. 1:1-2

Solomon points out both truth and error as taught among the people of his day. He notes that most of the things done and taught under the sun or in the world, was of an evil nature, and caused vexation of spirit. Many of the false doctrines taught were responsible for the evils that existed. The following scriptures show that Solomon was pointing out many of the evils:

1. All works under the sun is vanity and vexation of spirit ....Eccles. 1:14

2. Wickedness in the place of judgment under the sun ....Eccles. 3:16

3. No more remembrance of the wise than of the fool ....Eccles. 2:16-21

4. Sore evil that man goes out of this life as he came in ....Eccles. 5:16

5. Vanity to teach that a wicked man receiveth the same as righteous man ....Eccles. 8:14-15

6. Further evil pointed out, that there is one event happeneth to all and the dead know not anything, and that in the grave there is no wisdom, or knowledge or learning ....Eccles. 9:1-10

In contrast to the above evils, Solomon points out many truths. (See Eccles. 3:1-15; 9:11-18; and chapters 7, 10 and 11.)

NOTE—Solomon throughout condemns the doctrine that one event happeneth to all and that in all ways as a man came into the world so shall he go, and that the wise and righteous man would have no more profit than the wicked. It was belief in the unconscious condition of the dead that caused the people of Solomon's time to accept as a way of life, "Eat, drink and be merry for tomorrow we die." But Solomon pointed out that God would bring all men to judgment.

Objections Raised Against the Gospel Being Preached to the Dead:

(a) Shall thy loving kindness or thy truth be declared in the grave? ....Psalms 30:9; 6:5

(b) They that go down to the pit cannot hope for thy truth ....Isaiah 38:18

(c) A great gulf separates the righteous and the wicked, and the righteous cannot visit the wicked to declare the Gospel ....Luke 16:19-31

Explanation of Objections:

(a) and (b). Those who were destroyed by the Flood and went down to the pit or prison were without hope of receiving the truth. So likewise was the condition of all other wicked before Christ fulfilled his mission. They were separated from the righteous by a great gulf, and by prison doors.

(c) However, part of Christ's mission was to bridge the gulf, and to open the prison doors, that the prisoners might come out of the prison house. (See: Isaiah 42:6, 7; 62:1, and John 5:25-28.) That Christ did fulfill this part of His mission is attested in I Peter 3:18-20 and 4:6. It was Christ who brought the hope and opened the way for the truth to be preached to the dead.

Miscellaneous Works Recommended

The Progress of Man, by Joseph Fielding Smith.

The Way to Perfection, by Joseph Fielding Smith.

Teachings of the Prophet Joseph Smith, by Joseph Fielding Smith.

Junior and Senior Manuals, by The Genealogical Society of Utah.

The Great Temple, by Duncan M. McAllister.

The House of the Lord, by James E. Talmage.

Temples: Ancient and Modern, by J. M. Sjodahl.

The Vision, by N. B. Lundwall.

Mormonism and Masonry, by E. Cecil McGavin.

Documentary History of the Church, Vol. 7.

Doctrine and Covenants, Sections 128, 132.

President David O. McKay

President David O. McKay is one of the most effective missionaries the Church has ever had. His knowledge of the Gospel, his sincerity, his courage to stand for his beliefs, his sympathetic understanding of people and their problems, his keen sense of humor, his charming personality, his exemplary life, his noble appearance, and his humility appeal alike to the great ones of the earth and to the lowly ones. Some of his undertakings are: His world-wide tour of the missions of the Church in 1920-21, in which he and his companion, Elder Hugh J. Cannon, brought unspeakable joy to many who had never before met an Apostle, was an outstanding experience; his presidency of the European mission; the Temples dedicated by him have afforded wonderful opportunities for missionary work, especially among local and national government officials; the many chapels dedicated by him and his many duties and responsibilities as President of the Church — all of these demonstrate his wonderful capacity to do good by precept and by example as a true servant of God.

ADDENDA

The Key to Successful Temple Work

Another interesting feature of the conference (August 16, 1841. See Millennial Star, Vol. 18:630) was the report made by the Prophet, of the Church property in his charge as Trustee-in-Trust for the Church. He also took occasion to report the amount of his own earthly possessions, of which the following is a copy:

"Old Charley, a horse given to him several years before in Kirtland; two pet deers; two old turkeys and four young ones; an old cow given to him by a brother in Missouri; old Major, a dog; his wife, children, and a little household furniture."*

The greatest benefactor to the human race, the Redeemer of the world, stated of his possessions: "The foxes have holes and the birds of the air have nests, but the Son of Man hath nowhere to lay His head."

Other great characters, such as Adam, Abraham, Enoch, Alma, Moses, John The Baptist, the Apostles of the eastern, western, and those contemporary with the Prophet Joseph, and many other great spiritual leaders, have had but meagre worldly possessions, but their works and names will live forever. Alma, the great Nephite Prophet, when going through the land preaching the gospel, being spit upon, imprisoned, persecuted, "wading through much tribulation," came to the door of a home and said: "Will you give a humble servant of God something to eat?" (Alma 8:10-19.) Physical wealth and spiritual wealth are not twin companions. As a rule, spirituality decreases as wealth increases. The lust for the things of the world at the present time, for stocks and bonds, for bank accounts, for mortgages, for the empty praise of the world, is the reason why a larger degree of spirituality is not enjoyed among those professing to be Saints.

"We ought to care no more for the silver and the gold, and the property that is so much sought for by the wicked world, than for the soil, or the gravel upon which we tread: 'For all that is in the world, the lust of the flesh, and the lust of the eyes, and the pride of life, is not of the Father, but is of the world, and the

---

*Rise and Fall of Nauvoo, by B. H. Roberts, p. 111.

world passeth away, and the lust thereof; but he that doeth the will of God abideth forever.' 'If any man love the world, the love of the Father is not in him.' * * * Ye merchants, and lawyers, and doctors and speculators, be careful that you secure to yourselves eternal life in the kingdom of God in preference to doing anything else. That perfect union, which must ultimately be enjoyed by the Latter-day Saints, can only be brought about by every man and woman living so as to keep their minds pure and unspotted like a piece of clean white paper, being constantly free from the love of the world, that the spirit of revelation, may easily indite upon the heart whatever is the mind and the will of the Lord. We cannot be truly the members of Christ's mystical body without living in this way, that the Spirit may indite as easily upon the heart the things of God, as these brethren, our reporters, can write with ink on paper. In this way you have the witness within yourself, 'and need that no man teach you only as the same anointing teacheth you of all things, and is truth, and is no lie, and even as it hath taught you, ye shall abide in him.' "

Brigham Young, J. D., 11:19.

Benevolence and Justice of God

By Brigham Young

The punishment of God is God-like. It endures forever, because there never will be a time when people ought not to be damned, and there must always be a hell to send them to. How long the damned remain in hell, I know not, nor what degree of suffering they endure. If we could by any means compute how much wickedness they are guilty of, it might be possible to ascertain the amount of suffering they will receive. They will receive according as their deeds have been while in the body. God's punishment is eternal, but that does not prove that a wicked person will remain eternally in a state of punishment.

All the doctrines of life and salvation are as plain to the understanding as the geographical lines of a correctly executed map. This doctrine, revealed in these latter times, is worthy of the attention of all men. It gives the positive situation in which they will stand before the Heavens when they have finished their earthly career. Generation after generation is constantly coming and passing away. They all possess more or less intelligence, which forms the foundation within them for the reception of an eternal increase of intelligence. The endowments that human beings have received from their Great Creator are to them inestimable blessings. How wonderful and how excellent they are! What priceless blessings and exquisite enjoyments they secure to man, if by truth and righteousness they are made honorable in the sight of God. By the means of his wonderful and God-like endowments, man can drink at the fountain of eternal wisdom and bask in everlasting felicity.

But hundreds of millions of human beings have been born, lived out their short earthly span, and passed away, ignorant alike of themselves and of the plan of salvation provided for them. It gives great consolation, however, to know that this glorious plan, devised by Heaven, follows them into the next existence, offering for their acceptance eternal life and exaltation to thrones, dominions, principalities, and powers in the presence of their Father and God, through Jesus Christ his Son. How glorious—how ample is the Gospel plan in its saving properties and merciful designs. This one revelation, containing this principle, is worth world on worlds to mankind. It is worth forsaking fathers, mothers, sisters and brothers, wives and children, houses and lands, for the knowledge it reveals; and this is but one item in the great plan of human redemption. * * *

Can you tell me how much better "Mormonism" is than other religions and isms of the present day? More or less truth may be found in them all, both in civilized and barbarous nations. How has it transpired that the logical truth is thus so widely disseminated? It is because God was once known on the earth among his children of mankind, as we know one another. Adam was as conversant with his Father who placed him upon this earth as we are conversant with our earthly parents. The Father frequently came to visit his son Adam, and talked and walked with him; and the children of Adam were more or less acquainted with their Grandfather, and their children were more or less acquainted with their Great-Grandfather; and things that pertain to God and to heaven were as familiar among mankind, in the first ages of their existence on the earth, as these mountains are to our mountain boys, as our gardens are to our wives and children, or as the road to the Western Ocean is to the experienced traveler. From this source mankind have received their religious traditions.

I will tell you in a few words what I understand "Mormonism" to be. Our religion is called "Mormonism" because the ancient records revealed to Joseph Smith were entitled the Book of Mormon, according to the instructions given to him by the Lord; but I will call it the plan of salvation devised in the heavens for the redemption of mankind from sin, and their restoration to the presence of God. It is contained in the New Testament, Book of Mormon, Book of Doctrine and Covenants, and in all the revelations that God has hitherto given, and will give in the future.

It embraces every fact there is in the heavens and in the heaven of heavens—every fact there is upon the surface of the earth, in the bowels of the earth, and in the starry heavens; in fine, it embraces all truth there is in all the eternities of the Gods. How, then, can we deny it? We cannot. Were we arraigned face to face with the terrors of death, and called upon to deny our religion or die, we might speak a lie and say "Mormonism" is untrue, and might continue the same testimony all the time we were in hell; but that would make no difference with the truth. The devils and damned spirits in hell cannot deny the truth of "Mormonism" and speak the truth. I wish all those who profess to believe it did as much as the devils in hell do.

"Mormonism" embraces all truth that is revealed and that is unrevealed, whether religious, political, scientific, or philosophical. No matter how many deny their God and their religion, God is the same, His holy religion is the same, and all the truth is the same. There is no plan, no device, no possible way in which we can get rid of "Mormonism," only by taking the downward road which leads to hell, until spiritually and temporally the whole organized being is dissolved and the particles thereof have returned again to native elements. We read in the Scriptures of the second death not having power over certain ones. The first death is the separation of the spirit from the body; the second death is, as I stated, the dissolution of the organized particles which compose the spirit, and their return to their native element. The wicked spirit will have to endure the wrath of the Almighty, until it has paid the uttermost farthing where the "worm dieth not and the fire is not quenched." Every debt that has been contracted by it must be cancelled.   J. D., Vol. 9:147-9.

A Truism Eternities Old

By Brigham Young

The Latter-day Saints who turn their attention to money-making soon become cold in their feeling toward the ordinances of the house of God. They neglect their prayers, become unwilling to pay any donations; the law of Tithing gets too great a task for them; and they finally forsake their God, and the providences of heaven seem to be shut out from them—all in consequence of this lust after the things of this world, which will certainly perish in handling, and in their use they will fade away and go from us.

How vain it is in man to allow himself to think that he can make himself happy with the pleasures of this world. There is no lasting pleasure here, unless it is in God. * * *

When men leave the kingdom of God, their lives are filled with bitterness, their thoughts are full of fearfulness, and they are sorrowful, day by day. They may tell you they are happy; but when you probe them, and find out the innermost recesses of the heart, it is a cup of gall; they are not happy. They may seek, to the uttermost parts of the earth, for happiness, but they find it not. Where is happiness, real happiness? Nowhere but in God. By possessing the spirit of our holy religion, we are happy in the morning; we are happy at noon; we are happy in the evening; for the spirit of love and union is with us, and we rejoice in the spirit because it is of God, and we rejoice in God, for He is the giver of every good thing. Each and every Latter-day Saint, who has experienced the love of God in his heart, after having received the remission of his sins, through baptism, and the laying on of hands, realizes that he is filled with joy, and happiness, and consolation. He may be in pain, in error, in poverty, or in prison, if necessity demands, still, he is joyful. This is our experience, and each and every Latter-day Saint can bear witness to it.   J. D., Vol. 18:213-4

Why the Redeemer Sweat Blood

I ask, is there a reason for men and women being exposed more constantly and more powerfully to the power of the enemy by having visions than by not having them? There is and it is simply this—God never bestows upon His people, or upon an individual, superior blessings without a severe trial to prove them, to prove that individual or that people, to see whether they will keep their covenants with Him and keep in remembrance what He has shown them. Then the greater the vision, the greater the display of the power of the enemy. And when such individuals are off their guard they are left to themselves as Jesus was. For this express purpose the Father withdrew His spirit from His Son, at the time He was to be crucified. Jesus had been with His Father, talked with Him, dwelt in His bosom, and knew all about heaven, about making the earth, about the transgression of men, and what would redeem the people, and that He was the character who was to redeem the sons of earth, and the earth itself from all sin that had come upon it. The light, knowledge, power and glory with which He was clothed were far above or exceeded that of all others who had been upon the earth after the fall, consequently at the very moment, at the hour when the crises came for Him to offer up His life, the Father withdrew Himself, withdrew His spirit, and cast a veil over Him. That is what made Him sweat blood. If He had had the power of God upon Him, He would not have sweat blood; but all was withdrawn from Him, and a veil was cast over Him. And He then plead with the Father not to forsake Him. "No," says the Father, "You must have your trials as well as others."

So when individuals are blessed with visions, revelations and great manifestations, look out, then the devil is nigh you and you will be tempted in proportion to the vision, revelation or manifestation you have received. Hence thousands when they are off their guard give way to the severe temptations which come upon them and behold they are gone. Brigham Young, J. D., Vol. 3:205-6.

Death-Bed Repentance and Immediate Exaltation a Heresy

By Pres. Joseph F. Smith

We have a few people amongst us who are so wrapped up in and devoted to some of their kindred who have been guilty of every species of abomination and wickedness in the world, that, the moment they are dead they will come and ask us for permission to go into the house of God to perform the ordinances of the Gospel for their redemption. I do not blame them for their affection for their dead, nor do I blame them for the desire in their heart to do something for their salvation, but I do not admire their wisdom, nor can I agree with their conception of right and justice. You cannot take a murderer, a suicide, an adulterer, a liar, or one who was or is thoroughly abominable in his life here, and simply by the performance of an ordinance of the Gospel, cleanse him from sin and usher him into the presence of God. God has not instituted a plan of that kind, and it cannot be done. He said you shall repent of your sins. The wicked will have to repent of their wickedness. Those who die without the knowledge of the Gospel will have to come to the knowledge of it, and those who sin against light will have to pay the uttermost farthing for their transgression and their departure from the Gospel, before they can ever get back to it. Do not forget that. Do not forget it, you Elders in Israel, nor you, mothers in Israel either, and, when you seek to save either the living or the dead, bear it in mind that you can only do it on the principle of their repentance, and acceptance of the plan of life. That is the only way in which you can succeed.

General Conference Report, Oct. 4, 1907, pp. 6-7.

Angelic Beings Sanctified Through Suffering

By Brigham Young

With regard to the obedience of heavenly beings, to which reference has been made today: they live pure and holy, and they have attained unto this power through suffering. Many of them have drunk of the bitter cup even to the dregs. They have learned that righteousness will prevail, that truth is the foundation of their very existence. They have learned that their Father and God never commits an evil, that He never proposes an evil, and that whatever He dictates is for their good. When an angel is appointed to perform a duty, to go to the earth to preach the Gospel, or to do anything for the advancement of his Father's kingdom in any part of the great domain of heaven, the vision of that angel is opened to see and understand the magnitude of the work that is expected of him to perform, and the grand results which will grow out of it. That is the reason why the angels are of one heart and of one mind, in their faithfulness and obedience to the requirements of their Father and God. They can desire and ask for nothing that will make them happy, good and great that is withheld from them; and life eternal is theirs. Why, then, should they not be of one heart and of one mind? They see alike, understand alike, and know alike, and all things are before them, and, as far as their knowledge and experience extend, they see the propriety of all the works of God, and the harmony and beauty thereof.   J. D., Vol. 11:15.

Building of Temples Gives Increased Power and Protection

I fully believe that when that temple (Salt Lake Temple) is once finished there will be a power and manifestation of the goodness of God unto this people such as they have never before experienced. Every work of this kind that we have accomplished has been attended with increased and wonderful results unto us as a people—an increase of power and of God's blessings upon us. It was so in Kirtland and at Nauvoo; at both places the Elders had an increase of power, and the Saints, since the completion of, and the administration of ordinances in those buildings, have had a power they never possessed previously. * * *

Whence, I ask, my brethren and sisters, has this power come? Whence has it been derived? I attribute it to the blessings and the power and the authority and the keys which God gave unto His Saints, and which he commenced to give in the Temple at Nauvoo. The Elders of Israel there received keys, endowments and authority which they have not failed to exercise in times of extremity and danger; and clouds have been shattered and storms blown over, and peace and guidance, and all the blessings which have been desired have been bestowed upon the people, according to the faith that has been exercised. Others may attribute these things to other causes; but I attribute them to this, and I feel to give God the glory; and I trace these deliverances to the power that the Elders received in that temple and previously. I fully believe also, as I have said, that when this and other temples are completed, there will be an increase of power bestowed upon the people of God, and that they will, thereby, be better fitted to go forth and cope with the powers of darkness and with the evils that exist in the world and to establish the Zion of God never more to be thrown down.

George Q. Cannon, J. D., Vol. 14:125-6.

Temples to Be Erected In Zion and Jerusalem

For it is ordained that in *Zion and in her stakes*, and in *Jerusalem*, those places which I have appointed for refuge, shall be the places for your baptisms for your dead.

And again, verily I say unto you, how shall your washings be acceptable unto me, except ye perform them in a house which you have built to my name?

For, for this cause I commanded Moses that he should build a tabernacle, that they should bear it with them in the wilderness, and to build a house in the land of promise, that those ordinances might be revealed which had been hid from before the world was.

Therefore, verily, I say unto you, that your anointings, and your washings, and your baptisms for the dead, and your solemn assemblies, and your memorials for your sacrifices by the sons of Levi,[1] and for your oracles in your most holy places wherein you receive conversations, and your statues and judgments for the beginning of the revelations and foundation of Zion, and for the glory, honor, and endowment of all her municipals, are ordained by the ordinance of my holy house, which my people are always commanded to build unto my holy name.

D. & C., Sec. 124:36-39.

[1]It is very prevalent opinion that the sacrifices which were offered were entirely consumed. This was not the case; if you read Leviticus, second chapter, second and third verses, you will observe that the priests took a part as a memorial and offered it up before the Lord, while the remainder was kept for the maintenance of the priests; so that the offerings and sacrifices are not all consumed upon the altar—but the blood is sprinkled, and the fat and certain other portions are consumed.

These sacrifices, as well as every ordinance belonging to the Priesthood, will, when the Temple of the Lord shall be built, and the sons of Levi be purified, be fully restored and attended to in all their powers, ramifications and blessings. This ever did and ever will exist when the powers of the Melchizedek Priesthood are sufficiently manifest; else how can the restitution of all things spoken of by the holy Priesthood be brought to pass? It is not to be understood that the law of Moses will be established again with all its rites and variety of ceremonies; this has never been spoken of by the Prophets; but those things which existed prior to Moses' day, namely, sacrifice, will be continued.

It may be asked by some, what necessity for sacrifice, since the Great Sacrifice was offered? In answer to which, if repentance, baptism, and faith existed prior to the days of Christ, what necessity for them since that time? The Priesthood has descended in a regular line from father to son, through their succeeding generations.   Joseph the Prophet, D. H. C., Vol. 4, p. 211-2.

See also: Mediation and Atonement by John Taylor, pp. 119-123. Liahona, June 1, 1926, by Chas. W. Penrose.

The Path to Joy or Sorrow

By Brigham Young

No blessing that is sealed upon us will do us any good unless we live for it. Whereas, if we are faithful, there is nothing which is calculated to please the eye, to gladden the heart, to cheer and comfort the body and spirit of man, everything in the heavens, with the fulness of the earth, its pleasures and enjoyments, with perfect health, without pain, with appetites made pure, all this, and more that has not yet entered into the heart of man to conceive, the Lord has in store for His children. This earth, when it shall be made pure and holy, and sanctified and glorified and brought back into the presence of the Father and the Son, from whence it came at the time of the fall, will become celestial, and be the glorified habitation of the faithful of this portion of the great family of our Heavenly Father.

Abraham was faithful to the true God. He overthrew the idols of his father and obtained the Priesthood after the order of Melchizedek, which is after the order of the Son of God, and a promise that of the increase of his seed there should be no end. When you obtain the Holy Priesthood, which is after the order of Melchizedek, sealed upon you and the promise that your seed shall be numerous as the stars in the firmament, or as the sands upon the seashore, and of your increase there shall be no end, you have got the promise of Abraham, Isaac and Jacob, and all the blessings that were conferred upon them.

How many of the youth of our land are entitled to all the blessings of the kingdom of Heaven, without first receiving the law of adoption? When a man and woman have received their endowments and sealings, and then had children born to them afterwards, those children are legal heirs to the kingdom and to all its blessings and promises, and they are the only ones that are on this earth. There is not a young man in our community who would not be willing to travel from here to England to be married right, if he understood things as they are; there is not a young woman in our community, who loves the gospel and wishes its blessings, that would be married in any other way; they would live unmarried until they could be married as they should be, if they lived until they were as old as Sarah before she had Isaac born to her. Many of our brethren have married off their children without taking this into consideration, and thinking it a matter of little importance. I wish we all understood this in the light in which heaven understands it.

J. D., Vol. 11:117-18.

The Purpose of Marriage and the Destiny of Man
By Parley P. Pratt

The object of the union of the sexes is the propagation of their species, or procreation; also for mutual affection, and the cultivation of those eternal principles of never ending charity and benevolence, which are inspired by the Eternal Spirit; also for mutual comfort and assistance in this world of toil and sorrow, and for mutual duties towards their offspring.

"Marriage and its duties are therefore not a mere matter of choice or of convenience, or of pleasure to the parties, but to marry and multiply is a positive command of Almighty God, binding on all persons of both sexes who are circumstanced and conditioned to fulfill the same. To marry, propagate our species, do our duty to them, and to educate them in the light of truth, are among the chief objects of our existence on the earth. To neglect these duties is to fail to answer the end of our creation, and is a very great sin.

"While to pervert our natures, and to prostitute ourselves and our strength to mere pleasures, or to unlawful communion of the sexes, is alike subversive of health, of pure, holy and lasting affection, of moral and social order, and of the laws of God and nature.

"If we except murder, there is scarcely a more damning sin on the earth than the prostitution of female virtue or chastity at the shrine of pleasure or brutal lust, or that promiscuous and lawless intercourse which chills and corrodes the heart, perverts and destroys the pure affections, cankers and destroys, as it were, the well springs, the fountains or issues of life.

"A man who obeys the ordinances of God, and is without blemish or deformity, who has sound health and mature age, and enjoys liberty and access to the elements of life, is designed to be the head of a woman, a father, and a guide of the weaker sex and of those of tender age, to mansions of eternal life and salvation.

"A woman under similar circumstances is designed to be the glory of some man in the Lord, to be led and governed by him as her head in all things, even as Christ is the head of the man, to honor, obey, love, serve, comfort and help him in all things, to be a happy wife, and, if blessed with offspring, a faithful and affectionate mother, devoting her life to the joys, care and duties of her domestic sphere. * * *

"O candidates for celestial glory! Would your joys be full in the countless years of eternity without forming the connections, the relationship, the kindred ties which concentrate in the domestic circle, and branch forth, and bud and blossom, and bear the fruits of eternal increase?

"Would that eternal emotion of charity and benevolence which swells your bosoms be satisfied to enjoy 'in single blessedness,' without an increase of posterity, those exhaustless stores of never-ending riches and enjoyments? Or, would you, like your Heavenly Father, prompted by eternal benevolence and charity, wish to fill countless millions of worlds with your begotten sons and daughters, and to bring them through all the gradations of progressive being, to inherit immortal bodies and eternal mansions in your several dominions?

"If such be your aspirations, remember that this present probation is the world of preparation for joys eternal. This is the place where family organization is first formed for eternity, and where the kindred sympathies, relationships and affections take root, spring forth, shoot upward, bud, blossom and bear fruit to ripen and mature in eternal ages.

"Here, in the holy temples and sanctuaries of our God, must the everlasting covenants be revealed, ratified, sealed, bound, and recorded in the holy records, and guarded and preserved in the archives of God's Kingdom, by those who hold the keys of eternal apostleship, who have power to bind on earth that which shall be bound in heaven, and to record on earth that which shall be recorded in the archives of heaven, in the Lamb's book of life.

"Here, in the holy sanctuary, must be revealed, ordained and anointed the kings and queens of eternity.

"All vows, covenants, contracts, marriages, or unions, not formed by revelation, and sealed for time and all eternity, and recorded in the holy archives of earth and heaven, by the ministration of the holy and eternal Priesthood, will be dissolved by death, and will not be recognized by the eternal authorities, after the parties have entered through the vail into the eternal world.

"This is heaven's eternal law, as revealed to the ancients of all ages, who held the keys of eternal Priesthood, after the order of the Son of God, and as restored with the Priesthood to the Saints of this age."

Key to Theology, pp. 151-6, Ed. 1883.

The Path to Exaltation

I say, all the revelations of God teach simply this—son, daughter, you are the workmanship of mine hands: walk and live before me in righteousness, let your conversations be chaste; let your daily deportment be according to my law; let your dealings one with another be in justice and equity; let my character be sacred in your mouth and do not profane my holy name and trample upon mine authority; do not despise any of my sayings for I will not be disgraced. I wish to send one of my servants to visit you. What for? That you may see and know as others have —that you may see as you are seen—that you may understand those principles pertaining more particularly to the kingdom you are in. You have descended below all things. I have, in my wisdom, reduced you; I have caused that you should drink of the dregs of the bitter cup. I have placed you in the depths of ignorandce and have surrounded you with weakness, to prove you. I have subjected you to all misery that can be endured. I have caused you to come upon this earth where misery and darkness and every species of unbelief and wickedness reign to prove you, that you may understand and know the good from evil and be capable of judging between these with a righteous judgment. I have caused all this to be done; and now, son and daughter, the inhabitants of the whole earth that have lived from the days of Adam until now, the first and the last—the grand aim of all that I, the Lord, have revealed is to instruct you to live so that I can come and visit you, or send my angels, that they can enter into your habitations, walk and converse with you and they not be disgraced. By so doing you shall be made partakers of all knowledge and wisdom, power and glory that the sanctified or glorified beings enjoy. And this is, first of all, what the Lord wishes of the people.   Brigham Young, J. D., Vol. 6:284-5.

Recorded in the Lamb's Book of Life

You have heard a great deal about having your names written in the Lamb's Book of Life. When we were Christians, according to the common acceptance of the word, we used to preach a great deal about getting our names written in that Book.

I will tell you how it is. The names of every son and daughter of Adam are already written in the Lamb's Book of Life. Is there ever a time when they will be taken out of it? Yes, when they become sons of Perdition and not till then. Every person has the privilege of retaining it there for ever and ever. If they neglect that privilege, then their names will be erased and not till then. All the names of the human family are written there, and the Lord will hold them there until they come to the knowledge of the truth, that they can rebel against Him, and can sin against the Holy Ghost; then they will be thrust down to hell, and their names be blotted out from the Lamb's Book of Life.

Brigham Young, J. D., Vol. 6:297.

The Winding-Up Scene

"Why does not your God do thus and so? Why does He delay? Why does he permit the enemy to hold possession of the dominion of the Savior?"—with many other inquiries that rest in the minds of the people. Perhaps some of you have satisfactorily answered these questions to yourselves, and perhaps you have heard them satisfactorily answered in your minds and understanding by the Elders of Israel. There is a reason for all this. I have not time this afternoon, and do not wish to confine myself, to say all that my mind would be lead to say on the subject. I can say at once, if Jesus had taken the kingdom in the days when He was upon the earth, He would have spoiled the whole plan—He would have ruined the object for which He came into the world. If He had established His kingdom directly after the flood and reigned triumphantly on the earth, the earth could never have answered the ends of its creation; the inhabitants of the earth could not have been accountable. If He had to take possession of the earth at this present time, He would ruin His own scheme—thwart His own plans. It may be a mystery; it is with the many, why the Lord permits this and that, and dictates thus and so. This is for want of intelligence in the intelligent beings that are upon the earth. If they understood the object of the creation of this earth and the inhabitants upon it, these matters would be an easy and pleasing theme to their understandings; they would become natural principles to them, easy to be understood. They would comprehend the design of the Almighty in the forma-tion of these intelligent beings, in the direction of them, the ob-ject of the creation of the earth and the final issue in the end, when all that has been designed of this earth and all consigned to this earth have come upon it; and the work is completed—the winding-up scene has come, when Jesus shall have finished His work pertaining to man and his agency—you will then see that the kingdom will be taken possession of, and that very quickly.

Every mortal being must stand up as an intelligent, organ-ized capacity, and choose or refuse the good, and thus act for himself. All must have that opportunity, no matter if all go into the depths of wickedness. Whether they sustain the kingdom of God and promote the gospel of salvation or not, the earth must remain in the hands of man, liable to be acted upon continually by a superior power and authority. Man's independence must be held inviolate, it must be reserved to each and every individual, all must have the privilege of acting upon it. Until the last spirit that has been designed to come here and take a tabernacle has come upon the earth, the winding-up scene cannot come. I have not time to say what I would like to upon this subject, but will leave it to your own reflection.

Marvel not that the kingdom of God is not in its fulness. Marvel not that you see every man and woman subject to the passions that belong to fallen nature. There never was a prophet on the earth but what was subject to passions as we are. Every son and daughter of Adam that has come into this world, has been subject to sin, and prone to wander. They must have their times and seasons; and when the day has come in which all things are to be gathered in one, the Lord will gather those things. When the day comes in which Jesus will take possession of the earth—He will take possession of it when the time comes that Satan will be ejected from the inheritance of the children—of the legal heirs—you will find that ejectment will be served, and will be effectual. It will be effectual upon every tenant or occupant upon the premises of the Almighty, and they will be forthwith removed. But the time is not yet come—the work is not yet finished. Be patient; be co-workers with our Savior and Master until this work is accomplished, and we shall be blessed in our deeds.   Brigham Young, The Deseret News, Vol. 11, No. 6, p. 41, April 10, 1861.

The Heart Throbs of Many Fathers and Mothers

A PRAYER:

O Father, help me understand,
And know the reason why
The boy that Thou didst give to me,
So early had to die;
Why one whose life had been so pure,
Who never knew deceit,
Should droop and wither like a flower
Crushed under ruthless feet.

O Father, help me understand
Thy purposes Divine,
In letting death, with ruthless hand,
Tear his dear heart from mine.
O let me see the veil beyond,
Where dwells his spirit pure
And know he's happy where he's gone;
O let me feel secure.

Forgive the surging doubts that rise
Within my aching heart,
And take the dimness from mine eyes,
Let darkness all depart.
Let light and knowledge come to me
From heaven, Thy home on high,
O help me put my trust in Thee:
O Father, tell me, why.

Perhaps I sin in asking this,
More faith should show in Thee;
But, O, I miss his loving kiss,
He was so dear to me.
Just let me know that I sometime
Shall find him once again,
And clasp again his form in mine:
I ask in Jesus' name.

THE ANSWER:

> Grieve not, my son, for time shall be
>   When death shall be no more.
> Thy loved one I'll return to thee,
>   To cherish evermore.
> 'Twas in the plan that man should die,
>   And slumber in the grave,
> But rise again, as even I,
>   For this my life I gave.

> For mortal life is but a part
>   Of God's eternity,
> In which the souls of men embark
>   To find felicity.
> What men call death is but a step
>   From low to higher plane,
> And all who in the dust have slept,
>   Through me shall live again.

> Then grieve not for the one that's gone,
>   Nor let your heart despair;
> For God in wisdom called your son,
>   To work for Him up there;
> The prison gates to open wide
>   For those who died in sin,
> And through repentance them to guide
>   Again to worship Him.

> Let this then be your answer, why,
>   And let your heart rejoice,
> For unto God they do not die,
>   Who answer to His voice;
> But walk with Him in realms of love,
>   Where all the righteous be.
> Be comforted, for there above,
>   Thy boy will welcome thee.

—REY L. PRATT

Was Temple Work Done in the Days of the Old Prophets?

By Joseph Fielding Smith

QUESTION: *"Was temple work done in the days of the old prophets? Did they have the sealing powers or was all of this work left for the Church in this dispensation? If they had it, was it done in temples?"*

ANSWER: The detailed history of the performance of the saving ordinances of the gospel as practised in ancient times was never recorded in any detail, because such ordinances are sacred and not for the world. There are, however, in the Old Testament references to covenants and obligations under which the members of the Church in those days were placed, although the meaning is generally obscure. For example in Exodus 40:12-15, Numbers 25:11-13, and Jeremiah 31:31-33, we have reference to sacred covenants.

The fact that Adam and Noah, long after they were dead, appeared to Daniel as Michael and Gabriel (Dan. 10:13, 21; 8:16); and to Zacharias and Mary, (Luke 1:11 19; and 1:26-31) is evidence that they had received the fulness of blessings that entitled them to stand in the presence of God. Likewise the appearance of Moses and Elias on the mount of transfiguration with our Redeemer and his apostles, Peter, James, and John, is evidence that they also had obtained the fulness of the blessings of exaltation. Moreover, the fact that Elijah was the last of the ancient prophets to hold the keys of the sealing power before the coming of our Savior in his ministry, is evidence that this power was exercised in the interest of Israel in ancient times. Because of the fact that Elijah held this sealing authority, the Lord inspired Malachi to prophesy of Elijah's coming in the last days to restore these keys of authority in the following words:

"Behold, I will send you Elijah the prophet before the coming of the great and dreadful day of the Lord.

"And he shall turn the heart of the fathers to the children, and the heart of the children to their fathers, lest I come and smite the earth with a curse." (Malachi 4:5-6.)

We know that this prophecy was fulfilled, for on the third day of April, 1836, Elijah came to Joseph Smith and Oliver

Cowdery in the Kirtland Temple and conferred upon them this sealing authority. Since that day the hearts of the children have turned to their fathers, and without doubt the hearts of the fathers have turned to their children and this influence is felt throughout the world causing the children to search the records of their dead. This fact is so definitely apparent that it cannot be denied. Today we have the privilege of going into our temples and there sealing children to parents and parents to each other that we all may, as Paul declared, bow our knees " . . . unto the Father of our Lord Jesus Christ.

"Of whom the whole family in heaven and earth is named, . . ." (Eph. 3:14-15.)

That ordinances for Israel might be performed, the Lord commanded Moses to build a portable tabernacle — at times called the temple — in the wilderness in which sacred ordinances could be performed. The purpose of this building, in which Samuel officiated, has been declared in our day in these words: "For, for this cause I commanded Moses that he should build a tabernacle, that they should bear it with them in the wilderness, and to build a house in the land of promise, that those ordinances might be revealed which had been hid from before the world was." (D & C 124:38.)

There is a sufficient reason why the ordinance of baptism is not more clearly revealed in the Old Testament, and it is that in the repeated copying of the ancient records and their repeated translations, scribes and translators took from the record the plain and precious parts because they were contrary to their beliefs or comprehension. The Book of Mormon makes this clear; and in the writings of Moses, as they are given to us, we have them restored; and we know that baptism was taught to Adam, and he taught it to his children. There are some references in the Old Testament to washings, which could well mean baptisms, and the evidence of the font in the temple of Solomon is a mute witness that baptisms must have been practised in it; these are spoken of as washings. The Book of Mormon makes the fact very clear that baptism was practised among the Jews, and in the writings of Moses which have been restored, we learn that baptism was taught to Adam, and he was commanded to teach it to his children.

Improvemnt Era, November, 1955.

Temples for which Dedicatory Prayers were offered
by President David O. McKay.

Swiss Temple ....: See Improvement Era — November 1955:
Deseret News-Sept. 12, 1955.

Los Angeles Temple: .... See Improvement Era — April 1956:
Deseret News-March 31, 1956.

New Zealand Temple: ....:
Deseret News-May 10, 1958.

London Temple ....: See Improvement Era — October 1958:
Deseret News-Sept. 8, 1958.

Oakland Temple ....: See Improvement Era — January 1965:
Deseret News-Nov. 21, 1964.

The Blind Shall Enjoy Reading the Book
"Temples of the Most High"

On February 19, 1964, an "Application For Permission to Record on Magnetic Tape", the Book "Temples of The Most High", for the benefit of the blind, was received from the Chief of the Division for the Blind, Library of Congress. This permission was gladly and gratuitously given. The hearts of many thousands will thus be made glad, which will also gladden the heart of the Compiler of this Book.

ADDENDA B

(Note: The following pages were added to this book for the first time in the fifth edition. The value of the data incorporated will justify its publication, especially to those who are students of historical and doctrinal subjects pertaining to the Church of Jesus Christ of Latter-day Saints.)

None Qualified at Present to Build the Great Temple

By Brigham Young
(From discourse delivered in Salt Lake City, June 3, 1860.)

Let every mechanic and every scientific man of all classes and occupations, and every woman, improve to the best of their ability, faithfully living their religion, and we shall be none too well qualified to build up Zion when that time arrives. I never saw a stonemason who thoroughly understood his trade. We have not a quarryman who fully understands getting out rock for the Temple walls. Then how, amid such ignorance, are you going to properly lay the foundation of the New Jerusalem—the Zion of our God? What do you know about building the Great Temple that is yet to be built, upon which the glory of God will rest by day and by night? Where is the man that knows how to lay the first rock in that Temple, or to get out the first stick of timber for it? Where is the woman that knows how to make a single part of its interior decorations? *That knowledge is not now here*; and unless you wisely improve upon your privileges day by day, you will not be prepared, when called upon, to engage to the best advantage in the building up of Zion.

J. D., Vol. 8:278.

Ordinances in the Kirtland Temple

By Orson Pratt
(From discourse delivered at Logan, Utah, May 20, 1877.)

The Lord told us when we were living in the State of New York, to go to the Ohio; there to build a Temple to the name of the Most High. And there the Lord condescended to bestow upon his servants and people a great endowment, a blessing such as was not known among the children of men. And from thence they should go to the nations of the earth, and publish these tidings. We went to the Ohio; and after we had been sufficiently taught and instructed, the Lord commanded us through Joseph, to build a Temple, giving the pattern thereof, and the size thereof, the size of the inner and outer courts, the size of the several rooms and apartments, and the form of the pulpits and everything pertaining to it was given by the inspiration of the Almighty that rested upon Joseph, and upon those associated with him.

When the Temple was built, the Lord did not see proper to reveal all the ordinances of the Endowments, such as we now understand. He revealed little by little. No rooms were prepared for washings; no special place prepared for the anointings, such as you understand, and such as you comprehend at this period of the history of the Church! Neither did we know the necessity of the washings, such as we now receive. It is true, our hands were washed, our faces and our feet. The Prophet Joseph was commanded to gird himself with a towel, doing this in the Temple. What for? That the first Elder might witness to our Father and God, that we were clean from the blood of that wicked generation, that then lived. We had gone forth according to our best ability, to publish glad tidings of great joy, for thousands of miles, upon this continent. After this we were called in, and this washing of hands and feet was to testify to God that we were clean from the blood of this generation. The holy anointing was placed upon the heads of his servants, but not the full development of the Endowments in the anointings. These administrations in the Kirtland Temple were revealed, little by little, corresponding with what I have already been saying, that the Lord does not give the fulness at once, but imparts to us according to his own will and pleasure. Great were the blessings received. We were commanded to seek and behold the face of the Lord; to seek after revelation; to seek after the spirit of prophecy, and the gifts of the Spirit; and many testify to what they saw. But yet they were inexperienced; they had not proven themselves in their religion long enough. They obtained blessings greater than some of them were prepared to receive. They perhaps might have been faithful if they had exercised the agency which God gave them. But how easily are mankind toppled first this way, then that way; and are led astray, even after the heavens were opened and chariots and horses of fire as well as angels were seen; still many of those brethren apostatized.

God Received His Endowments Millions of Years Ago

By Wilford Woodruff

(From discourse delivered in Salt Lake City, January 25, 1857.)

———

Some of the people have looked upon the law of tithing as a kind of tax and burden laid upon them, but who is it for? Our tithing, our labor, and all that we do in the Kingdom of God, who is it all for? The tithing is not to exalt the Lord, or to feed or clothe Him. *He has had His endowments long ago; it is thousands and millions of years since He received His blessings,* and if He had not received them, we could not give them to Him, for He is far in advance of us. I want the brethren to understand this one thing, that our tithing, our labor, our works are not for the exaltation of the Almighty, but they are for us. Not but what the Lord is pleased to see us obey His commandments because by doing this it will place us in a position that will fulfill and accomplish the object of our creation, and bring about the end designed by our coming to take tabernacles here in the flesh. Again, when we do wrong, the Lord knows we shall inherit sorrow and misery if we continue in that wrong. Then I say, brethren, let us understand this as it is and we shall do well. In paying our tithing, in obeying every law that is given to exalt us and to do us good, it is all for our individual benefit and the benefit of our children, and it is not of any particular benefit to the Lord, only as He is pleased in the faithfulness of His children and desires to see them walk in the path which leads to salvation and eternal life.   J. D., Vol. 4:192-3; also Vol. 19:298-9; 22:209.

———

Jesus Gave His Disciples Their Endowments

By Heber C. Kimball

(From discourse delivered in Salt Lake City, July 19, 1863.)

———

Jesus says, "Verily, verily, I say unto thee, except a man be born again, he cannot see the kingdom of God." It is very easy to understand that a man can see very little of a kingdom unless he goes into it, and a man to see and understand the Kingdom of God must first become a member of the Church of Christ, and then he progresses until he has an opportunity of looking into the kingdom, of becoming acquainted with its officers and laws, and hence it is that Jesus says: "Verily, verily, I say unto thee, except a man be born of water and of the Spirit, he cannot enter the Kingdom of God." When the Kingdom of God is organized upon the earth, it is done to protect the Church of Christ in its rights and privileges, so that you see the Church makes a government to protect itself, but who knows what that government is? All those to whom it has been revealed, and no others. Let the Saints reflect upon these matters which I am laying before them. Think of your holy endowments and what you have been anointed to become and reflect upon the blessings which have been placed upon you *for they are the same in part that were placed upon Jesus; he was the one that inducted his Apostles into these ordinances*; it was he who set up the kingdom of which we are subjects. This is the kingdom of which all the Prophets spake, and to which Daniel alluded when he said: "And in the days of these kings shall the God of Heaven set up a kingdom, which shall never be destroyed; and the kingdom shall not be left to other people, but it shall break in pieces and consume all these kingdoms, and it shall stand forever." It is a blessing to have the privilege of entering into the Kingdom of God and partaking of the privileges and blessings that are bestowed upon its members.   J. D., Vol. 10:240-1.

When Endowments Prove a Curse

By Heber C. Kimball
(From discourse delivered in Salt Lake City, March 23, 1852.)

The most of those present have received their endowments, their washings and anointings and have made covenants to their God and their brethren, before witnesses, that they would be faithful, that they would be true, that they would listen to all the counsels of the Lord's servants, and cease to do evil. All who have done this have been pronounced clean, and will they then go and pollute themselves with the wicked? I am sorry to say that a few are unwise enough to do so.

Both men and women have also covenanted that they will have no unlawful intercourse with each other. After all this, do any of you make a practice of speaking evil one of another, of cheating one another, of lying and deceiving? Yes, some who are under the covenants just named actually indulge in those evil practices, and I say to all such that if they do not repent of their follies and sins, *their washings and anointings will prove a curse instead of a blessing, and will expedite their condemnation.*

If a man sins to that degree that he is cut off from the Church, he forfeits the blessings promised on condition of keeping his covenants. When a man loses his membership in this Church, he also loses his Priesthood, and of course the blessings of his endowments. Do not flatter yourself that you can retain the blessings of the Gospel, and at the same time pursue a wicked course, for you cannot do it.   J. D., Vol. 3:269.

Giving Endowments to Some Proves Their Overthrow

By Brigham Young
(From discourse delivered in Salt Lake City, June 28, 1857.)

Giving endowments to a great many proves their overthrow through revealing things to them which they cannot keep. They are not worthy to receive them. Brother Heber takes the lead in giving endowments, and you may ask, "Why do you give such folks their endowments?" To qualify them to be devils, if they wish to be. The plan of salvation is calculated to make devils as well as Saints; for by and by we shall need some to serve as devils; and it takes almost as much knowledge to make a complete devil as it does to fit a man to go into the celestial kingdom of God, and become an heir to His kingdom. We want to complete the education of a number of such fellows; they are running to the States, to California, and elsewhere, and are trying to reveal this, that, and the other; but I defy any one of them to give any idea of what is taught them in their endowments, except a garbled mass of trash. God takes that knowledge from their minds. * * *

I will tell you a truth; it is God's truth; it is eternal truth; neither you nor I would ever be prepared to be crowned in the celestial kingdom of our Father and our God, without devils in this world. Do you know that the Saints never could be prepared to receive the glory that is in reserve for them, without devils to help them to get in? Men and women never could be prepared to be judged and condemned out of their own mouths, and be set upon the left hand, or to have it said to them, "Go away into everlasting darkness," without the power both of God and the devil. We are obliged to know and understand them, one as well as the other, in order to prepare us for the day that is coming, and for our exaltation. Some of you may think that this is a curious principle, but it is true. Refer to the Book of Mormon, and you will find that Nephi and others taught that we actually need evil, in order to make this a state of probation. We must know the evil, in order to know the good. There must needs be an opposition in all things. All facts are demonstrated by their opposites. You will learn this in the Bible, the Book of Mormon, and in the revelations given through Joseph. We must know and understand the opposition that is in all things, in order to discern, choose, and receive that which we do know will exalt us to the presence of God. You cannot know the one without the other. This is a true principle.   J. D., Vol. 4:372-3.

Those Who Slew the Prophet Joseph Had Their Endowments

By Wilford Woodruff
(From discourse delivered in Salt Lake City, December 21, 1856.)

I remember what Joseph said a short time before he was slain in one of the last sermons I ever heard him preach. Said he: *"Men are here today who are seeking my blood, and they are those who have held the Priesthood and have received their washings and anointings; men who have received their endowments."* I saw the faces of those men at that time, and they had a hand in slaying the Prophet. There are men who now possess the same spirit and the same desire.   J. D., Vol. 4:149.

Ten Tribes to Receive Endowments Through Those Present

By Wilford Woodruff
(From discourse delivered in Salt Lake City, February 22, 1857.)

Again, here are the ten tribes of Israel. We know 1.othing about them only what the Lord has said by His Prophets. There are Prophets among them, and by and by they will come along, and they will smite the rocks, and the mountains of ice will flow down at their presence, and a highway will be cast up before them, and they will come to Zion, receive their endowments, and be crowned under the hands of the children of Ephraim, and *there are persons before me in this assembly today who will assist to give them their endowments.* They will receive their blessings and endowments, from under the children of Ephraim, who are the first fruits of the Kingdom of God in this dispensation, and the men will have to be ordained and receive their Priesthood and endowments in the land of Zion, according to the revelations of God.   J. D., Vol. 4:231-2.

Revelation in Building Temples

By Brigham Young
(From discourse delivered in Salt Lake City, February 14, 1853.)

Concerning revelations pertaining to building temples, I will give you the words of our beloved Prophet while he was yet living upon the earth. Many of us that are here today were with him from the commencement of the Church. He was frequently speaking upon the building of temples in Kirtland, Missouri, and Illinois. When the people refused in Kirtland to build a temple, unless by a special revelation, it grieved his heart that they should be so penurious in their feelings as to require the Lord to command them to build a house to His name. It was not only grievous to him, but to the Holy Spirit also. He frequently said, that if it were not for the covetousness of the people, the Lord would not give revelations concerning the building of temples, for we already knew all about them; the revelations giving us the order of the Priesthood make known to us what is wanting in that respect at our hands. * * *

The Prophet's feelings were often wounded because he was under the necessity of giving commandments concerning duties that were already before the people, until the temple was completed; but had he not done so, the temple would not have been built; had he waited until the minds of the people were opened, and they were led to see and do their duty, without commandment, he would have been slain before the keys of the Priesthood could have been committed to others, but the Lord put into his heart to give this power to his brethren before his martyrdom.

J. D., Vol. 1:277-8.

Parley P. Pratt to Build Temples in Scotland

By Brigham Young

(From discourse delivered in Salt Lake City, September 11, 1853.)

I will venture to say, that Brother Parley P. Pratt has a job on hand infinitely more extensive than the walling in of the whole territory of Utah. His work was given to him sixteen years ago, by the Prophet Joseph Smith, in the Kirtland Temple. Parley P. Pratt has yet to build temples in old Scotland. The Scotch brethren might say, "What is the use then of our coming to these distant valleys, so far from our native country?" Had you not better write to your brethren who are still in Scotland to stay where they are, think you? He has to build temples there of greater magnitude than we have yet contemplated. When he will do it I do not know; it is certain he will do it if he is faithful; but whether he will do it after the earth is glorified, or before that time, I do not know.

J. D., Vol. 1:77.

Instructions on the Sealing Ordinance

By Brigham Young

(From discourse delivered at Franklin, Idaho, September 4, 1873.)

The remarks that I shall make to you this evening will be upon the salvation of the people. There are a few ideas that I will relate to you, that the brethren and sisters should understand. There are many of the ordinances of the House of God that must be performed in a Temple that is erected expressly for the purpose. There are other ordinances that we can administer without a Temple. You know that there are some which you have received—baptism, the laying on of hands, the gifts of the Holy Ghost, such as the speaking in and interpretation of tongues, prophesying, healing, discerning of spirits, etc., and

many blessings bestowed upon the people, we have the privilege
of receiving without a Temple. There are other blessings that
will not be received, and ordinances that will not be performed
according to the law that the Lord has revealed, without their
being done in a Temple prepared for that purpose. We can, at
the present time, go into the Endowment House and be baptized
for the dead, receive our washings and anointings, etc., for there
we have a font that has been erected, dedicated expressly for
baptizing people for the remission of sins, for their health and
for their dead friends; in this the Saints have the privilege of
being baptized for their friends. We also have the privilege of
sealing women to men, without a Temple. This we can do in the
Endowment House; but when we come to our sealing ordinances, ordinances pertaining to the Holy Priesthood, to connect
the chain of the Priesthood from Father Adam until now, by
sealing children to their parents, being sealed for our forefathers,
etc., they cannot be done without a Temple. But we can seal
women to men, but not men to men, without a Temple. When
the ordinances are carried out in the Temples that will be
erected, men will be sealed to their fathers, and those who have
slept clear up to Father Adam. This will have to be done, because of the chain of the Priesthood being broke upon the earth.
The Priesthood has left the people, but in the first place the
people left the Priesthood. They transgressed the laws, changed
the ordinance, and broke the everlasting covenant, and the
Priesthood left them; but not until they had left the Priesthood.
This Priesthood has been restored again, and by its authority we
shall be connected with our fathers, by the ordinance of sealing,
until we shall form a perfect chain from Father Adam down to
the closing up scene. This ordinance will not be performed anywhere but in a Temple; neither will children be sealed to their
living parents in any other place than a Temple. For instance, a
man and his wife come into the Church, and they have a family
of children. These children have been begotten out of the covenant, because the marriages of their parents are not recognized
by the Lord as performed by His authority; they have, therefore,
to be sealed to their parents, or else they cannot claim them in
eternity; they will be distributed according to the wisdom of the
Lord, who does all things right. When we had a Temple prepared in Nauvoo, many of the brethren had their children who
were out of the covenant sealed to them, and endowments were
given. Then parents, after receiving their endowments, and being

sealed for time and all eternity, and they have other children, who are begotten and born under the covenant, and they are the rightful heirs to the kingdom, they possess the keys of the kingdom. Children born unto parents before the latter enter into the fulness of the covenants, have to be sealed to them in a Temple to become legal heirs of the Priesthood. It is true they can receive the ordinances, they can receive their endowments and be blessed in common with their parents; but still the parents cannot claim them legally and lawfully in eternity unless they are sealed to them. Yet the chain would not be complete without this sealing ordinance being performed.   J. D., Vol. 16:185-7.

Salvation for the Dead Not All Revealed at Once

By Brigham Young
(From discourse delivered at Paris, Idaho, August 31, 1875.)

Do you recollect that in about the year 1840-41, Joseph had a revelation concerning the dead? He had been asked the question a good many times: "What is the condition of the dead, those that lived and died without the Gospel?" It was a matter of inquiry with him. He considered this question not only for himself, but for the brethren and the Church. "What is the condition of the dead? What will be their fate? Is there no way today by which they can receive their blessings as there was in the days of the Apostles, and when the Gospel was preached upon the earth in ancient days?" When Joseph received the revelation that we have in our possession concerning the dead, the subject was opened to him, not in full but in part, and he kept on receiving. When he had first received the knowledge by the spirit of revelation how the dead could be officiated for— there are brethren and sisters here, I can see quite a number here who were in Nauvoo—and you recollect that when this doctrine was first revealed, and in hurrying in the administration of baptism for the dead, sisters were baptized for their male friends, for their fathers, their grandfathers, their mothers and their grandmothers, etc. I just mention this so that you will understand, that as we knew nothing about this matter at first; the old Saints recollect, there was little by little given, and the subject was made plain, but little was given at once. Consequently, in the first place people were baptized for their friends and no record was kept. Joseph afterwards kept a record, etc. Then women were baptized for men and men for women, etc. It would be very strange, you know, to the eyes of the wise and they that understood the things pertaining to eternity, if we were called upon to commence a work that we could not finish. This, therefore, was regulated and all set in order; for it was revealed that if a woman was baptized for a man, she could not be ordained for him, neither could she be made an Apostle or a Patriarch for the man, consequently the sisters are to be baptized for their own sex only. This doctrine of baptism for the dead is a great doctrine, one of the most glorious doctrines that was ever revealed to the human family; and there are light, power, glory, honor and immortality in it.   J. D., Vol. 16:165-6.

Segregation of the Spirits in the Spirit World

By Brigham Young
(From discourse delivered in Salt Lake City, December 3, 1854.)

It is understood, and is so written, that when the inhabitants of the earth pass through what is called the valley of death, that which is in the tabernacle leaves it, and goes into the world of spirits, which is called hades or hell. The spirits that dwell in these tabernacles on this earth, when they leave them, go directly into the world of spirits. What, a congregated mass of inhabitants there in spirit, mingling with each other, as they do here? Yes, brethren, they are there together, and if they associate together, and collect together in clans and in societies as they do here, it is their privilege. No doubt they yet, more or less, see, hear, converse, and have to do with each other both good and bad. Jesus himself went to preach to the spirits in prison; now, as he went to preach to them, he certainly associated with them; there is no doubt of that. If the prophets went and preached to the spirits in prison, they associated with them; if the Elders of Israel in these latter times go and preach to the spirits in prison, they associate with them, precisely as our Elders associate with the wicked in the flesh, when they go to preach to them. * * *

When the light of the knowledge of God comes to a man and he rejects it, that is his condemnation. When I have told all I have been authorized to declare to him in the name of the Lord, if he does not have the visions of eternity, it is all nonsense to him. To know the truth of my testimony he must have the visions and revelations of God for himself. And when he gets them, and turns aside, becoming a traitor to the cause of righteousness, the wrath of God will beat upon him, and the vengeance of the Almighty will be heavy upon him. This comes, not because their fathers lived in darkness before them, and the ancestors of their fathers before them; not because the nations have lived and died in ignorance; but because the Lord pours the spirit of revelation upon them, and they reject it. Then they are prepared for the wrath of God, and *they are banished to another part of the spirit world, where the devil has power and control over them.*   J. D., Vol. 2:137, 140-1.

Unnatural Infamies

By President John Taylor
(From discourse delivered on October 6, 1884.)

No woman murderer, no man murderer can have a place among the Latter-day Saints, and I speak of it that the presidents of stakes and the bishops may be apprized of these things. And some of these people would try to pass by the bishops, and then by the presidents of stakes, and then by the president of the Church, and crawl with all their slime and damnable hypocrisy into the temples of the living God. They may pass by these, but they will have to pass by the angels and the Gods before they get through, and they will never inherit the Kingdom of God. Hear it, you sisters! Hear it, you brethren! Hear it, you bishops, and you presidents of stakes! Watch well and know well what you are doing, when you sign recommends for doubtful characters to go into these holy places. We do not want them there. It is not their place, and you will have to account for your acts if you permit these things knowingly. It is necessary that you should be particular about these matters, for you will have

to answer for your doings as I have for mine. We cannot, because of relationship because somebody is a cousin, or an uncle,
or an aunt, or a brother, or a sister, or a son or a daughter, or a
father or a mother, we cannot admit and will not admit them to
any of these holy places unless they are worthy. I call upon you
if you know of adulterers or adulteresses, or people that practice these unnatural infamies, to sever them from the Church;
they shall not have a place in the Church and Kingdom of God.

ADDENDA C

The Burning of the Nauvoo Temple
By Robert Aveson

The following article, under the heading "Burning of the Nauvoo Temple," was taken from the Fort Madison (Iowa) *Democrat* many years ago. I herewith reproduce it from my scrapbook.

George H. Rudsill, now of Bowling Green, Florida, but once a Ft. Madison boy, tells of the destruction of the Nauvoo Temple, which occurred fifty years ago, in the following words:

"Well, to the burning of the Temple. I will give it in Mr. J. B. Agnew's own words, as near as I can recollect, which was just before his death in the fall of 1870. After telling me his story he asked me as a friend not to let it be known until after his death of all parties concerned, as they had pledged themselves to secrecy in the matter. This I told him I would do, and now that these parties are all dead, it will be no harm to let it be known, and it will satisfy many an old settler's curiosity.

"Mr. Agnew was in failing health at the time he came to me. He told me that he was going to die soon, which I thought was true. I asked him if he had repented of his wrongdoings and he smiled and said: 'Yes, all but one thing.' I asked what that was and he said it was the burning of the Nauvoo Temple. Says I: Did you do that? And he said: 'Yes, I did it with my own hands. Sit down and I will tell you about it,' which is as follows, as near as I can give it in his own words:

" 'The reason why I burned it was that there was a continual report in circulation that the Mormons were coming back to Nauvoo and we were afraid they might take it into their heads to do so, and as we had had all the trouble with them we wanted, Judge Sharp of Carthage, Hyrum McCauley of Appanooce, and myself of Pontoosue, determined the destruction of their Temple and by so doing they would not be able ever again to try and come back.

" 'So on the afternoon of the night that the Temple was burned, in order to make arrangements we three met on the prairie five miles south of Fort Madison, in Illinois, the judge coming from Carthage, the squire from Appanooce, and I from Pentoosue, and we met about where the Mormon Church stood, five miles south of Appanooce, and there we pledged ourselves to destroy the Temple if it cost us our lives. So we journeyed toward it on horseback, and on the way tried to perfect some plan to work on. After a while we decided to get the steward to show us through the Temple, and then watch our chance to get in our work. So we hid our horses in the bushes in a secluded place a mile from town and walked in. We looked about town until 4 o'clock in the afternoon, and in the meantime had prepared a bundle of kindling by taking a corn sack and cutting arm holes in it so I could put it on like a coat under my coat. I then stuck in as many tarred rags on sticks as I could carry without being noticed. I then put it on and secured some matches from a store to light my pipe and we were ready. We had but little trouble to find the steward and after laboring with him some time he at last consented to show us through the Temple. We claimed to be strangers in the country and were going away that night and it would be our last chance perhaps of ever having an opportunity to visit the Temple. So on these conditions he would oblige us, provided we would hurry, which we agreed to do, as it was getting late and it would be dark before we could get through. So after a good deal of delay the key was at last inserted, it not seeming to fit, but at last the door swung open. We went in with a rush and kept a going, the man being left behind working with the door. He called out for us to stop but we kept on going and I noticed that he left the door with the key in it.

" 'I stepped back in a side room, and the other two kept on. The man ran on after them, and after he had passed me, I went back to the door and unlocked it and put the key in my pocket and then ran after them. By this time the man had discovered that I was missing, but when I came up to them and explained that I had stopped to look at the crucifixion, he seemed to be satisfied but looked suspicious at me, and from that time on he kept close to my side and would not allow us to stop but walked us right on around and out. It was getting dusk and we had no chance for me to light my fire and I saw that it was telling on my companions—that they were bitterly disappointed when we were compelled to walk out. I told them to come on in haste, that we were late and would miss our boat that we were going on. So they came along and we stopped behind a house, where I told them what I had done, which made them two of the happiest fellows I ever saw. We had to watch but a few minutes until we saw the steward start away on a run, and we knew he was going for a key or some one, and that that this was our chance, so leaving the judge and squire on guard, I ran back to the Temple.

" 'I started for the top which I soon gained and found a good place to start my fire where it would get a good start before it would shed any light and be seen from the outside. After seeing it start to success I began to retrace my steps with joy and a light heart, for I was sure that the Temple was as good as burned, with a chance for me to burn with it, for I had lost my way and did not know which way to turn to get out, although I had been through the Temple a number of times before. I had thought if I would succeed at last in getting out, that I would be sure to get caught by the steward, for he would soon be back and in all probability would have help with him, for I was certain that he would lay the missing key to us. You can imagine my feeling, being left in the burning Temple, and in case I did escape the fire I was sure of an arrest. I ran first one way, then the other, in hopes of gaining some passage that I would know so as to find my way out, but all to no purpose. I was getting worse lost all the time, and I could not tell one direction from another, for it was as dark as an Egyptian night. At last I came to the stairway going up and I took it with the hope that it would lead me back to where I had started the fire and I could then take a new start. After going up two pairs of stairs and through many halls I came to a square turn and a light shone way down the passage in the opposite direction from what I wanted to go, but I thought it best to go and see what it was or who it was, and I soon discovered that it was my fire which was burning at a fearful rate, sending its fiery tongue clear across the hall.

" 'I drew as near as I could and I happened to see Squire McCauley's bandana handkerchief lying on the floor a short distance from the fire on the opposite side of me. So I knew that my way led through the fire as that room was the end of our trip. Now what was I to do? I knew no other way out but through the fire. I became horror stricken. Was I to be burned up by my own hands? O God, what shall I do? Not knowing as it were what I did, I threw my coat over my head and made a dive through that hell of fire, striking my full length on the floor and I rolled over and over until I got out of the reach of the fire. When I got to my feet I took off my coat and extinguished the fire that caught in the lining, after which I put it on again. With difficulty I tried to run, for I seriously hurt my arm and one of my legs from my fall on the floor, but was so excited at the time that I did not realize the pain until afterwards. With the assistance of a few matches I had, that I now thought of, I kept striking them along the way, and at last reached the door that I had been going through and found it standing open. The squire had come and thrown it open in hopes I might be able to see a star from without.

" 'They were satisfied that something had happened on account of my delay. You can imagine our feelings when I stepped through the door. I pulled the door to and locked it and ran away in an easterly direction, the judge and squire following. I was sore, lame and burned and almost choked, not being able to speak and when I came to a well about one hundred yards away, I drank and threw the key in the well. I then told the boys to scatter and go to the horses, which they did. They got there long before I did for I was almost beyond going at all. After reaching the horses I told them the job was done and for them to go in different directions and get home as soon as possible and avoid meeting anyone. They objected to leaving me as they were afraid I was hurt internally, which I was fearful was the case, I had inhaled the fire and thought my time had come. I told them to go, that I would pull through all right. So the squire took the river road up the river to Appanooce ten miles distant; the judge took the road to Carthage, about sixteen miles distant to the south; while I took the prairie road in the direction of Pontoosue, twelve miles distant.

" 'After going about one-half mile, I looked toward Nauvoo and I saw a flickering light and the next minute the flames burst through the roof and lit up the country for miles as light as day. I put my horse into a dead run in the direction of the Missouri timber, which I gained in time without being seen, as the people on the road were all in bed, but I had no sooner jumped my horse over a fence into a field and secreted myself behind some bushes, when along came seven horsemen on their way to the fire, which had by this time been discovered twenty miles around. After they had passed I again tried to mount my horse, but found it impossible and found my leg had swollen so that I could not walk. I was in a fix, sure enough. What to do I did not know, but I had to do something, so I got down on my hands and knees and crawled on toward a cluster of trees, leading my horse. When I arrived at the timber I fortunately found a large tree which had been cut down, leaving a high stump; crawling upon this stump I managed to get on the back of my horse, and went back, jumping my horse over the fence back into the road.

" 'I was suffering so terribly that I could but just cling to my saddle. I turned my horse in the direction of Squire McCauley's cabin, where I arrived just before daybreak, and found that the squire had got home nearly two hours before. He was surprised to be called out by me, but after giving him to understand my condition, he cried like a child. He took me in and hid me away for a week, where he and his wife cared for me, as they would for one of their own, until I was able to go about without suspicion. The judge got home the night following the night the Temple was burned, having to ride in the woods on Rock Creek all day, which was on the south side of Rock Creek township.'

"So after nearly fifty years the true history of the burning of the great Mormon Temple is made known. The narrator of this story, as told by Mr. Agnew, was a small boy at the time of the burning of the Temple, living with his mother just west of Ft. Madison, Iowa, and he recollects seeing the light from the burning building on that memorable night. Over twenty years after the destruction of the Temple I became intimately acquainted with all the parties connected with this narrative."—George H. Rudsill, Bowling Green, Florida.

(A few years after the burning of the Temple, Elders George A. Smith and Erastus Snow visited Nauvoo, and from Lewis A. Bidamon, landlord of the Nauvoo Mansion, were told that the inhabitants of several of the surrounding settlements—previous to the burning of the sacred edifice—were jealous of Nauvoo, and fearing it would continue to retain its superior influence as a town, and the Mormons be induced to return, they contributed a purse of $500 which they gave to this man Joseph Agnew to perform the diabolical act, and that he was the wretch who set fire to the building. Mr. Bidamon told the brethren that the burning of the Temple did certainly have the effect of diminishing the importance of Nauvoo, for his hotel did not have one-fourth the custom after the burning as it had before the destruction of that magnificent structure.)

ADDENDA D—The Oakland Temple

Historical Data on the Oakland Temple

The events connected with the selection and acquisition of a site for the erection of a temple in Oakland, California, are, like other temples having similar experiences, very inspiring, and indicate that God inspired those who chose these locations for the temples concerned.

By permission of W. Aird Macdonald, I quote from the May 1964 issue of the *Improvement Era* respecting the interesting events connected with the acquisition of the site for the Oakland temple, this article having been prepared by Harold W. Burton, Church Supervising Architect, and Elder Macdonald. This write-up also records the history of events leading up to and including the dedication of the Temple.

Forty years ago this summer, in 1924, the late President George Albert Smith, then a member of the Council of the Twelve, was in San Francisco attending regional Boy Scout meetings. As the president of the little Oakland Branch of the California Mission, I [Aird Macdonald] was invited to meet him at the Fairmont Hotel, high atop Nob Hill. We sat on the roof terrace facing the East Bay, discussing affairs concerning the little church organization across the bay.

From the Fairmont terrace we had a wonderful panorama of the great San Francisco Bay, nesting at our feet. The setting sun seemed to set the whole eastern shore afire, until the Oakland hills were ablaze with golden light. As we admired the beauty and majesty of the scene, President Smith suddenly grew silent, ceased talking, and for several minutes gazed intently toward the East Bay hills.

"Brother Macdonald, I can almost see in vision a white temple of the Lord high upon those hills," he exclaimed rapturously, "an ensign to all the world travelers as they sail through the Golden Gate into this wonderful harbor." Then he studied the vista for a few moments as if to make sure of the scene before him. "Yes, sir, a great white temple of the Lord," he confided with calm assurance, "will grace those hills, a glorious ensign to the nations to welcome our Father's children as they visit this great city."

A few years later, President David O. McKay, then one of the Twelve, visited Oakland at one of our first stake conferences, and asked to see the place where Brother Smith had envisioned a temple. I accompanied him to the hill, a point high above the Dimond district off Mountain Boulevard, the present site of the Oakland Temple. Following President McKay's visit, negotiations for the purchase of the property countined for several years, until the Church finally acquired the hill where Brother Smith saw the vision of a temple that summer evening in 1924.

The vision of a "White Temple" on the East Bay hills persisted and became the dream of the local church colony. After the visit of President McKay, efforts to buy the site continued over a period of fourteen years. But many circumstances developed to block the ownership of the hilltop by the Church. One private owner refused to sell his essential parcel. It was not until after his death that a settlement among his heirs finally made the property available. Once the site was pre-empted by the school board for an elementary school building. When plans changed, the property fell into the hands of a real estate housing promoter, whose plans were approved by city, county and state officials, but because of the Korean War he was not able to proceed with the project.

Later, Brother A. B. Graham (a realtor) received word that the site was for sale. On November 16, 1942, a letter signed by President Heber J. Grant and President David 'O. McKay (then the second counselor in the First Presidency) was received by President Eugene Hilton who was then President of the Oakland Stake, which stated that they had concluded to purchase this site for a temple, and enclosed a check for $100.00 as assurance of good faith. On January 28, 1943, the balance due on the purchase price was sent, which then amounted to a little over $18,-000.00 as the total cost of the site which thereafter was called "Temple Hill." Other parcels of land were later added in order to enlarge the site.

On Monday, January 23, 1961, President David O. McKay flew to San Francisco to a pre-arranged meeting at the Hilton Hotel near the San Francisco airport. Stake presidencies to the area from Fresno on the south to Klamath on the north and Reno on the east, were present. At that time there were nineteen stakes in the area. Now, three years later, there are twenty-five. President McKay announced that the First Presidency and the Council of the Twelve had approved a temple for Oakland. Harold W. Burton, supervising architect of the Church building committee, had been appointed architect for the temple, the fifteenth to be erected by the Church in this dispensation.

The stake presidencies were overjoyed with this announce- ment and pledged to President McKay that they would raise not less than five hundred thousand dollars toward the construction of the temple. One stake president recalls making a mental calcu- lation that the pledge would mean more than five dollars per capita for the 92,000 church members of the area. (Later, Pres. O. Leslie Stone reported that $635,000.00 had been subscribed.)

At this meeting a temple committee was named with Presi- dent O. Leslie Stone of the Oakland-Berkeley Stake as chairman, President David B. Haight of the Palo Alto Stake, vice chairman, Presidents Dallas A. Tueller of the Fresno Stake and Carroll William Smith of Klamath (Oregon) Stake as members. Paul F. Warnick of the Oakland-Berkeley Stake was named executive secretary of the committee, and Sister Nell Smith was appointed publicity chairman.

President McKay returned to Oakland, Saturday, May 26, 1962, when he officially broke ground for the structure, at which time he also dedicated the site. All members of the First Presi- dency and many of the General Authorities were present. Ap- proximately seven thousand were in attendance at this service. Construction on the building started the following Monday morn- ing.

President Joseph Fielding Smith of the Council of the Twelve laid the cornerstone on Saturday, May 25, 1963. The Salt Lake Tabernacle Choir (then on a concert tour in California) sang at the services, which were attended by an estimated seven thou- sand.

The temple was designed by Harold W. Burton and was erected by the Leon M. Wheatley Co., Inc., and the Jacobsen Construction Co., Inc., as a joint venture. Superintendent of construction was Robert C. Loden. Arthur Price was resident architect supervisor during the construction of the temple.

The First Presidency, on January 4, 1964, announced the appointment of Elder Delbert F. Wright as president of the Oakland Temple, with Sister Wright as temple matron.

The temple was dedicated by President David O. McKay on Tuesday morning, Nov. 17, 1964. The dedicatory prayer was repeated at each of the following sessions. Two sessions were held each day for three days, November 17, 18, and 19. President McKay also addressed each of the six sessions. He was assisted in conducting the dedicatory services by his counselors, President Hugh B. Brown and President N. Eldon Tanner. They also spoke as did all members of the Council of the Twelve in attendance and others of the General Authorities.

The Temple was opened for ordinance work on Tuesday, January 5, 1965. A staff of 250 ordinance workers were trained to perform the necessary functions essential in this sacred structure.

Physical Description of the Temple

by

HAROLD W. BURTON, *Suprevising Architect*

and

W AIRD MACDONALD

The Oakland Temple differs from the older type of temple in that there will be but two ordinance rooms. The ceremonies that are performed in four rooms in other temples are consolidated into each of these two rooms. The ceremonies in these two ordinance rooms will be alternated at one hour and fifteen minute intervals. The celestial room will be common to both ordinance rooms, which will make it possible for one group of temple workers to officiate in both rooms.

The celestial room in the Oakland Temple, located directly under the central tower and spire, is thirty-eight feet square. The room has a thirty-five foot high ceiling. The walls are covered in *giallo sienna,* a beautiful golden-toned marble imported from Italy. The wall panels are of light-colored South American wood, known as Prima Vera. This Prima Vera wood has a golden glaze which harmonizes perfectly with the beautiful Italian marble. The floor is carpeted with a deep pile velvet carpet in a golden hue that harmonizes with the marble and wood paneling.

Beneath the celestial room is the baptistry in the exact center of the building, in the lowest part of the temple. The floor of the baptistry is marble, the sixteen supporting columns that carry the weight of the central tower and spire is covered with a traver-tine marble which is quarried in Utah. It is crystalline formation with onyx and other crystals, which gives it a rich bronze-like effect.

The font itself is supported on the backs of twelve life-sized oxen covered with pure gold leaf. The oxen have the appearance of emerging from reeded foliage, which is polychromed in natural foliage colors. The oxen are typical of those used by the early Mormon pioneers in crossing the plains.

There are ten sealing rooms in the building, two of which have a seating capacity of sixty, four with a seating of twenty-two each, and four seating sixteen each. The sealing rooms are carpeted wall to wall. All four walls are paneled with silk-covered panels and mirrors. These mirrors give the symbolic effect of eternity because of the repeated reflections on all sides of the rooms.

The ground floor of the temple is devoted to the initiatory ceremonies. The west wing contains the Bureau of Information and a reception room for temple patrons. The temple chapel and the other administrative offices are in the east wing.

The exterior of the building from the base to the top of the central tower is faced with sierra white granite, which is quar-ried at Raymond, California, approximately 175 miles from the temple site.

The temple proper sits on the stylobate 210 feet from east to west and 190 feet from north to south. It faces two and one-half degrees west off true north. The central tower rises 170 feet from ground level to the tip of the finial or spire. There are four lesser spires directly over the four corner towers. These spires reach heavenward ninety-six feet. The towers are perfo-rated and are covered in a blue glass mosaic and gold leaf. They present a very striking effect in the sun light and at night will be illuminated from the interior of the spires, transmitting rays of lacy light which stream through the perforations. The temple will present a stirring sight, especially at night, for viewers from miles away.

A feature of the exterior of the temple is two sculptured panels, thirty-five feet wide and thirteen feet, one inch high. The sculptured figures in these panels, one on the north facade and one on the south facade, are heroic in size.

The panel on the approach, or north side of the building, depicts Jesus of Nazareth in Palestine; the one on the south facade shows Jesus appearing to the Nephites in the Land Bountiful. These panels grow out of the face of the building and are executed in the same granite as the rest of the building, and thereby have the appearance of being an integral part of the temple.

From the stylobate projecting northward are two wings, thirty-feet by 149 feet, enclosing a fore-court 80 feet wide and 116 feet long. There is a reflecting pool in the center of the fore-court thirty-six feet wide and ninety-seven feet long. This is fed by a waterfall coming from the top of the stylobate down the face of the building into a catch basin, overflowing into the reflecting pool. The stylobate is beautifully landscaped with exotic plantings. From this point, the visitor gets a breath-taking panoramic view of the entire bay area. The fore-court is landscaped with a variety of citrus trees typical of California.

The cost of this temple was $3½ million.

Public Interest in the Temple

More than 347,000 visitors went through the Oakland Temple during the four weeks in October it was opened for public viewing. This was an average of 16,000 per day. The largest number came on the first Saturday, October 10, when there were 24,000 visitors.

Excellent weather prevailed except for the last two or three days at the close of the month. Despite the rain more than 17,000 visitors went through the building on the final Saturday.

In raincoats and sheltered by umbrellas, people stood in line for nearly two hours at times to enter the beautiful structure.

The reporter of the Oakland Tribune, Bill Rose, stated in the October 15th issue: " 'Fantastically beautiful, exquisite, inspiring, overwhelming and gorgeous' were a few of the superlatives used by some of the 12,000 persons who viewed the Oakland Mor' mon Temple last night."

Grand View of Nearby Cities

The Oakland Temple commands a sweeping view of the entire bay area. The Golden Gate is directly to the west. The city of San Francisco lies some eighteen miles distant. Seen also from the temple grounds are the cities of Piedmont, Berkeley and Rich' mond to the north; San Jose and Palo Alto to the south; and San Leandro and Hayward to the east.

References

For detailed accounts of the construction and dedication of the Oakland Temple, consult the following:

Special Dedication Section of the *Deseret News* for Nov. 21, 1964.

Church News for October 24, October 31, November 7, and November 28, 1964.

The Improvement Era for May 1964 and January 1965.

A book, all in colors, was sold which described the Temple in detail.

OAKLAND TEMPLE

OAKLAND TEMPLE

ADDENDA E.

Additional Information Pertaining to The Construction of Temples Listed In This Book; Also Data on Alterations and Additions to Temples Concerned.

Appreciation and gratitude is expressed to Harold W. Burton, Edward O. Anderson, Arthur Price, and Emil B. Fetzer, Architects, and to W. Aird Macdonald and ElRay L. Christiansen for their generous assistance rendered and interest manifested in the recording in this Book, the information embodied in this Addenda E, which will be of value in years to come. Detailed information may be had for each Temple in the Chapters preceding this Addenda.

KIRTLAND TEMPLE.

The Kirtland Temple was dedicated on March 27, 1836.

"On June 6, 1833, a conference of High Priests assembled in Kirtland and instructed the building committee (Hyrum Smith, Jared Carter and Reynolds Cahoon) to proceed immediately to obtain stone, brick, lumber and other materials for the building, which they did, and on July 23, 1833 (the same day on which the Saints in Missouri made a treaty with the mob, and agreed to leave Jackson Conuty) the corner stones of the Lord's House, or the Kirtland Temple, were laid after the order of the Holy Priesthood.

"At that time," writes Sister Eliza R. Snow, "the Saints were few in number and most of them very poor; and, had it not been for the assurance that God had spoken, and had commanded that a house should be built to his name, of which he not only revealed the form, but also designated the dimensions, an attempt towards building that Temple, under the then existing circumstances, would have been, by all concerned, pronounced preposterous.

"Although many sections of the world abounded with mosques, churches, synagogues and cathedrals, built professedly for worship, this was the first instance, for the lapse of many centuries, of God having given a pattern, from the heavens, and manifested by direct revelation how the edifice should be constructed, in order that he might accept and acknowledge it as his own. This knowledge inspired the Saints to almost superhuman efforts, while through faith and union they acquired strength."

"One striking feature of the (dedicatory) ceremonies, was the grand shout of hosanna, which was given by the whole assembly, in standing position, with uplifted hands. The form of the shout is as follows: 'Hosanna — hosanna — hosanna — to God and the Lamb —

amen — amen, and amen.' The foregoing was deliberately and emphatically pronounced, and three times repeated, and with such power as seemed almost sufficient to raise the roof from the building.

"A singular incident in connection with this shout may be discredited by some, but it is verily true. A notice had been circulated that children in arms would not be admitted at the dedication of the Temple. A sister who had come a long distance with her babe, six weeks old, having, on her arrival, heard of the above requisition, went to the Patriarch Joseph Smith, sen., in great distress, saying that she knew no one with whom she could leave her infant; and to be deprived of the privilege of attending the dedication seemed more than she could endure. The ever generous and kind-hearted father volunteered to take the responsibility on himself, and told her to take her child, at the same time giving the mother a promise that her babe should make no disturbance; and the promise was verified. But when the congregation shouted hosanna, that babe joined in the shout. As marvelous as that incident may appear to many, it is not more so than other occurrences on that occasion.

"The ceremonies of that dedication may be rehearsed, but no mortal language can describe the heavenly manifestations of that memorable day. Angels appeared to some, while a sense of divine presence was realized by all present, and each heart was filled with 'joy inexpressible and full of glory.' "

(The reader is here referred to 3 Nephi 26:16, now quoted:

"Behold, it came to pass on the morrow that the multitude gathered themselves together, and they both saw and heard these children; yea, even babes did open their mouths and utter marvelous things; and the things which they did utter were forbidden that there should not any man write them.")

Besides being devoted to general meetings for worship and the celebration of the Lord's Supper every first day of the week, the Temple was occupied by crowded assemblies on the first Thursday in each month, that day being observed strictly, by the Latter-day Saints, as a day of fasting and prayer. These, called fast-meetings, were hallowed and interesting beyond the power of language to describe. Many, many were the pentecostal seasons of the outpouring of the spirit of God on those days, manifesting the gifts of the Gospel and the power of healing, prophesying, speaking in tongues, the interpretation of tongues, etc.

"I have there," continues Sister Snow, "seen the lame man, on being administered to, throw aside his crutches and walk home perfectly healed; and not only were the lame made to walk, but the blind to see, the deaf to hear, the dumb to speak, and evil spirits to depart."

Historical Record, By Andrew Jensen, 5:74-80

Architect's rendering of Nauvoo Temple
by William Weeks

NAUVOO TEMPLE

The Nauvoo Temple was officially dedicated on May 1, 1846 by Orson Hyde and Wilford Woodruff. The word of the Lord concerning the building of this Temple and the ordinances to be performed therein, was given in a revelation to the Prophet Joseph Smith on January 19, 1841. In this revelation the Lord said:

"And I will show unto my servant Joseph ALL THINGS pertaining to this house, and the priesthood thereof and the place whereon it shall be built."

The Lord, therefore, was the Architect and Designer of this Temple; the Prophet Joseph Smith was the Supervising Architect; and William Weeks was the Contractor, which statement the following item will verify:

"In the afternoon, Elder William Weeks (whom I had employed as architect of the Temple), came in for instruction. I instructed him in relation to the circular windows designed to light the offices in the dead work on the arch between stories. He said that round windows in the broad side of a building were a violation of all known rules of architecture, and contended that they should be semi-circular — the building was too low for round windows. I told him I would have the circles, if he had to make the Temple ten feet higher than it was originally caculated; that one light at the center of each circular window would be sufficient to light the whole room; that when the whole building was thus illuminated, the effect would be remarkably grand. I wish you to carry out my designs. I HAVE SEEN IN VISION THE SPLENDID APPEARANCE OF THAT BUILDING ILLUMINATED, AND WILL HAVE IT BUILT ACCORDING TO THE PATTERN SHOWN ME."

"The matter of building a Temple was laid before the general conference held at Commerce, Oct. 6, 1840, when the Church voted to commence the work immediately. On this day also the conference appointed Alpheus Cutler, Elias Highbee and Reynolds Cahoon as a committee of three to carry the business into operation and to oversee the work. During the conference, which lasted three days, the Prophet Joseph explained to the Saints the law of tithing and the plan upon which the building of the Temple was to be conducted.

"In February, 1841, Elder Alpheus Cutler, assisted by Elder Reynolds Cahoon and others, laid out the foundation of the Temple. On the 18th of that month the brethren began to dig the cellar. As it was the wish of President Smith that the corner stones of the Temple should be laid on the 6th day of April next, the corners for the foundation were first excavated; and about the 1st day of March the cellar walls were commenced. On April 6, 1841, the corner stones were laid. (See Historical Record, 8:858-860, for detailed account of this event.)

"Elders Cahoon and Cutler hired the laborers, superintended the work and kept an oversight of the entire business."

"On Sept. 25, 1841, Elders Alpheus Cutler and Peter Haws started for the pine country to obtain lumber for the Temple and Nauvoo House. They took with them Tarlton Lewis, Jabes Durfee, Hardin Wilson, Wm. L. Cutler, Horace Owens, Octavius Pauket, Blakely B. Anderson, James M. Flack, Nathaniel Child, Brother Child's wife and daughter, and Peter W. Conover. These brethren spent the winter in the pine forests, and toiled diligently in their appointed work. They suffered some because of the cold in that northern region, but they made good progress. By the following July, they had succeeded in making up and bringing to Nauvoo a large raft of first-rate pine lumber. Ibid p. 860.

"In the revelation given Jan. 19, 1841, the Lord stated:

" 'For a baptismal font there is not upon the earth, that they, my Saints, may be baptized for those who are dead.' etc., etc. "In the summer and fall of the year 1841, in conformity with the foregoing item of law, the brethren entered into measures to build a baptismal font in the cellar floor near the east end of the Temple. President Smith approved and accepted a draft for the font, made by Brother Wm. Weeks; and on August 18, 1841, Elder Weeks began to labor on the construction of the font with his own hands.'** August 11th Brother Weeks began carving the oxen, twelve in number, upon which the font was to stand. After carving for six days, he consigned this branch to Brother Elijah Fordham, the principal carver, who continued until they were finished. On Nov. 8, 1841, at 5 o'clock in the evening, the font was dedicated by Joseph Smith." This font was constructed of pine timber and was built for the baptisms for the dead until the Temple "shall be finished when a more durable one will supply its place." Ibid p. 862.

The following is from the pen of William Clayton:

"After the dedication of the font Reuben McBride was the first person baptized, under the direction of the President, Brother Samuel Rolfe, who was seriously afflicted with a felon upon one of his hands, was present. President Smith instructed him to wash in the font and told him that the hand would be healed. The doctors had told him that he could not recover before spring, and had advised him to have his hand cut. He dipped his hand in the font, and within a week he was perfectly healed."

"After this time baptisms were continued in the font, and many Saints realized great blessings — both spiritually and bodily." Ibid p. 862.

"From the beginning Albert P. Rockwood, assisted by Charles Drury, was in charge of the crews working in the quarries." Times and Seasons, Apr. 15, 1841).

William W. Player was an expert stone layer, and as soon as he arrived from England in the spring of 1842, he superintended the rock work on the Temple. He came from England for the express purpose of doing this work. Ibid p. 862.

"After the excitement incident to the martyrdom of Joseph and Hyrum Smith, the work on the Temple ceased for two weeks, all the hands having to watch and stand on guard night and day. The work was suspended about June 20, 1844. On the second Sabbath after the murder (July 7th) the subject of the Temple was brought into consideration, and the Church voted to commence work again and finish the building as speedily as possible.

"Consequently, on July 8, 1844, the laborers resumed their work, although the committee had not so much as a bushel of meal, nor a pound of flour, nor a pound of meat to feed the hands with; but the Saints seemed determined to go to work and trust in God for the means. On July 5th a large raft of pine lumber, containing 87,732 feet, was landed at Nauvoo for the Temple. Shortly after another raft, containing 67,952 feet of lumber, was received and hauled to the Temple." For more detailed history of this Temple, see Historical Record, volume (8); Documentary History of the Church, vol. 4:229, 326-331, 443-444, 7:456-457.

This priceless architectural drawing of the Nauvoo Temple by William Weeks, architect of the Nauvoo Temple, was loaned to the compiler of this book by Edward O. Anderson, Church Architect. This is probably the first time the original drawing of the Nauvoo Temple has ever been printed.

ST. GEORGE TEMPLE

Truman O. Angel, Church architect, drew the plans for the building; Miles P. Romney was general superintendent of construction; Edward Lloyd Parry had charge of the stone cutting and laying; William Carter of the device for pounding to solidity the foundation bottoms; George Jarvis had charge of all scaffold making and hoisting devices at the quarries and at the temple; William Burt had charge of the plastering; David Milne supervised the painting and decorating; Albert Foremaster and Et Wiltbank supervised the production and delivery of lime; Robert Gardner superintended the getting out of the lumber at Mt. Trumbull and Pine Valley; and Arch McNeil was overseer at the quarries. The mule teams of James Andrus, Edward M. Brown, Thomas Judd and Daniel D. McArthur hauled much of the stone, the larger pieces being slung under the wagons. Benjamin and Frederick Blake were the noted drivers of large ox teams that brought in the lumber from Mt. Trumbull. This Temple was dedicated on April 6, 1877, by Elder Daniel H. Wells.

ALTERATION PROGRAM FOR ST. GEORGE TEMPLE

By

Edward O. Anderson, Architect

In 1947, the Church approved an extensive renovation program on the exterior of this Temple. As noted in the pervious narrations, the exterior walls are surfaced with a red stone Ashler, which in turn was covered with a limeplaster finish. Over the years this plaster finish failed, especially on horizontal and sloping surfaces.

In 1947, the Church authorized the removal of all this lime plaster on the exterior of the building down to the red sandstone, and then apply a new cement plaster, under the direction of Howard J. McKean, Contractor, Don Carlos Young, Architect, and Edward O. Anderson, Church Supervising Architect. The California *Granolux* Co. applied a cement plaster with air gun to the surface, all of which had been reinforced with heavy steel welded mesh, attached to reinforcing bars anchored to the stone. A Brother Kuntz, plaster Contractor from California, applied a finish coat of white cement and white silica sand plaster. This finish plaster failed on horizontal and sloped surfaces, but recently has been corrected by using epoxy adheasive to the stone and sealing the plaster with silicone transparent damp proofing.

In 1956, Edward O. Anderson, Architect, Lloyd Leon Jennings, Contractor, David O. Woodbury, Supervisor, and Clair Stirling, carried out an extensive Annex Addition to the Temple which was a much needed addition.

On the Main Floor:

1. An ample entrance vestibule and foyer
2. Chapel
3. Kitchen-Dining Room
4. Rest rooms with toilet facilities
5. President's Office
6. Laundry-Sewing Room
7. Storage room, suit case storage rooms

In the Basement: Reading rooms and storage rooms.

During the excavation of the basement, spring water stood in the bottom of the excavation. On further examination it was found this water could be drained off into the original water drain around the Temple. This made it possible to complete a basement under the entire Annex. Later this space has been finished and is now used as a Childrens' Room.

This Annex Addition was finished under the direction of **Harold W**. Burton, Supervising Architect for the Church Building Department.

In 1964 adequate rooms were prepared in the Bureau of Information Building, and is now used by the area Genealogical organization for research and recording.

These improvements were recommended by Harold S. Snow, President of the St. George Temple from 1937 to 1963, and by Rudger C. Atkin who succeeded President Snow.

LOGAN TEMPLE

This Temple was dedicated on May 17, 1884, by President John Taylor. Truman O. Angell was the Architect; Charles O. Card was the Superintendent of Construction.

ALTERATIONS AND ADDITIONS

In 1945 the Celestial room, two of the sealing rooms and the main hallway and certain areas were completely redecorated by the Otto Wolfe Company at a cost of $10,395.00.

In 1946 the Temple was closed from August 9 to December 1 in order to correct a structural fault which developed because of the settling of the inner walls of the temple. At the time of the fire in 1917, the great wooden beams and arches were soaked with water which ran down the footings. Over the years dry rot occurred and the walls settled. To correct this condition, eleven tons of steel beams were placed alongside the original beams. It was also necessary to put new ceilings in the Creation and Garden Rooms.

In 1947 all the old foundation planting of shrubbery and trees were removed. A flood-lighting system for the entire exterior was installed, at which time appropriate ceremonies were had.

In 1948 the rock masonry of the entire building, from top to bottom, was pointed up and every crack filled. Cement footings were poured under the entire building to prevent caving-in of the gravel where trenches for passageways exist. The old furnace was relined with fire brick and a new stoker installed. A new floor was placed in the Groom's room and also redecorated. A new electrical switch board replaced the old control box. The metal fence around the Temple was painted; and the front Assembly Room and main hallway were redecorated.

In the year 1949, Lorenzo S. Young was appointed as Architect for the alterations and additions to this Temple. He was assisted by Arnold H. Ehlers, Architect, under the direction of Edward O. Anderson, Supervising Architect.

During the year 1949-1950, nearly a third of a million dollars was spent in providing extensive improvements. Only a few of the many are here noted: a well equipped laundry; enlarged meeting room with new ventilation system; Baptismal room was tiled and redecorated; the ceiling lowered with adequate lighting; new lighting and ventilating system throughout the Temple; a new public address system for ceremonies; new veils with new lighting; an elevator for all four floors; store rooms for food and supplies in basement of Annex and fruit and vegetable cellars were built. Radiation was installed in the large Assembly Room upstairs; acoustical tile placed on the ceilings and the walls replastered and painted white, again making the room beautiful and useful; a new dining room and cefeteria, with new fixtures and equipment.

In carrying on these improvements, 600 tons of rock were hauled out of the mountains, 3300 tons of gravel and 150 tons of rock were taken out of the basement and building; 600 foot sewer 10 to 14 feet deep constructed; 45,000 bricks used in new chimney and 250 tons of cement was used.

These improvements were recommended and constructed during the period in which President ElRay L. Christiansen was president of this Temple — (1943-1952).

In 1952 the Bride's Room was enlarged and redecorated with new carpets, drapes, furniture, mirrors, pictures, and lamps. A new floor was installed in the large Assembly Room, and all small upper rooms painted and acoustical tile placed on all ceilings. A new telephone system was installed, with connections to each department. This portion of the work was accomplished during the administration of President A. George Raymond.

MANTI TEMPLE

The Manti Temple was dedicated on May 21, 1888 by Elder Lorenzo Snow. W. H. Folsom was the Architect and Superintendent of Construction; Edward L. Parry was master mason, and William Asper was designer of stairways and interior decorator.

ALTERATIONS AND ADDITIONS

By

Edward O. Anderson, Architect

During the early 1940's, Don Carlos Young, Jr., Architect, and Howard J. McKean, Contractor, conducted alterations and additions to this Temple, especially to the finishing of the large Assembly Room on the upper floor and rooms in the west and east towers.

During 1956 and 1957, alterations and additions were made to the Annex. This work was done by Edward O. Anderson, Architect, Oakland Construction Co., Contractors, and Clarence W. Silver, Electrical Contractor, under the direction of Howard J. McKean, Chairman of the Church Building Committee.

President Robert D. Young (1933-1943) and President Lewis R. Anderson (1943-1959) were Presidents of the Temple during this period of construction.

SALT LAKE TEMPLE

The Salt Lake Temple was dedicated on April 6, 1893 by President Wilford Woodruff. Truman O. Angell was the Architect. Cyrus Dallin designed the figure of the angel Moroni on the capstone of the east center tower.

Truman O. Angell was sent to Europe by the First Presidency of the Church, to study design and construction of important buildings, and obtain information on the inverted arch-type of construction for stone foundations. This type of work was performed on the River Thames, and was used in the design of the Salt Lake Temple footings.

ALTERATIONS AND ADDITIONS

By

Edward O. Anderson, Architect

(The need for added facilities and improvements were envisioned and recommended by the Temple President, ElRay L. Christiansen (1954-1962) and his councilors who collaborated with the Architects over a period of four years before the final plans were approved by the First Presidency — David O. McKay, J. Reuben Clark, Jr., and Henry D. Moyle. The alterations were completed during the presidency of Willard R. Smith (1962-1964) and Howard S. McDonald (1964-   ).

The Salt Lake Temple Alterations and additions extending from the year 1958 to the present time (1965) have been extensive. The work was divided into two parts: First, alterations and additions to the Temple itself; and, second, the addition of a Temple Sealing Room Annex, and a Chapel and Office Annex.

After a careful examination of the Temple, it was found the electrical system was in a bad state of repair and in many places presented a fire hazard; the heating system (especially the piping) was rusted; and the ventilating system was inadequate. Some of the second floor wood girders were damaged by dry rot. The wood floors and joists around the Baptismal font and under wash rooms, were very badly rotted.

On account of the location of the Temple, and because of increased patronage, all facilities of the Temple and the Annex were overtaxed. This was especially true in the lack of sufficient lockers, initiatory ordinance rooms and Sealing Rooms.

In 1958, Harold W. Burton, Church Supervising Architect, and Arthur Price ,Architect, started studies of the many problems connected with the proposed work. These studies culminated in a complete set of preliminary drawings indicating plan arrangements, and the architectural design of the additions to the Temple that were to be in harmony with the architectural style of the Temple. These preliminary drawings were approved by the First Presidency. Later, Edward O. Anderson, Architect, was commissioned to complete working drawings and specifications in accordance with the preliminary designs prepared under the directions of the Supervising Architect.

After these documents were completed they were presented by the Church Building Committee (Howard Barker in charge), for bidding and on July 27, 1962, contracts were entered into with Jensen Construction Co., Arthur M. Jensen representing the General Contractor, Higham-Hilton, Raymond F. Hilton, and Harding H. Higham, representing the Mechanical Contractor. Under the General Contract, Claire L. Neves, Engineer, and Harman B. Jensen supervised this work. The Wasatch Electrical Co., Richard Bertoch representing the Electrical Contractor. Western Automatic Sprinkling Co., David E. Dahn, representing Automatic Fire Control, Contractor, and Elevator Supply Co., J. Eugene Russon, Manager, Electrical Contractor.

SUB-CONTRACTORS: Henry L. Ashton and Sons, Stone work; Lee Falmo and Norman Faldmo, Plastering Contract; Pons and Davis, sheet metal work; Clarence Godwin, painting.

At the time the above work was started, Wendell B. Mendenhal, Chairman of the Church Building Committee, was very helpful in coordinating this work.

After work was commenced on the Temple's interior, the repair work became more extensive to protect the foundations, and reinforced concrete retaining walls were installed, both on the interior and exterior of the Temple. As noted in the written history of the Temple and in many articles written on the same, it was found that footings under exterior walls were 16' 0" wide, and up to a height of about 7' 0" were tapered (sloped) to a width of 9' 0" and were of a hard tough silica stone. Above this was started the historical 9' 0" thick cut granite foundations.

All existing electrical cables, wiring, insulations, etc., were removed. All plumbing and heating pipe (except cast iron pipe) were removed. The inadequate and faulty ventilating system was removed. Many plaster ceilings were removed to make way for a forced air ventilating metal duct system, with the ceiling replaced at a lower level in their original design. Two new air conditioning units were installed in special rooms in the sub-basement, furnishing cool or warm air to each room. Each room in turn is provided with a thermostat to control the room temperature automatically. All plumbing with its steel piping and fixtures are new. All electrical conduits, panel boards wiring, wiring boxes and some lighting fixtures are new. Almost all original electrical fixtures were taken down, rewired, refinished and were rehung at the finish of the building.

The Baptismal Font with its twelve oxen were removed, blasted, cleaned and repaired, and then refinished with a coat of molten bronze applied with heated pressure torch. New marble floors and stairs with bronze railings were installed. A new filtered chlorinated water system was attached to the bowl of the font.

The whole of the interior of the Temple was first vacuumed, cleaned from sub-basement to attic, and where necessary, washed, and then given the required first class paint finish. The work was so extensive it required the painting force of four painting contractors:

Wheat Bros. Painting and Decorating Co., Alfred A. Lippold Painting and Decorating Co., H. J. Bloomquist Painting and Decorating Co., Otto Wolffe, Jr., Painting and Decorating Co.

A great deal of defective plaster along with the mural paintings were removed from ordinance rooms No. 1, No. 2 and No. 3.

After being replastered, Ival C. Thompson, Artist, restored and re-painted these walls.

For some time the Temple has been over-crowded in Sealing Rooms. After due consideration, the First Presidency authorized the Sealing Room Annex to the north side of the Temple. A proper *function* of the Temple required this Addition. The design of this necesarily became a challenge. Native Utah Cottonwood granite from the same quarries as the original temple granite was quarried, cut and installed by Wilford Hansen Stone Company.

The Chapel and Office Annex, with outer and inner foyers and halls are above ground level. These are faced on the exterior with a granite facing similar to the Sealing Room Annex.

The entire area under the above annexes and lawn and garden areas, is excavated and is occupied with Temple annex facilities. It is an area of about 120,000 square feet. Under this is a sub-basement.

IDAHO FALLS TEMPLE

ALTERATIONS AND ADDITIONS

By

Emil B. Fetzer, Architect

In 1962 under the direction of Brother Harold W. Burton, Church Architect, Fetzer & Fetzer, Architects of Salt Lake City, Utah, prepared drawings for additions and alterations to the Idaho Falls Temple. Temple President William L. Killpack consulted with the Architects on the planning work. This work was done to facilitate the temple work and make it more convenient for the Temple Patrons and for the Temple Workers. The Dressing and Washing Rooms were enlarged and air-conditioned and Lounges and Locker Rooms for the Men and Women Temple Workers were provided and comfortably furnished. The Additions were constructed on the west side of the building and were built of the same material and in the same design as the original building so that it is not apparent from the exterior of the building that the additions constructed at a later date than the original building.

The Construction was done under the direction of Brother Lyle Peterson, Contractor of Rigby, Idaho, and supervised by Fetzer & Fetzer, Architects.

INDEPENDENCE TEMPLE SITE

This site was dedicated on August 3, 1831, by Joseph Smith the Prophet.

"And thus saith the Lord your God; if you will receive wisdom here is wisdom. Behold, the place which is now called Independence is the center place, and the spot for the temple is lying westward, upon a lot which is not far from the courthouse. (Doc. and Cov. 57:3.)

"Verily this is the word of the Lord that the city Jew Jerusalem shall be built by the gathering of the saints, beginning at this place, even the place of the temple, which temple shall be reared in this dispensation.

"For verily this generation shall not all pass away until an house shall be built unto the Lord, and a cloud shall rest upon it, which cloud shall be even the glory of the Lord, which shall fill the house." (Doc. and Cov. 84:4-5.)

FAR WEST TEMPLE SITE

This site was dedicated on July 4, 1838, by Brigham Young. It was re-dedicated on April 26, 1839. At that time Alpheus Cutler placed a stone near the Southeast corner of the site. The word of the Lord was: "And let a house be built unto my name *according to the pattern which I will show unto them.* And if my people build it not according to the pattern which I shall show unto their presidency, I will not accept it at their hands.

"But if my people do build it according to the pattern which I shall show unto their Presidency, even my servant Joseph and his counselors, then I will accept it at the hands of my people." (Doc. and Cov. 115:14-16.)

If mobocracy and persecution had not interferred in the construction of this Temple, the Lord would have been the designer of the same.

TEMPLE SITE AT ADAM-ONDI-AHMAN

"After hearing of the mobbing, burning and robbing in Gallatin, Daviess County, and the region round about, the brethren went directly to Adam-ondi-Ahman, which is on the west fork of Grand River. Thomas B. Marsh, David W. Patten, Brigham Young, myself, Parley P. Pratt and John Taylor amongst the number. When we arrived there we found the Prophet Joseph, Hyrum Smith and Sidney Rigdon, with hundreds of others of the Saints preparing to defend themselves from the mob, who were threatening the destruction of our people. Men, women, and children were fleeing to that place for safety from every direction; their houses and property were burned and they had to flee half naked, crying, and frightened nigh unto death, to save their lives.

"While there we laid out a city on a high elevated piece of land, and set the stakes for the four corners of a temple block, which was dedicated, Brigham Young being mouth. There were from three to five hundred men present on the occasion, under arms. This elevated spot was probably from two hundred and fifty to five hundred feet above the level of Grand River, so that one could look east, west, north, or south, as far as the eye could reach; it was one of the most beautiful places I ever beheld.

Life of Heber C. Kimball, by Orson F. Whitney," pp. 221-222.

For "Alterations and Additions" to the Hawaiian Temple, see pages 152-153.

For "Alterations and Additions" to the Alberta Temple, see pages 162-164.

INDEX

A

ABRAHAM, seen in vision in Kirland Temple, 17; Resoration of Gospel of, 89; How A. became great, 295-6; Chosen before he was born, 296; What are blessings of A., 374.

ABRAHAM, Book of, 263, 355.

ADAM, opens gate to celestial city, 25.

ADAM-ONDI-AHMAN, Temple block dedicated in, 348.

AGNEW, JOSEPH, Burns Nauvoo Temple, 45, 397.

ALBANY, To be destroyed by fire, 98.

ALBERTA TEMPLE, Dedicatory prayer of, 155; Physical and historical description of, 161; Foretold the building of, 164; Loved ones beyond the veil give message in, 166; Presidents of, 168.

ALDRICH, HAZEN, Apostasy of, 32.

ALTAR, new, dedicated in Nauvoo Temple, 67.

ANCIENT RECORDS bring forth light, 260.

ANCIENT TEMPLES in Western Hemisphere, 358-9.

ANDERSON, EDWARD O., architect, at Swiss Temple ceremonies, 200; At London Temple ceremonies, 224; Architect of Los Angeles Temple, 203; Architect of Swiss Temple, 200; Architect of London Temple, 223; Was present at dedication of London and Swiss Temple sites, 202, 224.

ARCHITECTURAL FORUM MAGAZINE, Article on Kirtland Temple from, 11, 14.

ANGELS in Kirtland Temple, 16, 18, 19, 23, 25; A. can come from God, 321; Our kindred dead are A., 317; A. are sanctified through suffering, 370.

ANOINTINGS and washings to be performed in temples, 43.

ANOINTING ORDINANCE in Kirtland temple, 24, 28.

APOSTASY in Kirtland, 27-41.

APOSTATES, Character of, 30-34; Guided by peep stones, 33, 40; A. break into Kirtland temple, 39.

APOSTLES seen in tribulation, 18, 25; Welcomes to celestial city by Adam, 25.

ARIZONA TEMPLE, Dedicatory prayer of, 169; Physical and historical description of, 176; Presidents of, 178; Manifestations in, 181.

ARMIES OF HEAVEN will protect Zion in her redemption, 18.

ATHEISM defined by Orson Pratt, 292.

ATHEISTS, two classes of, 291.

B

BATTLEFIELDS where wicked have slain the wicked, 328, 331.

BAPTISMS for dead to be performed in temple, 43; Performed in Mississippi River, 44, 49; B. first performed in Nauvoo Temple, 45, 49.

BAPTISMAL FONT in Nauvoo Temple, description of, 49; Made ready for use, 45; Dedicated by Brigham Young, 49.

BECK, JOSEPH E., Benefactor to Orson Hyde, 258.

BIBLE, References on temples in, 351.

BLESSINGS sealed will do no good unless we live for them, 373.

BOGGS, Gov. LILBURN W., Exterminating order of, 42, 252.

BOOK OF ABRAHAM, References on translation of, 355.

BOOK OF MORMON, References on temple in, 352.

BOSTON to be swept into sea, 98.

BOYNTON, JOHN, Apostasy of, 32, 33, 36.

BRONGHURST, SAMUEL E., was at Swiss Temple construction, 197.

BROWN, CAPT., tells of Nauvoo Temple, 47.

C

CAHOON, REYNOLDS, to superintend construction of Kirtland Temple, 15.

CARTER, JARED, to superintend construction of Kirtland Temple, 15.

CELESTIAL GLORY obtained after being resurrected, 339.

CELESTIAL KINGDOM, Heirs of, 17.

CHANDLER, MICHAEL H., left legacy of ancient papyrus and mummies, 260; Exhibits mummies at Kirtland, 261; Orson Pratt's account of papyrus and mummies, 266.

CHASE, DARWIN, ordained a Seventy, 250, 252; Mortally wounded by Indians, 252.

CHILDREN saved in celestial kingdom, 18.

CHURCH to come forth out of wilderness of darkness, 6; Name by which C. shall be called, 250.

CLOVEN TONGUES of fire seen in Kirtland Temple, 25.

COMMERCE, Ill., Arrival of Saints at, 42.

CONFINED in a Missouri dungeon, 298.

CONSTITUTION, Prayer for, in Kirtland Temple, 5; Framers of C. appeared in St. George Temple, 82.

COE, JOSEPH, Apostasy of, 32; Was present at dedication of Independence Temple site, 231, 233.

COURTHOUSE mentioned in revelation, 231.

COVENANTS, Eternal, to be sealed in temples only, 375.

COWDERY, OLIVER, Apostasy of 36; Was present at dedication of Independence Temple site, 231, 233; Was scribe in translating papyrus, 263.

COWDERY, M. F., Apostasy of, 32.

COWDERY, W. D., Apostasy of, 32.

CREATION, Catholic philosophy on, 288; Earliest account of, 264.

421

H

HAPPINESS defined, 368.

HARRIS, MARTIN, goes with Prophet, 35; Was present at dedication of Independence Temple site, 231, 233; Commanded to repent, 294.

HAWAIIAN TEMPLE, Dedicatory prayer of, 143; Remarks made at dedicatory services of, 152; Physical and historical description of, 151; Presidents of, 152.

HEAD, Anointing of in Kirtland Temple, 28.

HEAVENLY BEINGS obtained holiness and protection through suffering, 370.

HIEROGLYPHICS, Translation of, 261-277; Could only be translated by Joseph the Prophet, 264.

HOSANNA SHOUT given, 18, 19, 24, 52, 78.

HYDE, JOSEPH S., relates vision of Orson Hyde, 255.

HYDE, ORSON, Dedicates Nauvoo Temple, 45; Vision given to, 255; Dedicates land of Palestine, 255; His vision of wicked spirits, 319.

I

IDAHO FALLS TEMPLE, Dedicatory prayer of, 182; Physical description of, 191; Historical description of, 194; Presidents of, 195.

IMMATERIAL GOD is nothing, 292.

IMMATERIALISTS, Belief of, 291.

IMPROVEMENT ERA MAGAZINE, References to temples and temple work, 354.

INDEPENDENCE TEMPLE, to be reared in this generation, 231, 233! Described by Orson Pratt, 236; To be eternal, 242; To be built before the second coming of the Savior, 244; Many now living will assist in building it, 245; To endure forever, 238; Cornerstones laid for, 247; Glory of, 147; Many will see Jesus when built, 245; None qualified now to build it, 384; Sacred records to be stored in, 232; Seen in vision, 240.

INDEPENDENCE TEMPLE SITE, Photograph of, 233; Designated and dedicated, 234; Persons present when cornerstones were laid, 231, 233.

INFIDELS, Belief of, 291.

INSANE woman in Kirtland Temple rebuked, 20.

J

JACOBSEN, SOREN, is supervisor of construction of Los Angeles Temple, 205.

JARED, Things shown to brother of, 309.

JACKSON COUNTY to be built up in this generation, 231; Location defined, 235; Fertility of soil of, 235; Resources of, 235. J. C. courthouse, 231.

JACKSON COUNTY TEMPLE, See Independence Temple.

JOSEPH CITY, Same as Nauvoo, 54.

JESUS suffered in body for sins committed by the body, 294; J. suffered for sins committed in spiritual world, 295; J. was fore-ordained before foundation of the world, 295.

JERUSALEM to be redeemed, 5, 256.

JOHN THE BELOVED seen at Kirtland Temple dedication, 24.

JOHNSON, LUKE, Apostasy of, 32, 34.

JOHNSON, LYMAN, Apostasy of, 32.

JOHNSON, ORSON, Apostasy of, 32.

K

KANE, THOMAS L., Lecture on Mormons by, 60.

KEYS of this dispensation restored, 17.

KEYS of all dispensations restored, 175.

KIMBALL, HEBER C., Labors on Kirtland Temple, 14, 57; Missionary labors in England, 33-34; Dedicates Endowment House, 227; Prophecies of, 138, 228, 230; Lost Diary of, 316; Dictates his history, 316; Sees world of wicked spirits, 318; Saw Jesus and Apostles preaching to spirits, 330.

KINGDOM OF GOD to fill the whole earth, 6; Those blessed who build, 56.

KIRTLAND BANK, Cause of failure of, 30.

KIRTLAND TEMPLE, Construction of, 7, 11, 22; Architecture of, 11, 14, 22-23; Plans revealed of God for, 7, 34; Women faithful in construction of, 11, 14; Builders inspired who constructed, 14; Poverty of the Saints in Kirtland, 26; Constructed in poverty, 11, 14, 23, 34, 57; An historic American building, 11; Committee who superintended construction of, 15; Divine manifestations in, 16-25; Angel present to accept dedication of, 23; Cost of, 21, 27; Heber C. Kimball labors on, 15, 57; Wicked cursed in, 29; Accepted of the Lord, 16; Cloven tongues of fire seen in, 25; Builders slept on weapons while constructing, 33; Plaster of, glistened like diamonds, 38; Authorized to sell, 39; Visited by Richard W. Young, 39; Keys restored in, 49; Defiled, 42-43; Apostates break into, 39; Restored to former appearance by Reorganized Church, 40; Apostasy seen in vision by the Prophet Joseph, 35; Polluted, 274; Ordinances performed in, 384; Pulpits in, covered with straw, 37.

KNIGHT, NEWELL, was present at dedication of Independence Temple site, 231, 233.

L

LAMANITES, to be converted from savage condition, 6; Prayer for, in Arizona Temple, 173.

LAMB'S BOOK OF LIFE, 376.

LAMBERT, CHARLES, sees Lucifer in Nauvoo, 54.

LIGHT, rejection of, is man's condemnation, 395.

LOGAN TEMPLE, Dedication of, 87; Historical and physical description of, 94; Construction of, foretold, 97; Spirit of discernment in, 100; Sound doctrine advocated in, 101; Presidents of, 96; Sacred ordinances performed in, 96.